Onward and Downward

OTHER BOOKS BY JIM TOOMEY

Sherman's Lagoon: Ate That, What's Next?

Poodle: The Other White Meat

An Illustrated Guide to Shark Etiquette

Another Day in Paradise

Greetings from Sherman's Lagoon

Surf's Up!

The Shark Diaries

Catch of the Day

A Day at the Beach

Surfer Safari

Planet of the Hairless Beach Apes

Yarns & Shanties (and Other Nautical Baloney)

Sharks Just Wanna Have Fun

Confessions of a Swinging Single Sea Turtle

Discover Your Inner Hermit Crab

Never Bite Anything That Bites Back

Think Like a Shark

Here We Go Again

Lunch Wore a Speedo

Tales From the Deep: That Are Completely Fabricated

Happy as a Clam

TREASURIES

Sherman's Lagoon 1991 to 2001: Greatest Hits and Near Misses

In Shark Years I'm Dead: Sherman's Lagoon Turns Fifteen

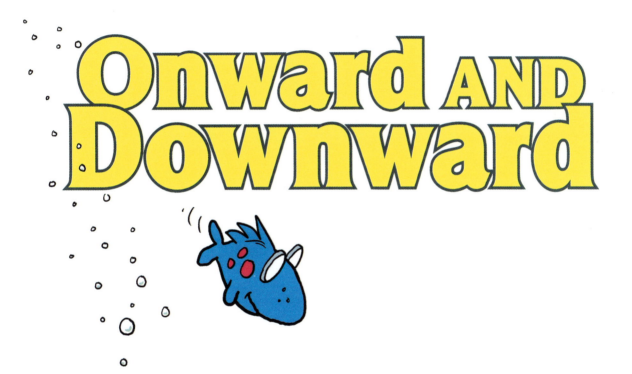

Onward and Downward

The Twenty-Second Sherman's Lagoon Collection

JIM TOOMEY

Andrews McMeel
PUBLISHING®

Sincere thanks to my good friend and fellow ocean advocate Dr. Sylvia Earle for allowing me to use her battle cry "Onward and Downward" as the title for this book.

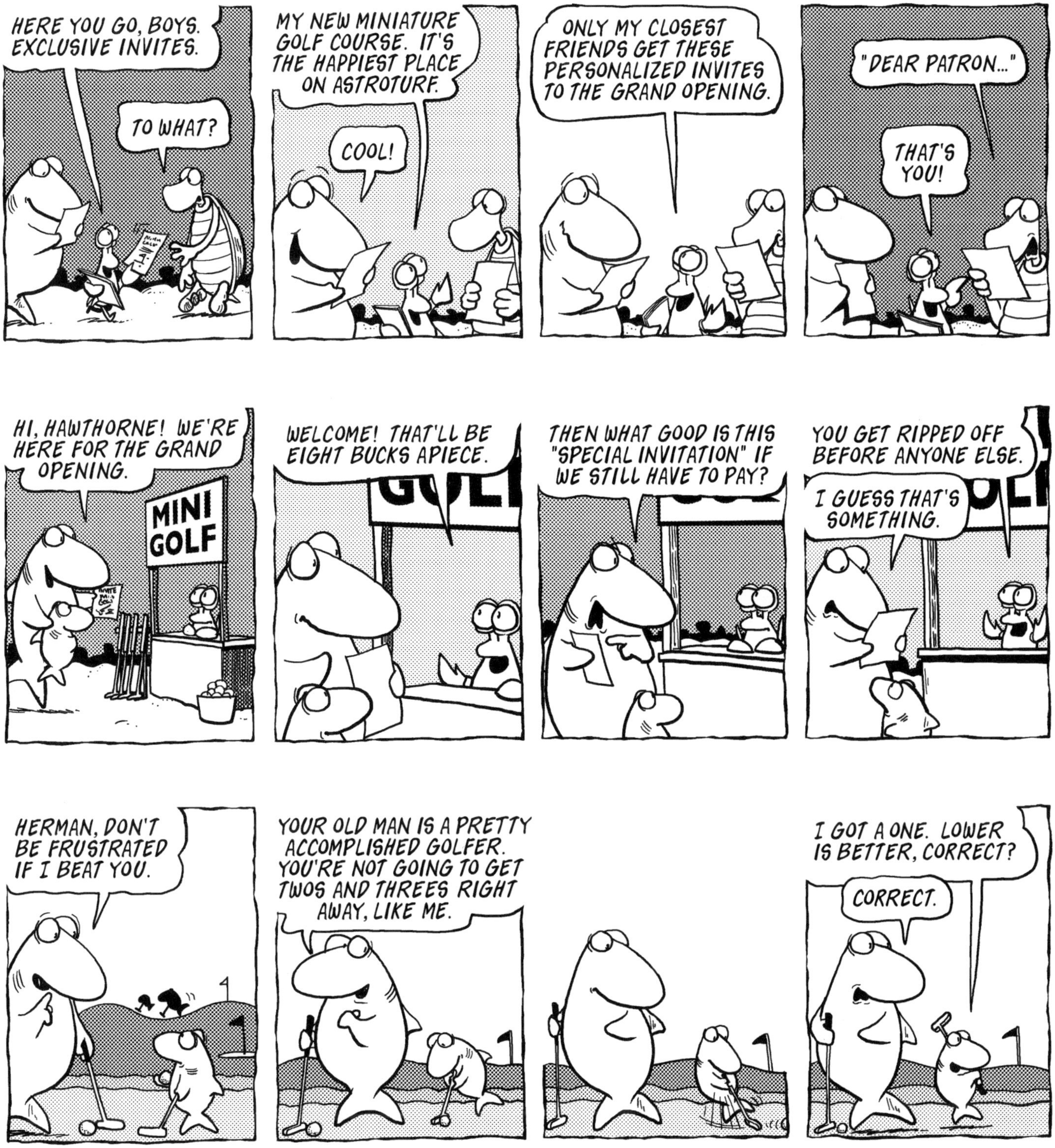
HERE YOU GO, BOYS. EXCLUSIVE INVITES.
TO WHAT?
MY NEW MINIATURE GOLF COURSE. IT'S THE HAPPIEST PLACE ON ASTROTURF.
COOL!
ONLY MY CLOSEST FRIENDS GET THESE PERSONALIZED INVITES TO THE GRAND OPENING.
"DEAR PATRON..."
THAT'S YOU!
HI, HAWTHORNE! WE'RE HERE FOR THE GRAND OPENING.
MINI GOLF
WELCOME! THAT'LL BE EIGHT BUCKS APIECE.
THEN WHAT GOOD IS THIS "SPECIAL INVITATION" IF WE STILL HAVE TO PAY?
YOU GET RIPPED OFF BEFORE ANYONE ELSE.
I GUESS THAT'S SOMETHING.
HERMAN, DON'T BE FRUSTRATED IF I BEAT YOU.
YOUR OLD MAN IS A PRETTY ACCOMPLISHED GOLFER. YOU'RE NOT GOING TO GET TWOS AND THREES RIGHT AWAY, LIKE ME.
I GOT A ONE. LOWER IS BETTER, CORRECT?
CORRECT.

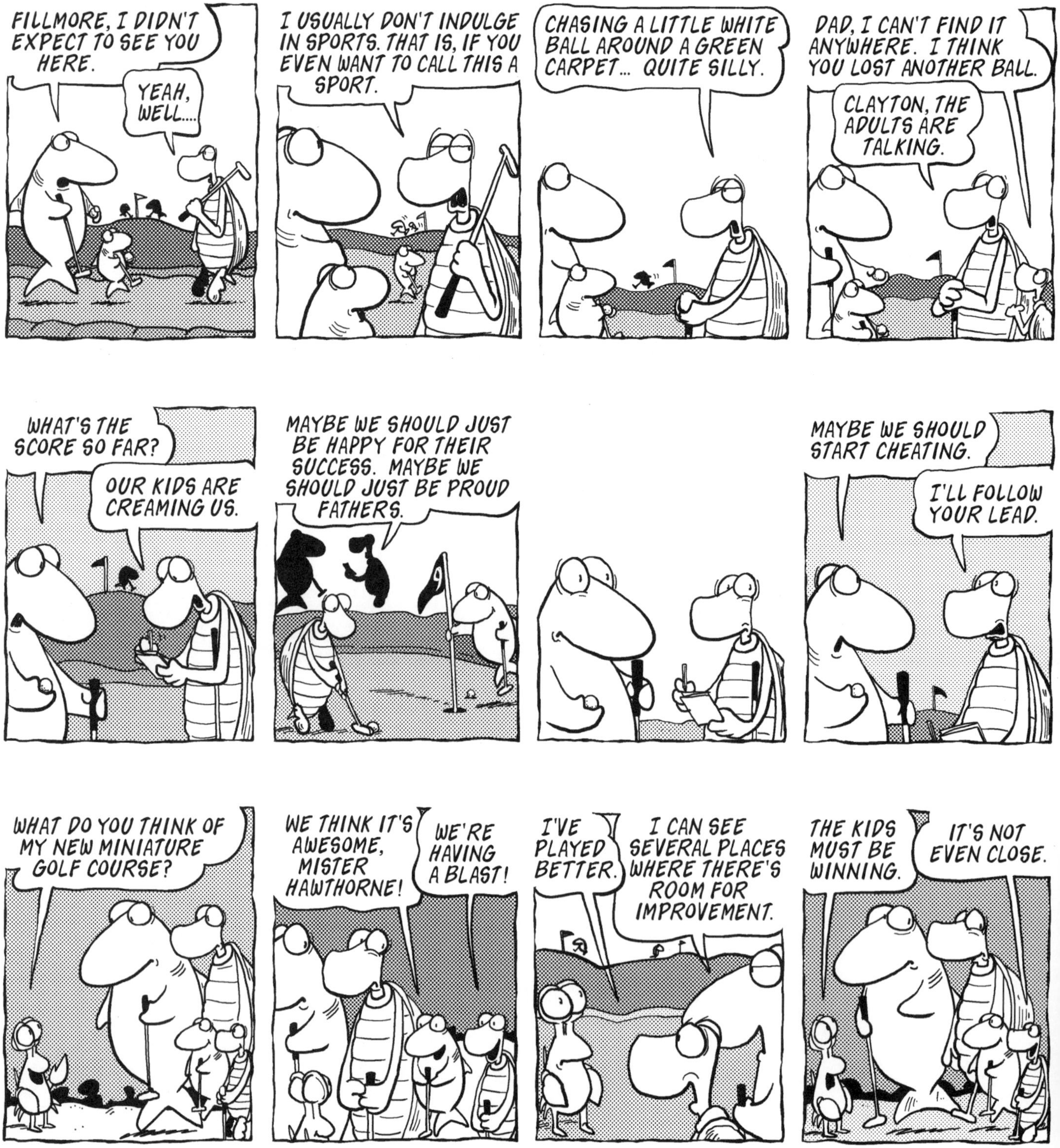

FILLMORE, I DIDN'T EXPECT TO SEE YOU HERE.
YEAH, WELL....
I USUALLY DON'T INDULGE IN SPORTS. THAT IS, IF YOU EVEN WANT TO CALL THIS A SPORT.
CHASING A LITTLE WHITE BALL AROUND A GREEN CARPET... QUITE SILLY.
DAD, I CAN'T FIND IT ANYWHERE. I THINK YOU LOST ANOTHER BALL.
CLAYTON, THE ADULTS ARE TALKING.
WHAT'S THE SCORE SO FAR?
OUR KIDS ARE CREAMING US.
MAYBE WE SHOULD JUST BE HAPPY FOR THEIR SUCCESS. MAYBE WE SHOULD JUST BE PROUD FATHERS.
MAYBE WE SHOULD START CHEATING.
I'LL FOLLOW YOUR LEAD.
WHAT DO YOU THINK OF MY NEW MINIATURE GOLF COURSE?
WE THINK IT'S AWESOME, MISTER HAWTHORNE!
WE'RE HAVING A BLAST!
I'VE PLAYED BETTER.
I CAN SEE SEVERAL PLACES WHERE THERE'S ROOM FOR IMPROVEMENT.
THE KIDS MUST BE WINNING.
IT'S NOT EVEN CLOSE.

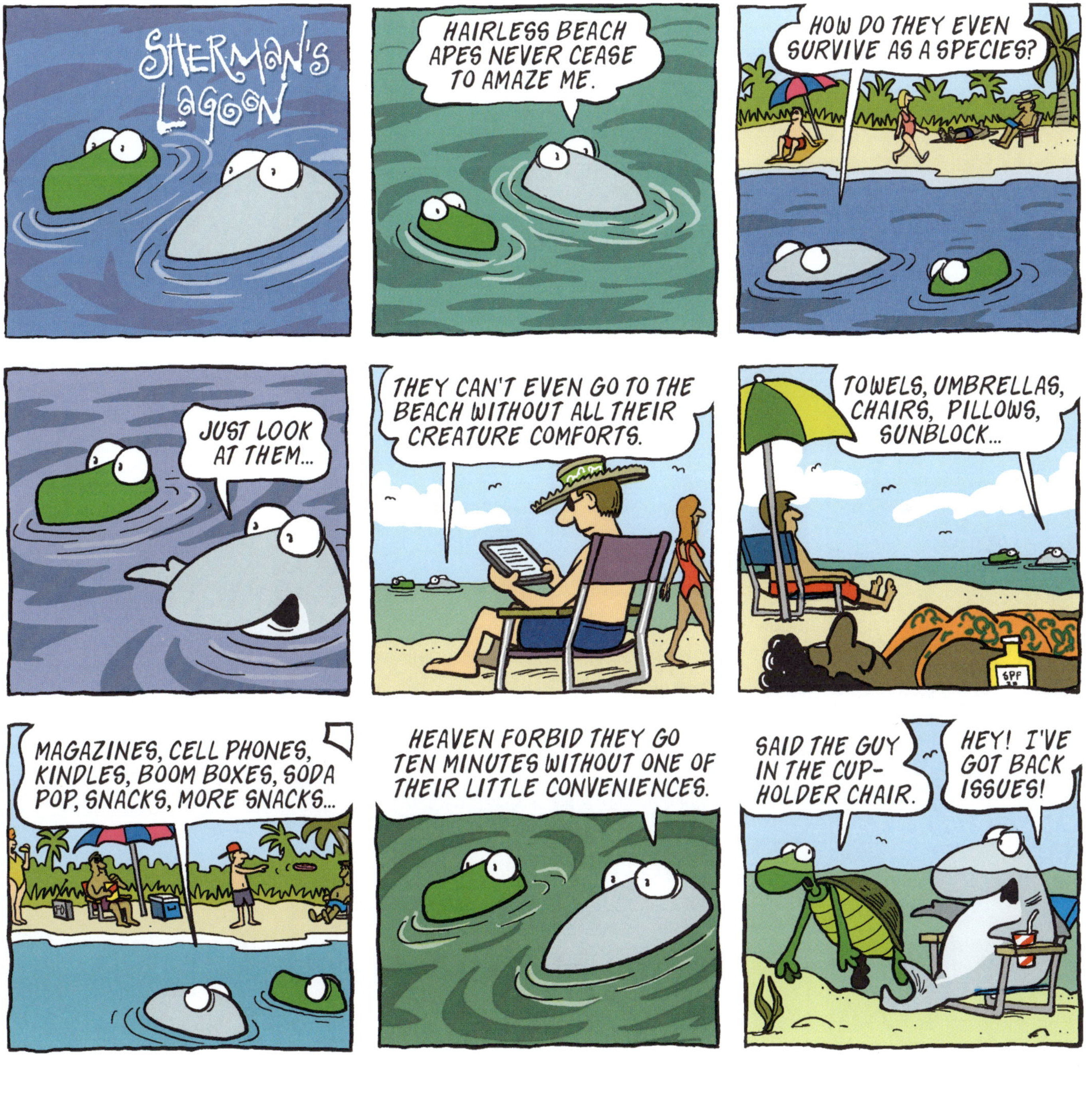
SHERMAN'S LAGOON
HAIRLESS BEACH APES NEVER CEASE TO AMAZE ME.
HOW DO THEY EVEN SURVIVE AS A SPECIES?
JUST LOOK AT THEM...
THEY CAN'T EVEN GO TO THE BEACH WITHOUT ALL THEIR CREATURE COMFORTS.
TOWELS, UMBRELLAS, CHAIRS, PILLOWS, SUNBLOCK...
SPF
MAGAZINES, CELL PHONES, KINDLES, BOOM BOXES, SODA POP, SNACKS, MORE SNACKS...
HEAVEN FORBID THEY GO TEN MINUTES WITHOUT ONE OF THEIR LITTLE CONVENIENCES.
SAID THE GUY IN THE CUP-HOLDER CHAIR.
HEY! I'VE GOT BACK ISSUES!

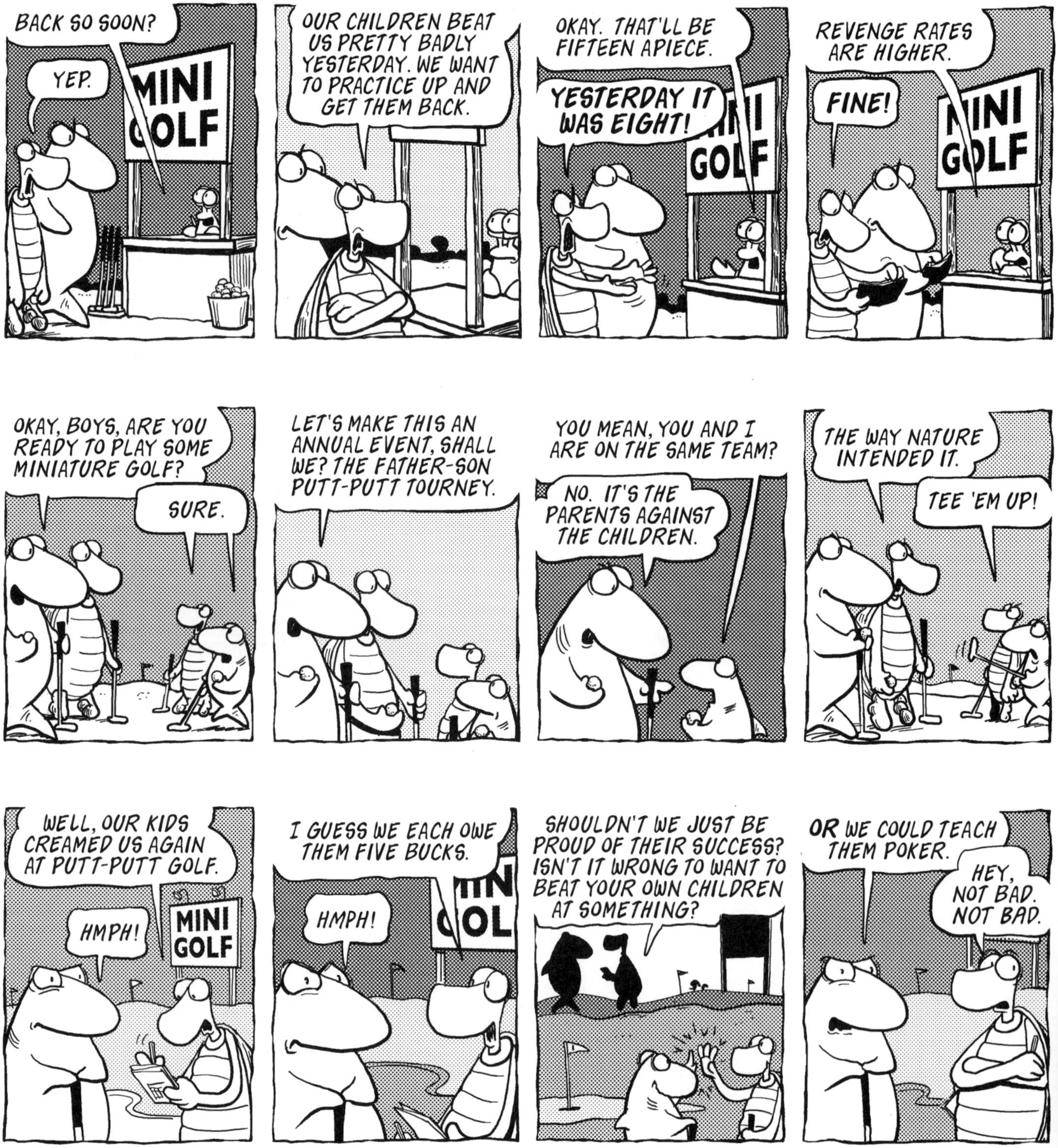
BACK SO SOON?
YEP.
MINI GOLF
OUR CHILDREN BEAT US PRETTY BADLY YESTERDAY. WE WANT TO PRACTICE UP AND GET THEM BACK.
OKAY. THAT'LL BE FIFTEEN APIECE.
YESTERDAY IT WAS EIGHT!
REVENGE RATES ARE HIGHER.
FINE!
OKAY, BOYS, ARE YOU READY TO PLAY SOME MINIATURE GOLF?
SURE.
LET'S MAKE THIS AN ANNUAL EVENT, SHALL WE? THE FATHER-SON PUTT-PUTT TOURNEY.
YOU MEAN, YOU AND I ARE ON THE SAME TEAM?
NO. IT'S THE PARENTS AGAINST THE CHILDREN.
THE WAY NATURE INTENDED IT.
TEE 'EM UP!
WELL, OUR KIDS CREAMED US AGAIN AT PUTT-PUTT GOLF.
HMPH!
MINI GOLF
I GUESS WE EACH OWE THEM FIVE BUCKS.
HMPH!
SHOULDN'T WE JUST BE PROUD OF THEIR SUCCESS? ISN'T IT WRONG TO WANT TO BEAT YOUR OWN CHILDREN AT SOMETHING?
OR WE COULD TEACH THEM POKER.
HEY, NOT BAD. NOT BAD.

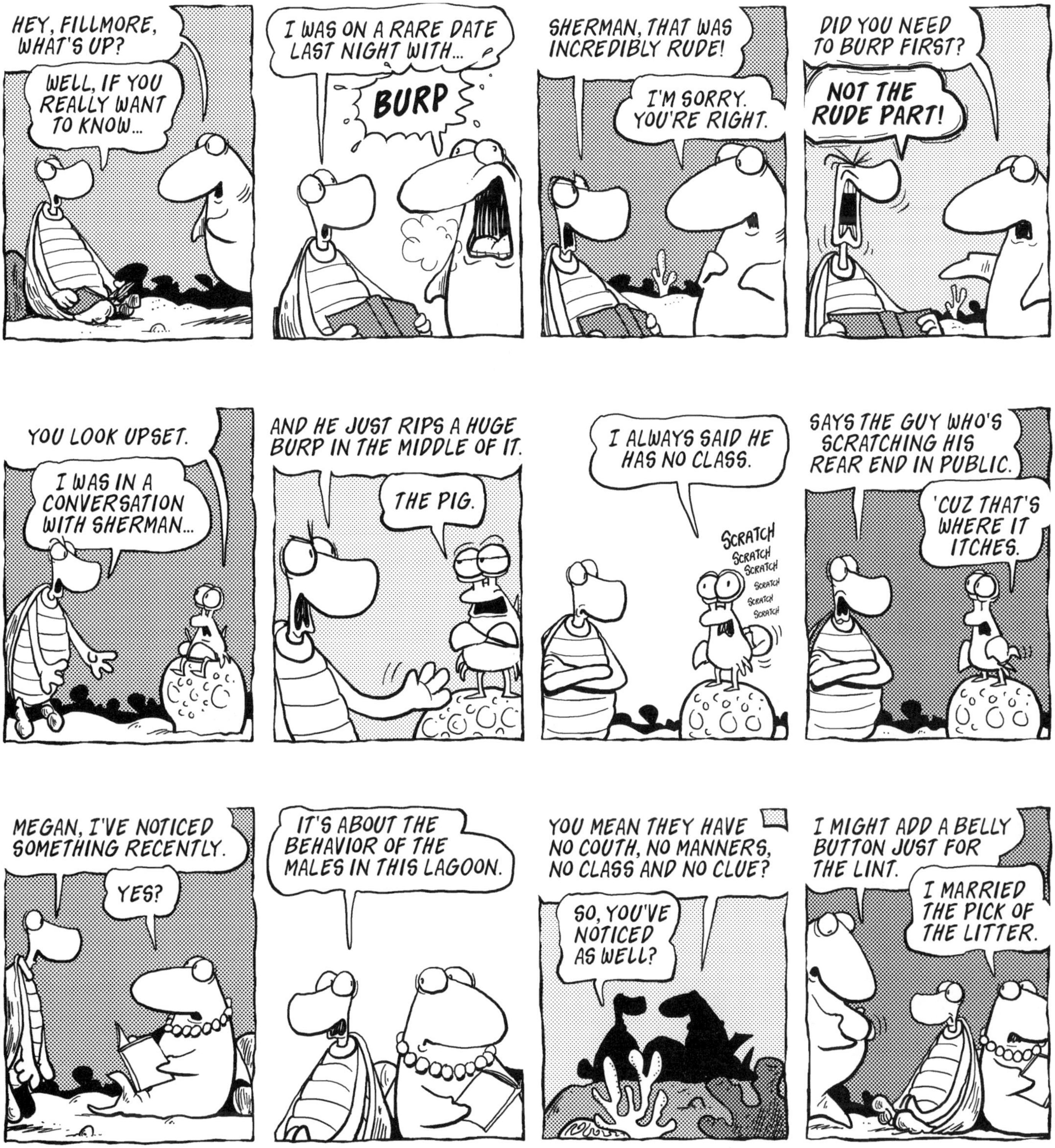

HEY, FILLMORE, WHAT'S UP?
WELL, IF YOU REALLY WANT TO KNOW...
I WAS ON A RARE DATE LAST NIGHT WITH...
BURP
SHERMAN, THAT WAS INCREDIBLY RUDE!
I'M SORRY. YOU'RE RIGHT.
DID YOU NEED TO BURP FIRST?
NOT THE RUDE PART!
YOU LOOK UPSET.
I WAS IN A CONVERSATION WITH SHERMAN...
AND HE JUST RIPS A HUGE BURP IN THE MIDDLE OF IT.
THE PIG.
I ALWAYS SAID HE HAS NO CLASS.
SCRATCH SCRATCH SCRATCH SCRATCH SCRATCH SCRATCH
SAYS THE GUY WHO'S SCRATCHING HIS REAR END IN PUBLIC.
'CUZ THAT'S WHERE IT ITCHES.
MEGAN, I'VE NOTICED SOMETHING RECENTLY.
YES?
IT'S ABOUT THE BEHAVIOR OF THE MALES IN THIS LAGOON.
YOU MEAN THEY HAVE NO COUTH, NO MANNERS, NO CLASS AND NO CLUE?
SO, YOU'VE NOTICED AS WELL?
I MIGHT ADD A BELLY BUTTON JUST FOR THE LINT.
I MARRIED THE PICK OF THE LITTER.

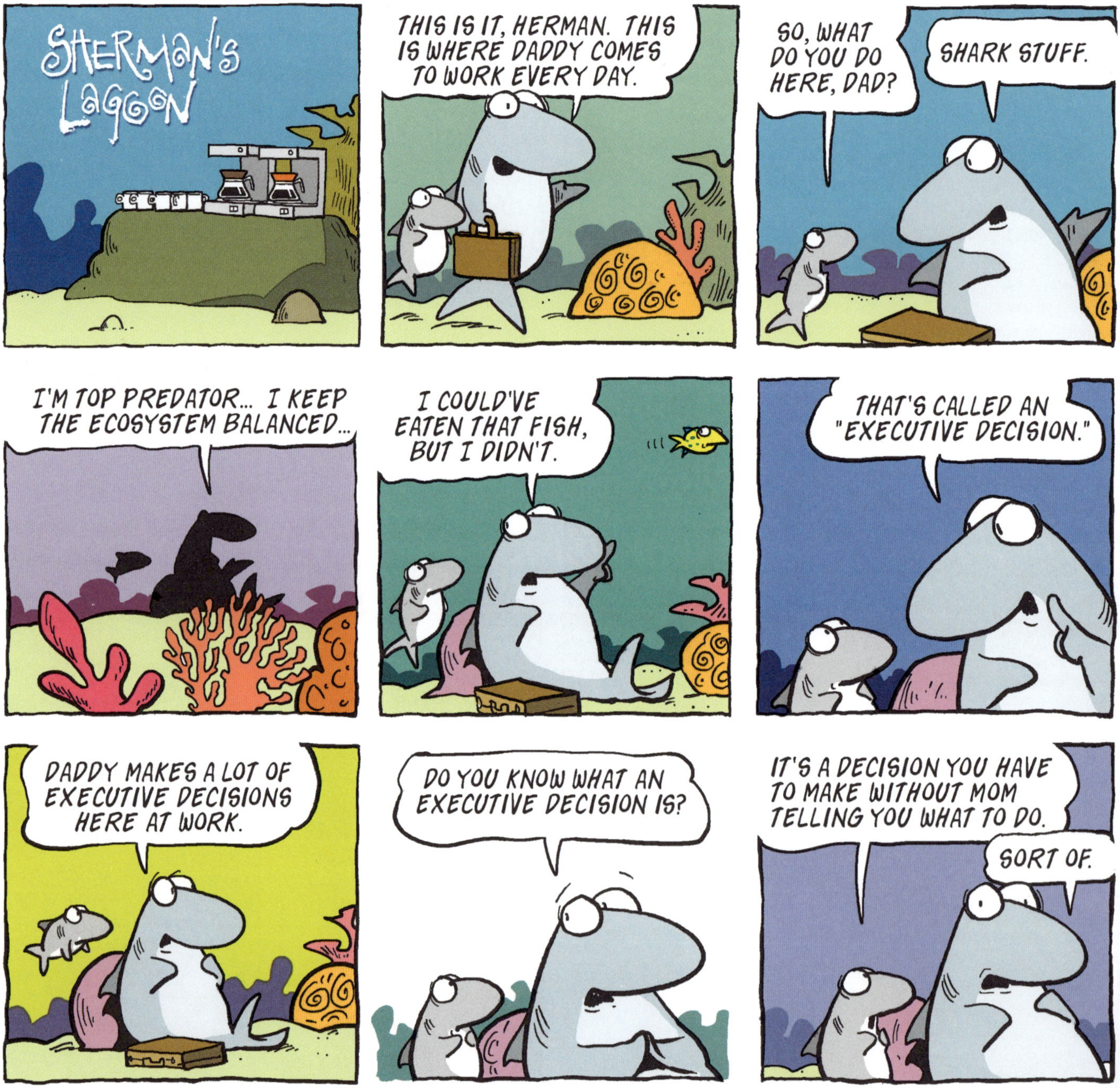
SHERMAN'S LAGOON
THIS IS IT, HERMAN. THIS IS WHERE DADDY COMES TO WORK EVERY DAY.
SO, WHAT DO YOU DO HERE, DAD?
SHARK STUFF.
I'M TOP PREDATOR... I KEEP THE ECOSYSTEM BALANCED...
I COULD'VE EATEN THAT FISH, BUT I DIDN'T.
THAT'S CALLED AN "EXECUTIVE DECISION."
DADDY MAKES A LOT OF EXECUTIVE DECISIONS HERE AT WORK.
DO YOU KNOW WHAT AN EXECUTIVE DECISION IS?
IT'S A DECISION YOU HAVE TO MAKE WITHOUT MOM TELLING YOU WHAT TO DO.
SORT OF.

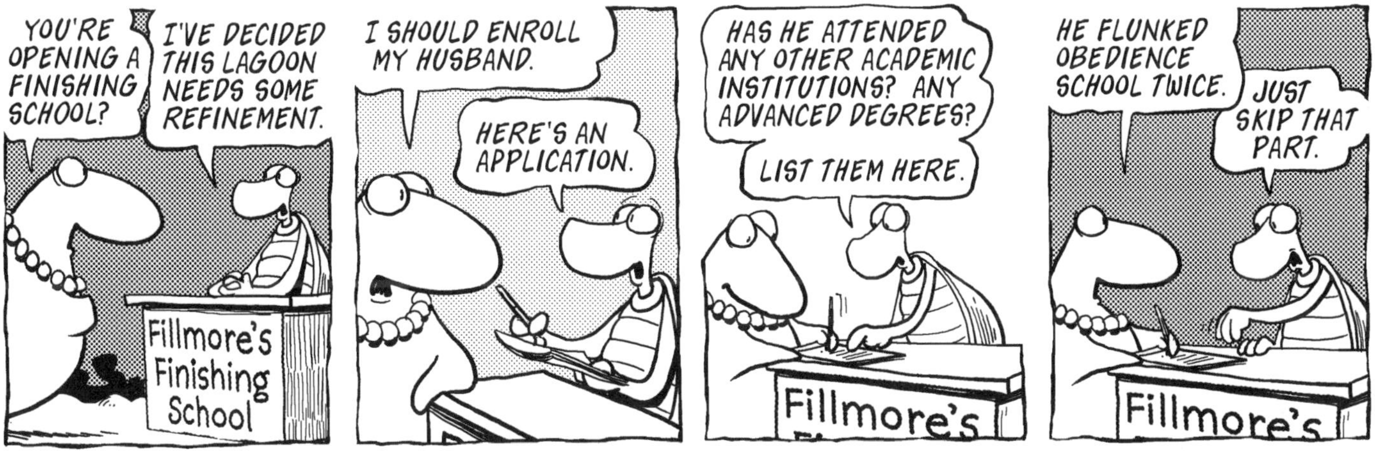
YOU'RE OPENING A FINISHING SCHOOL?
I'VE DECIDED THIS LAGOON NEEDS SOME REFINEMENT.
Fillmore's Finishing School
I SHOULD ENROLL MY HUSBAND.
HERE'S AN APPLICATION.
HAS HE ATTENDED ANY OTHER ACADEMIC INSTITUTIONS? ANY ADVANCED DEGREES?
LIST THEM HERE.
Fillmore's
HE FLUNKED OBEDIENCE SCHOOL TWICE.
JUST SKIP THAT PART.
Fillmore's

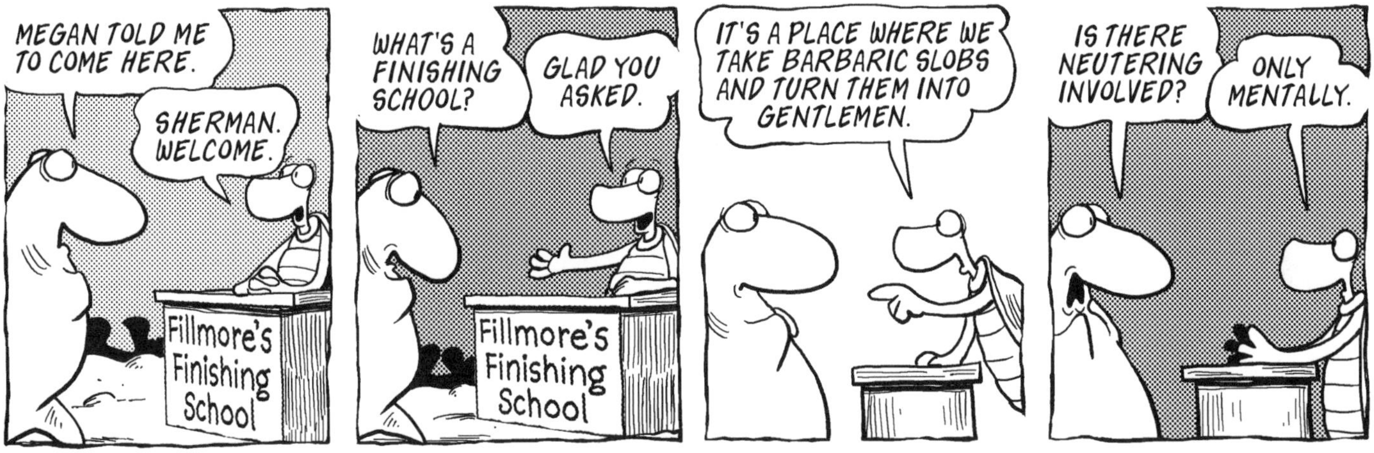
MEGAN TOLD ME TO COME HERE.
SHERMAN. WELCOME.
Fillmore's Finishing School
WHAT'S A FINISHING SCHOOL?
GLAD YOU ASKED.
Fillmore's Finishing School
IT'S A PLACE WHERE WE TAKE BARBARIC SLOBS AND TURN THEM INTO GENTLEMEN.
IS THERE NEUTERING INVOLVED?
ONLY MENTALLY.

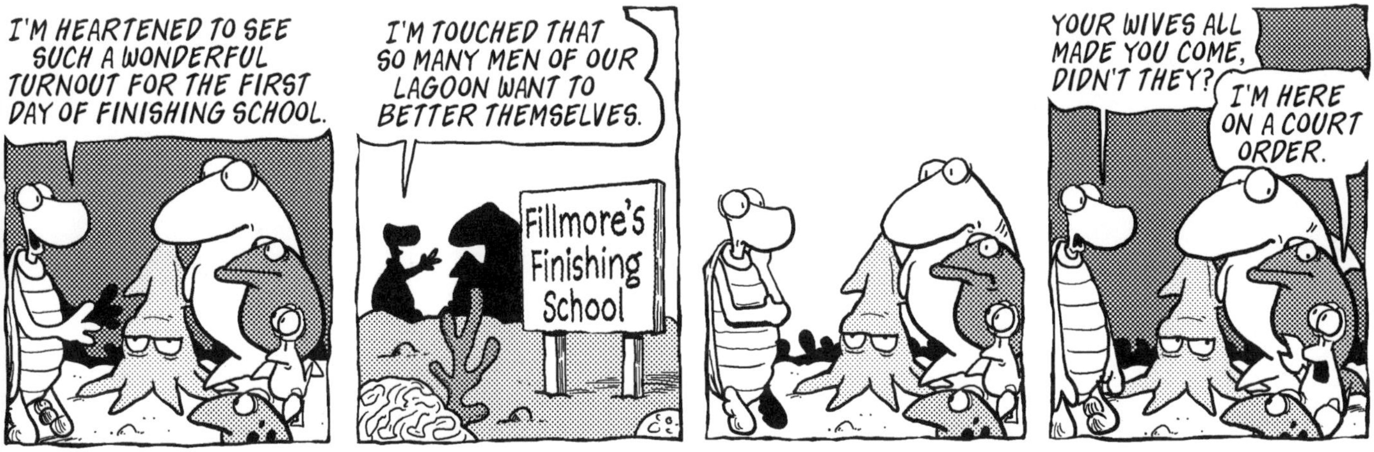
I'M HEARTENED TO SEE SUCH A WONDERFUL TURNOUT FOR THE FIRST DAY OF FINISHING SCHOOL.
I'M TOUCHED THAT SO MANY MEN OF OUR LAGOON WANT TO BETTER THEMSELVES.
Fillmore's Finishing School
YOUR WIVES ALL MADE YOU COME, DIDN'T THEY?
I'M HERE ON A COURT ORDER.

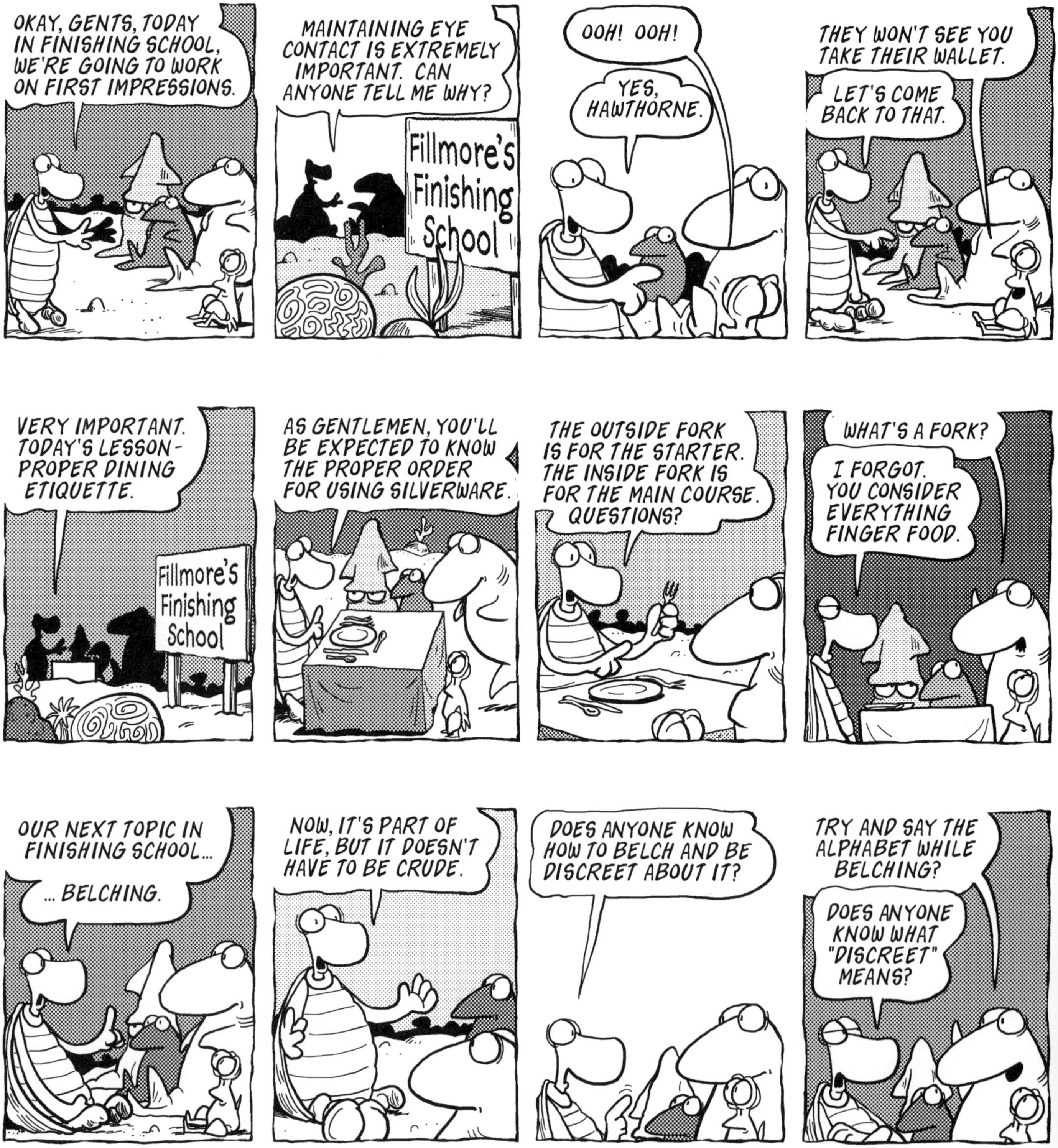

OKAY, GENTS, TODAY IN FINISHING SCHOOL, WE'RE GOING TO WORK ON FIRST IMPRESSIONS.
MAINTAINING EYE CONTACT IS EXTREMELY IMPORTANT. CAN ANYONE TELL ME WHY?
Fillmore's Finishing School
OOH! OOH!
YES, HAWTHORNE.
THEY WON'T SEE YOU TAKE THEIR WALLET.
LET'S COME BACK TO THAT.
VERY IMPORTANT. TODAY'S LESSON - PROPER DINING ETIQUETTE.
Fillmore's Finishing School
AS GENTLEMEN, YOU'LL BE EXPECTED TO KNOW THE PROPER ORDER FOR USING SILVERWARE.
THE OUTSIDE FORK IS FOR THE STARTER. THE INSIDE FORK IS FOR THE MAIN COURSE. QUESTIONS?
WHAT'S A FORK?
I FORGOT. YOU CONSIDER EVERYTHING FINGER FOOD.
OUR NEXT TOPIC IN FINISHING SCHOOL...
... BELCHING.
NOW, IT'S PART OF LIFE, BUT IT DOESN'T HAVE TO BE CRUDE.
DOES ANYONE KNOW HOW TO BELCH AND BE DISCREET ABOUT IT?
TRY AND SAY THE ALPHABET WHILE BELCHING?
DOES ANYONE KNOW WHAT "DISCREET" MEANS?

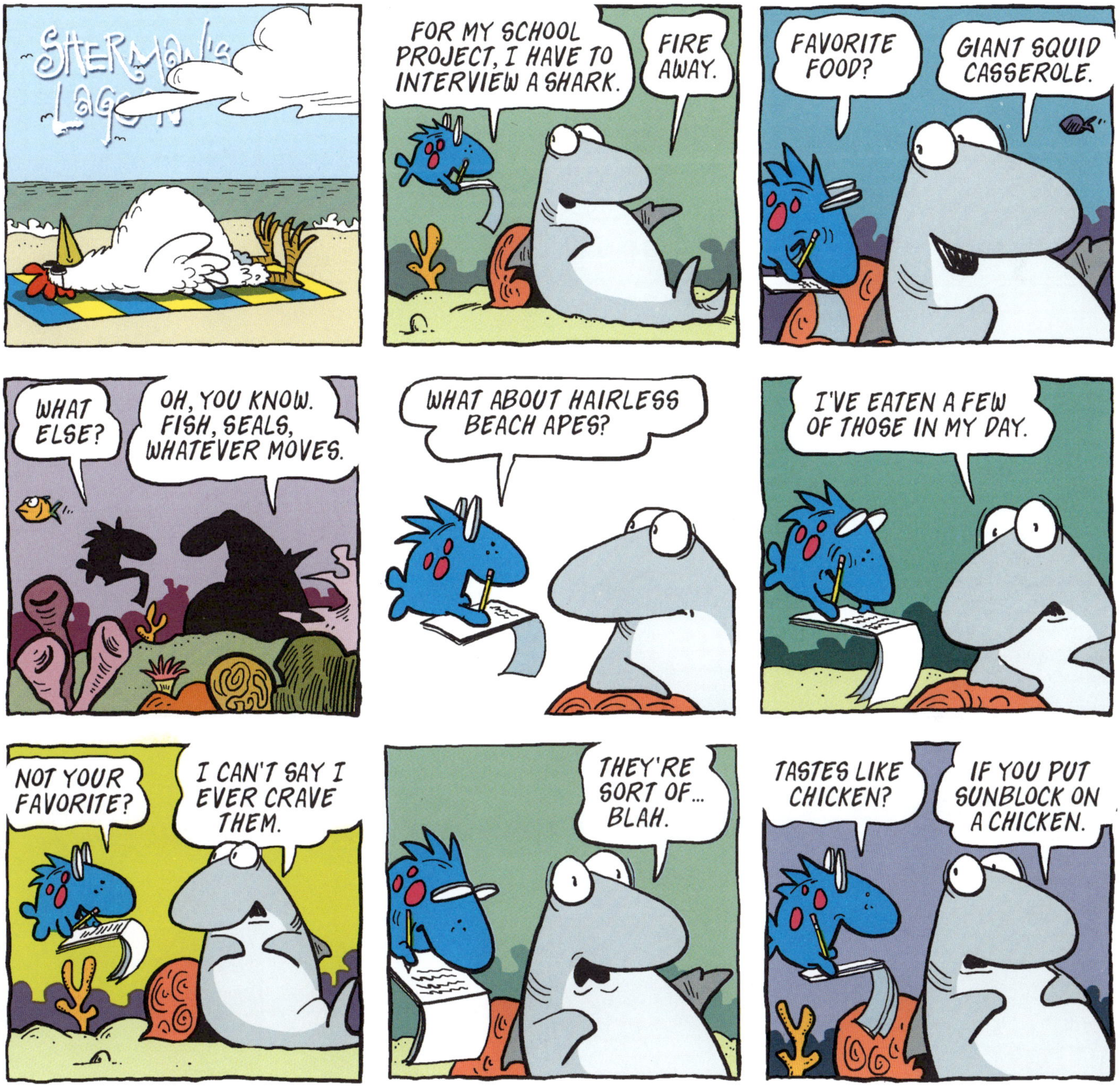
Sherman's Lagoon
FOR MY SCHOOL PROJECT, I HAVE TO INTERVIEW A SHARK.
FIRE AWAY.
FAVORITE FOOD?
GIANT SQUID CASSEROLE.
WHAT ELSE?
OH, YOU KNOW. FISH, SEALS, WHATEVER MOVES.
WHAT ABOUT HAIRLESS BEACH APES?
I'VE EATEN A FEW OF THOSE IN MY DAY.
NOT YOUR FAVORITE?
I CAN'T SAY I EVER CRAVE THEM.
THEY'RE SORT OF... BLAH.
TASTES LIKE CHICKEN?
IF YOU PUT SUNBLOCK ON A CHICKEN.

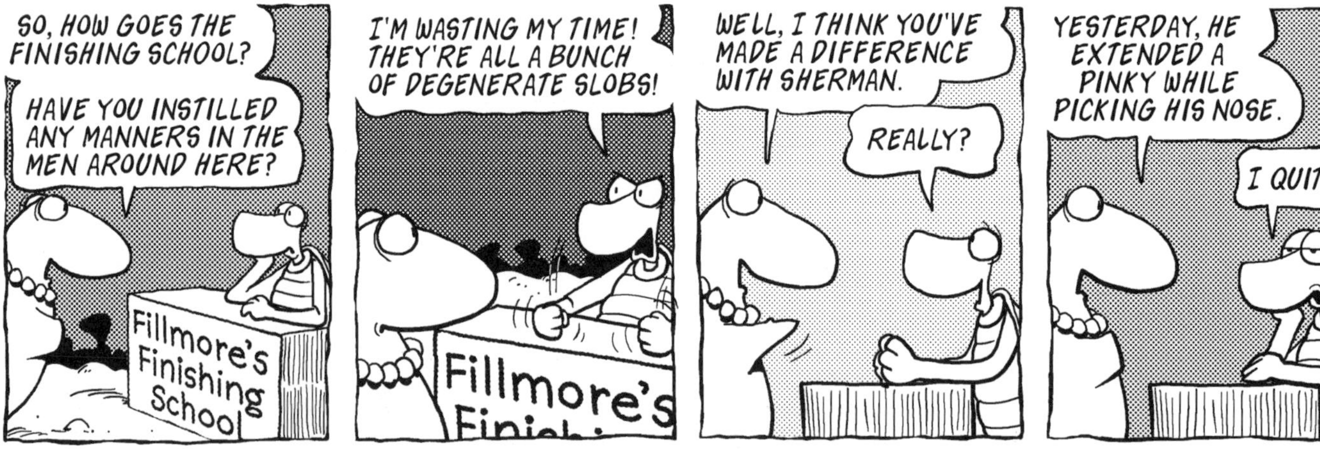
SO, HOW GOES THE FINISHING SCHOOL?
HAVE YOU INSTILLED ANY MANNERS IN THE MEN AROUND HERE?
Fillmore's Finishing School
I'M WASTING MY TIME! THEY'RE ALL A BUNCH OF DEGENERATE SLOBS!
Fillmore's
WELL, I THINK YOU'VE MADE A DIFFERENCE WITH SHERMAN.
REALLY?
YESTERDAY, HE EXTENDED A PINKY WHILE PICKING HIS NOSE.
I QUIT.

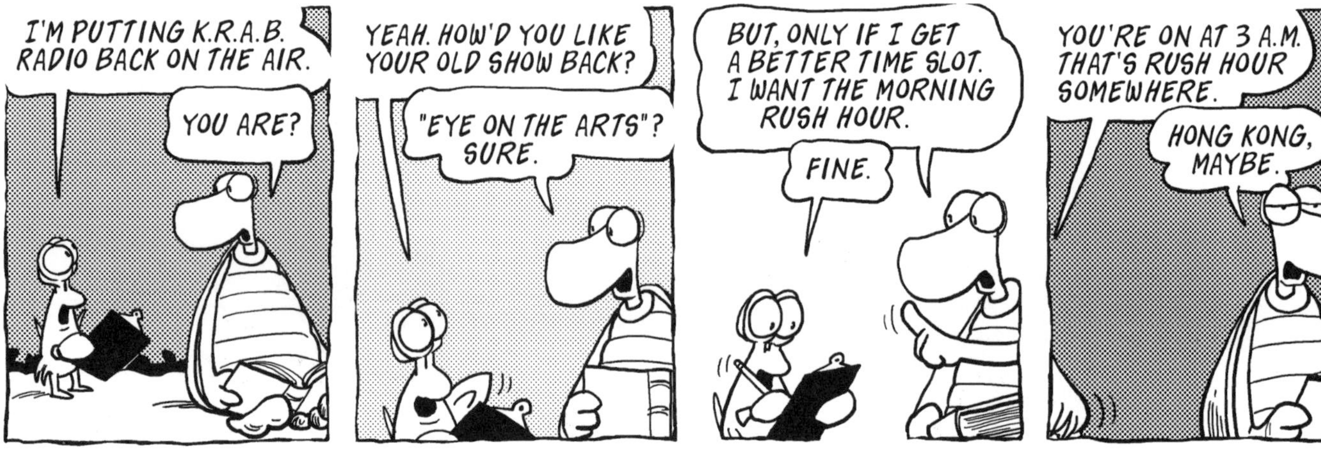
I'M PUTTING K.R.A.B. RADIO BACK ON THE AIR.
YOU ARE?
YEAH. HOW'D YOU LIKE YOUR OLD SHOW BACK?
"EYE ON THE ARTS"? SURE.
BUT, ONLY IF I GET A BETTER TIME SLOT. I WANT THE MORNING RUSH HOUR.
FINE.
YOU'RE ON AT 3 A.M. THAT'S RUSH HOUR SOMEWHERE.
HONG KONG, MAYBE.

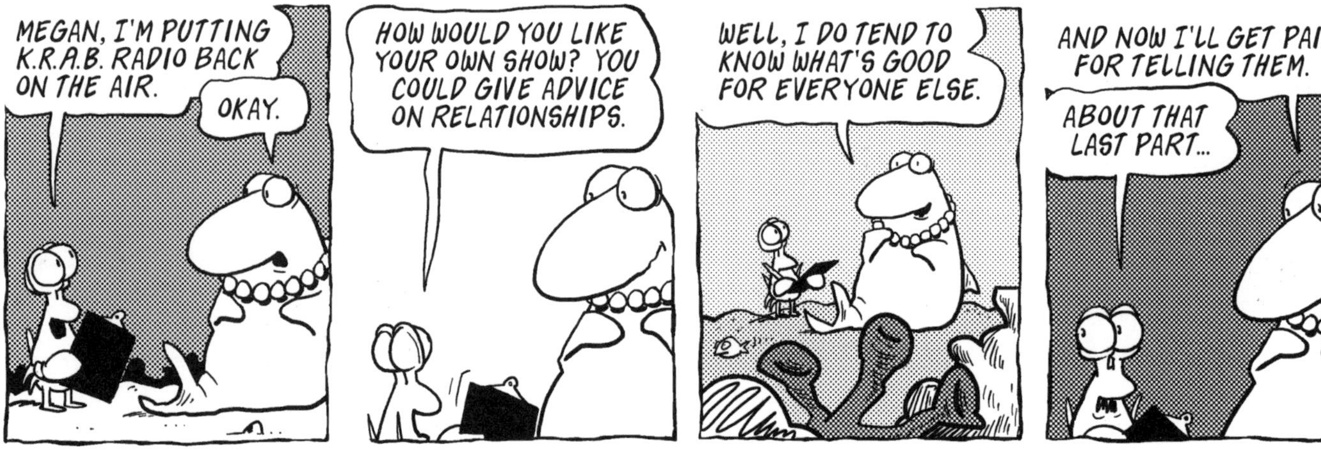
MEGAN, I'M PUTTING K.R.A.B. RADIO BACK ON THE AIR.
OKAY.
HOW WOULD YOU LIKE YOUR OWN SHOW? YOU COULD GIVE ADVICE ON RELATIONSHIPS.
WELL, I DO TEND TO KNOW WHAT'S GOOD FOR EVERYONE ELSE.
AND NOW I'LL GET PAID FOR TELLING THEM.
ABOUT THAT LAST PART...

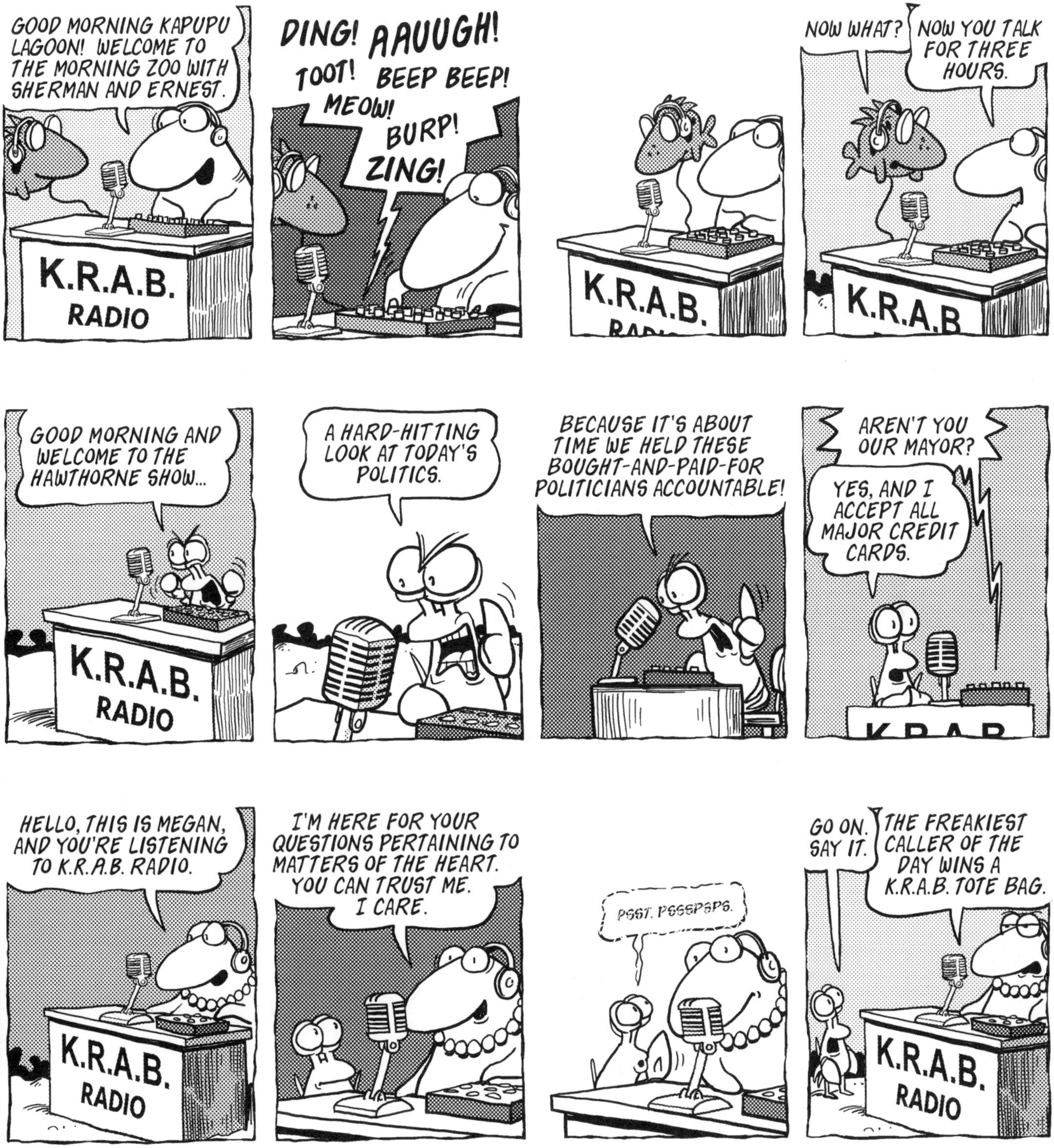
GOOD MORNING KAPUPU LAGOON! WELCOME TO THE MORNING ZOO WITH SHERMAN AND ERNEST.
K.R.A.B. RADIO
DING! AAUUGH!
TOOT! BEEP BEEP!
MEOW!
BURP!
ZING!
K.R.A.B.
NOW WHAT?
NOW YOU TALK FOR THREE HOURS.
K.R.A.B
GOOD MORNING AND WELCOME TO THE HAWTHORNE SHOW...
K.R.A.B. RADIO
A HARD-HITTING LOOK AT TODAY'S POLITICS.
BECAUSE IT'S ABOUT TIME WE HELD THESE BOUGHT-AND-PAID-FOR POLITICIANS ACCOUNTABLE!
AREN'T YOU OUR MAYOR?
YES, AND I ACCEPT ALL MAJOR CREDIT CARDS.
HELLO, THIS IS MEGAN, AND YOU'RE LISTENING TO K.R.A.B. RADIO.
K.R.A.B. RADIO
I'M HERE FOR YOUR QUESTIONS PERTAINING TO MATTERS OF THE HEART. YOU CAN TRUST ME. I CARE.
PSST. PSSSPSPS.
GO ON. SAY IT.
THE FREAKIEST CALLER OF THE DAY WINS A K.R.A.B. TOTE BAG.
K.R.A.B. RADIO

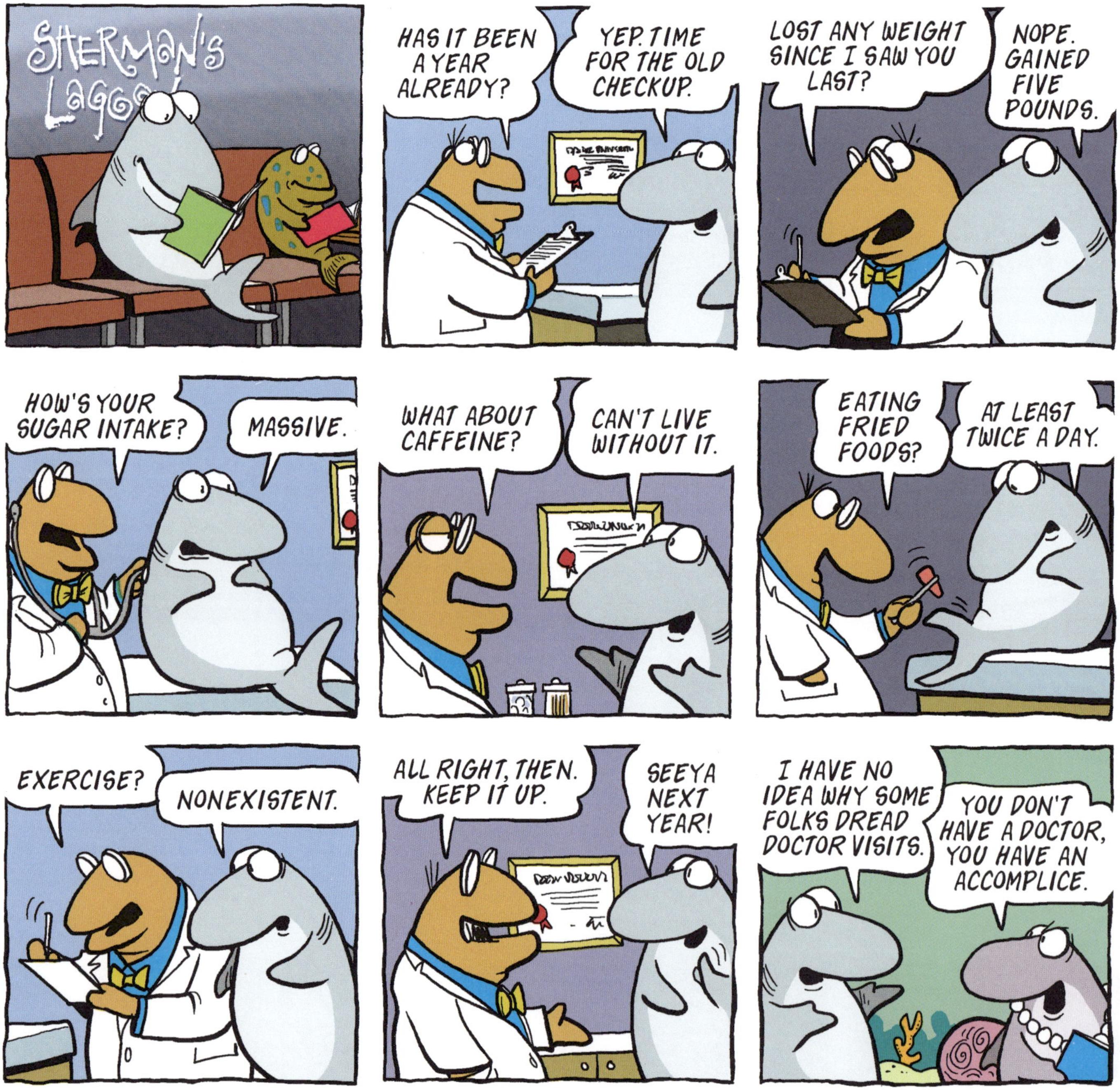
SHERMAN'S LAGOON
HAS IT BEEN A YEAR ALREADY?
YEP. TIME FOR THE OLD CHECKUP.
LOST ANY WEIGHT SINCE I SAW YOU LAST?
NOPE. GAINED FIVE POUNDS.
HOW'S YOUR SUGAR INTAKE?
MASSIVE.
WHAT ABOUT CAFFEINE?
CAN'T LIVE WITHOUT IT.
EATING FRIED FOODS?
AT LEAST TWICE A DAY.
EXERCISE?
NONEXISTENT.
ALL RIGHT, THEN. KEEP IT UP.
SEE YA NEXT YEAR!
I HAVE NO IDEA WHY SOME FOLKS DREAD DOCTOR VISITS.
YOU DON'T HAVE A DOCTOR, YOU HAVE AN ACCOMPLICE.

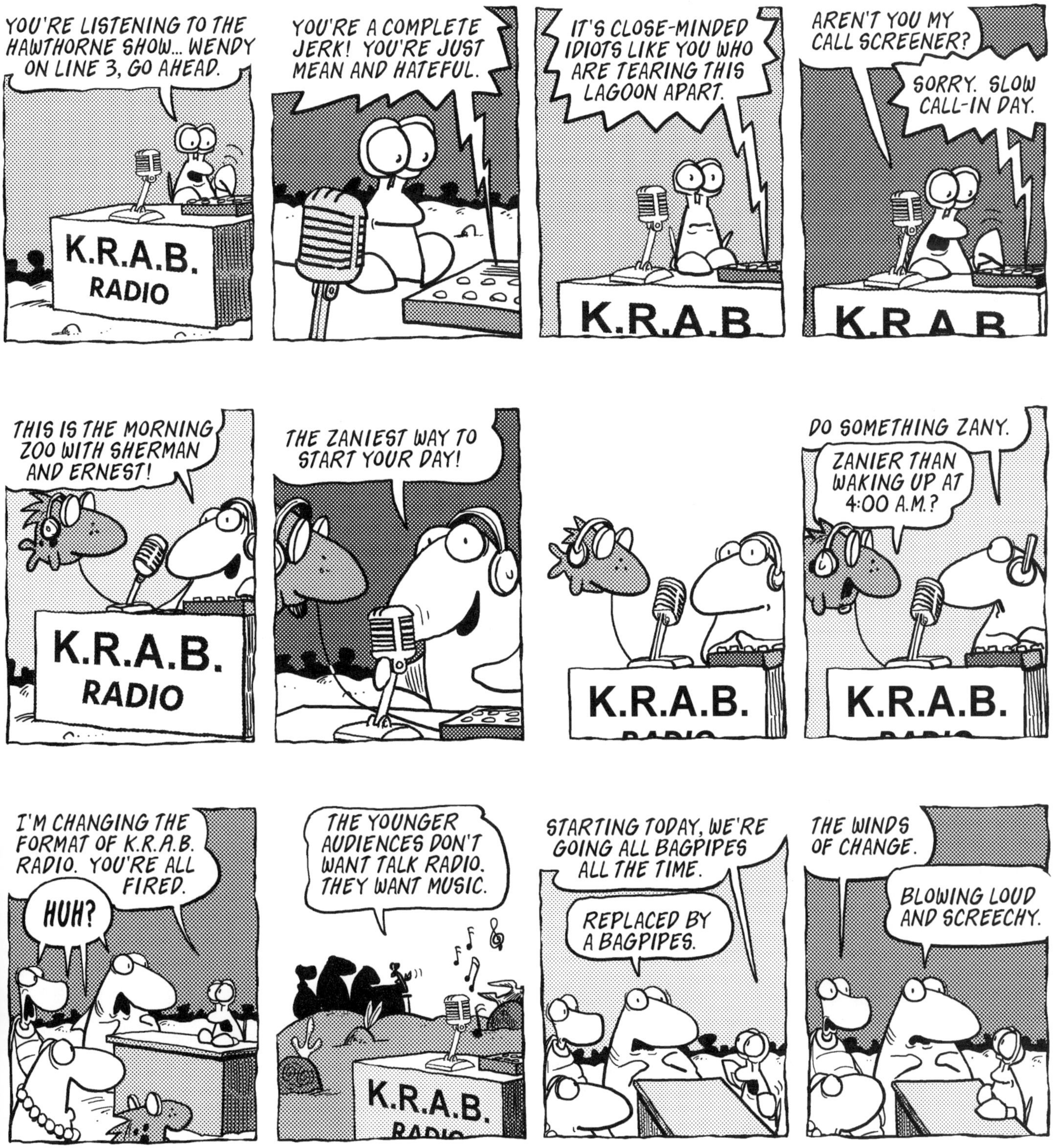
YOU'RE LISTENING TO THE HAWTHORNE SHOW... WENDY ON LINE 3, GO AHEAD.
K.R.A.B. RADIO
YOU'RE A COMPLETE JERK! YOU'RE JUST MEAN AND HATEFUL.
IT'S CLOSE-MINDED IDIOTS LIKE YOU WHO ARE TEARING THIS LAGOON APART.
K.R.A.B.
AREN'T YOU MY CALL SCREENER?
SORRY. SLOW CALL-IN DAY.
THIS IS THE MORNING ZOO WITH SHERMAN AND ERNEST!
K.R.A.B. RADIO
THE ZANIEST WAY TO START YOUR DAY!
K.R.A.B.
DO SOMETHING ZANY.
ZANIER THAN WAKING UP AT 4:00 A.M.?
K.R.A.B.
I'M CHANGING THE FORMAT OF K.R.A.B. RADIO. YOU'RE ALL FIRED.
HUH?
THE YOUNGER AUDIENCES DON'T WANT TALK RADIO. THEY WANT MUSIC.
K.R.A.B.
STARTING TODAY, WE'RE GOING ALL BAGPIPES ALL THE TIME.
REPLACED BY A BAGPIPES.
THE WINDS OF CHANGE.
BLOWING LOUD AND SCREECHY.

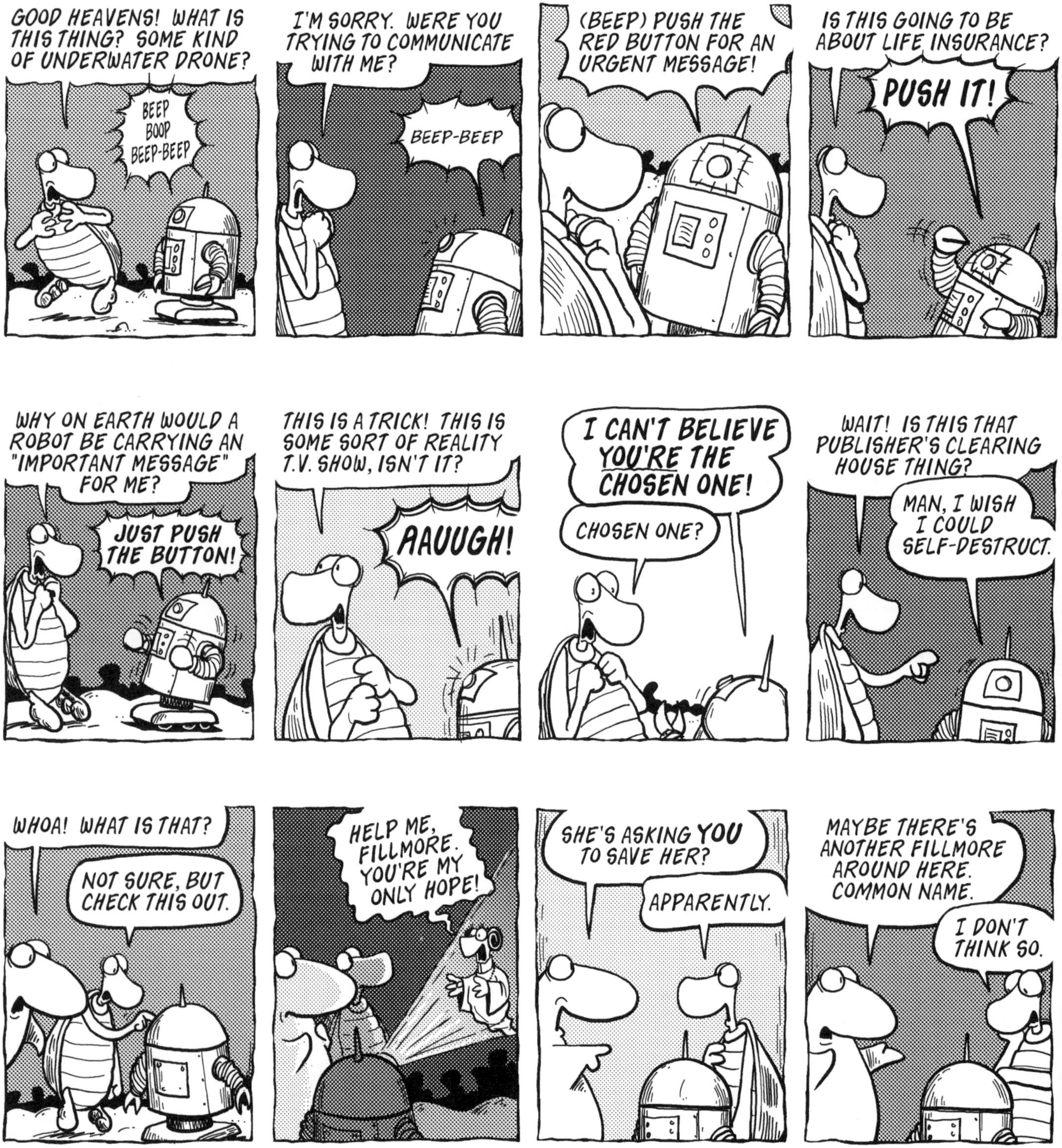
GOOD HEAVENS! WHAT IS THIS THING? SOME KIND OF UNDERWATER DRONE?
BEEP BOOP BEEP-BEEP
I'M SORRY. WERE YOU TRYING TO COMMUNICATE WITH ME?
BEEP-BEEP
(BEEP) PUSH THE RED BUTTON FOR AN URGENT MESSAGE!
IS THIS GOING TO BE ABOUT LIFE INSURANCE?
PUSH IT!
WHY ON EARTH WOULD A ROBOT BE CARRYING AN "IMPORTANT MESSAGE" FOR ME?
JUST PUSH THE BUTTON!
THIS IS A TRICK! THIS IS SOME SORT OF REALITY T.V. SHOW, ISN'T IT?
AAUUGH!
I CAN'T BELIEVE YOU'RE THE CHOSEN ONE!
CHOSEN ONE?
WAIT! IS THIS THAT PUBLISHER'S CLEARING HOUSE THING?
MAN, I WISH I COULD SELF-DESTRUCT.
WHOA! WHAT IS THAT?
NOT SURE, BUT CHECK THIS OUT.
HELP ME, FILLMORE. YOU'RE MY ONLY HOPE!
SHE'S ASKING YOU TO SAVE HER?
APPARENTLY.
MAYBE THERE'S ANOTHER FILLMORE AROUND HERE. COMMON NAME.
I DON'T THINK SO.

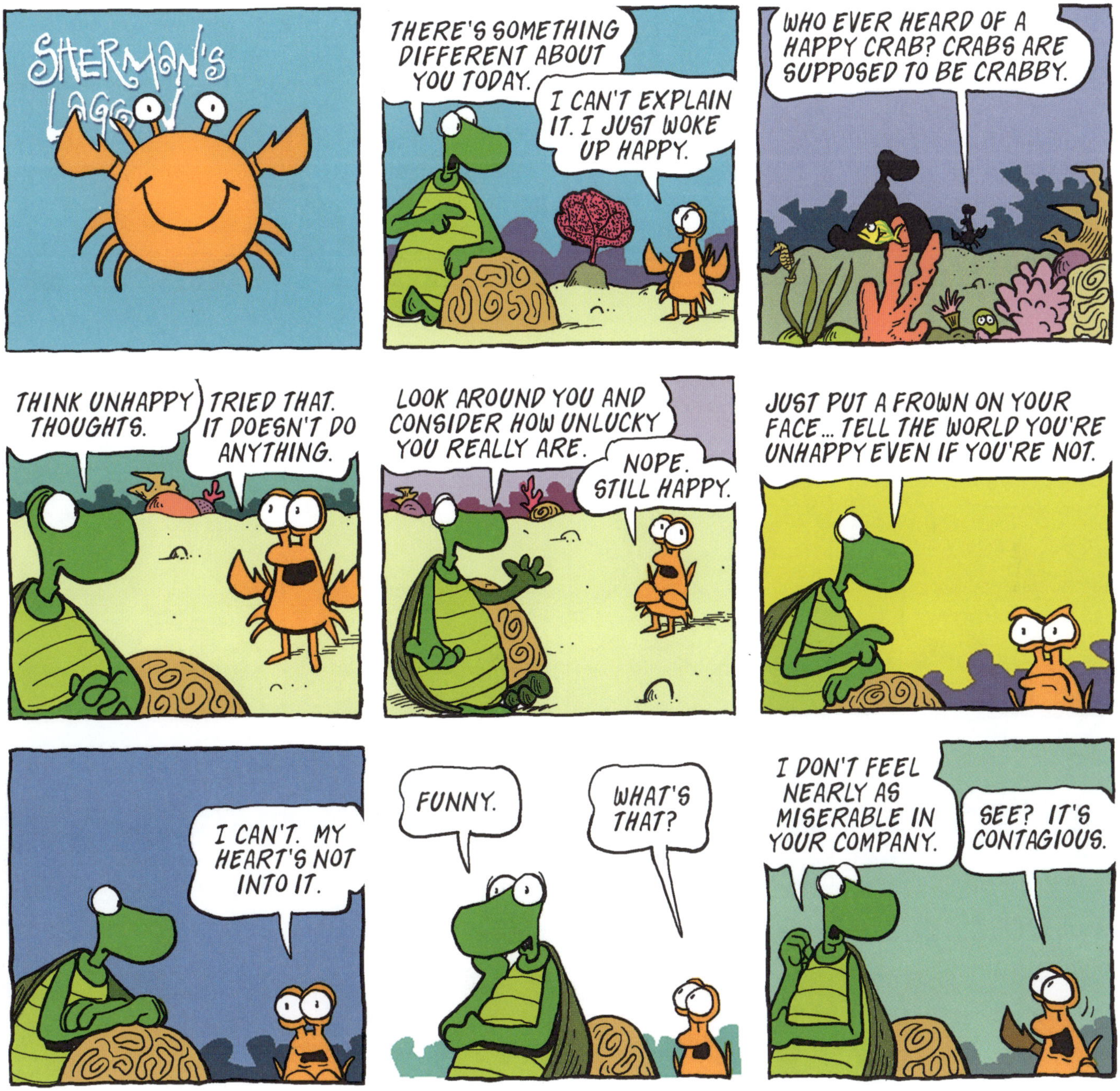
SHERMAN'S LAGOON
THERE'S SOMETHING DIFFERENT ABOUT YOU TODAY.
I CAN'T EXPLAIN IT. I JUST WOKE UP HAPPY.
WHO EVER HEARD OF A HAPPY CRAB? CRABS ARE SUPPOSED TO BE CRABBY.
THINK UNHAPPY THOUGHTS.
TRIED THAT. IT DOESN'T DO ANYTHING.
LOOK AROUND YOU AND CONSIDER HOW UNLUCKY YOU REALLY ARE.
NOPE. STILL HAPPY.
JUST PUT A FROWN ON YOUR FACE... TELL THE WORLD YOU'RE UNHAPPY EVEN IF YOU'RE NOT.
I CAN'T. MY HEART'S NOT INTO IT.
FUNNY.
WHAT'S THAT?
I DON'T FEEL NEARLY AS MISERABLE IN YOUR COMPANY.
SEE? IT'S CONTAGIOUS.

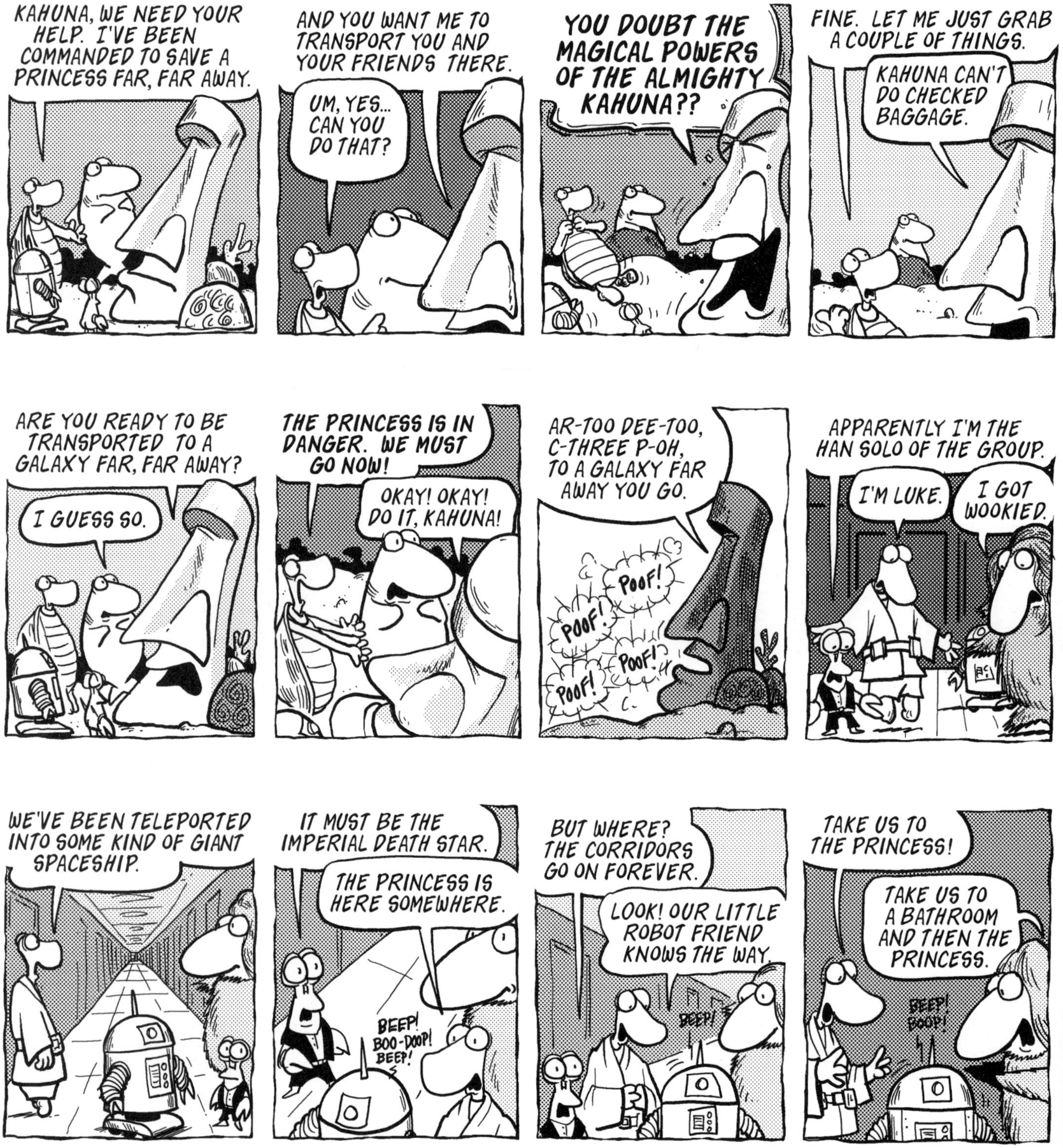
KAHUNA, WE NEED YOUR HELP. I'VE BEEN COMMANDED TO SAVE A PRINCESS FAR, FAR AWAY.
AND YOU WANT ME TO TRANSPORT YOU AND YOUR FRIENDS THERE.
UM, YES... CAN YOU DO THAT?
YOU DOUBT THE MAGICAL POWERS OF THE ALMIGHTY KAHUNA??
FINE. LET ME JUST GRAB A COUPLE OF THINGS.
KAHUNA CAN'T DO CHECKED BAGGAGE.
ARE YOU READY TO BE TRANSPORTED TO A GALAXY FAR, FAR AWAY?
I GUESS SO.
THE PRINCESS IS IN DANGER. WE MUST GO NOW!
OKAY! OKAY! DO IT, KAHUNA!
AR-TOO DEE-TOO, C-THREE P-OH, TO A GALAXY FAR AWAY YOU GO.
POOF!
POOF!
POOF!
POOF!
APPARENTLY I'M THE HAN SOLO OF THE GROUP.
I'M LUKE.
I GOT WOOKIED.
WE'VE BEEN TELEPORTED INTO SOME KIND OF GIANT SPACESHIP.
IT MUST BE THE IMPERIAL DEATH STAR.
THE PRINCESS IS HERE SOMEWHERE.
BEEP! BOO-DOOP! BEEP!
BUT WHERE? THE CORRIDORS GO ON FOREVER.
LOOK! OUR LITTLE ROBOT FRIEND KNOWS THE WAY.
BEEP!
TAKE US TO THE PRINCESS!
TAKE US TO A BATHROOM AND THEN THE PRINCESS.
BEEP! BOOP!

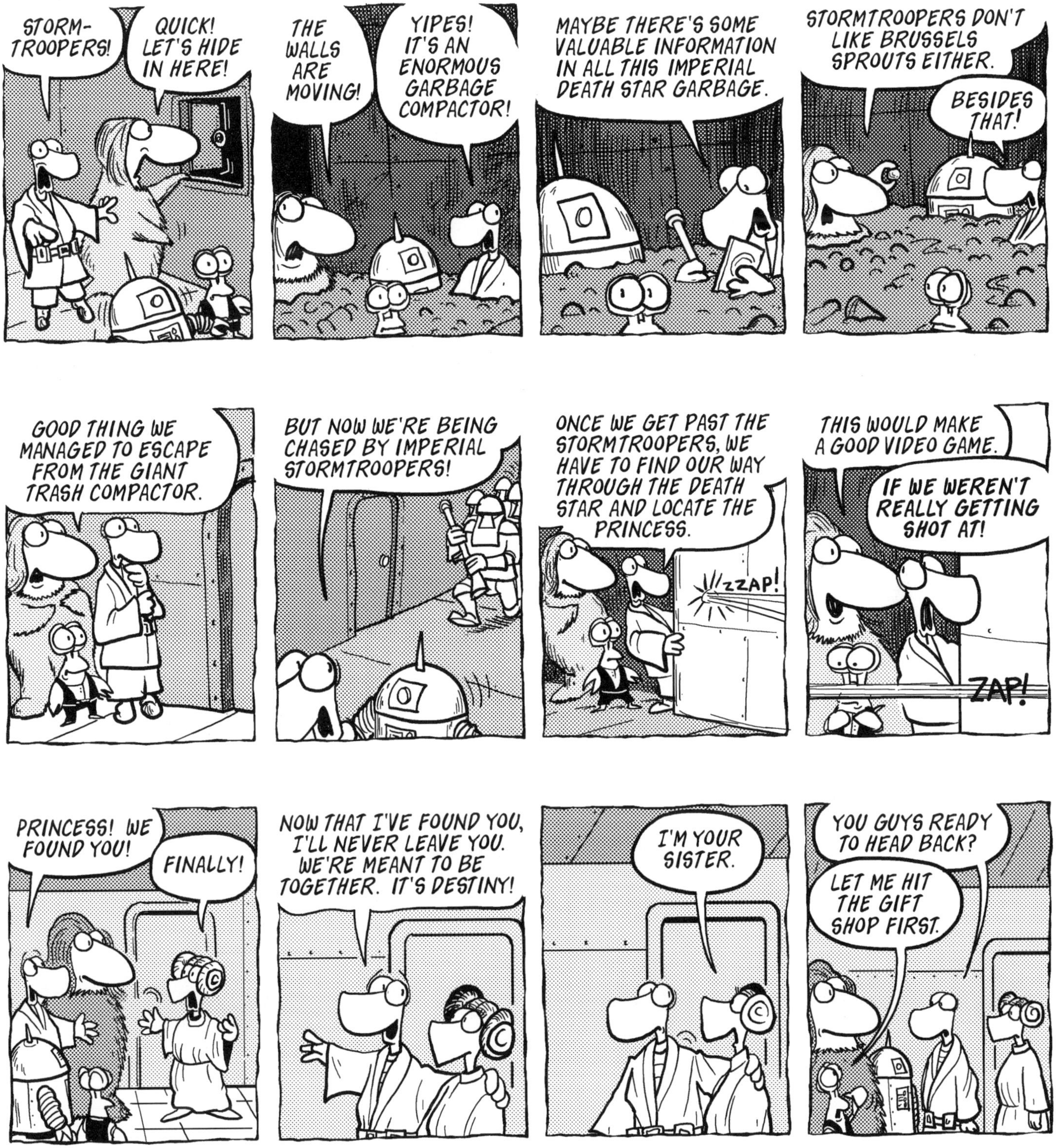
STORM-TROOPERS!
QUICK! LET'S HIDE IN HERE!
THE WALLS ARE MOVING!
YIPES! IT'S AN ENORMOUS GARBAGE COMPACTOR!
MAYBE THERE'S SOME VALUABLE INFORMATION IN ALL THIS IMPERIAL DEATH STAR GARBAGE.
STORMTROOPERS DON'T LIKE BRUSSELS SPROUTS EITHER.
BESIDES THAT!
GOOD THING WE MANAGED TO ESCAPE FROM THE GIANT TRASH COMPACTOR.
BUT NOW WE'RE BEING CHASED BY IMPERIAL STORMTROOPERS!
ONCE WE GET PAST THE STORMTROOPERS, WE HAVE TO FIND OUR WAY THROUGH THE DEATH STAR AND LOCATE THE PRINCESS.
ZZAP!
THIS WOULD MAKE A GOOD VIDEO GAME.
IF WE WEREN'T REALLY GETTING SHOT AT!
ZAP!
PRINCESS! WE FOUND YOU!
FINALLY!
NOW THAT I'VE FOUND YOU, I'LL NEVER LEAVE YOU. WE'RE MEANT TO BE TOGETHER. IT'S DESTINY!
I'M YOUR SISTER.
YOU GUYS READY TO HEAD BACK?
LET ME HIT THE GIFT SHOP FIRST.

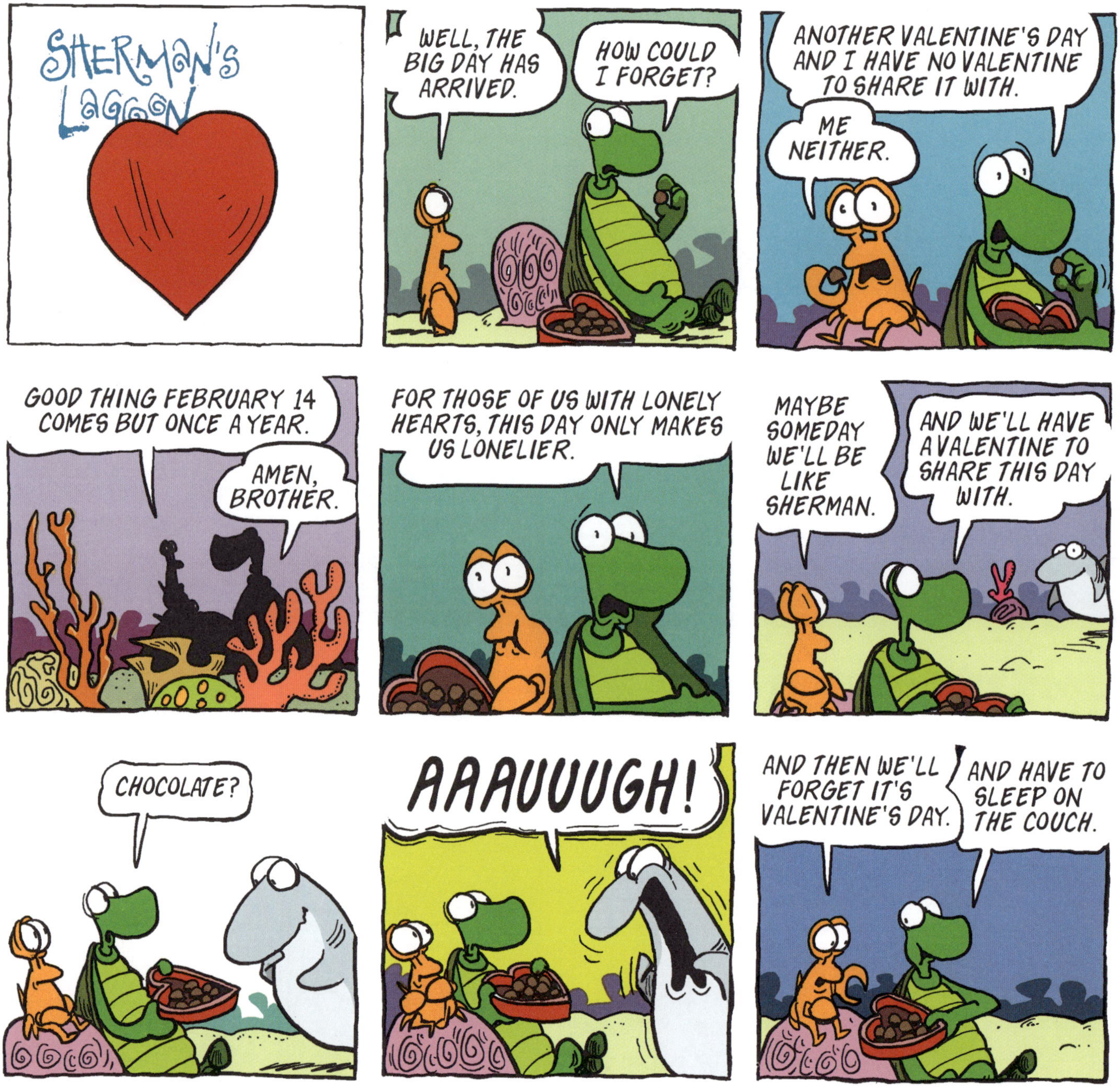
SHERMAN'S LAGOON
WELL, THE BIG DAY HAS ARRIVED.
HOW COULD I FORGET?
ANOTHER VALENTINE'S DAY AND I HAVE NO VALENTINE TO SHARE IT WITH.
ME NEITHER.
GOOD THING FEBRUARY 14 COMES BUT ONCE A YEAR.
AMEN, BROTHER.
FOR THOSE OF US WITH LONELY HEARTS, THIS DAY ONLY MAKES US LONELIER.
MAYBE SOMEDAY WE'LL BE LIKE SHERMAN.
AND WE'LL HAVE A VALENTINE TO SHARE THIS DAY WITH.
CHOCOLATE?
AAAUUUGH!
AND THEN WE'LL FORGET IT'S VALENTINE'S DAY.
AND HAVE TO SLEEP ON THE COUCH.

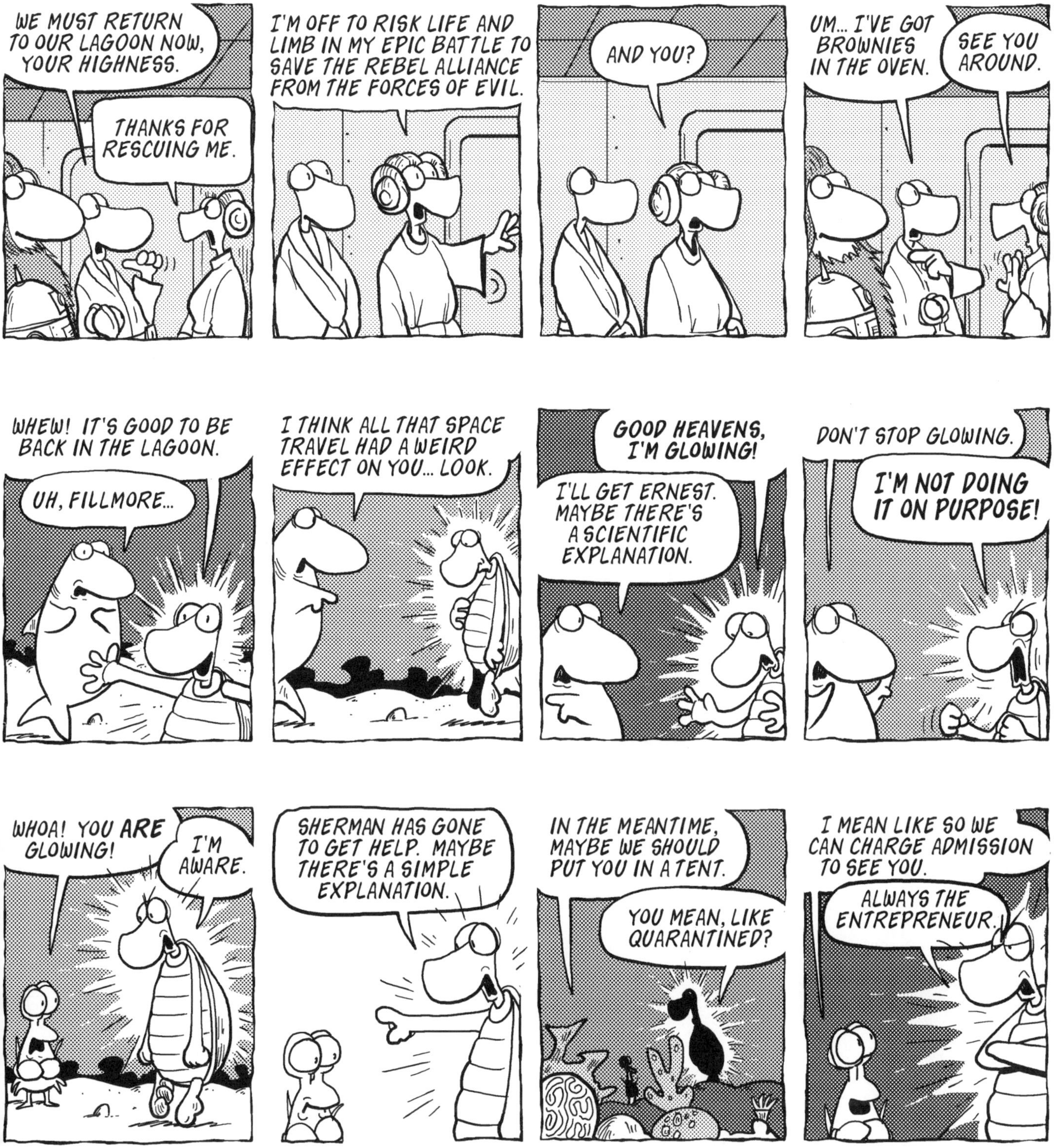
WE MUST RETURN TO OUR LAGOON NOW, YOUR HIGHNESS.
THANKS FOR RESCUING ME.
I'M OFF TO RISK LIFE AND LIMB IN MY EPIC BATTLE TO SAVE THE REBEL ALLIANCE FROM THE FORCES OF EVIL.
AND YOU?
UM... I'VE GOT BROWNIES IN THE OVEN.
SEE YOU AROUND.
WHEW! IT'S GOOD TO BE BACK IN THE LAGOON.
UH, FILLMORE...
I THINK ALL THAT SPACE TRAVEL HAD A WEIRD EFFECT ON YOU... LOOK.
GOOD HEAVENS, I'M GLOWING!
I'LL GET ERNEST. MAYBE THERE'S A SCIENTIFIC EXPLANATION.
DON'T STOP GLOWING.
I'M NOT DOING IT ON PURPOSE!
WHOA! YOU **ARE** GLOWING!
I'M AWARE.
SHERMAN HAS GONE TO GET HELP. MAYBE THERE'S A SIMPLE EXPLANATION.
IN THE MEANTIME, MAYBE WE SHOULD PUT YOU IN A TENT.
YOU MEAN, LIKE QUARANTINED?
I MEAN LIKE SO WE CAN CHARGE ADMISSION TO SEE YOU.
ALWAYS THE ENTREPRENEUR.

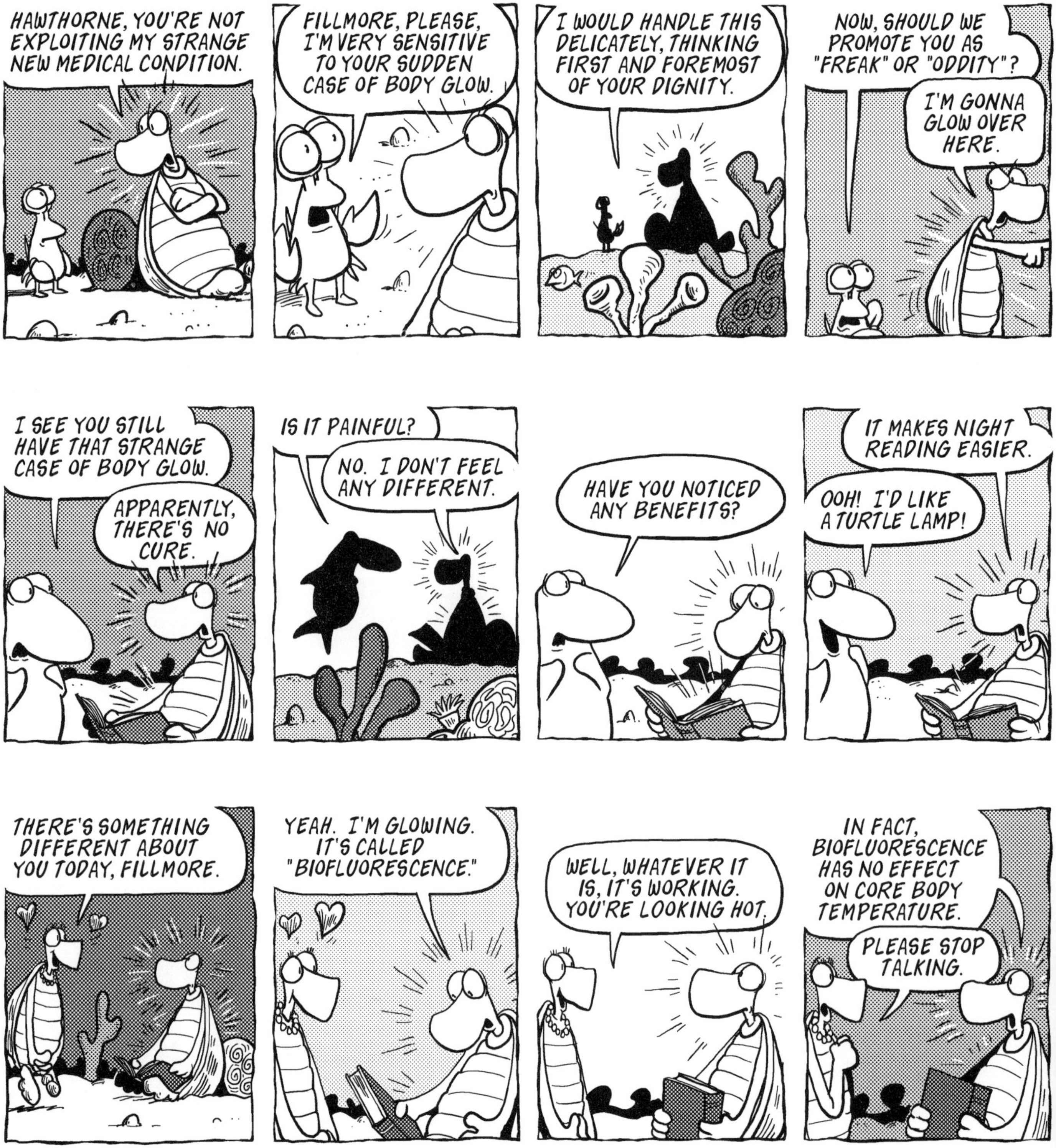
HAWTHORNE, YOU'RE NOT EXPLOITING MY STRANGE NEW MEDICAL CONDITION.
FILLMORE, PLEASE, I'M VERY SENSITIVE TO YOUR SUDDEN CASE OF BODY GLOW.
I WOULD HANDLE THIS DELICATELY, THINKING FIRST AND FOREMOST OF YOUR DIGNITY.
NOW, SHOULD WE PROMOTE YOU AS "FREAK" OR "ODDITY"?
I'M GONNA GLOW OVER HERE.
I SEE YOU STILL HAVE THAT STRANGE CASE OF BODY GLOW.
APPARENTLY, THERE'S NO CURE.
IS IT PAINFUL?
NO. I DON'T FEEL ANY DIFFERENT.
HAVE YOU NOTICED ANY BENEFITS?
IT MAKES NIGHT READING EASIER.
OOH! I'D LIKE A TURTLE LAMP!
THERE'S SOMETHING DIFFERENT ABOUT YOU TODAY, FILLMORE.
YEAH. I'M GLOWING. IT'S CALLED "BIOFLUORESCENCE."
WELL, WHATEVER IT IS, IT'S WORKING. YOU'RE LOOKING HOT.
IN FACT, BIOFLUORESCENCE HAS NO EFFECT ON CORE BODY TEMPERATURE.
PLEASE STOP TALKING.

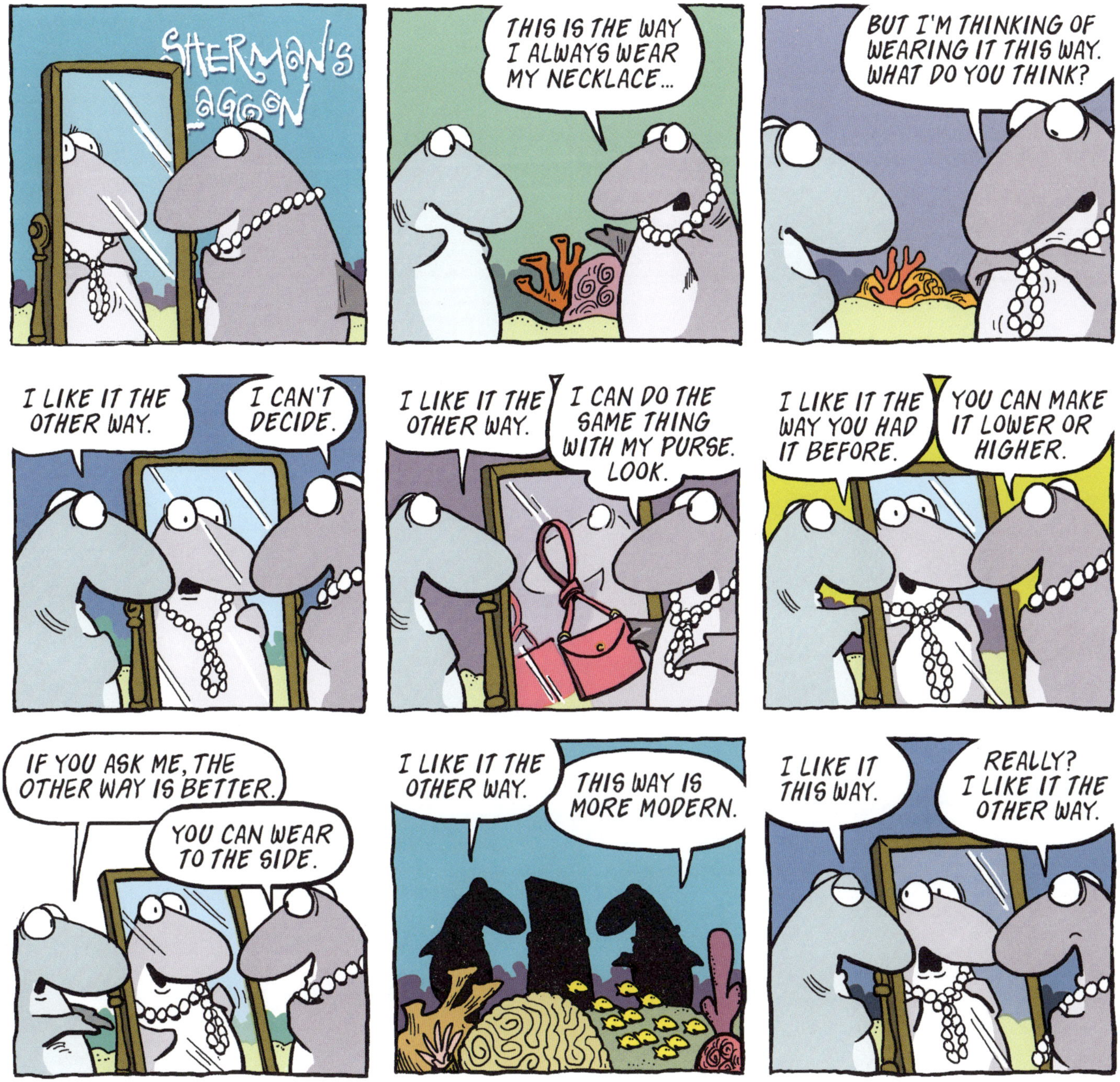
SHERMAN'S LAGOON
THIS IS THE WAY I ALWAYS WEAR MY NECKLACE...
BUT I'M THINKING OF WEARING IT THIS WAY. WHAT DO YOU THINK?
I LIKE IT THE OTHER WAY.
I CAN'T DECIDE.
I LIKE IT THE OTHER WAY.
I CAN DO THE SAME THING WITH MY PURSE. LOOK.
I LIKE IT THE WAY YOU HAD IT BEFORE.
YOU CAN MAKE IT LOWER OR HIGHER.
IF YOU ASK ME, THE OTHER WAY IS BETTER.
YOU CAN WEAR TO THE SIDE.
I LIKE IT THE OTHER WAY.
THIS WAY IS MORE MODERN.
I LIKE IT THIS WAY.
REALLY? I LIKE IT THE OTHER WAY.

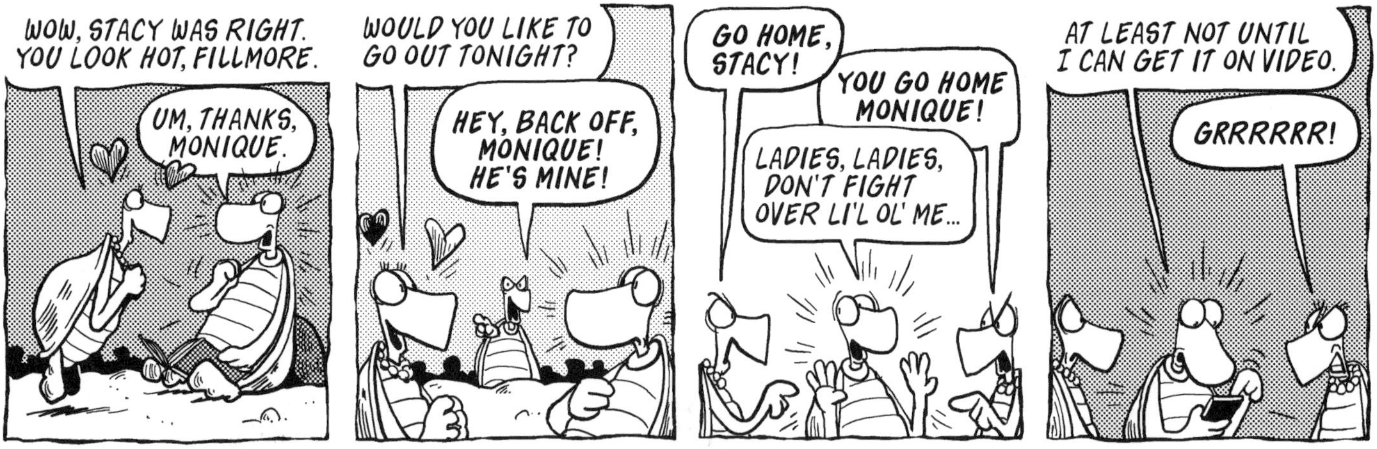
WOW, STACY WAS RIGHT. YOU LOOK HOT, FILLMORE.
UM, THANKS, MONIQUE.
WOULD YOU LIKE TO GO OUT TONIGHT?
HEY, BACK OFF, MONIQUE! HE'S MINE!
GO HOME, STACY!
YOU GO HOME MONIQUE!
LADIES, LADIES, DON'T FIGHT OVER LI'L OL' ME...
AT LEAST NOT UNTIL I CAN GET IT ON VIDEO.
GRRRRRR!

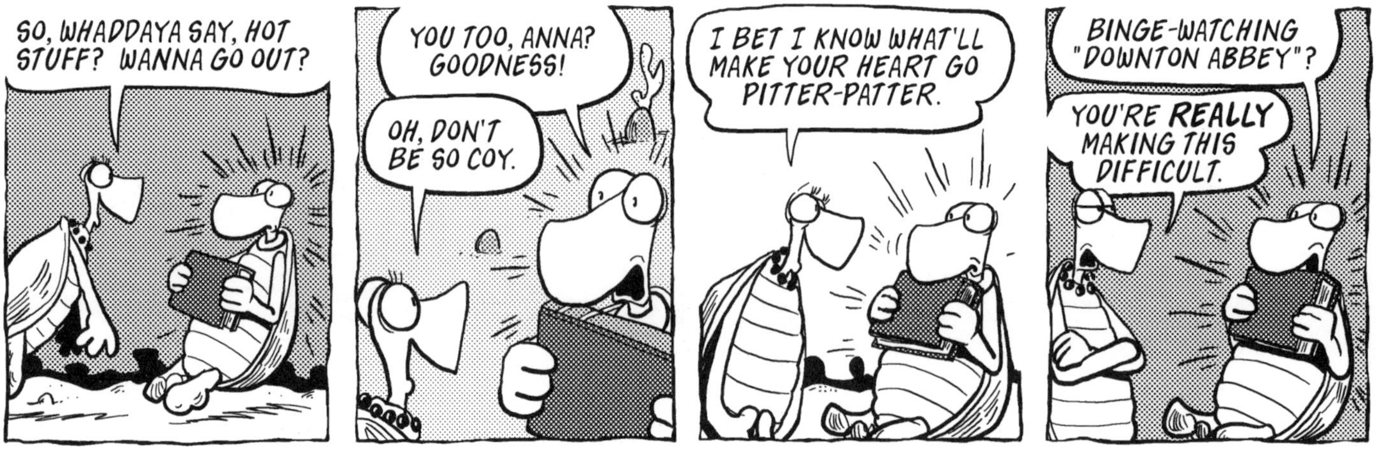
SO, WHADDAYA SAY, HOT STUFF? WANNA GO OUT?
YOU TOO, ANNA? GOODNESS!
OH, DON'T BE SO COY.
I BET I KNOW WHAT'LL MAKE YOUR HEART GO PITTER-PATTER.
BINGE-WATCHING "DOWNTON ABBEY"?
YOU'RE REALLY MAKING THIS DIFFICULT.

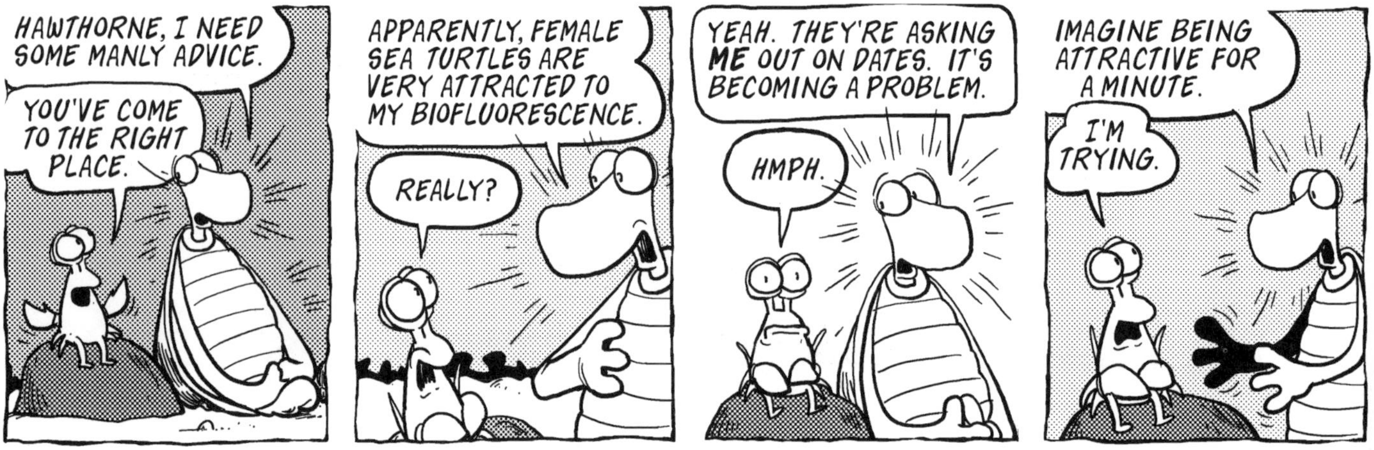
HAWTHORNE, I NEED SOME MANLY ADVICE.
YOU'VE COME TO THE RIGHT PLACE.
APPARENTLY, FEMALE SEA TURTLES ARE VERY ATTRACTED TO MY BIOFLUORESCENCE.
REALLY?
YEAH. THEY'RE ASKING ME OUT ON DATES. IT'S BECOMING A PROBLEM.
HMPH.
IMAGINE BEING ATTRACTIVE FOR A MINUTE.
I'M TRYING.

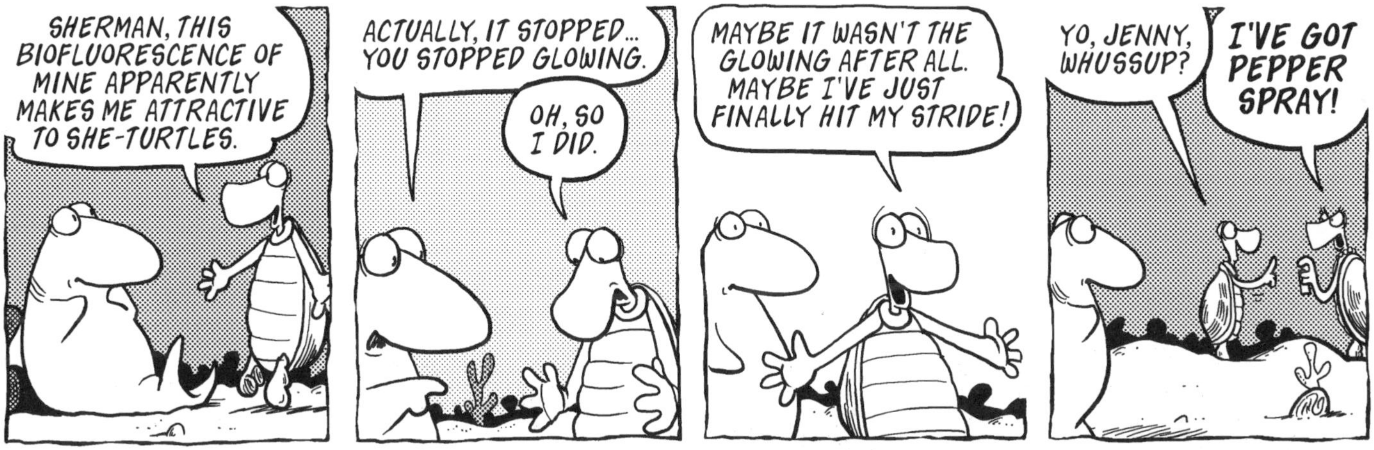
SHERMAN, THIS BIOFLUORESCENCE OF MINE APPARENTLY MAKES ME ATTRACTIVE TO SHE-TURTLES.
ACTUALLY, IT STOPPED... YOU STOPPED GLOWING.
OH, SO I DID.
MAYBE IT WASN'T THE GLOWING AFTER ALL. MAYBE I'VE JUST FINALLY HIT MY STRIDE!
YO, JENNY, WHUSSUP?
I'VE GOT PEPPER SPRAY!

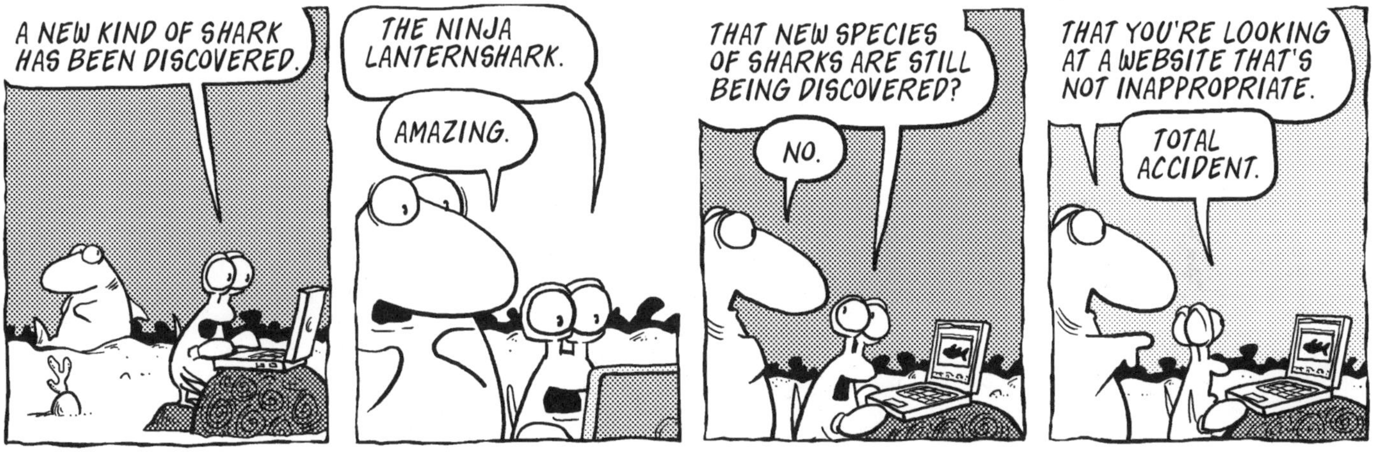
A NEW KIND OF SHARK HAS BEEN DISCOVERED.
THE NINJA LANTERNSHARK.
AMAZING.
THAT NEW SPECIES OF SHARKS ARE STILL BEING DISCOVERED?
NO.
THAT YOU'RE LOOKING AT A WEBSITE THAT'S NOT INAPPROPRIATE.
TOTAL ACCIDENT.

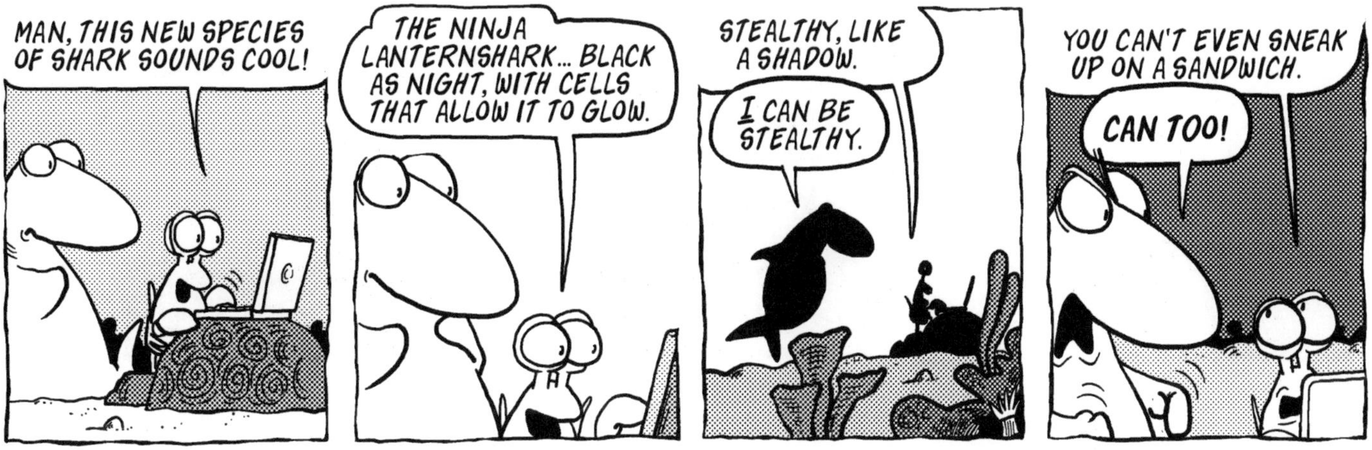
MAN, THIS NEW SPECIES OF SHARK SOUNDS COOL!
THE NINJA LANTERNSHARK... BLACK AS NIGHT, WITH CELLS THAT ALLOW IT TO GLOW.
STEALTHY, LIKE A SHADOW.
I CAN BE STEALTHY.
YOU CAN'T EVEN SNEAK UP ON A SANDWICH.
CAN TOO!

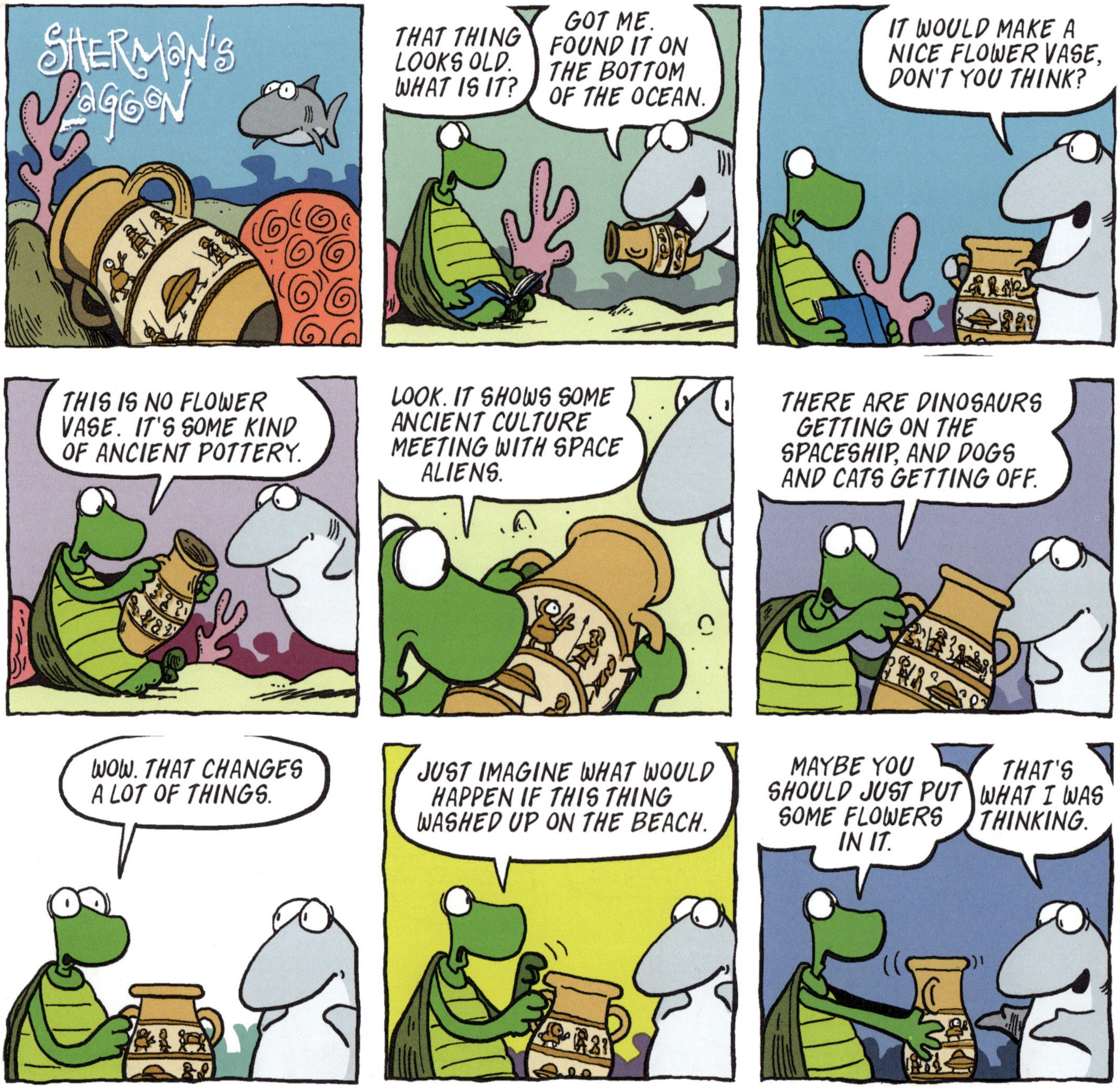
SHERMAN'S LAGOON
THAT THING LOOKS OLD. WHAT IS IT?
GOT ME. FOUND IT ON THE BOTTOM OF THE OCEAN.
IT WOULD MAKE A NICE FLOWER VASE, DON'T YOU THINK?
THIS IS NO FLOWER VASE. IT'S SOME KIND OF ANCIENT POTTERY.
LOOK. IT SHOWS SOME ANCIENT CULTURE MEETING WITH SPACE ALIENS.
THERE ARE DINOSAURS GETTING ON THE SPACESHIP, AND DOGS AND CATS GETTING OFF.
WOW. THAT CHANGES A LOT OF THINGS.
JUST IMAGINE WHAT WOULD HAPPEN IF THIS THING WASHED UP ON THE BEACH.
MAYBE YOU SHOULD JUST PUT SOME FLOWERS IN IT.
THAT'S WHAT I WAS THINKING.

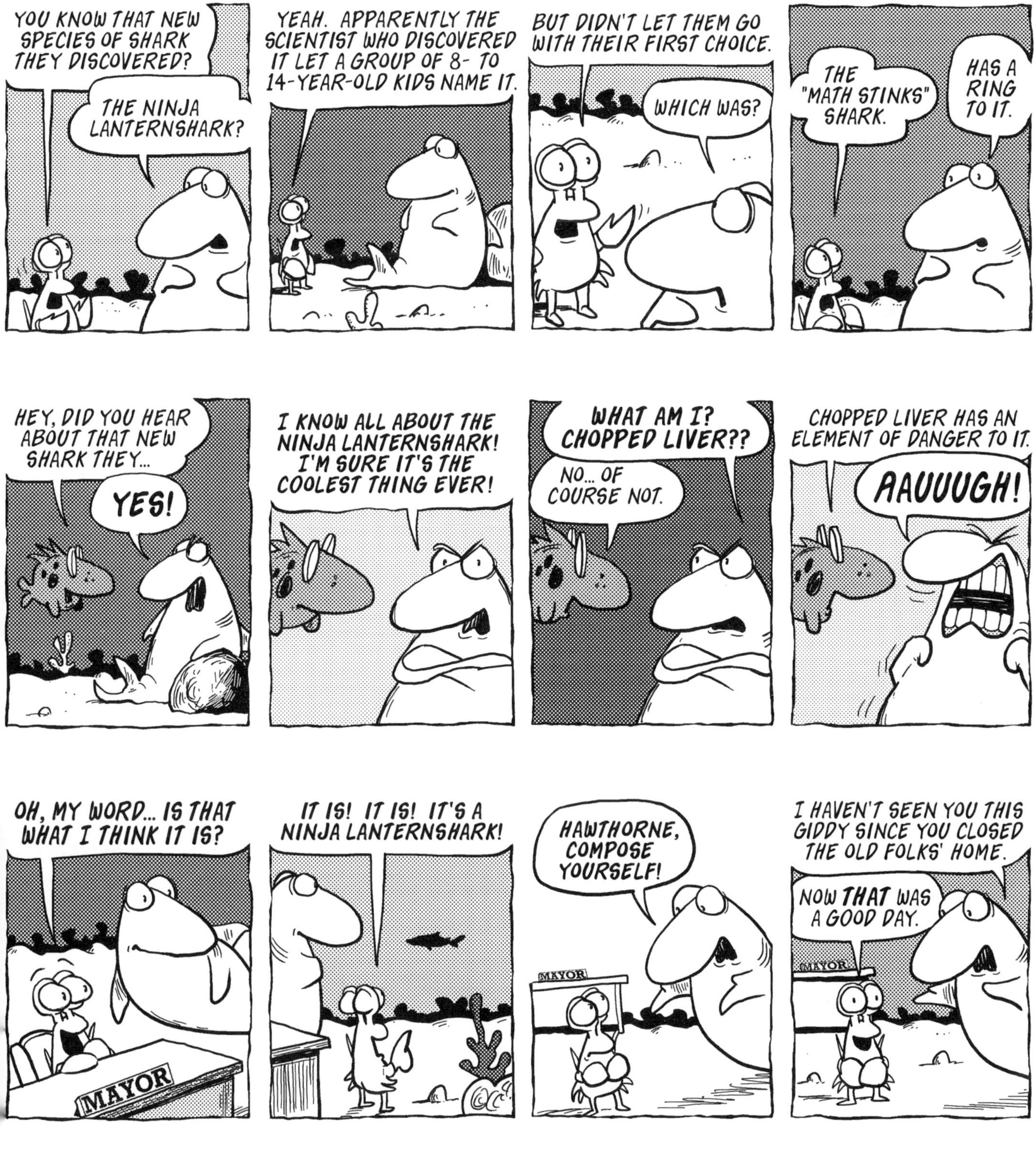
YOU KNOW THAT NEW SPECIES OF SHARK THEY DISCOVERED?
THE NINJA LANTERNSHARK?
YEAH. APPARENTLY THE SCIENTIST WHO DISCOVERED IT LET A GROUP OF 8- TO 14-YEAR-OLD KIDS NAME IT.
BUT DIDN'T LET THEM GO WITH THEIR FIRST CHOICE.
WHICH WAS?
THE "MATH STINKS" SHARK.
HAS A RING TO IT.
HEY, DID YOU HEAR ABOUT THAT NEW SHARK THEY...
YES!
I KNOW ALL ABOUT THE NINJA LANTERNSHARK! I'M SURE IT'S THE COOLEST THING EVER!
WHAT AM I? CHOPPED LIVER??
NO... OF COURSE NOT.
CHOPPED LIVER HAS AN ELEMENT OF DANGER TO IT.
AAUUUGH!
OH, MY WORD... IS THAT WHAT I THINK IT IS?
MAYOR
IT IS! IT IS! IT'S A NINJA LANTERNSHARK!
HAWTHORNE, COMPOSE YOURSELF!
MAYOR
I HAVEN'T SEEN YOU THIS GIDDY SINCE YOU CLOSED THE OLD FOLKS' HOME.
NOW THAT WAS A GOOD DAY.
MAYOR

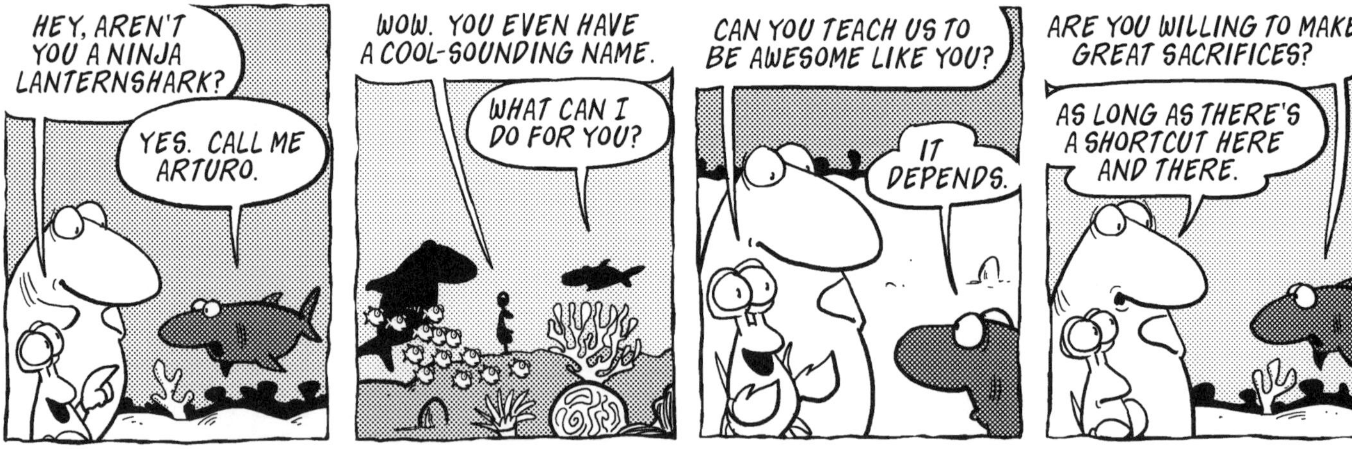
HEY, AREN'T YOU A NINJA LANTERNSHARK?
YES. CALL ME ARTURO.
WOW. YOU EVEN HAVE A COOL-SOUNDING NAME.
WHAT CAN I DO FOR YOU?
CAN YOU TEACH US TO BE AWESOME LIKE YOU?
IT DEPENDS.
ARE YOU WILLING TO MAKE GREAT SACRIFICES?
AS LONG AS THERE'S A SHORTCUT HERE AND THERE.

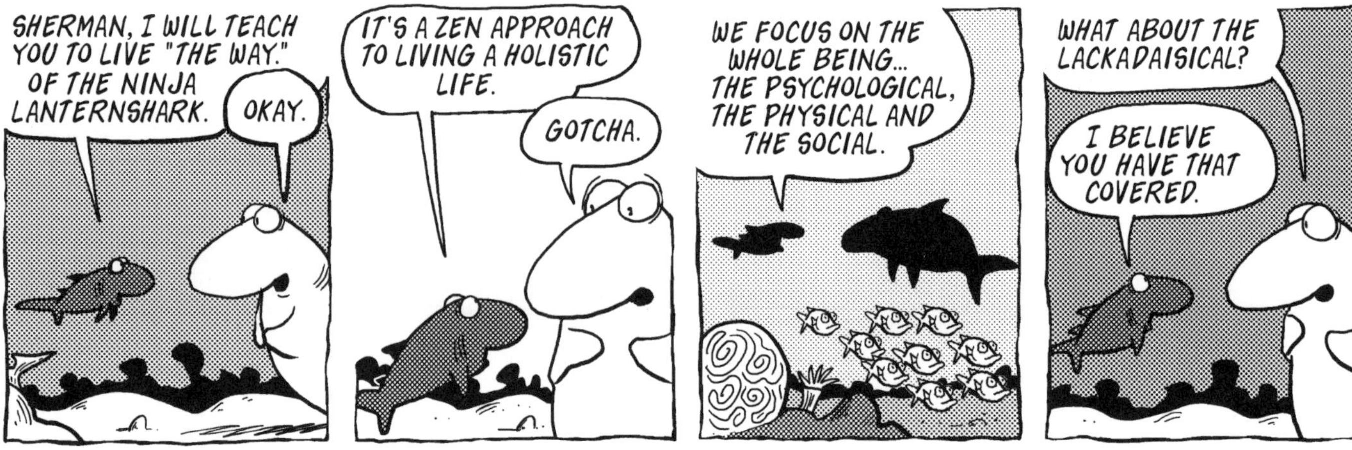
SHERMAN, I WILL TEACH YOU TO LIVE "THE WAY." OF THE NINJA LANTERNSHARK.
OKAY.
IT'S A ZEN APPROACH TO LIVING A HOLISTIC LIFE.
GOTCHA.
WE FOCUS ON THE WHOLE BEING... THE PSYCHOLOGICAL, THE PHYSICAL AND THE SOCIAL.
WHAT ABOUT THE LACKADAISICAL?
I BELIEVE YOU HAVE THAT COVERED.

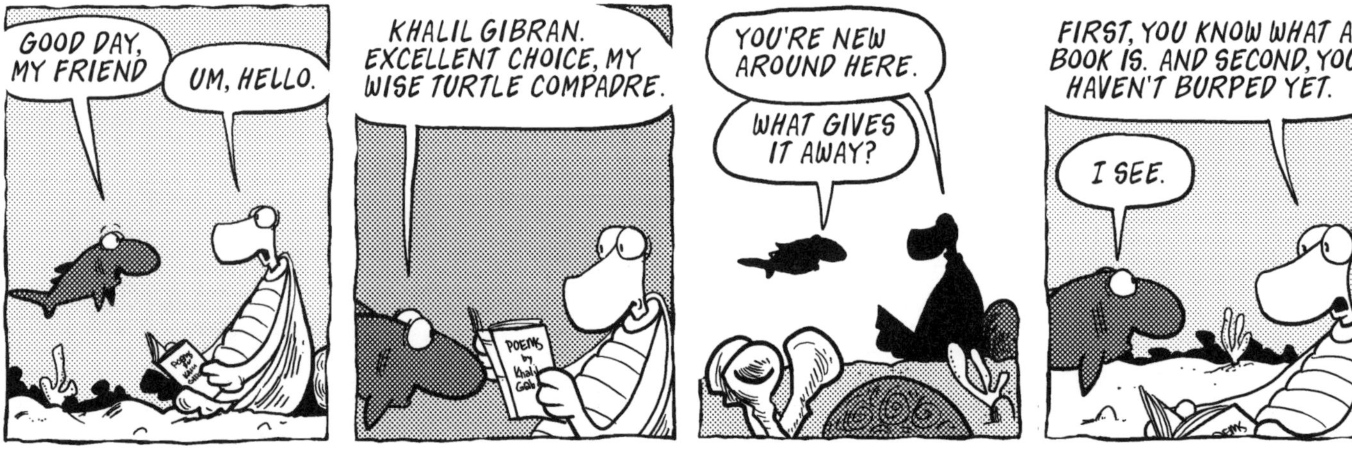
GOOD DAY, MY FRIEND
UM, HELLO.
KHALIL GIBRAN. EXCELLENT CHOICE, MY WISE TURTLE COMPADRE.
POEMS by Khalil Gib
YOU'RE NEW AROUND HERE.
WHAT GIVES IT AWAY?
FIRST, YOU KNOW WHAT A BOOK IS. AND SECOND, YOU HAVEN'T BURPED YET.
I SEE.

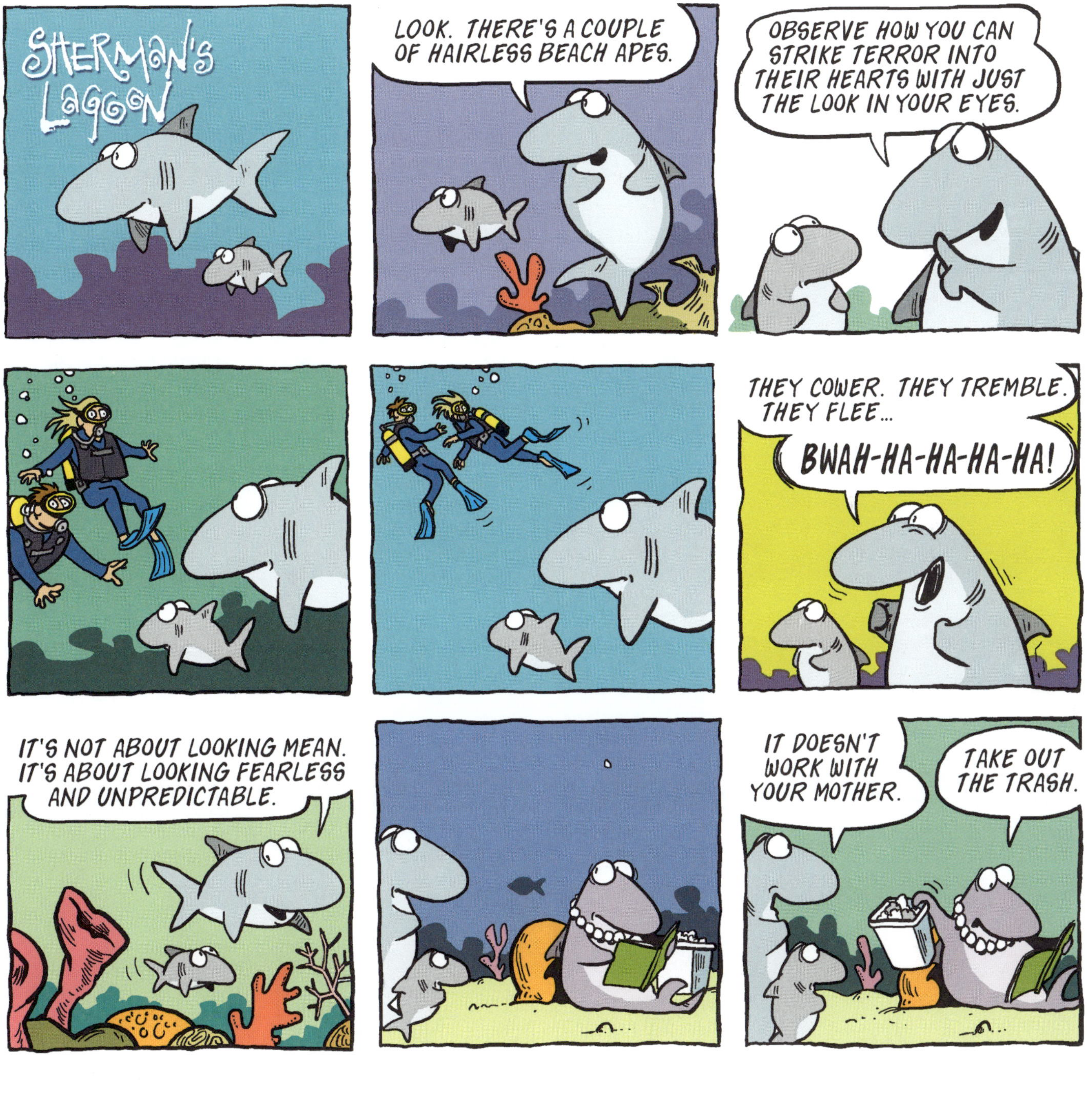
SHERMAN'S LAGOON
LOOK. THERE'S A COUPLE OF HAIRLESS BEACH APES.
OBSERVE HOW YOU CAN STRIKE TERROR INTO THEIR HEARTS WITH JUST THE LOOK IN YOUR EYES.
THEY COWER. THEY TREMBLE. THEY FLEE...
BWAH-HA-HA-HA-HA!
IT'S NOT ABOUT LOOKING MEAN. IT'S ABOUT LOOKING FEARLESS AND UNPREDICTABLE.
IT DOESN'T WORK WITH YOUR MOTHER.
TAKE OUT THE TRASH.

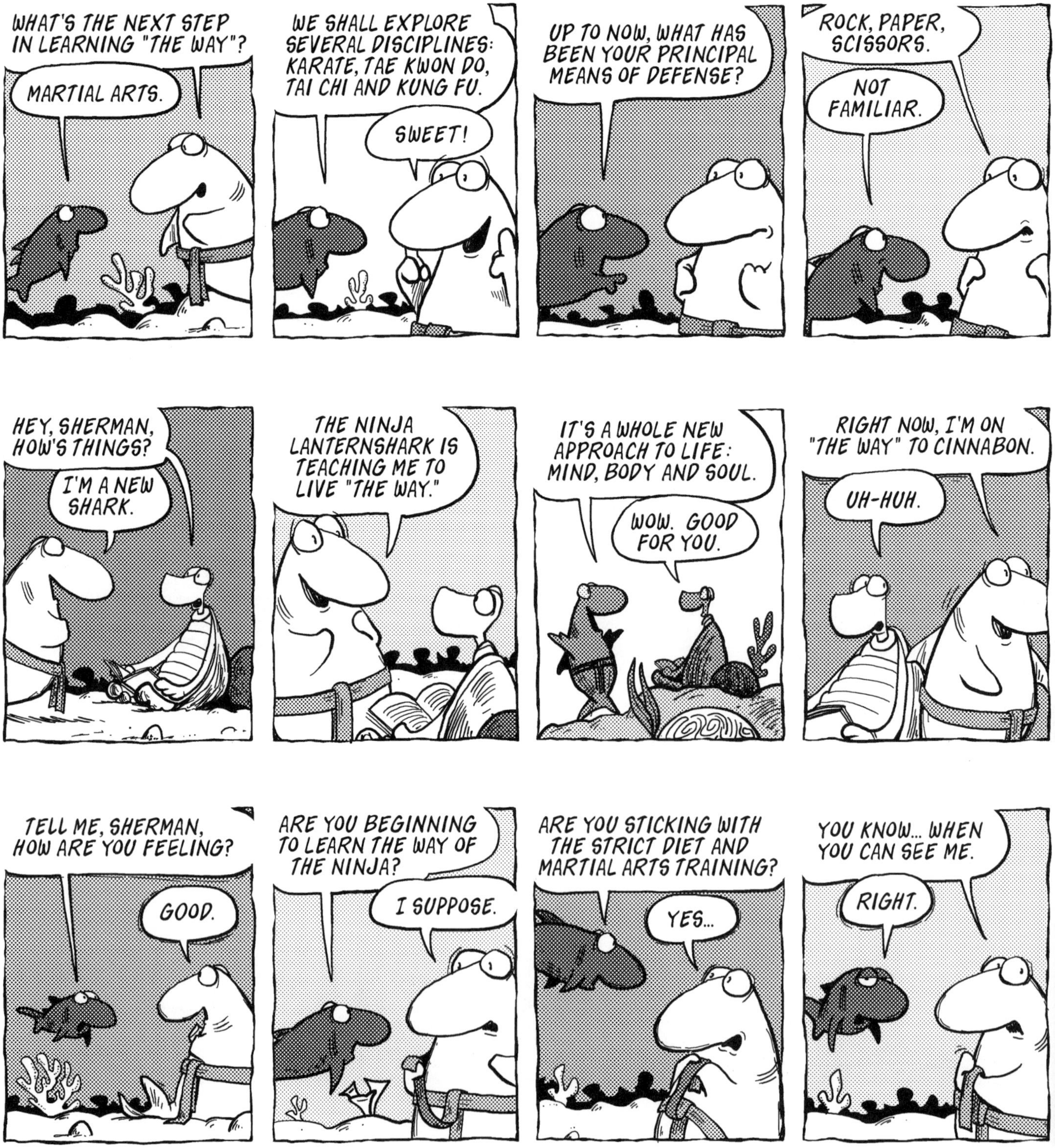
WHAT'S THE NEXT STEP IN LEARNING "THE WAY"?
MARTIAL ARTS.
WE SHALL EXPLORE SEVERAL DISCIPLINES: KARATE, TAE KWON DO, TAI CHI AND KUNG FU.
SWEET!
UP TO NOW, WHAT HAS BEEN YOUR PRINCIPAL MEANS OF DEFENSE?
ROCK, PAPER, SCISSORS.
NOT FAMILIAR.
HEY, SHERMAN, HOW'S THINGS?
I'M A NEW SHARK.
THE NINJA LANTERNSHARK IS TEACHING ME TO LIVE "THE WAY."
IT'S A WHOLE NEW APPROACH TO LIFE: MIND, BODY AND SOUL.
WOW. GOOD FOR YOU.
RIGHT NOW, I'M ON "THE WAY" TO CINNABON.
UH-HUH.
TELL ME, SHERMAN, HOW ARE YOU FEELING?
GOOD.
ARE YOU BEGINNING TO LEARN THE WAY OF THE NINJA?
I SUPPOSE.
ARE YOU STICKING WITH THE STRICT DIET AND MARTIAL ARTS TRAINING?
YES...
YOU KNOW... WHEN YOU CAN SEE ME.
RIGHT.

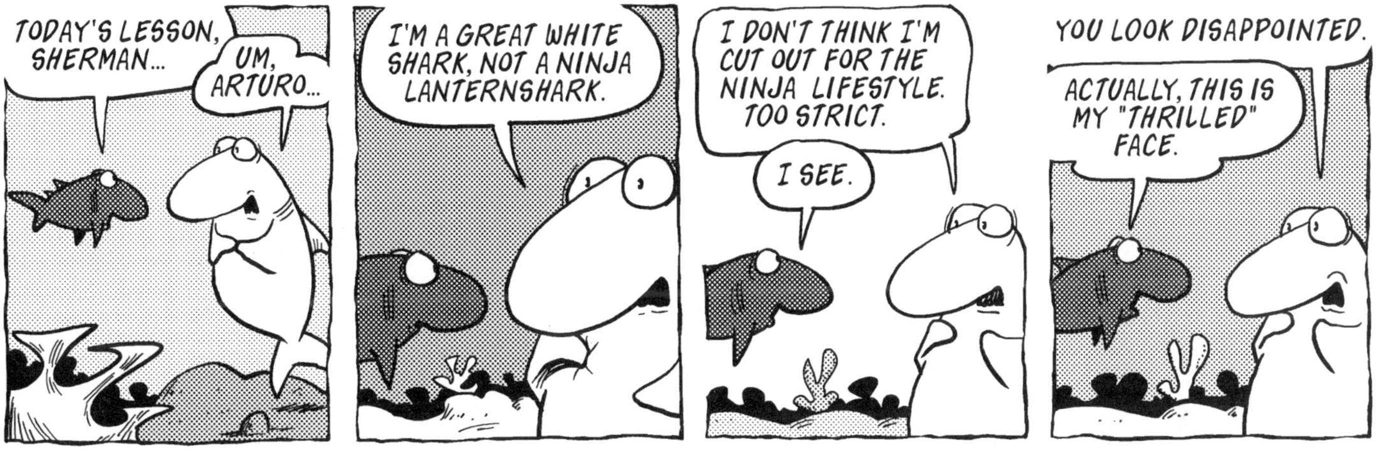
TODAY'S LESSON, SHERMAN...
UM, ARTURO...
I'M A GREAT WHITE SHARK, NOT A NINJA LANTERNSHARK.
I DON'T THINK I'M CUT OUT FOR THE NINJA LIFESTYLE. TOO STRICT.
I SEE.
YOU LOOK DISAPPOINTED.
ACTUALLY, THIS IS MY "THRILLED" FACE.

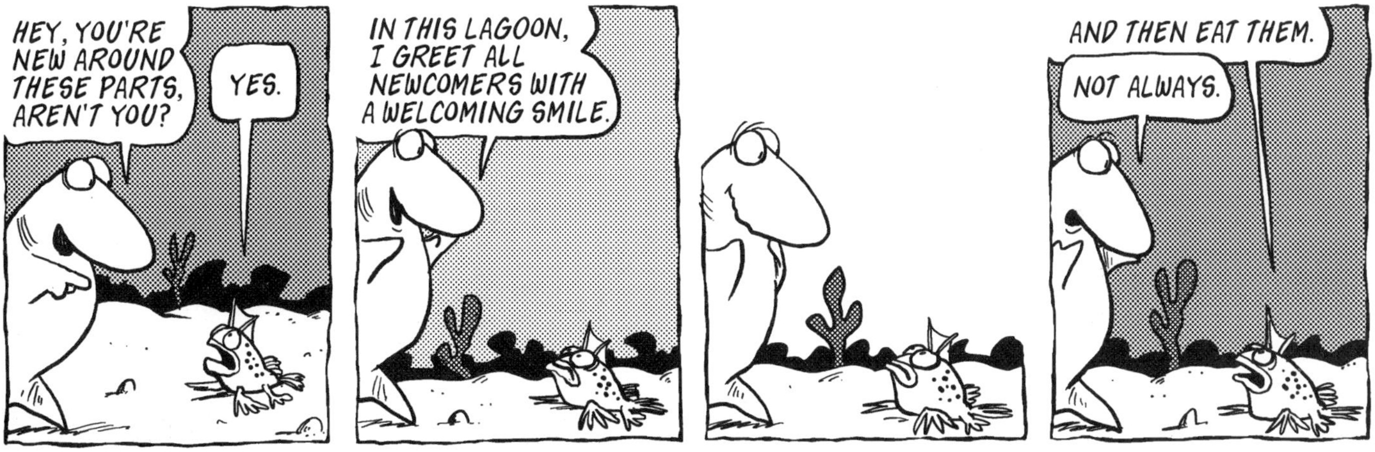
HEY, YOU'RE NEW AROUND THESE PARTS, AREN'T YOU?
YES.
IN THIS LAGOON, I GREET ALL NEWCOMERS WITH A WELCOMING SMILE.
AND THEN EAT THEM.
NOT ALWAYS.

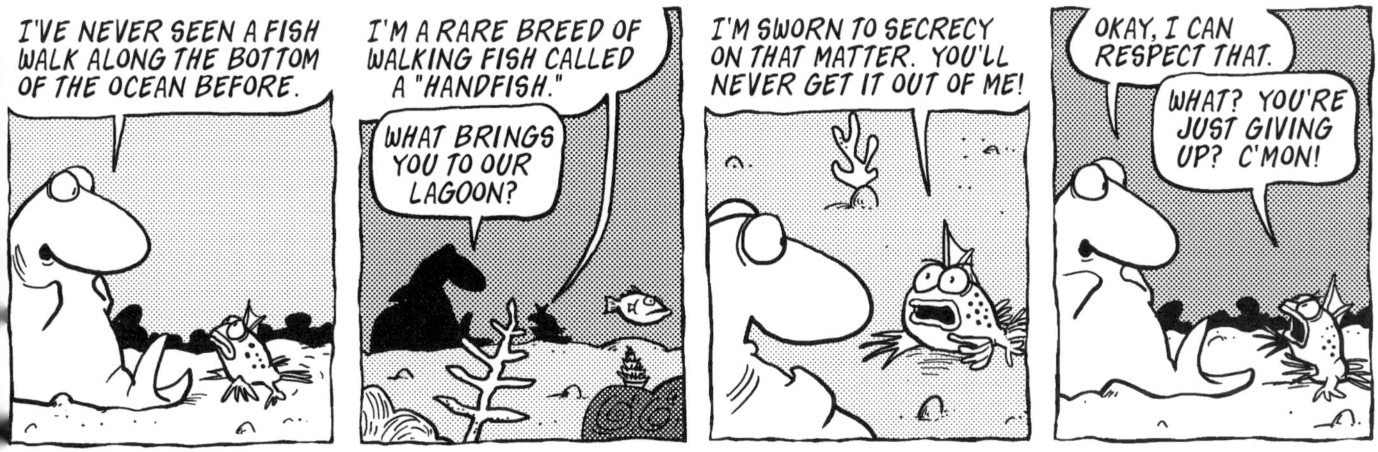
I'VE NEVER SEEN A FISH WALK ALONG THE BOTTOM OF THE OCEAN BEFORE.
I'M A RARE BREED OF WALKING FISH CALLED A "HANDFISH."
WHAT BRINGS YOU TO OUR LAGOON?
I'M SWORN TO SECRECY ON THAT MATTER. YOU'LL NEVER GET IT OUT OF ME!
OKAY, I CAN RESPECT THAT.
WHAT? YOU'RE JUST GIVING UP? C'MON!

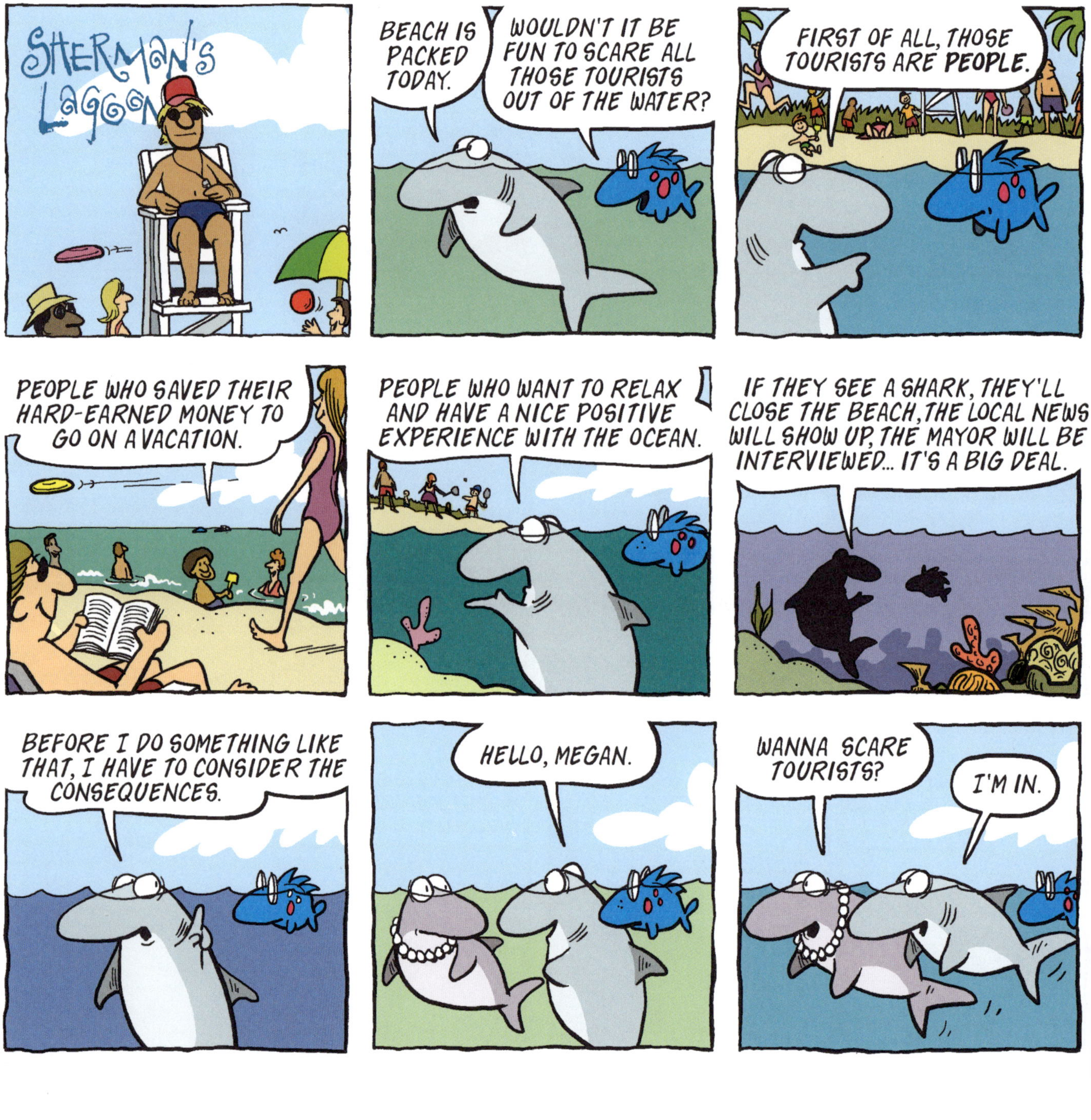
SHERMAN'S Lagoon
BEACH IS PACKED TODAY.
WOULDN'T IT BE FUN TO SCARE ALL THOSE TOURISTS OUT OF THE WATER?
FIRST OF ALL, THOSE TOURISTS ARE **PEOPLE**.
PEOPLE WHO SAVED THEIR HARD-EARNED MONEY TO GO ON A VACATION.
PEOPLE WHO WANT TO RELAX AND HAVE A NICE POSITIVE EXPERIENCE WITH THE OCEAN.
IF THEY SEE A SHARK, THEY'LL CLOSE THE BEACH, THE LOCAL NEWS WILL SHOW UP, THE MAYOR WILL BE INTERVIEWED... IT'S A BIG DEAL.
BEFORE I DO SOMETHING LIKE THAT, I HAVE TO CONSIDER THE CONSEQUENCES.
HELLO, MEGAN.
WANNA SCARE TOURISTS?
I'M IN.

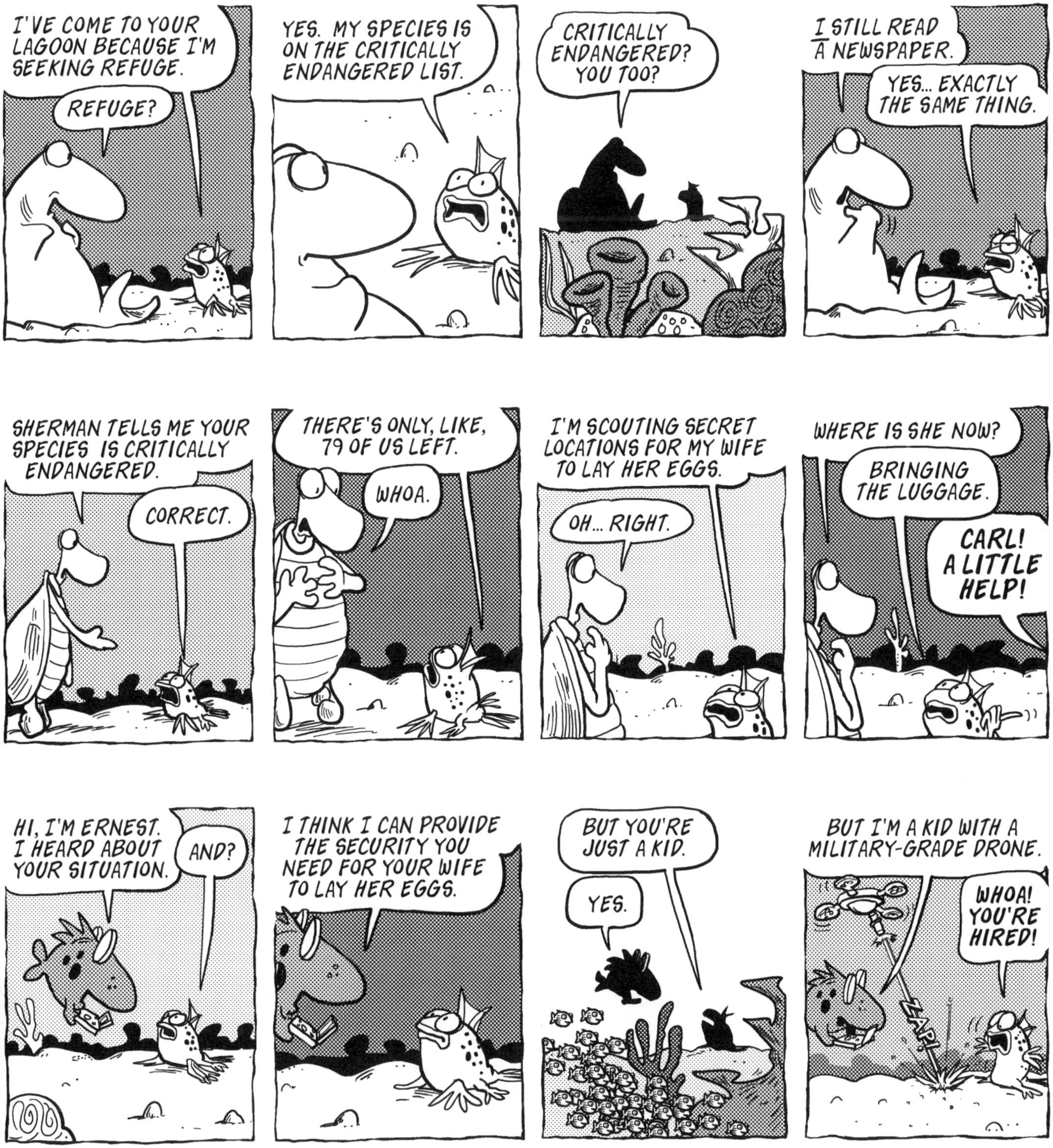
I'VE COME TO YOUR LAGOON BECAUSE I'M SEEKING REFUGE.
REFUGE?
YES. MY SPECIES IS ON THE CRITICALLY ENDANGERED LIST.
CRITICALLY ENDANGERED? YOU TOO?
I STILL READ A NEWSPAPER.
YES... EXACTLY THE SAME THING.
SHERMAN TELLS ME YOUR SPECIES IS CRITICALLY ENDANGERED.
CORRECT.
THERE'S ONLY, LIKE, 79 OF US LEFT.
WHOA.
I'M SCOUTING SECRET LOCATIONS FOR MY WIFE TO LAY HER EGGS.
OH... RIGHT.
WHERE IS SHE NOW?
BRINGING THE LUGGAGE.
CARL! A LITTLE HELP!
HI, I'M ERNEST. I HEARD ABOUT YOUR SITUATION.
AND?
I THINK I CAN PROVIDE THE SECURITY YOU NEED FOR YOUR WIFE TO LAY HER EGGS.
BUT YOU'RE JUST A KID.
YES.
BUT I'M A KID WITH A MILITARY-GRADE DRONE.
WHOA! YOU'RE HIRED!
ZAP!

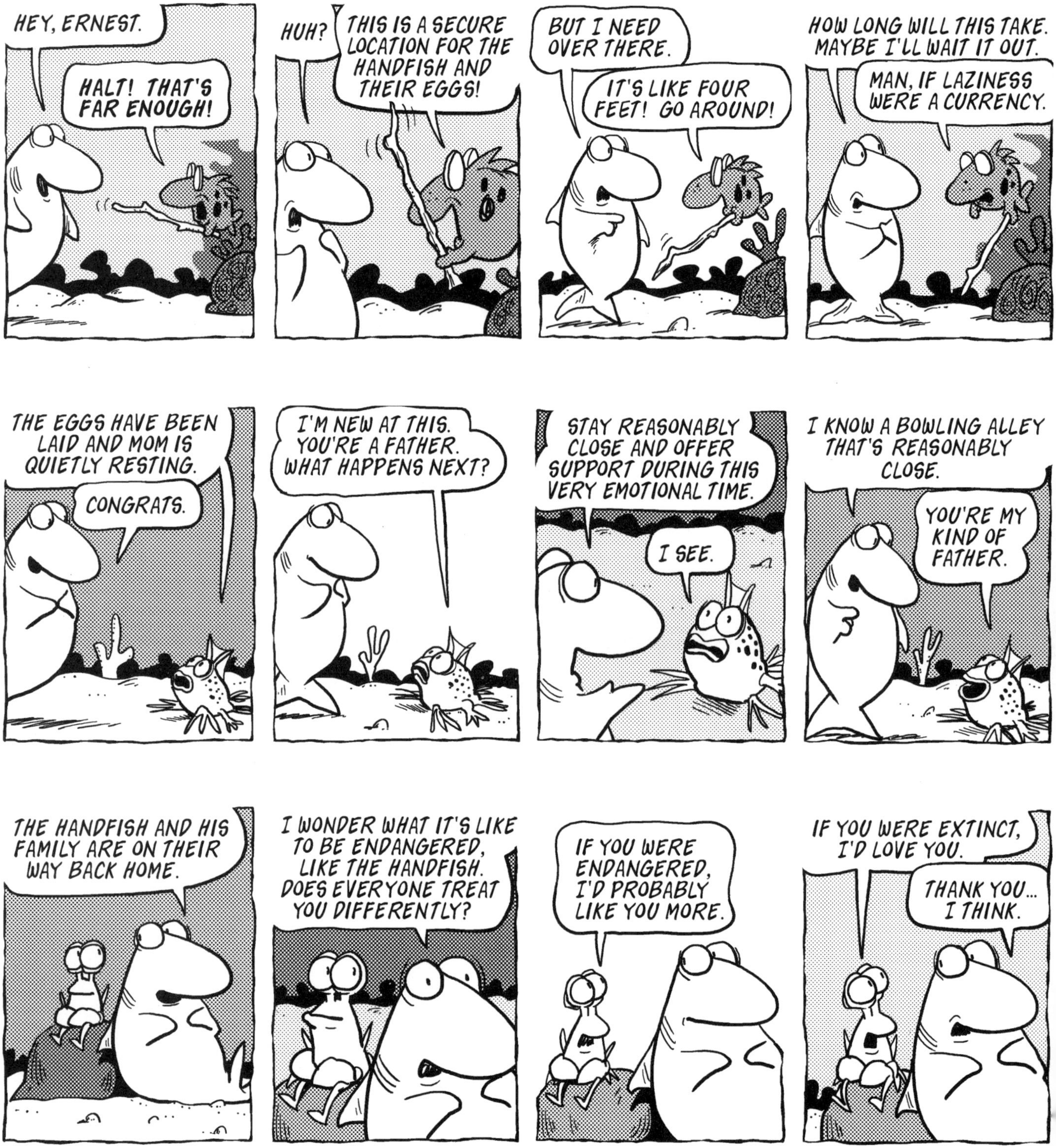
HEY, ERNEST.
HALT! THAT'S FAR ENOUGH!
HUH?
THIS IS A SECURE LOCATION FOR THE HANDFISH AND THEIR EGGS!
BUT I NEED OVER THERE.
IT'S LIKE FOUR FEET! GO AROUND!
HOW LONG WILL THIS TAKE. MAYBE I'LL WAIT IT OUT.
MAN, IF LAZINESS WERE A CURRENCY.
THE EGGS HAVE BEEN LAID AND MOM IS QUIETLY RESTING.
CONGRATS.
I'M NEW AT THIS. YOU'RE A FATHER. WHAT HAPPENS NEXT?
STAY REASONABLY CLOSE AND OFFER SUPPORT DURING THIS VERY EMOTIONAL TIME.
I SEE.
I KNOW A BOWLING ALLEY THAT'S REASONABLY CLOSE.
YOU'RE MY KIND OF FATHER.
THE HANDFISH AND HIS FAMILY ARE ON THEIR WAY BACK HOME.
I WONDER WHAT IT'S LIKE TO BE ENDANGERED, LIKE THE HANDFISH. DOES EVERYONE TREAT YOU DIFFERENTLY?
IF YOU WERE ENDANGERED, I'D PROBABLY LIKE YOU MORE.
IF YOU WERE EXTINCT, I'D LOVE YOU.
THANK YOU... I THINK.

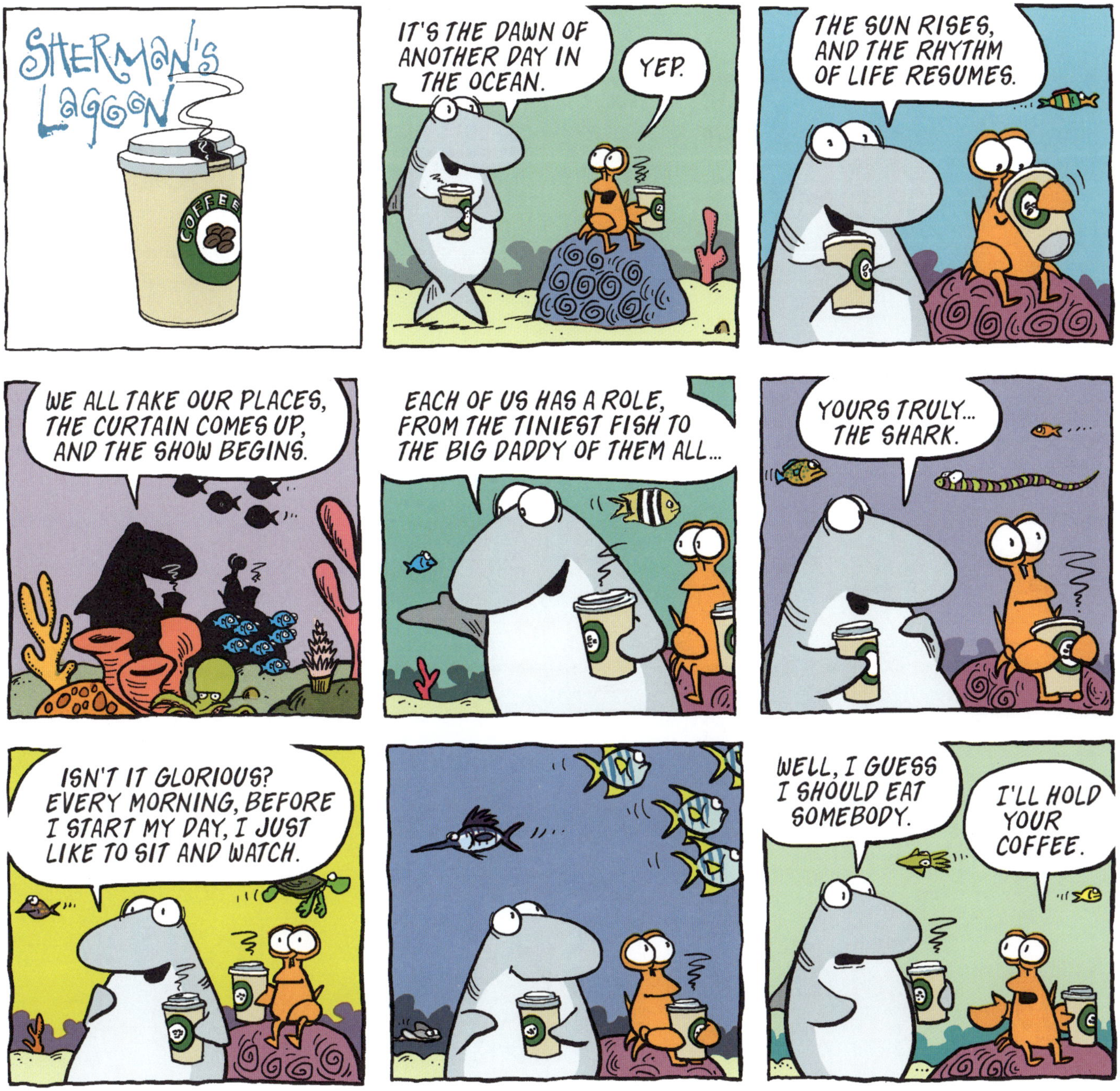
SHERMAN'S LAGOON
COFFEE
IT'S THE DAWN OF ANOTHER DAY IN THE OCEAN.
YEP.
THE SUN RISES, AND THE RHYTHM OF LIFE RESUMES.
WE ALL TAKE OUR PLACES, THE CURTAIN COMES UP, AND THE SHOW BEGINS.
EACH OF US HAS A ROLE, FROM THE TINIEST FISH TO THE BIG DADDY OF THEM ALL...
YOURS TRULY... THE SHARK.
ISN'T IT GLORIOUS? EVERY MORNING, BEFORE I START MY DAY, I JUST LIKE TO SIT AND WATCH.
WELL, I GUESS I SHOULD EAT SOMEBODY.
I'LL HOLD YOUR COFFEE.

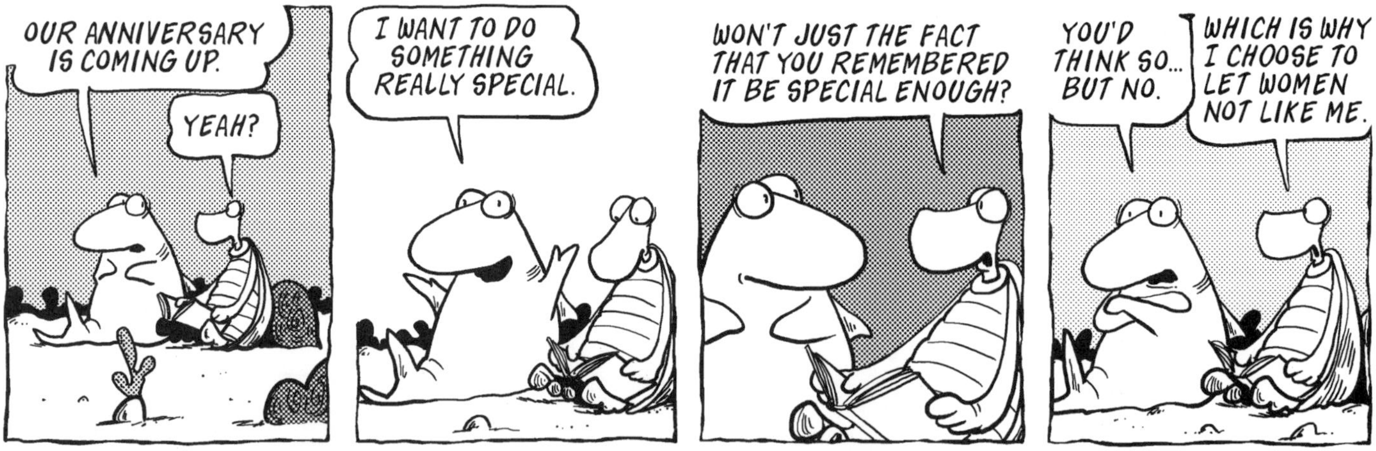
OUR ANNIVERSARY IS COMING UP.
YEAH?
I WANT TO DO SOMETHING REALLY SPECIAL.
WON'T JUST THE FACT THAT YOU REMEMBERED IT BE SPECIAL ENOUGH?
YOU'D THINK SO... BUT NO.
WHICH IS WHY I CHOOSE TO LET WOMEN NOT LIKE ME.

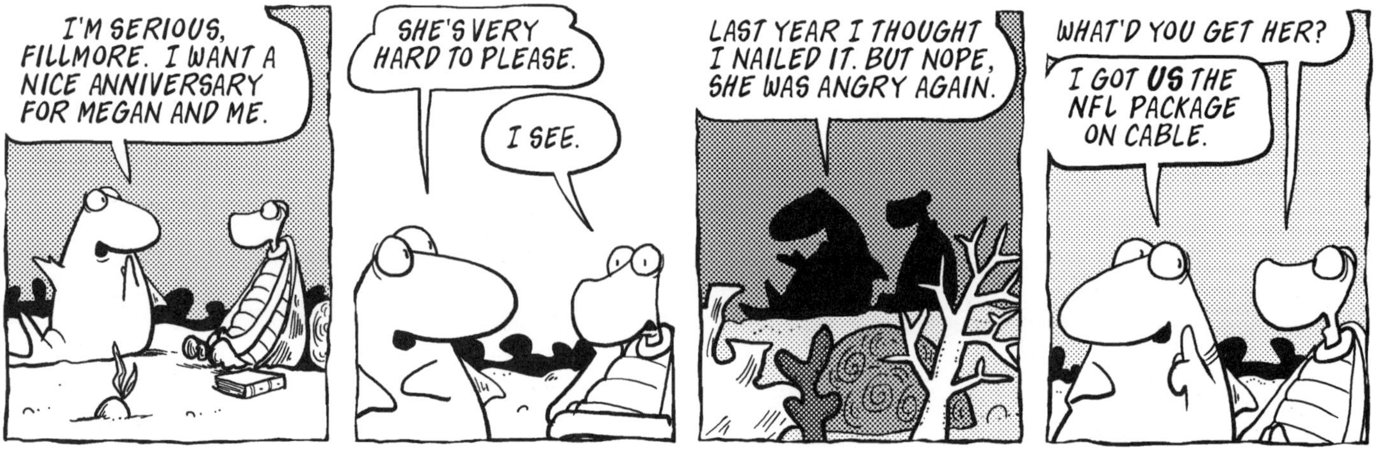
I'M SERIOUS, FILLMORE. I WANT A NICE ANNIVERSARY FOR MEGAN AND ME.
SHE'S VERY HARD TO PLEASE.
I SEE.
LAST YEAR I THOUGHT I NAILED IT. BUT NOPE, SHE WAS ANGRY AGAIN.
WHAT'D YOU GET HER?
I GOT **US** THE NFL PACKAGE ON CABLE.

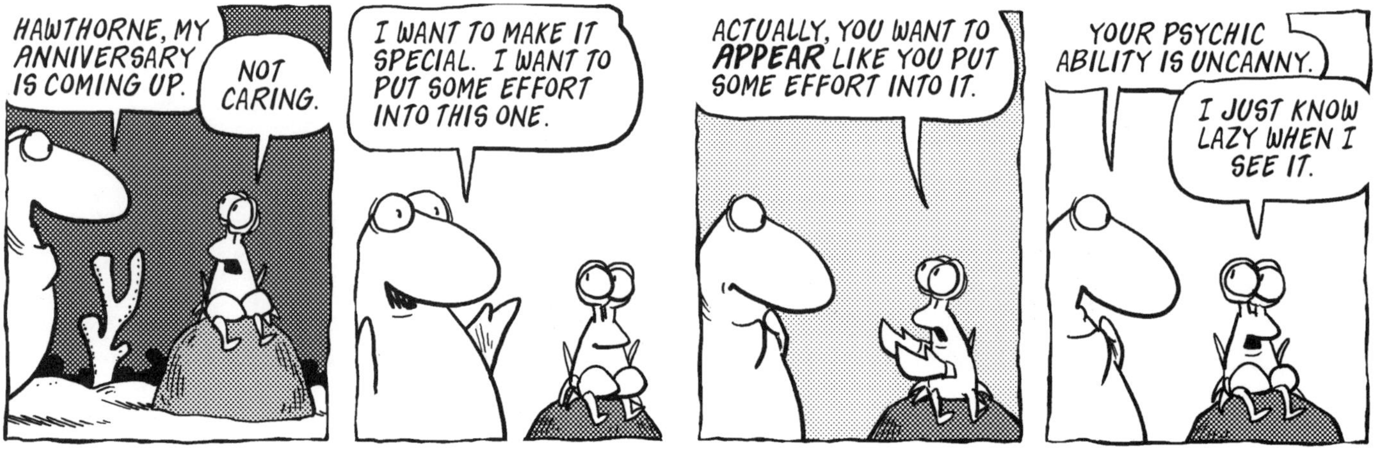
HAWTHORNE, MY ANNIVERSARY IS COMING UP.
NOT CARING.
I WANT TO MAKE IT SPECIAL. I WANT TO PUT SOME EFFORT INTO THIS ONE.
ACTUALLY, YOU WANT TO **APPEAR** LIKE YOU PUT SOME EFFORT INTO IT.
YOUR PSYCHIC ABILITY IS UNCANNY.
I JUST KNOW LAZY WHEN I SEE IT.

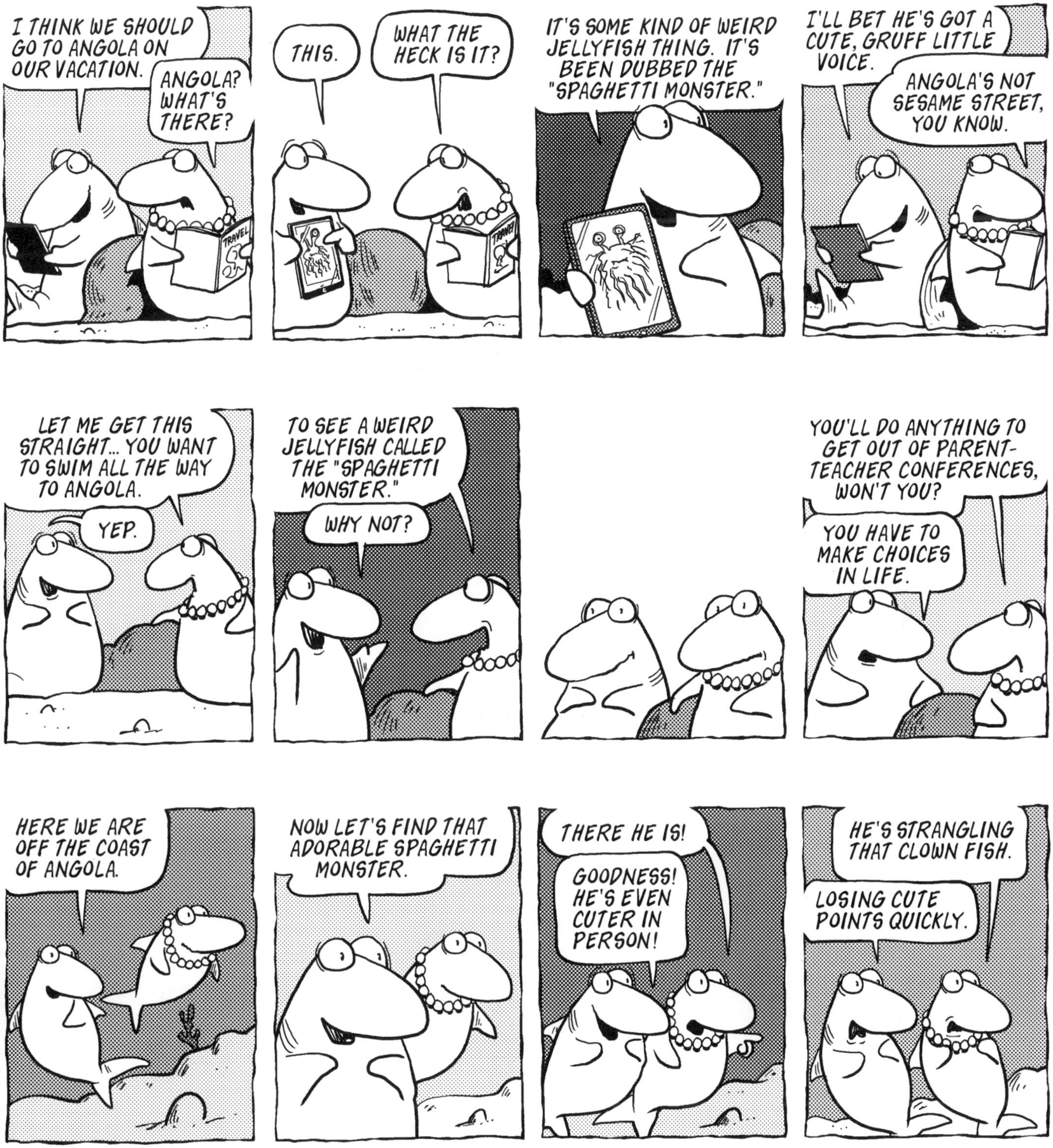
I THINK WE SHOULD GO TO ANGOLA ON OUR VACATION.
ANGOLA? WHAT'S THERE?
TRAVEL
THIS.
WHAT THE HECK IS IT?
TRAVEL
IT'S SOME KIND OF WEIRD JELLYFISH THING. IT'S BEEN DUBBED THE "SPAGHETTI MONSTER."
I'LL BET HE'S GOT A CUTE, GRUFF LITTLE VOICE.
ANGOLA'S NOT SESAME STREET, YOU KNOW.
LET ME GET THIS STRAIGHT... YOU WANT TO SWIM ALL THE WAY TO ANGOLA.
YEP.
TO SEE A WEIRD JELLYFISH CALLED THE "SPAGHETTI MONSTER."
WHY NOT?
YOU'LL DO ANYTHING TO GET OUT OF PARENT-TEACHER CONFERENCES, WON'T YOU?
YOU HAVE TO MAKE CHOICES IN LIFE.
HERE WE ARE OFF THE COAST OF ANGOLA.
NOW LET'S FIND THAT ADORABLE SPAGHETTI MONSTER.
THERE HE IS!
GOODNESS! HE'S EVEN CUTER IN PERSON!
HE'S STRANGLING THAT CLOWN FISH.
LOSING CUTE POINTS QUICKLY.

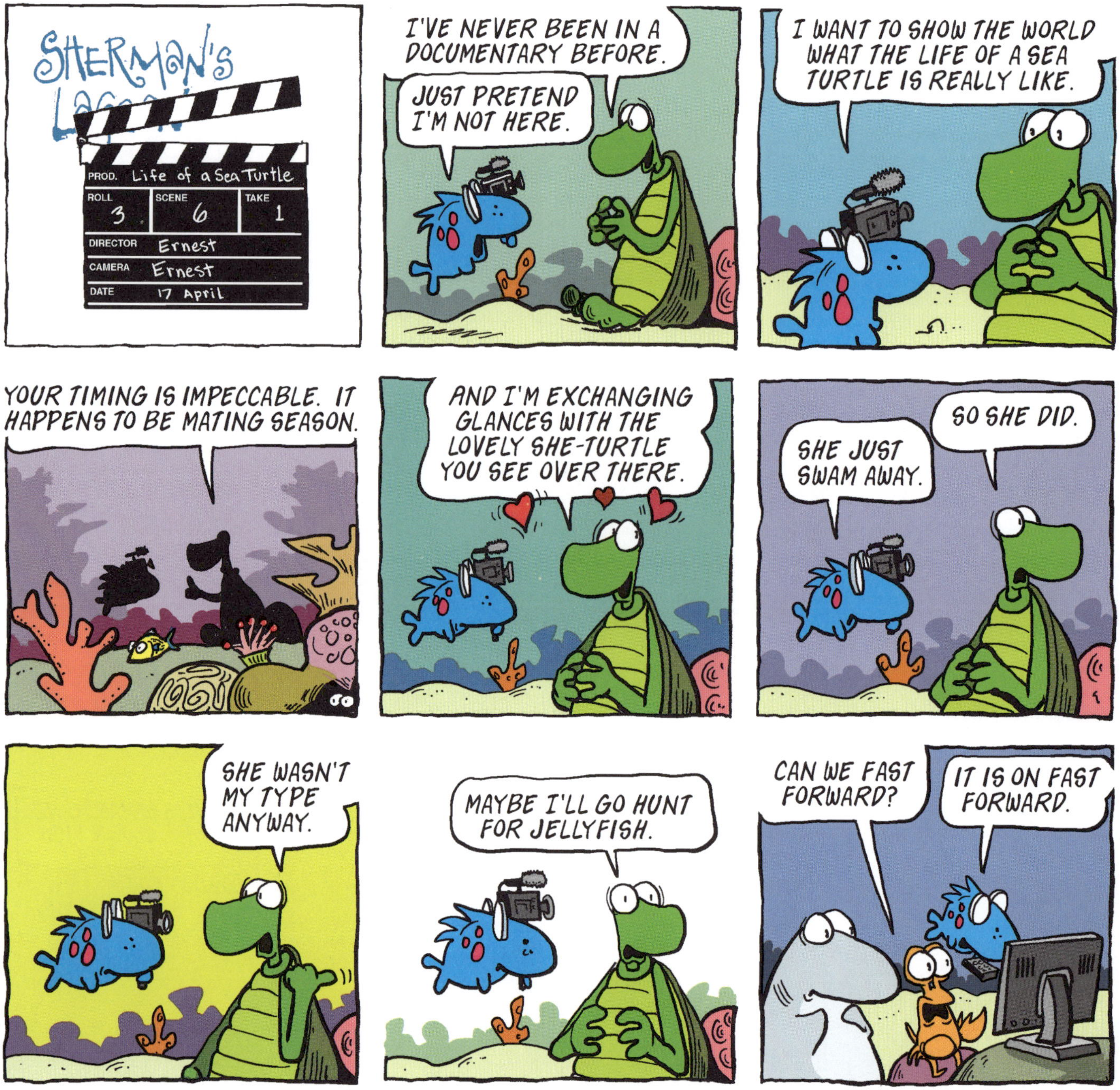
SHERMAN'S LAGOON
PROD. Life of a Sea Turtle
ROLL 3
SCENE 6
TAKE 1
DIRECTOR Ernest
CAMERA Ernest
DATE 17 April
I'VE NEVER BEEN IN A DOCUMENTARY BEFORE.
JUST PRETEND I'M NOT HERE.
I WANT TO SHOW THE WORLD WHAT THE LIFE OF A SEA TURTLE IS REALLY LIKE.
YOUR TIMING IS IMPECCABLE. IT HAPPENS TO BE MATING SEASON.
AND I'M EXCHANGING GLANCES WITH THE LOVELY SHE-TURTLE YOU SEE OVER THERE.
SHE JUST SWAM AWAY.
SO SHE DID.
SHE WASN'T MY TYPE ANYWAY.
MAYBE I'LL GO HUNT FOR JELLYFISH.
CAN WE FAST FORWARD?
IT IS ON FAST FORWARD.

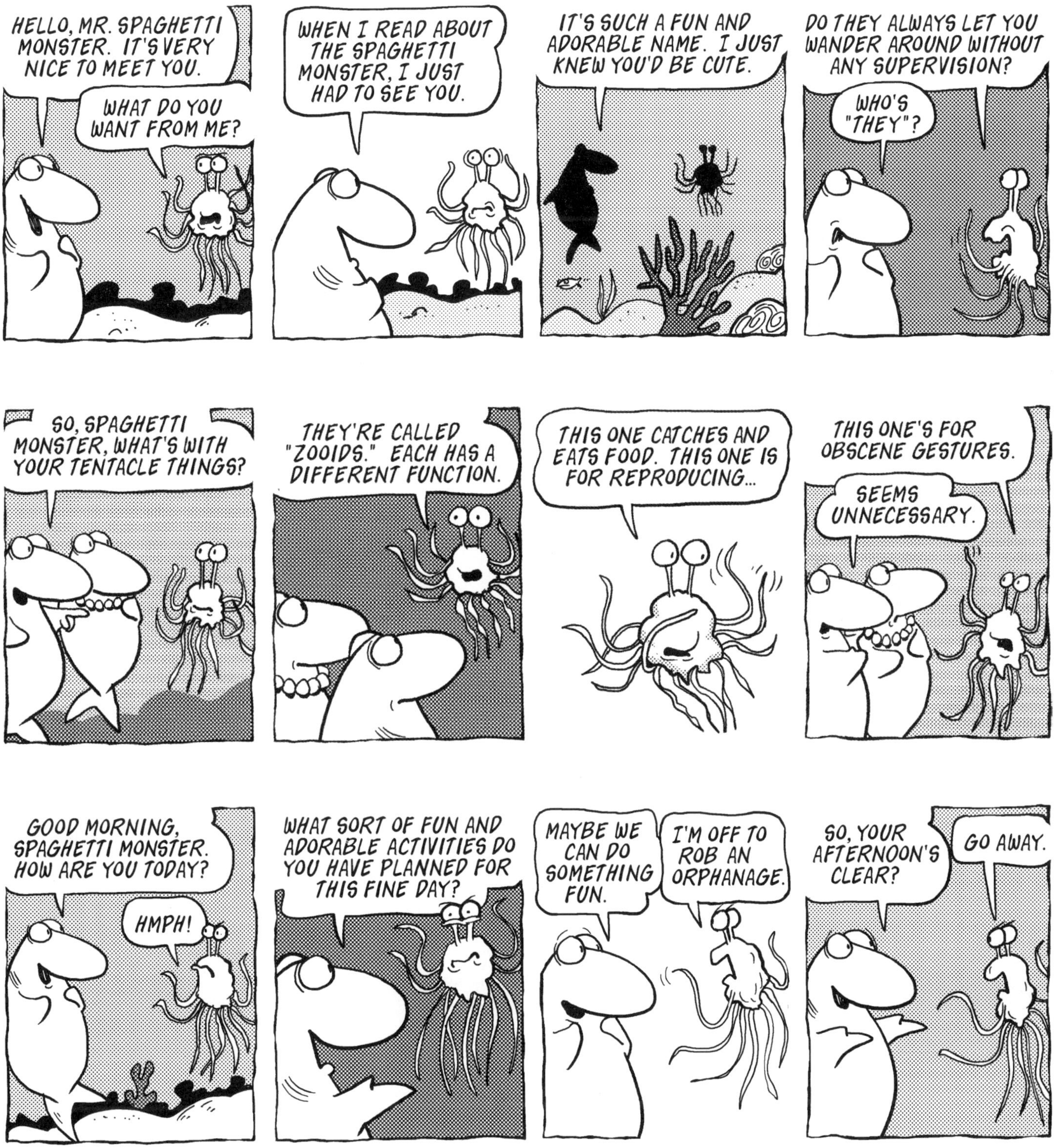
HELLO, MR. SPAGHETTI MONSTER. IT'S VERY NICE TO MEET YOU.
WHAT DO YOU WANT FROM ME?
WHEN I READ ABOUT THE SPAGHETTI MONSTER, I JUST HAD TO SEE YOU.
IT'S SUCH A FUN AND ADORABLE NAME. I JUST KNEW YOU'D BE CUTE.
DO THEY ALWAYS LET YOU WANDER AROUND WITHOUT ANY SUPERVISION?
WHO'S "THEY"?
SO, SPAGHETTI MONSTER, WHAT'S WITH YOUR TENTACLE THINGS?
THEY'RE CALLED "ZOOIDS." EACH HAS A DIFFERENT FUNCTION.
THIS ONE CATCHES AND EATS FOOD. THIS ONE IS FOR REPRODUCING...
THIS ONE'S FOR OBSCENE GESTURES.
SEEMS UNNECESSARY.
GOOD MORNING, SPAGHETTI MONSTER. HOW ARE YOU TODAY?
HMPH!
WHAT SORT OF FUN AND ADORABLE ACTIVITIES DO YOU HAVE PLANNED FOR THIS FINE DAY?
MAYBE WE CAN DO SOMETHING FUN.
I'M OFF TO ROB AN ORPHANAGE.
SO, YOUR AFTERNOON'S CLEAR?
GO AWAY.

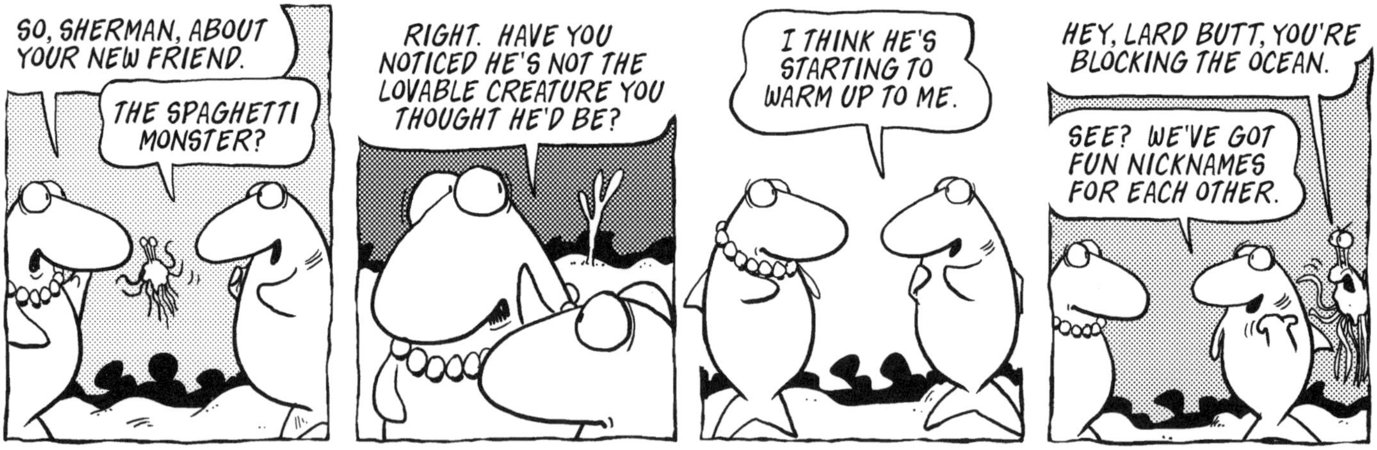
SO, SHERMAN, ABOUT YOUR NEW FRIEND.
THE SPAGHETTI MONSTER?
RIGHT. HAVE YOU NOTICED HE'S NOT THE LOVABLE CREATURE YOU THOUGHT HE'D BE?
I THINK HE'S STARTING TO WARM UP TO ME.
HEY, LARD BUTT, YOU'RE BLOCKING THE OCEAN.
SEE? WE'VE GOT FUN NICKNAMES FOR EACH OTHER.

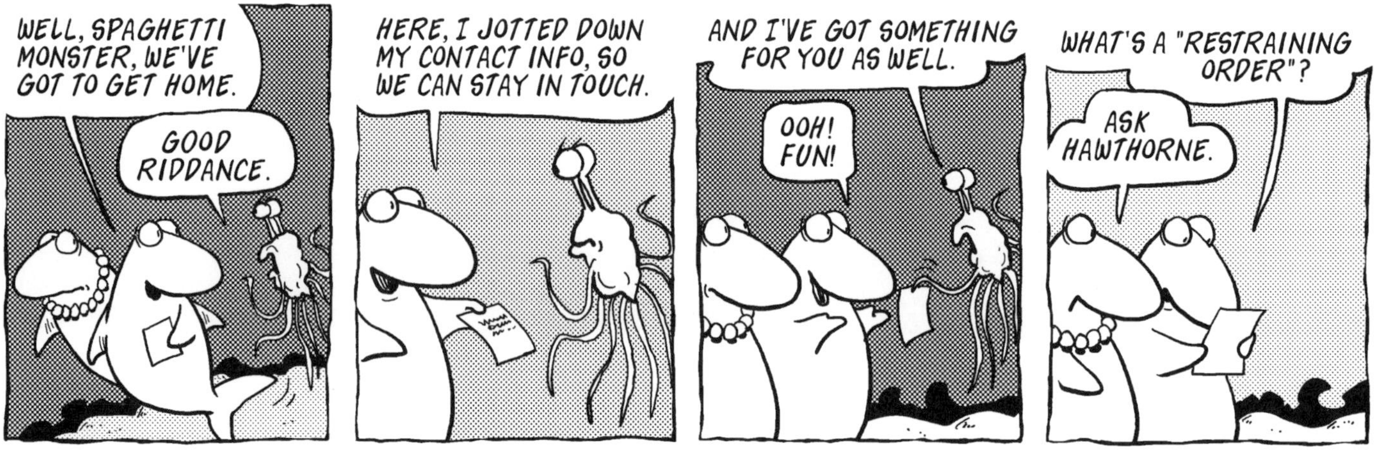
WELL, SPAGHETTI MONSTER, WE'VE GOT TO GET HOME.
GOOD RIDDANCE.
HERE, I JOTTED DOWN MY CONTACT INFO, SO WE CAN STAY IN TOUCH.
AND I'VE GOT SOMETHING FOR YOU AS WELL.
OOH! FUN!
WHAT'S A "RESTRAINING ORDER"?
ASK HAWTHORNE.

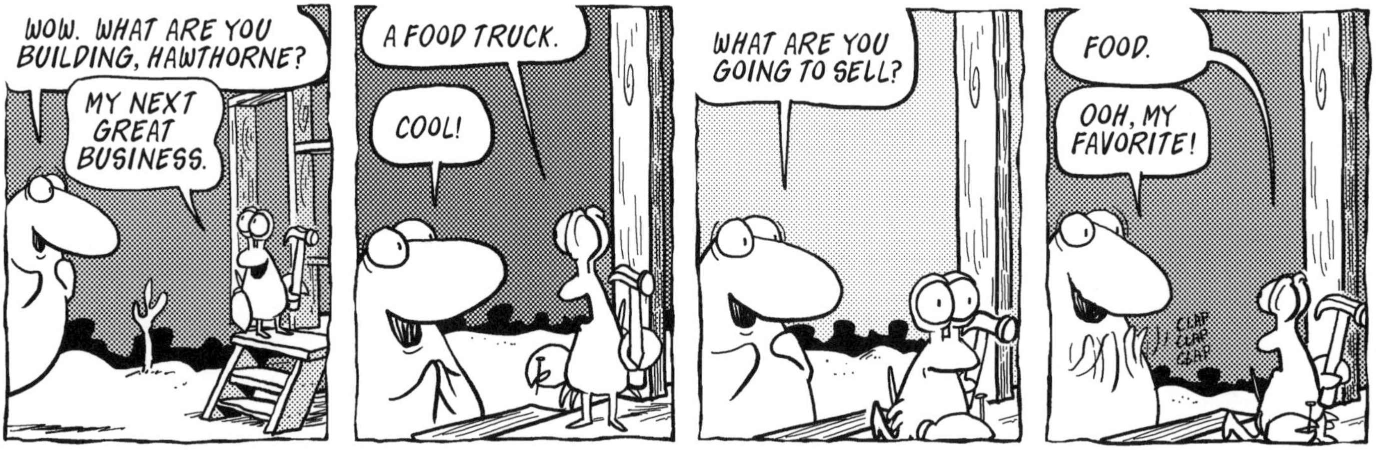
WOW. WHAT ARE YOU BUILDING, HAWTHORNE?
MY NEXT GREAT BUSINESS.
A FOOD TRUCK.
COOL!
WHAT ARE YOU GOING TO SELL?
FOOD.
OOH, MY FAVORITE!
CLAP CLAP CLAP

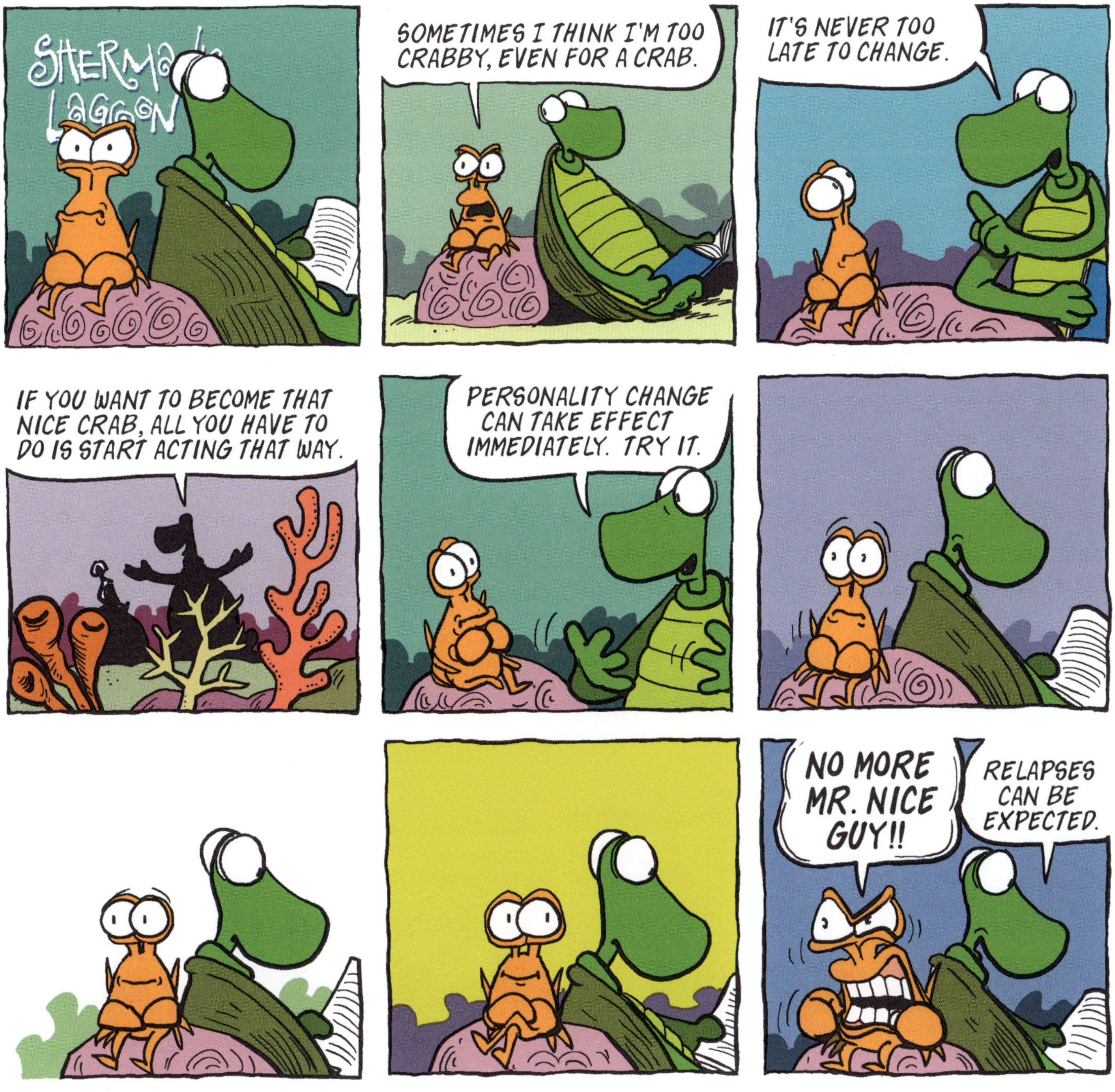
SHERMAN'S LAGOON
SOMETIMES I THINK I'M TOO CRABBY, EVEN FOR A CRAB.
IT'S NEVER TOO LATE TO CHANGE.
IF YOU WANT TO BECOME THAT NICE CRAB, ALL YOU HAVE TO DO IS START ACTING THAT WAY.
PERSONALITY CHANGE CAN TAKE EFFECT IMMEDIATELY. TRY IT.
NO MORE MR. NICE GUY!!
RELAPSES CAN BE EXPECTED.

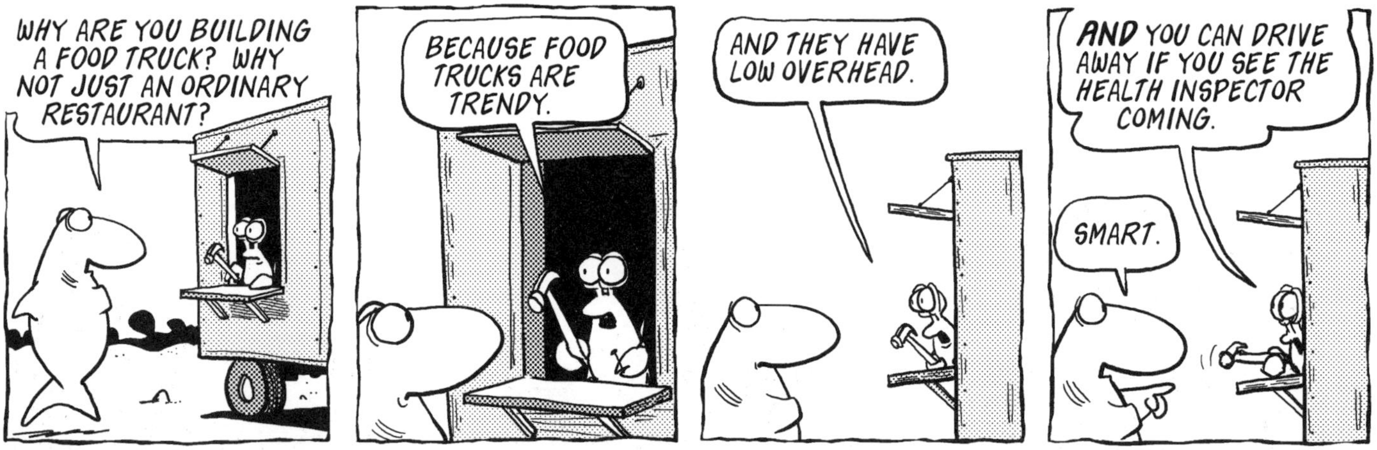
WHY ARE YOU BUILDING A FOOD TRUCK? WHY NOT JUST AN ORDINARY RESTAURANT?
BECAUSE FOOD TRUCKS ARE TRENDY.
AND THEY HAVE LOW OVERHEAD.
AND YOU CAN DRIVE AWAY IF YOU SEE THE HEALTH INSPECTOR COMING.
SMART.

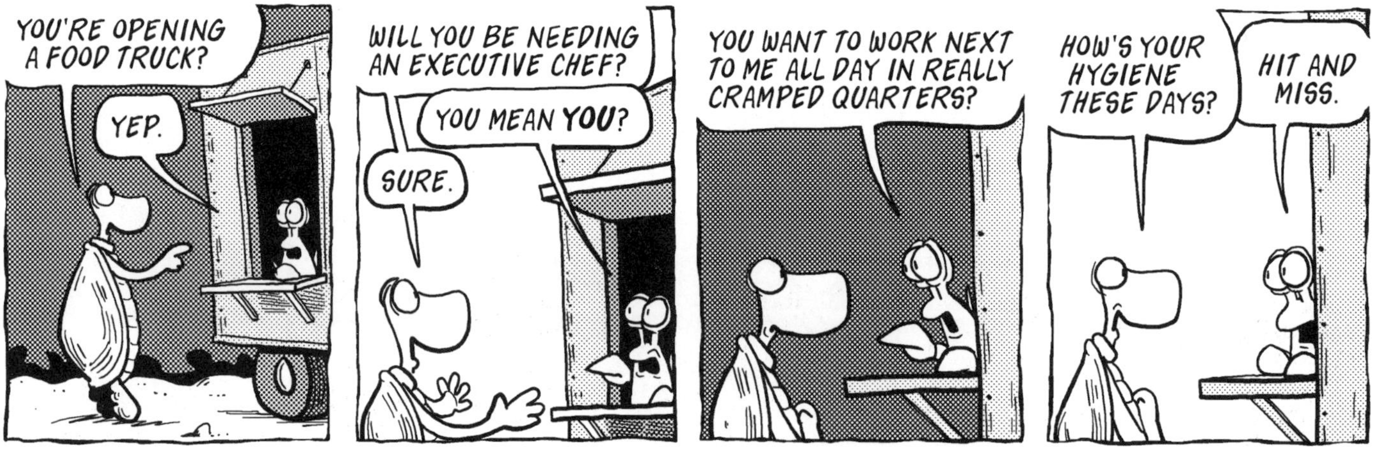
YOU'RE OPENING A FOOD TRUCK?
YEP.
WILL YOU BE NEEDING AN EXECUTIVE CHEF?
SURE.
YOU MEAN YOU?
YOU WANT TO WORK NEXT TO ME ALL DAY IN REALLY CRAMPED QUARTERS?
HOW'S YOUR HYGIENE THESE DAYS?
HIT AND MISS.

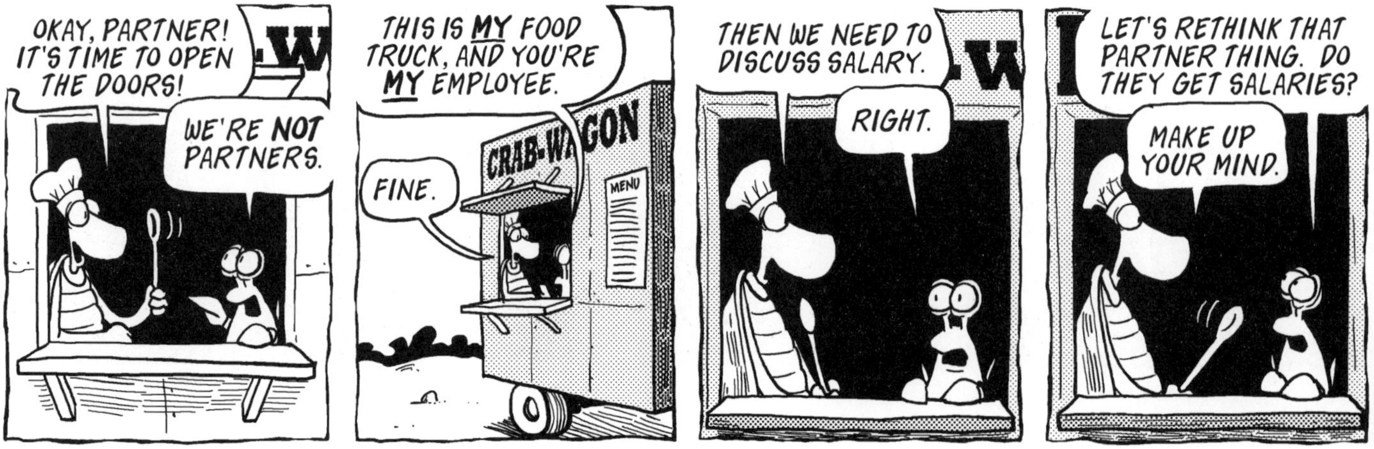
OKAY, PARTNER! IT'S TIME TO OPEN THE DOORS!
WE'RE NOT PARTNERS.
THIS IS MY FOOD TRUCK, AND YOU'RE MY EMPLOYEE.
FINE.
MENU
THEN WE NEED TO DISCUSS SALARY.
RIGHT.
LET'S RETHINK THAT PARTNER THING. DO THEY GET SALARIES?
MAKE UP YOUR MIND.

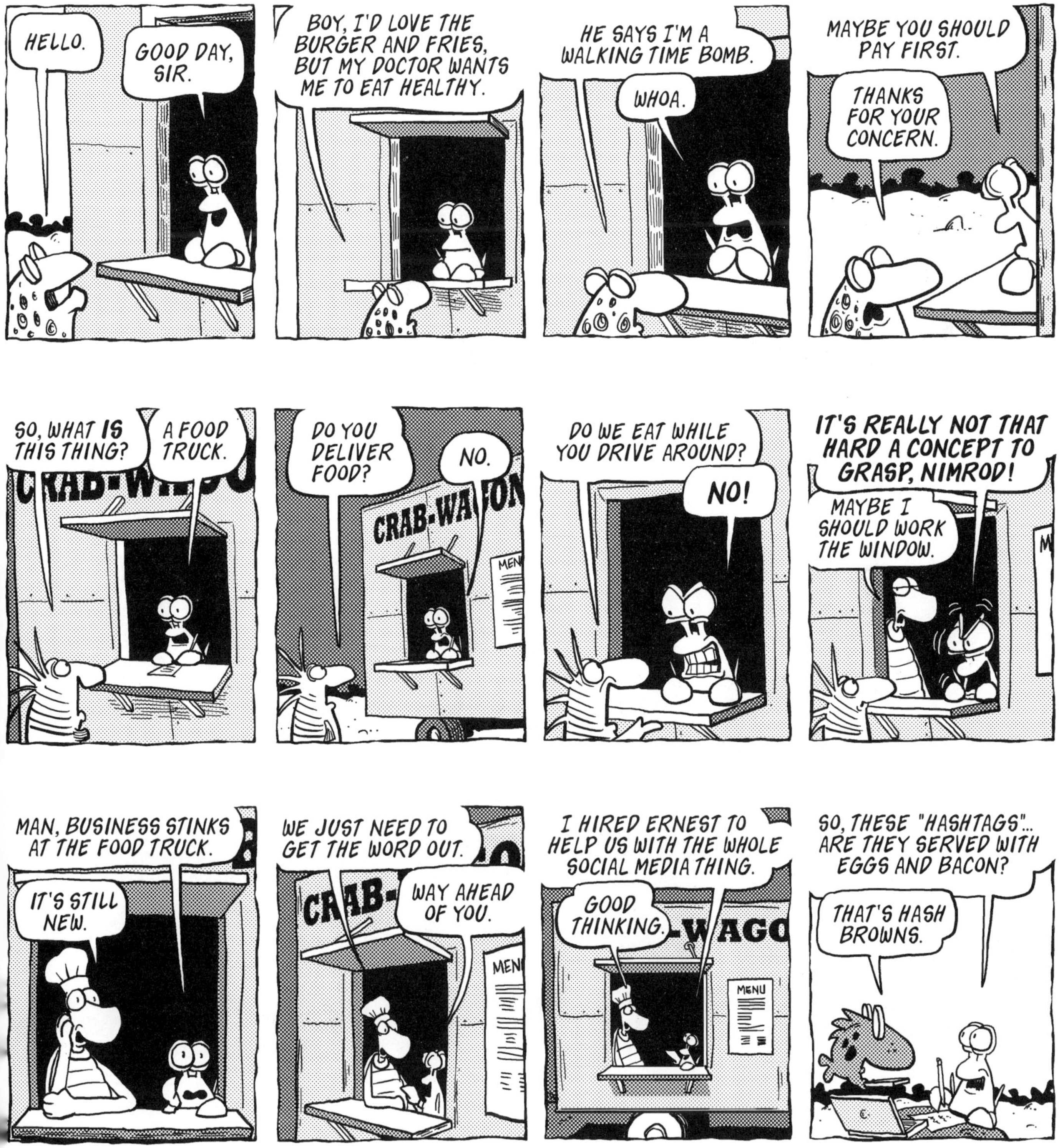
HELLO.
GOOD DAY, SIR.
BOY, I'D LOVE THE BURGER AND FRIES, BUT MY DOCTOR WANTS ME TO EAT HEALTHY.
HE SAYS I'M A WALKING TIME BOMB.
WHOA.
MAYBE YOU SHOULD PAY FIRST.
THANKS FOR YOUR CONCERN.
SO, WHAT IS THIS THING?
A FOOD TRUCK.
DO YOU DELIVER FOOD?
NO.
CRAB-WA
MENU
DO WE EAT WHILE YOU DRIVE AROUND?
NO!
IT'S REALLY NOT THAT HARD A CONCEPT TO GRASP, NIMROD!
MAYBE I SHOULD WORK THE WINDOW.
MAN, BUSINESS STINKS AT THE FOOD TRUCK.
IT'S STILL NEW.
WE JUST NEED TO GET THE WORD OUT.
WAY AHEAD OF YOU.
I HIRED ERNEST TO HELP US WITH THE WHOLE SOCIAL MEDIA THING.
GOOD THINKING.
-WAGO
MENU
SO, THESE "HASHTAGS"... ARE THEY SERVED WITH EGGS AND BACON?
THAT'S HASH BROWNS.

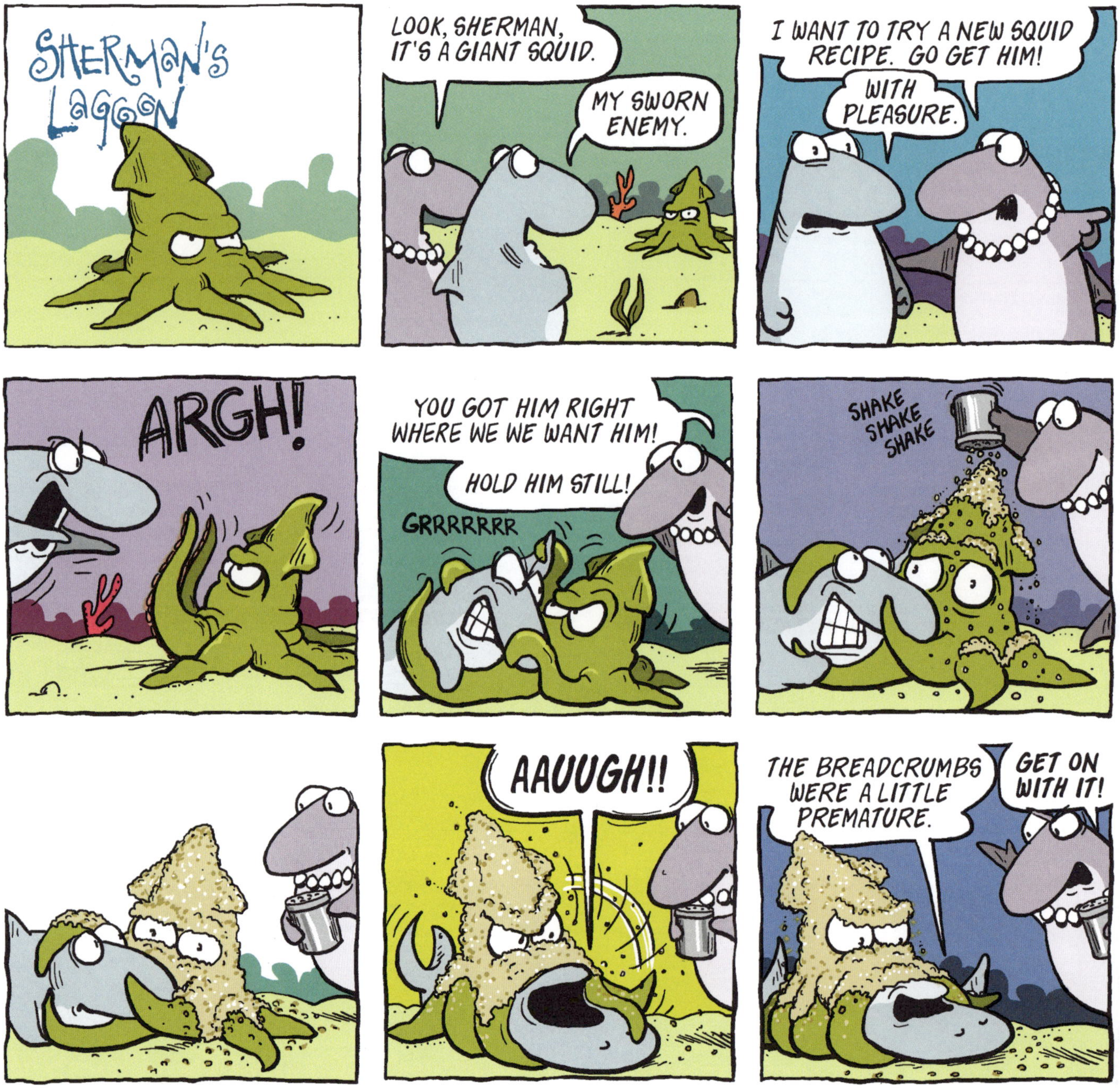
SHERMAN'S LAGOON
LOOK, SHERMAN, IT'S A GIANT SQUID.
MY SWORN ENEMY.
I WANT TO TRY A NEW SQUID RECIPE. GO GET HIM!
WITH PLEASURE.
ARGH!
YOU GOT HIM RIGHT WHERE WE WE WANT HIM!
HOLD HIM STILL!
GRRRRRRR
SHAKE SHAKE SHAKE
AAUUGH!!
THE BREADCRUMBS WERE A LITTLE PREMATURE.
GET ON WITH IT!

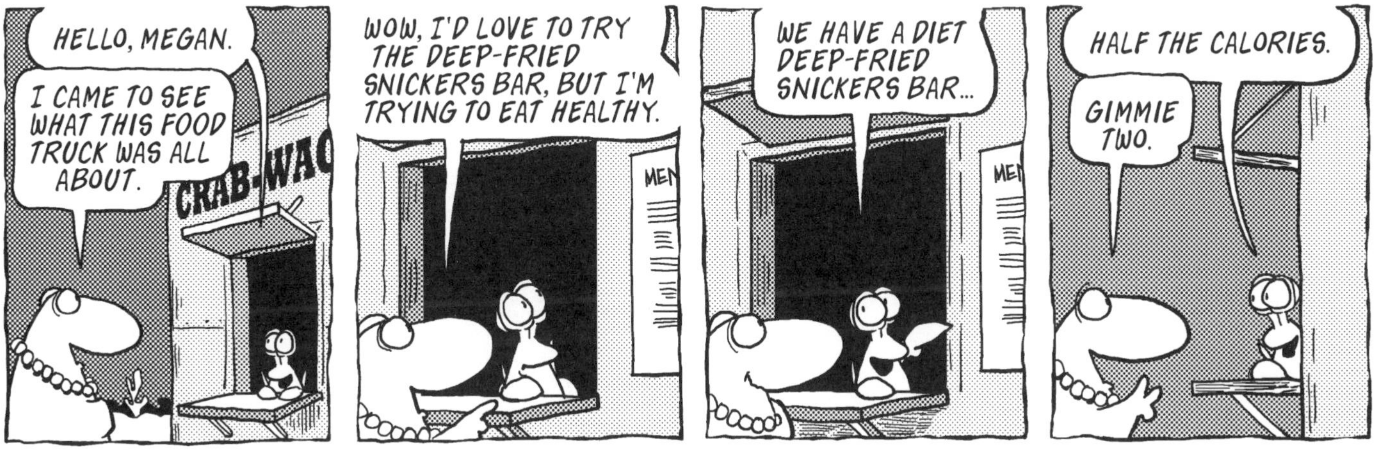
HELLO, MEGAN.
I CAME TO SEE WHAT THIS FOOD TRUCK WAS ALL ABOUT.
CRAB-WAG
WOW, I'D LOVE TO TRY THE DEEP-FRIED SNICKERS BAR, BUT I'M TRYING TO EAT HEALTHY.
WE HAVE A DIET DEEP-FRIED SNICKERS BAR...
HALF THE CALORIES.
GIMMIE TWO.

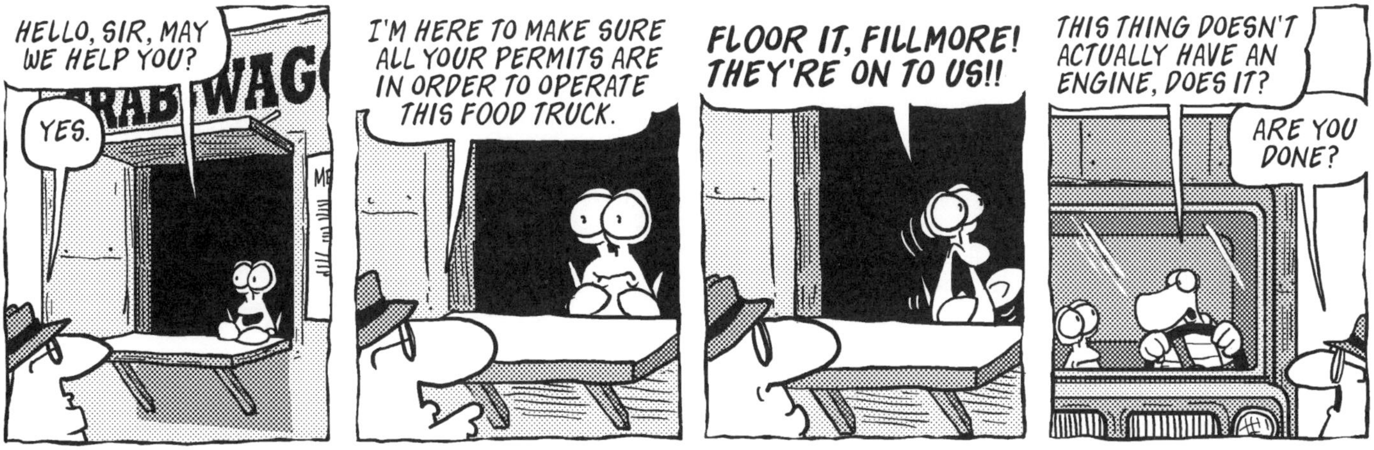
HELLO, SIR, MAY WE HELP YOU?
YES.
I'M HERE TO MAKE SURE ALL YOUR PERMITS ARE IN ORDER TO OPERATE THIS FOOD TRUCK.
FLOOR IT, FILLMORE! THEY'RE ON TO US!!
THIS THING DOESN'T ACTUALLY HAVE AN ENGINE, DOES IT?
ARE YOU DONE?

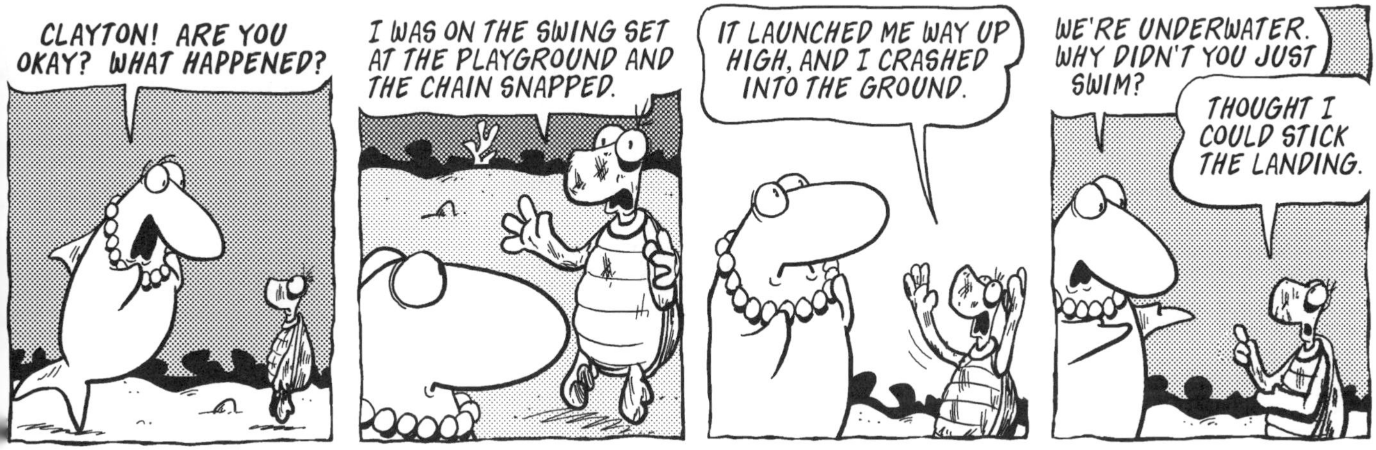
CLAYTON! ARE YOU OKAY? WHAT HAPPENED?
I WAS ON THE SWING SET AT THE PLAYGROUND AND THE CHAIN SNAPPED.
IT LAUNCHED ME WAY UP HIGH, AND I CRASHED INTO THE GROUND.
WE'RE UNDERWATER. WHY DIDN'T YOU JUST SWIM?
THOUGHT I COULD STICK THE LANDING.

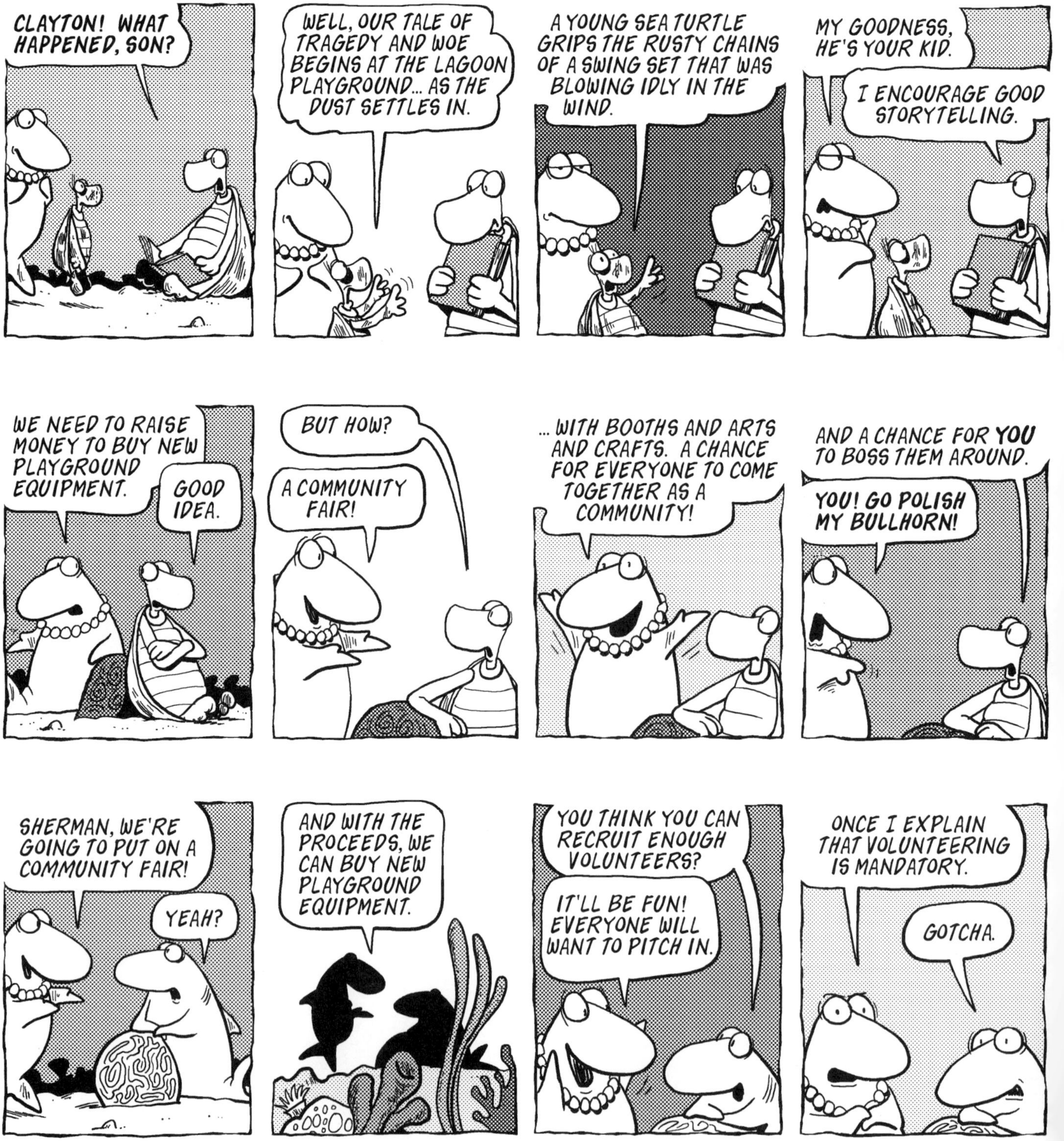
CLAYTON! WHAT HAPPENED, SON?
WELL, OUR TALE OF TRAGEDY AND WOE BEGINS AT THE LAGOON PLAYGROUND... AS THE DUST SETTLES IN.
A YOUNG SEA TURTLE GRIPS THE RUSTY CHAINS OF A SWING SET THAT WAS BLOWING IDLY IN THE WIND.
MY GOODNESS, HE'S YOUR KID.
I ENCOURAGE GOOD STORYTELLING.
WE NEED TO RAISE MONEY TO BUY NEW PLAYGROUND EQUIPMENT.
GOOD IDEA.
BUT HOW?
A COMMUNITY FAIR!
... WITH BOOTHS AND ARTS AND CRAFTS. A CHANCE FOR EVERYONE TO COME TOGETHER AS A COMMUNITY!
AND A CHANCE FOR YOU TO BOSS THEM AROUND.
YOU! GO POLISH MY BULLHORN!
SHERMAN, WE'RE GOING TO PUT ON A COMMUNITY FAIR!
YEAH?
AND WITH THE PROCEEDS, WE CAN BUY NEW PLAYGROUND EQUIPMENT.
YOU THINK YOU CAN RECRUIT ENOUGH VOLUNTEERS?
IT'LL BE FUN! EVERYONE WILL WANT TO PITCH IN.
ONCE I EXPLAIN THAT VOLUNTEERING IS MANDATORY.
GOTCHA.

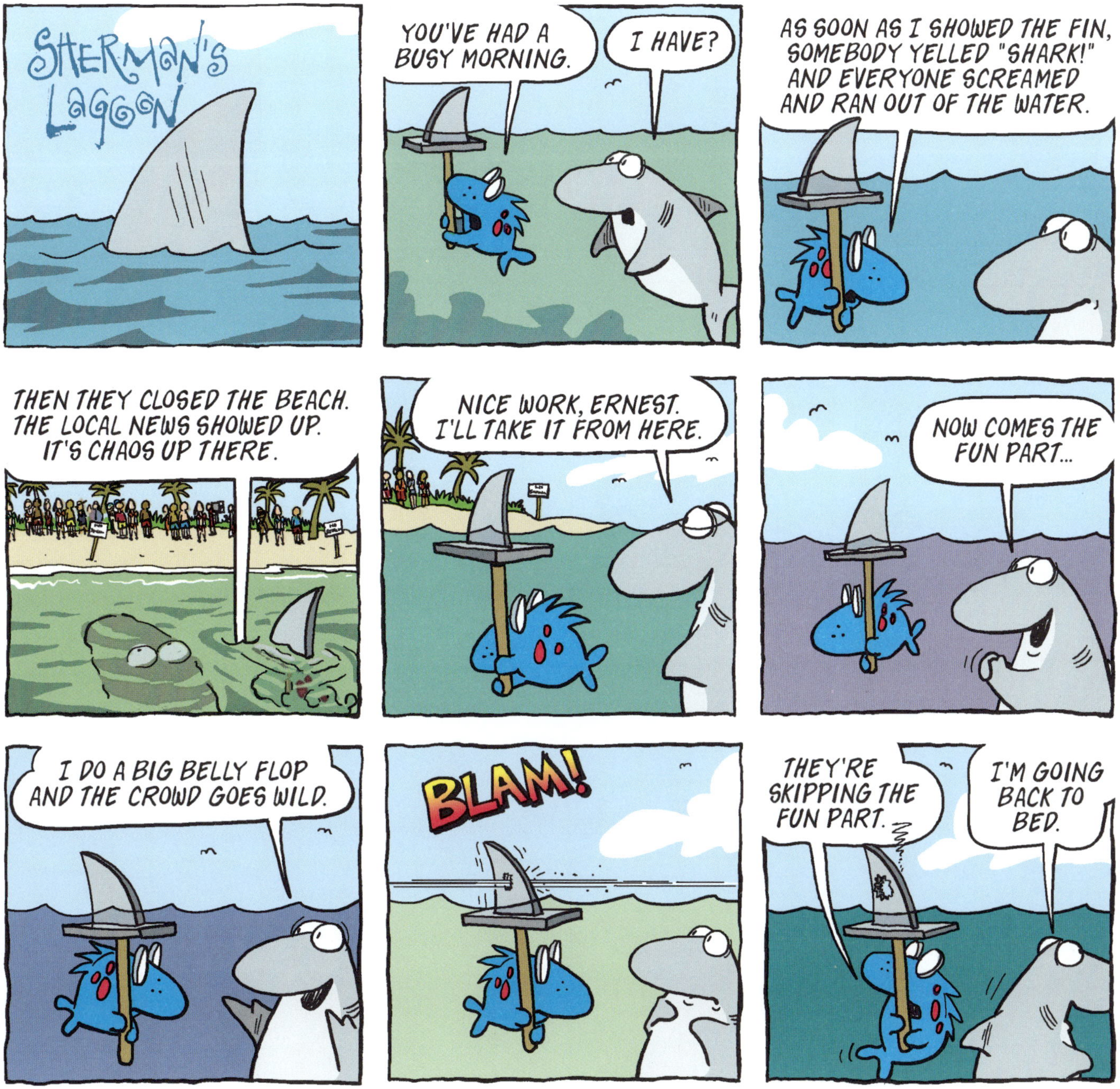
SHERMAN'S LAGOON
YOU'VE HAD A BUSY MORNING.
I HAVE?
AS SOON AS I SHOWED THE FIN, SOMEBODY YELLED "SHARK!" AND EVERYONE SCREAMED AND RAN OUT OF THE WATER.
THEN THEY CLOSED THE BEACH. THE LOCAL NEWS SHOWED UP. IT'S CHAOS UP THERE.
NICE WORK, ERNEST. I'LL TAKE IT FROM HERE.
NOW COMES THE FUN PART...
I DO A BIG BELLY FLOP AND THE CROWD GOES WILD.
BLAM!
THEY'RE SKIPPING THE FUN PART.
I'M GOING BACK TO BED.

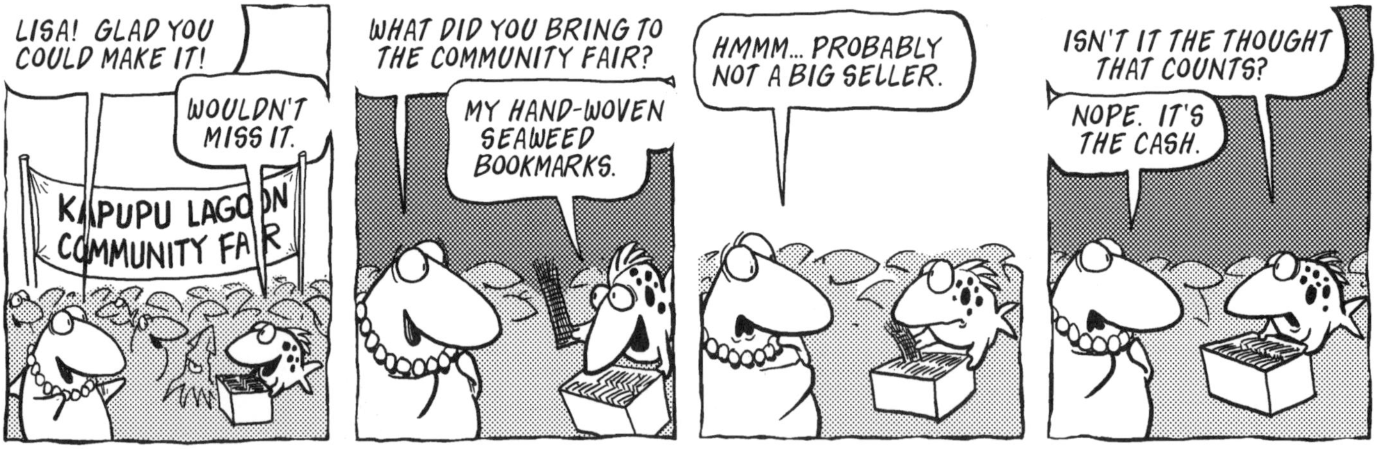
LISA! GLAD YOU COULD MAKE IT!
WOULDN'T MISS IT.
KAPUPU LAGOON COMMUNITY FAIR
WHAT DID YOU BRING TO THE COMMUNITY FAIR?
MY HAND-WOVEN SEAWEED BOOKMARKS.
HMMM... PROBABLY NOT A BIG SELLER.
ISN'T IT THE THOUGHT THAT COUNTS?
NOPE. IT'S THE CASH.

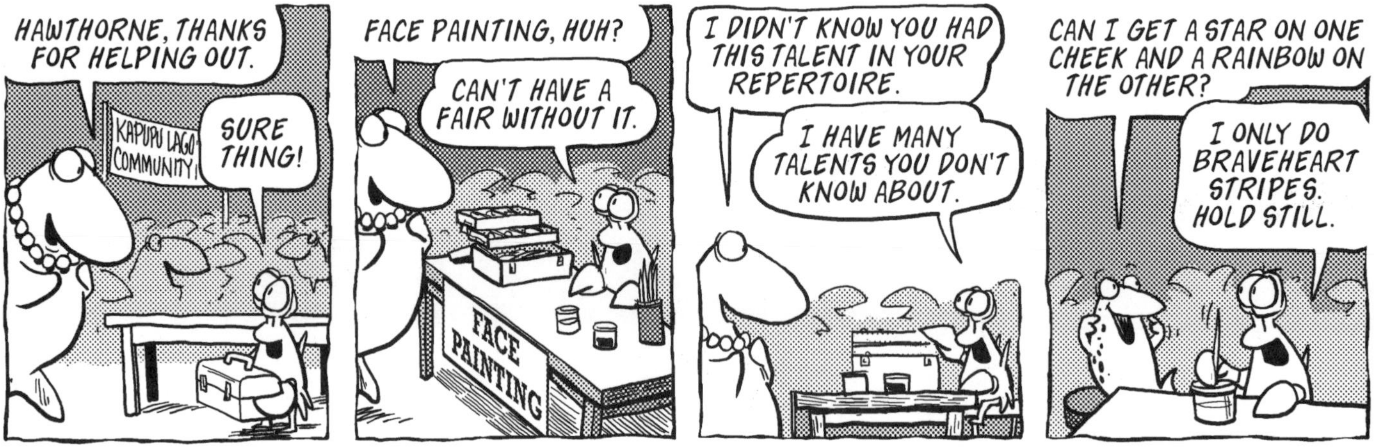
HAWTHORNE, THANKS FOR HELPING OUT.
SURE THING!
FACE PAINTING, HUH?
CAN'T HAVE A FAIR WITHOUT IT.
FACE PAINTING
I DIDN'T KNOW YOU HAD THIS TALENT IN YOUR REPERTOIRE.
I HAVE MANY TALENTS YOU DON'T KNOW ABOUT.
CAN I GET A STAR ON ONE CHEEK AND A RAINBOW ON THE OTHER?
I ONLY DO BRAVEHEART STRIPES. HOLD STILL.

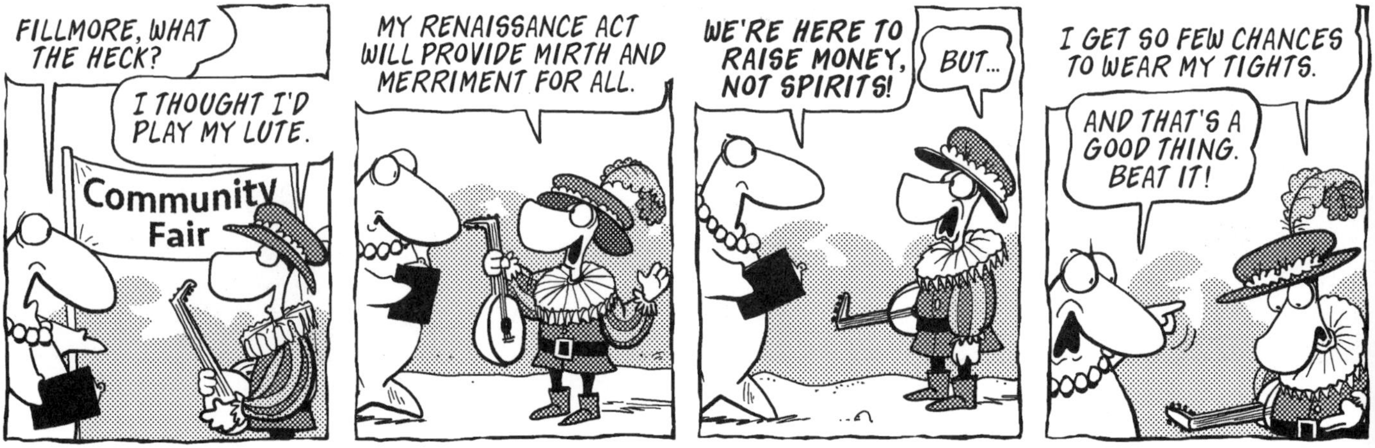
FILLMORE, WHAT THE HECK?
I THOUGHT I'D PLAY MY LUTE.
Community Fair
MY RENAISSANCE ACT WILL PROVIDE MIRTH AND MERRIMENT FOR ALL.
WE'RE HERE TO RAISE MONEY, NOT SPIRITS!
BUT...
I GET SO FEW CHANCES TO WEAR MY TIGHTS.
AND THAT'S A GOOD THING. BEAT IT!

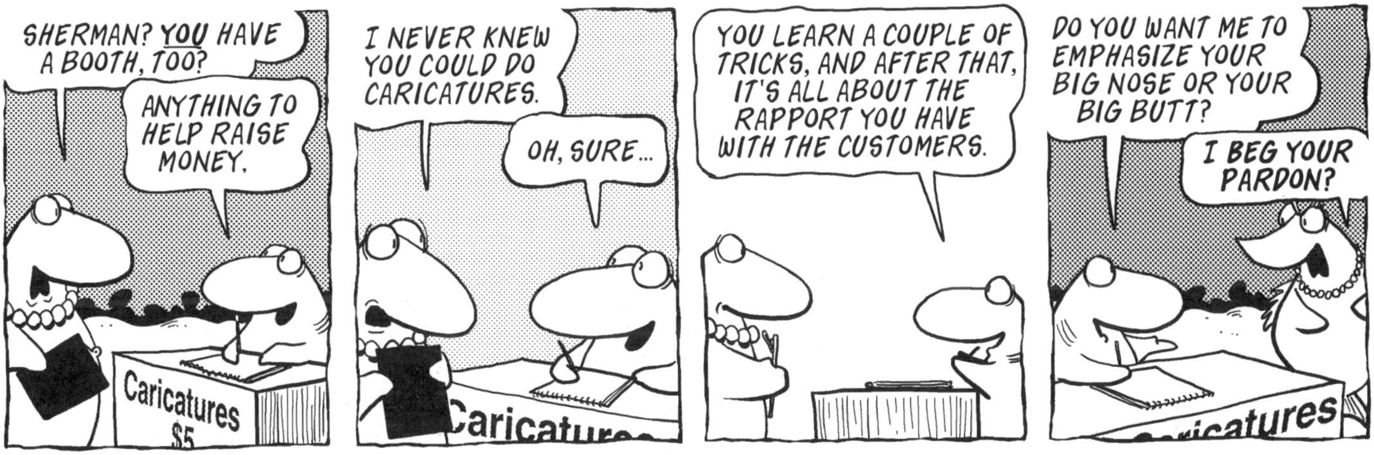
SHERMAN? YOU HAVE A BOOTH, TOO?
ANYTHING TO HELP RAISE MONEY.
Caricatures $5
I NEVER KNEW YOU COULD DO CARICATURES.
OH, SURE...
Caricatures
YOU LEARN A COUPLE OF TRICKS, AND AFTER THAT, IT'S ALL ABOUT THE RAPPORT YOU HAVE WITH THE CUSTOMERS.
DO YOU WANT ME TO EMPHASIZE YOUR BIG NOSE OR YOUR BIG BUTT?
I BEG YOUR PARDON?
Caricatures

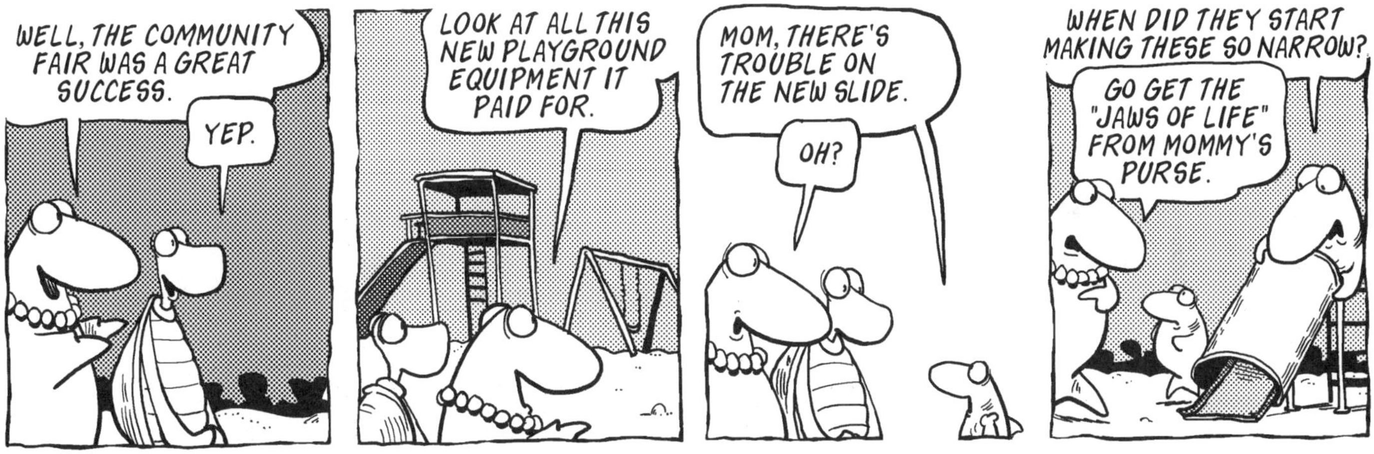
WELL, THE COMMUNITY FAIR WAS A GREAT SUCCESS.
YEP.
LOOK AT ALL THIS NEW PLAYGROUND EQUIPMENT IT PAID FOR.
MOM, THERE'S TROUBLE ON THE NEW SLIDE.
OH?
WHEN DID THEY START MAKING THESE SO NARROW?
GO GET THE "JAWS OF LIFE" FROM MOMMY'S PURSE.

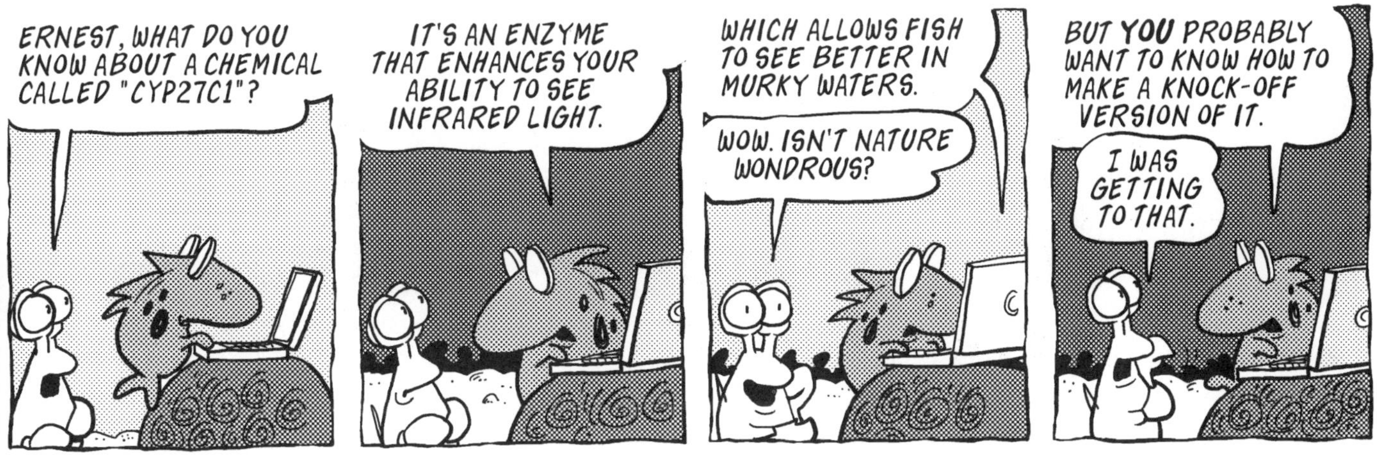
ERNEST, WHAT DO YOU KNOW ABOUT A CHEMICAL CALLED "CYP27C1"?
IT'S AN ENZYME THAT ENHANCES YOUR ABILITY TO SEE INFRARED LIGHT.
WHICH ALLOWS FISH TO SEE BETTER IN MURKY WATERS.
WOW. ISN'T NATURE WONDROUS?
BUT YOU PROBABLY WANT TO KNOW HOW TO MAKE A KNOCK-OFF VERSION OF IT.
I WAS GETTING TO THAT.

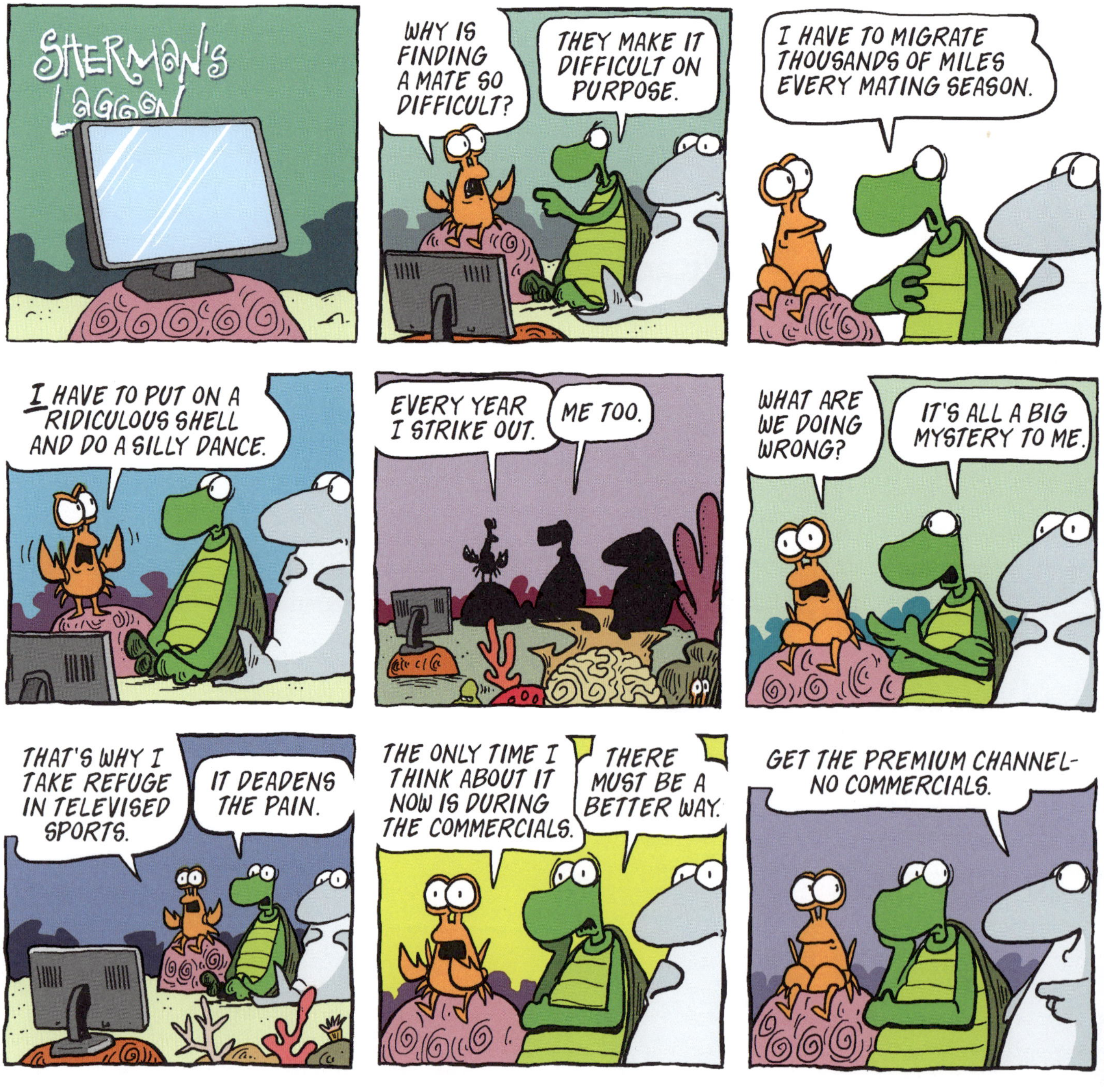
SHERMAN'S LAGOON
WHY IS FINDING A MATE SO DIFFICULT?
THEY MAKE IT DIFFICULT ON PURPOSE.
I HAVE TO MIGRATE THOUSANDS OF MILES EVERY MATING SEASON.
I HAVE TO PUT ON A RIDICULOUS SHELL AND DO A SILLY DANCE.
EVERY YEAR I STRIKE OUT.
ME TOO.
WHAT ARE WE DOING WRONG?
IT'S ALL A BIG MYSTERY TO ME.
THAT'S WHY I TAKE REFUGE IN TELEVISED SPORTS.
IT DEADENS THE PAIN.
THE ONLY TIME I THINK ABOUT IT NOW IS DURING THE COMMERCIALS.
THERE MUST BE A BETTER WAY.
GET THE PREMIUM CHANNEL- NO COMMERCIALS.

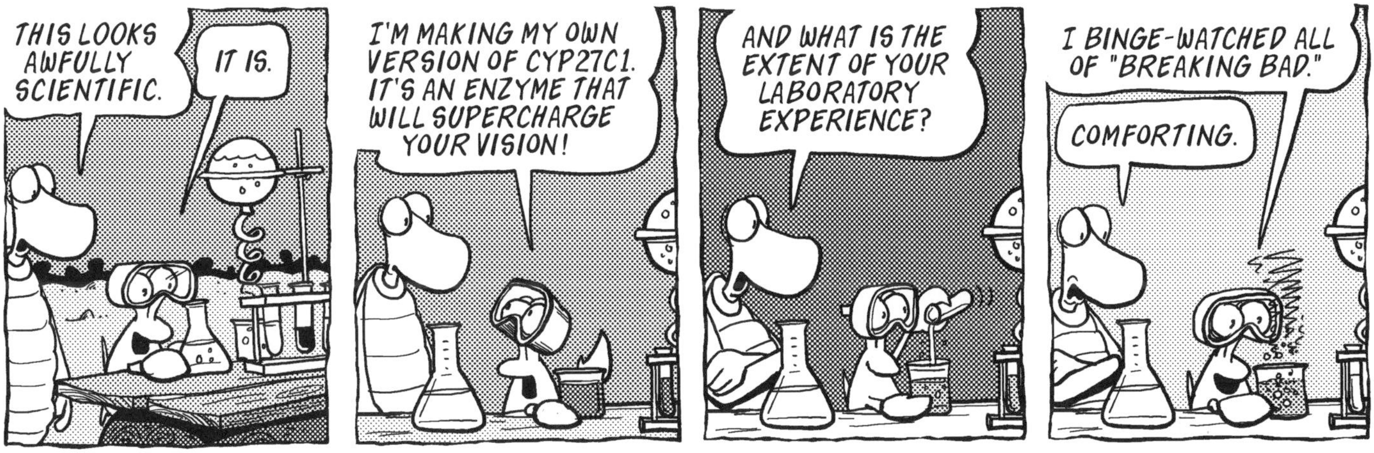
THIS LOOKS AWFULLY SCIENTIFIC.
IT IS.
I'M MAKING MY OWN VERSION OF CYP27C1. IT'S AN ENZYME THAT WILL SUPERCHARGE YOUR VISION!
AND WHAT IS THE EXTENT OF YOUR LABORATORY EXPERIENCE?
I BINGE-WATCHED ALL OF "BREAKING BAD."
COMFORTING.

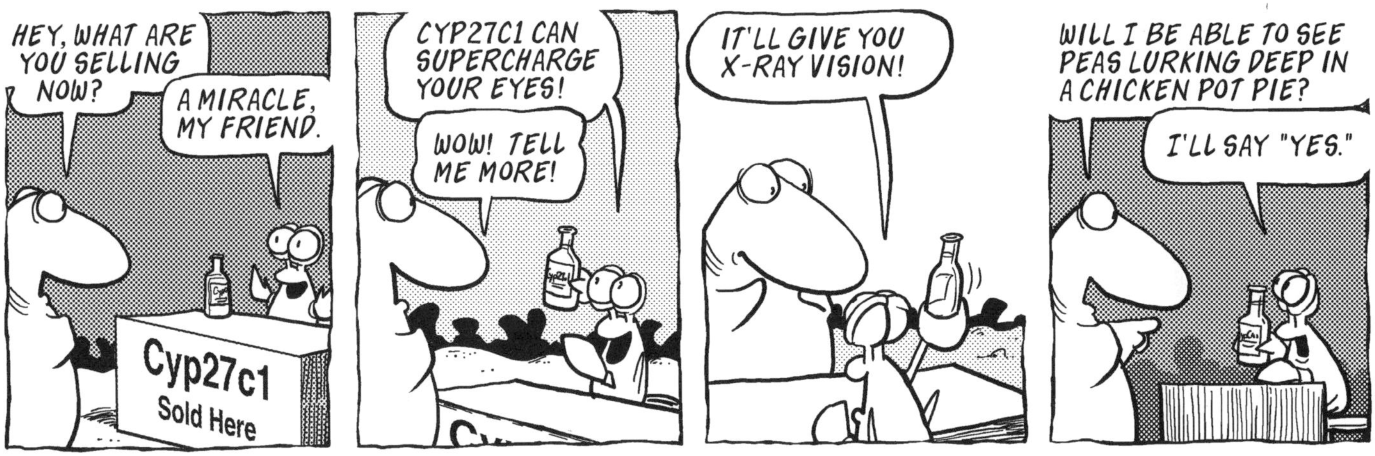
HEY, WHAT ARE YOU SELLING NOW?
A MIRACLE, MY FRIEND.
Cyp27c1
Sold Here
CYP27C1 CAN SUPERCHARGE YOUR EYES!
WOW! TELL ME MORE!
IT'LL GIVE YOU X-RAY VISION!
WILL I BE ABLE TO SEE PEAS LURKING DEEP IN A CHICKEN POT PIE?
I'LL SAY "YES."

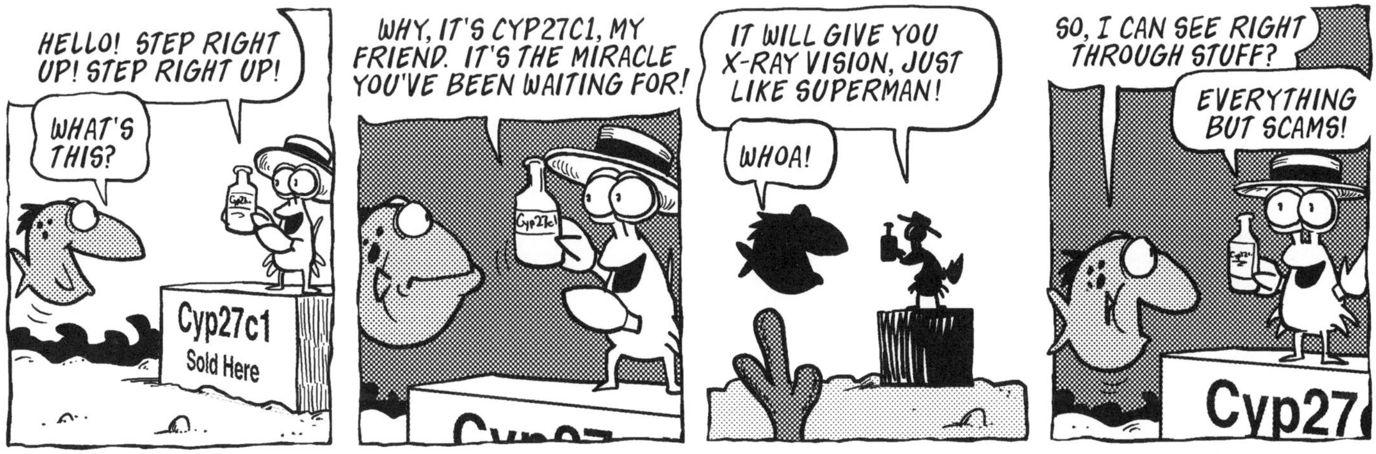
HELLO! STEP RIGHT UP! STEP RIGHT UP!
WHAT'S THIS?
Cyp27c1
Sold Here
WHY, IT'S CYP27C1, MY FRIEND. IT'S THE MIRACLE YOU'VE BEEN WAITING FOR!
IT WILL GIVE YOU X-RAY VISION, JUST LIKE SUPERMAN!
WHOA!
SO, I CAN SEE RIGHT THROUGH STUFF?
EVERYTHING BUT SCAMS!
Cyp27

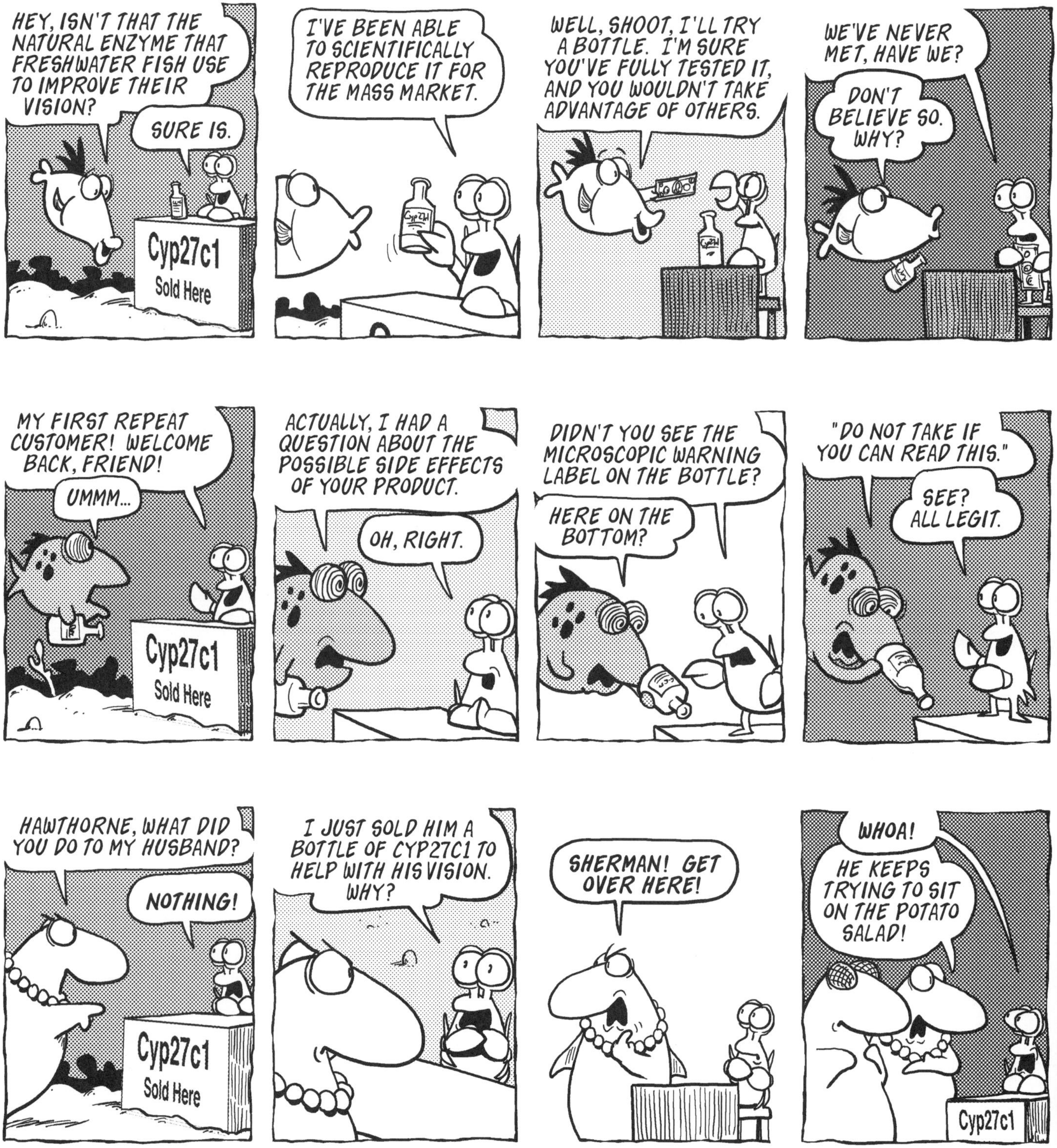
HEY, ISN'T THAT THE NATURAL ENZYME THAT FRESHWATER FISH USE TO IMPROVE THEIR VISION?
SURE IS.
Cyp27c1
Sold Here
I'VE BEEN ABLE TO SCIENTIFICALLY REPRODUCE IT FOR THE MASS MARKET.
WELL, SHOOT, I'LL TRY A BOTTLE. I'M SURE YOU'VE FULLY TESTED IT, AND YOU WOULDN'T TAKE ADVANTAGE OF OTHERS.
WE'VE NEVER MET, HAVE WE?
DON'T BELIEVE SO. WHY?
MY FIRST REPEAT CUSTOMER! WELCOME BACK, FRIEND!
UMMM...
Cyp27c1
Sold Here
ACTUALLY, I HAD A QUESTION ABOUT THE POSSIBLE SIDE EFFECTS OF YOUR PRODUCT.
OH, RIGHT.
DIDN'T YOU SEE THE MICROSCOPIC WARNING LABEL ON THE BOTTLE?
HERE ON THE BOTTOM?
"DO NOT TAKE IF YOU CAN READ THIS."
SEE? ALL LEGIT.
HAWTHORNE, WHAT DID YOU DO TO MY HUSBAND?
NOTHING!
Cyp27c1
Sold Here
I JUST SOLD HIM A BOTTLE OF CYP27C1 TO HELP WITH HIS VISION. WHY?
SHERMAN! GET OVER HERE!
WHOA!
HE KEEPS TRYING TO SIT ON THE POTATO SALAD!
Cyp27c1

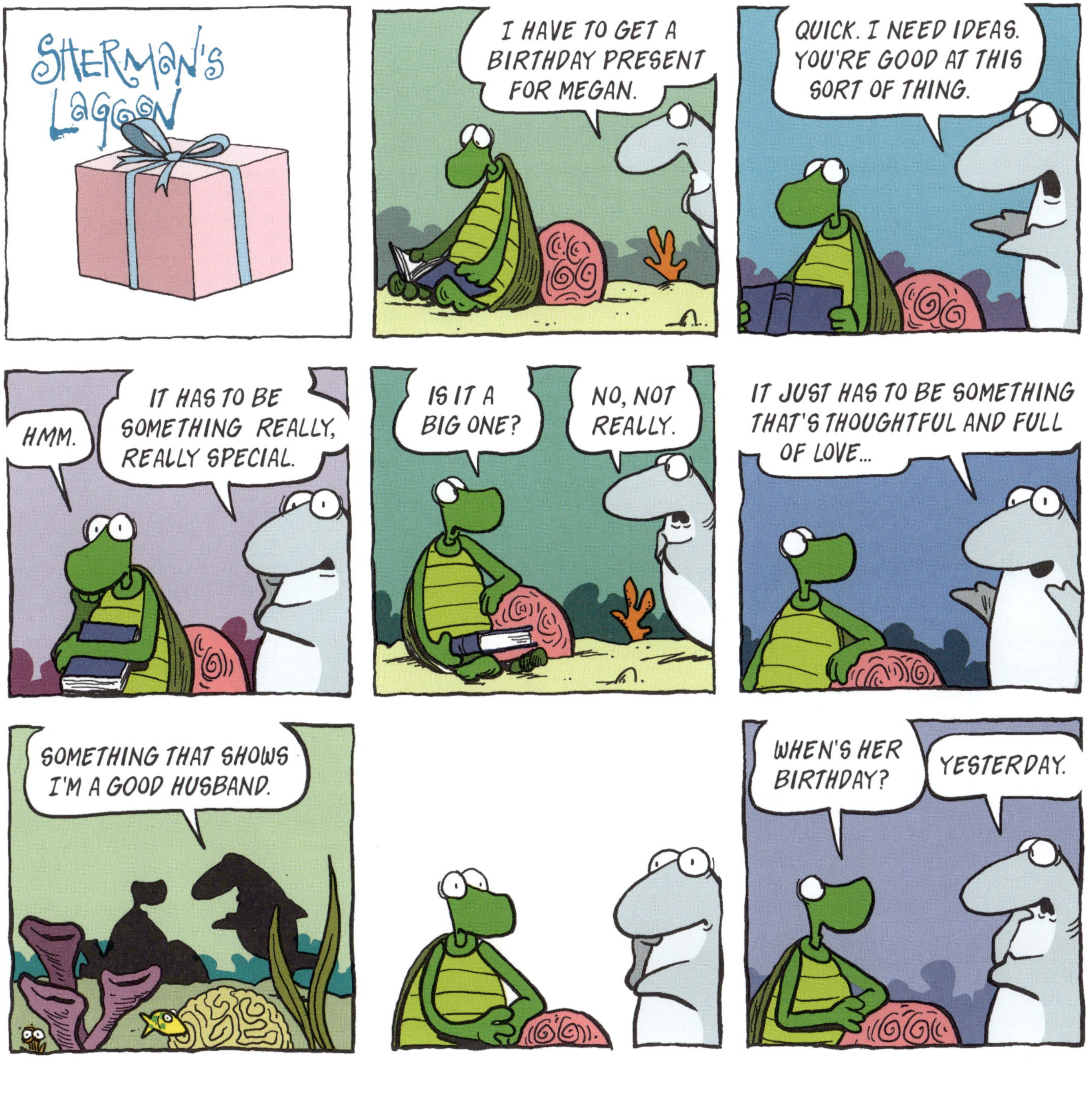
SHERMAN'S LAGOON
I HAVE TO GET A BIRTHDAY PRESENT FOR MEGAN.
QUICK. I NEED IDEAS. YOU'RE GOOD AT THIS SORT OF THING.
HMM.
IT HAS TO BE SOMETHING REALLY, REALLY SPECIAL.
IS IT A BIG ONE?
NO, NOT REALLY.
IT JUST HAS TO BE SOMETHING THAT'S THOUGHTFUL AND FULL OF LOVE...
SOMETHING THAT SHOWS I'M A GOOD HUSBAND.
WHEN'S HER BIRTHDAY?
YESTERDAY.

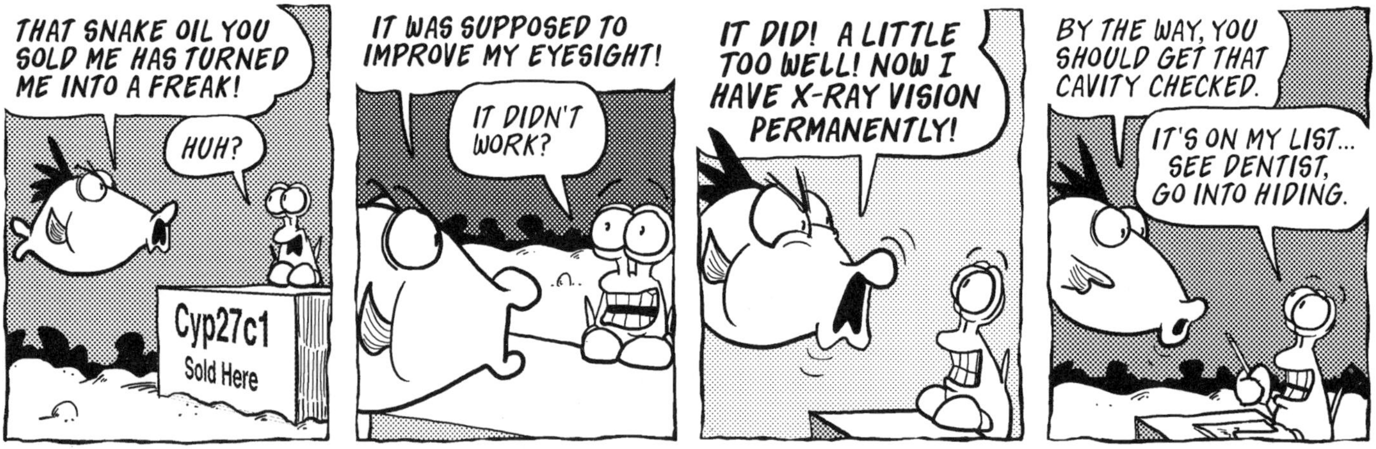
THAT SNAKE OIL YOU SOLD ME HAS TURNED ME INTO A FREAK!
HUH?
Cyp27c1 Sold Here
IT WAS SUPPOSED TO IMPROVE MY EYESIGHT!
IT DIDN'T WORK?
IT DID! A LITTLE TOO WELL! NOW I HAVE X-RAY VISION PERMANENTLY!
BY THE WAY, YOU SHOULD GET THAT CAVITY CHECKED.
IT'S ON MY LIST... SEE DENTIST, GO INTO HIDING.

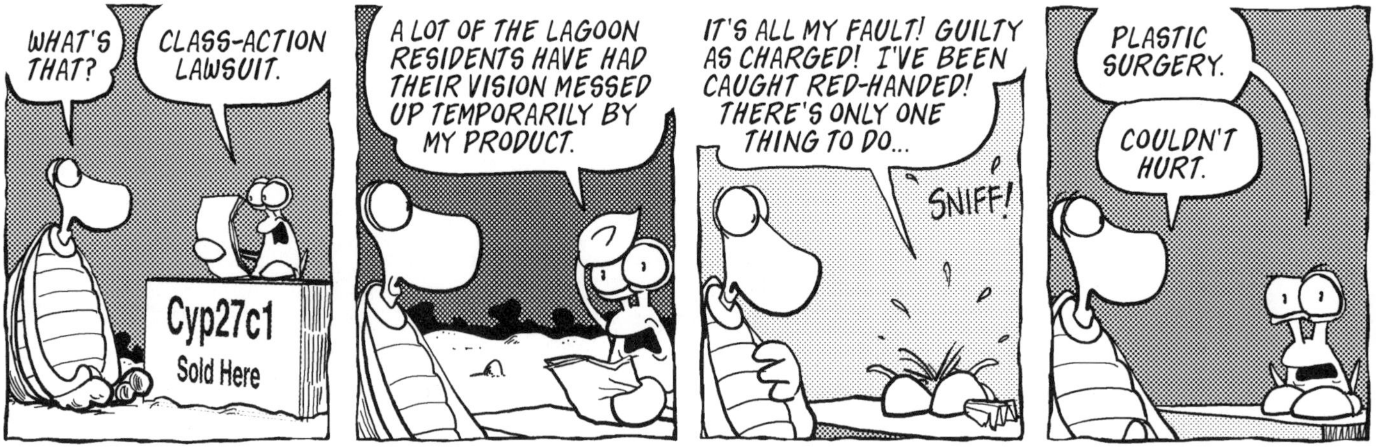
WHAT'S THAT?
CLASS-ACTION LAWSUIT.
Cyp27c1 Sold Here
A LOT OF THE LAGOON RESIDENTS HAVE HAD THEIR VISION MESSED UP TEMPORARILY BY MY PRODUCT.
IT'S ALL MY FAULT! GUILTY AS CHARGED! I'VE BEEN CAUGHT RED-HANDED! THERE'S ONLY ONE THING TO DO...
SNIFF!
PLASTIC SURGERY.
COULDN'T HURT.

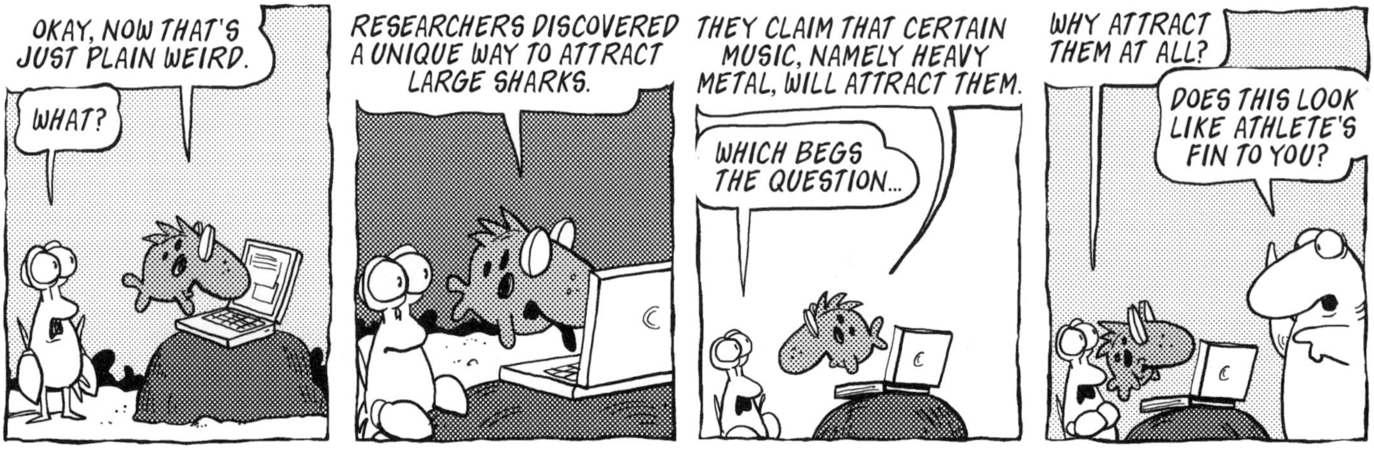
OKAY, NOW THAT'S JUST PLAIN WEIRD.
WHAT?
RESEARCHERS DISCOVERED A UNIQUE WAY TO ATTRACT LARGE SHARKS.
THEY CLAIM THAT CERTAIN MUSIC, NAMELY HEAVY METAL, WILL ATTRACT THEM.
WHICH BEGS THE QUESTION...
WHY ATTRACT THEM AT ALL?
DOES THIS LOOK LIKE ATHLETE'S FIN TO YOU?

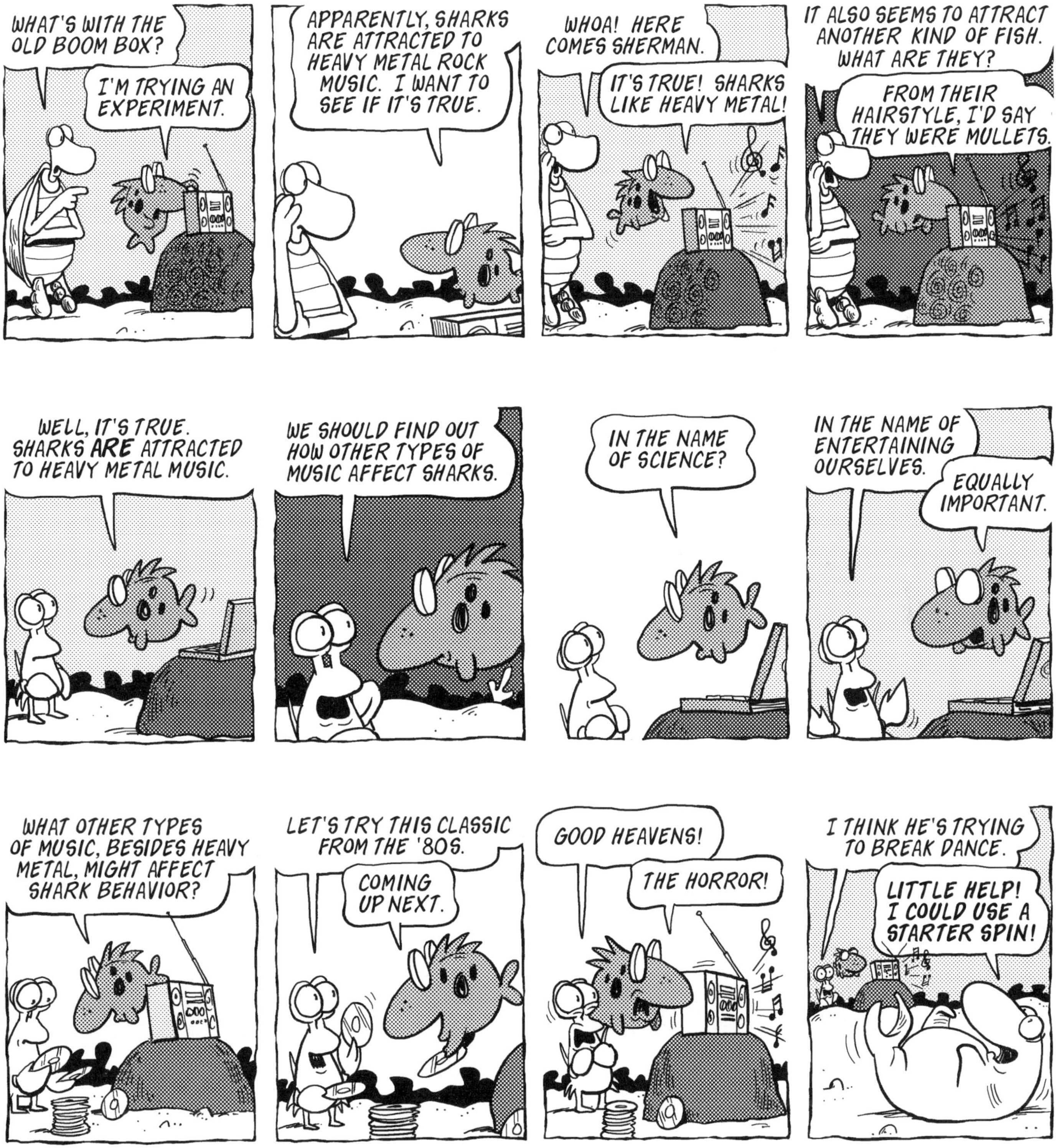
WHAT'S WITH THE OLD BOOM BOX?
I'M TRYING AN EXPERIMENT.
APPARENTLY, SHARKS ARE ATTRACTED TO HEAVY METAL ROCK MUSIC. I WANT TO SEE IF IT'S TRUE.
WHOA! HERE COMES SHERMAN.
IT'S TRUE! SHARKS LIKE HEAVY METAL!
IT ALSO SEEMS TO ATTRACT ANOTHER KIND OF FISH. WHAT ARE THEY?
FROM THEIR HAIRSTYLE, I'D SAY THEY WERE MULLETS.
WELL, IT'S TRUE. SHARKS ARE ATTRACTED TO HEAVY METAL MUSIC.
WE SHOULD FIND OUT HOW OTHER TYPES OF MUSIC AFFECT SHARKS.
IN THE NAME OF SCIENCE?
IN THE NAME OF ENTERTAINING OURSELVES.
EQUALLY IMPORTANT.
WHAT OTHER TYPES OF MUSIC, BESIDES HEAVY METAL, MIGHT AFFECT SHARK BEHAVIOR?
LET'S TRY THIS CLASSIC FROM THE '80S.
COMING UP NEXT.
GOOD HEAVENS!
THE HORROR!
I THINK HE'S TRYING TO BREAK DANCE.
LITTLE HELP! I COULD USE A STARTER SPIN!

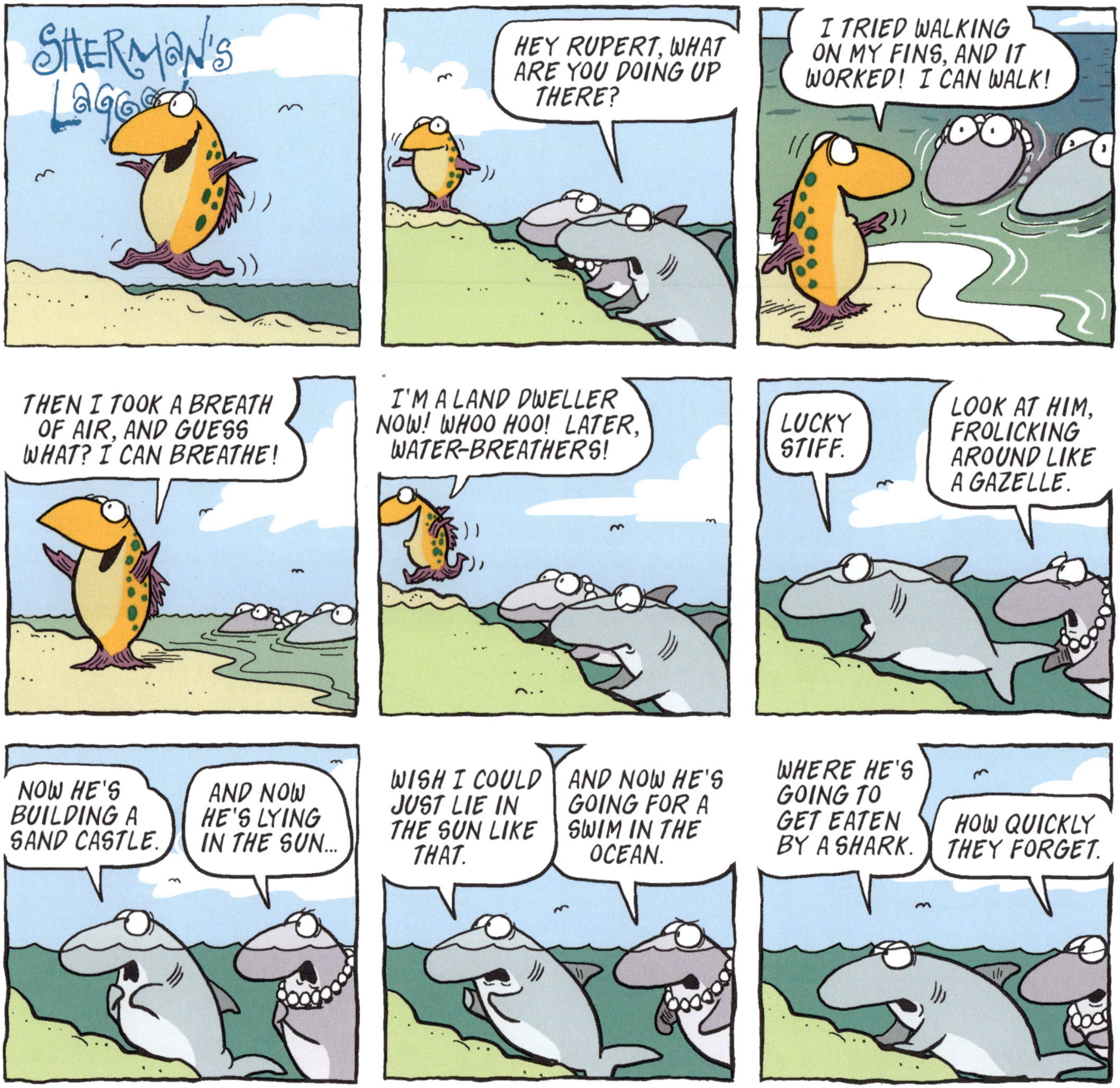
Sherman's Lagoon
HEY RUPERT, WHAT ARE YOU DOING UP THERE?
I TRIED WALKING ON MY FINS, AND IT WORKED! I CAN WALK!
THEN I TOOK A BREATH OF AIR, AND GUESS WHAT? I CAN BREATHE!
I'M A LAND DWELLER NOW! WHOO HOO! LATER, WATER-BREATHERS!
LUCKY STIFF.
LOOK AT HIM, FROLICKING AROUND LIKE A GAZELLE.
NOW HE'S BUILDING A SAND CASTLE.
AND NOW HE'S LYING IN THE SUN...
WISH I COULD JUST LIE IN THE SUN LIKE THAT.
AND NOW HE'S GOING FOR A SWIM IN THE OCEAN.
WHERE HE'S GOING TO GET EATEN BY A SHARK.
HOW QUICKLY THEY FORGET.

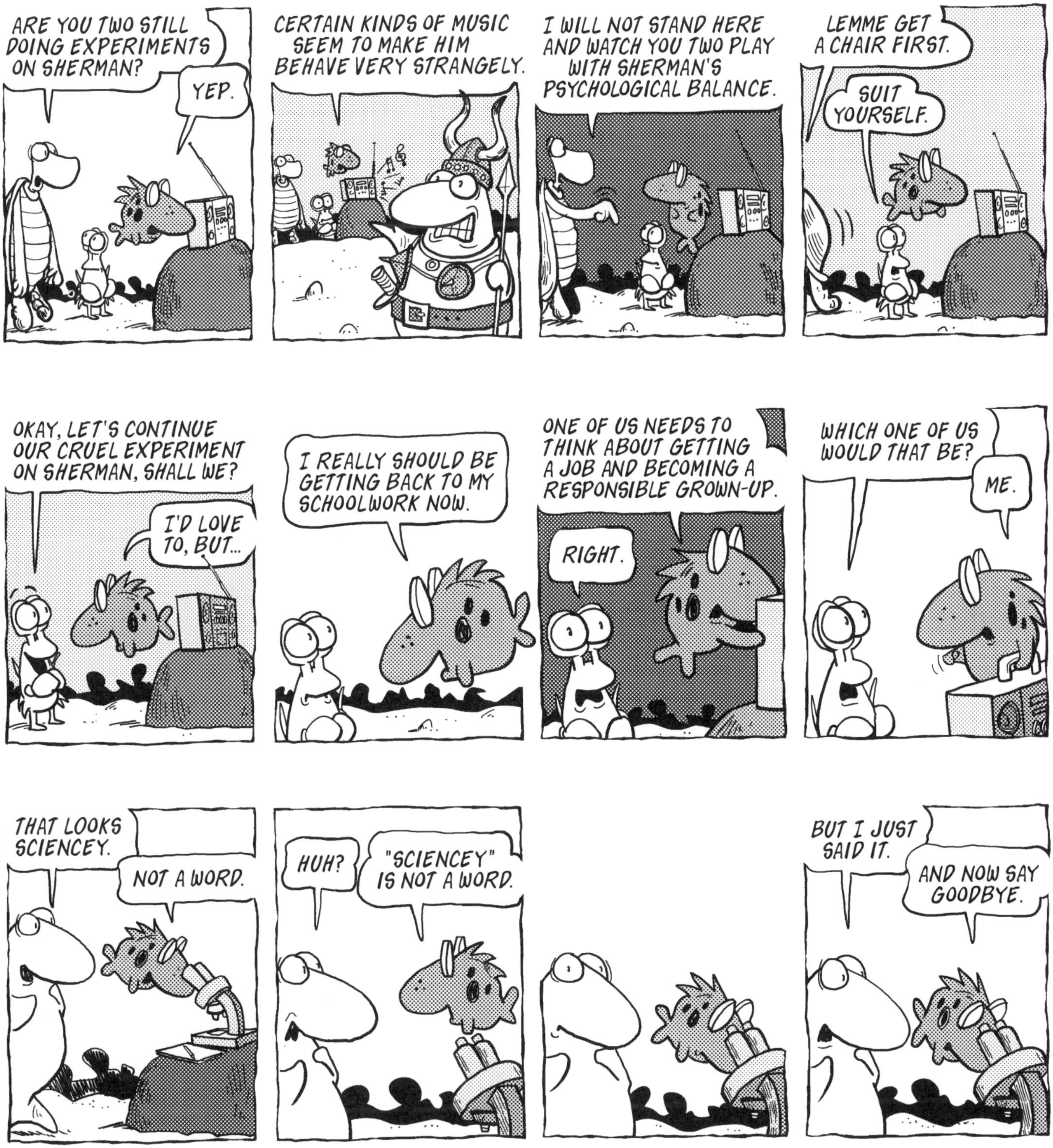
ARE YOU TWO STILL DOING EXPERIMENTS ON SHERMAN?
YEP.
CERTAIN KINDS OF MUSIC SEEM TO MAKE HIM BEHAVE VERY STRANGELY.
I WILL NOT STAND HERE AND WATCH YOU TWO PLAY WITH SHERMAN'S PSYCHOLOGICAL BALANCE.
LEMME GET A CHAIR FIRST.
SUIT YOURSELF.
OKAY, LET'S CONTINUE OUR CRUEL EXPERIMENT ON SHERMAN, SHALL WE?
I'D LOVE TO, BUT...
I REALLY SHOULD BE GETTING BACK TO MY SCHOOLWORK NOW.
ONE OF US NEEDS TO THINK ABOUT GETTING A JOB AND BECOMING A RESPONSIBLE GROWN-UP.
RIGHT.
WHICH ONE OF US WOULD THAT BE?
ME.
THAT LOOKS SCIENCEY.
NOT A WORD.
HUH?
"SCIENCEY" IS NOT A WORD.
BUT I JUST SAID IT.
AND NOW SAY GOODBYE.

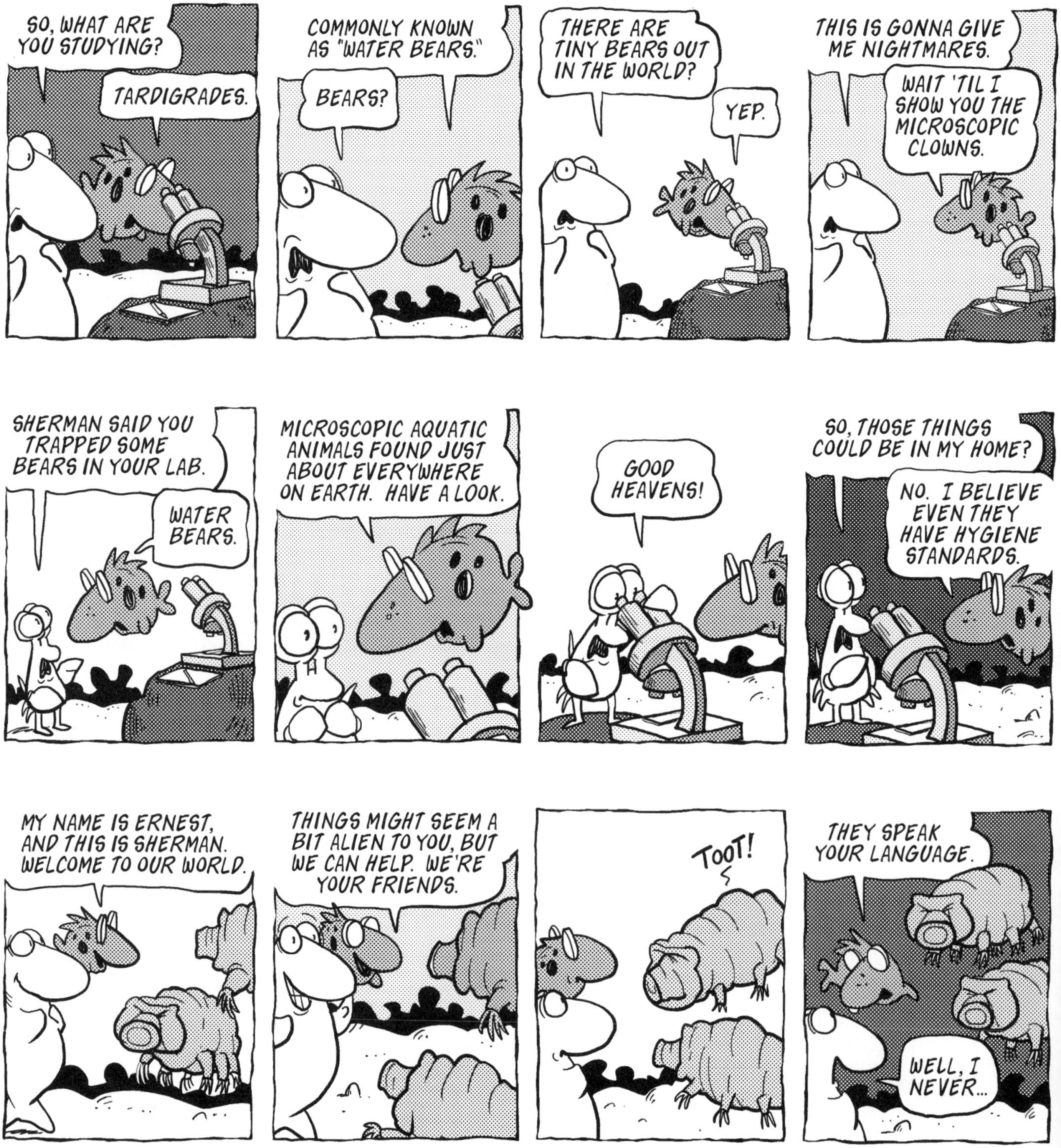
SO, WHAT ARE YOU STUDYING?
TARDIGRADES.
COMMONLY KNOWN AS "WATER BEARS."
BEARS?
THERE ARE TINY BEARS OUT IN THE WORLD?
YEP.
THIS IS GONNA GIVE ME NIGHTMARES.
WAIT 'TIL I SHOW YOU THE MICROSCOPIC CLOWNS.
SHERMAN SAID YOU TRAPPED SOME BEARS IN YOUR LAB.
WATER BEARS.
MICROSCOPIC AQUATIC ANIMALS FOUND JUST ABOUT EVERYWHERE ON EARTH. HAVE A LOOK.
GOOD HEAVENS!
SO, THOSE THINGS COULD BE IN MY HOME?
NO. I BELIEVE EVEN THEY HAVE HYGIENE STANDARDS.
MY NAME IS ERNEST, AND THIS IS SHERMAN. WELCOME TO OUR WORLD.
THINGS MIGHT SEEM A BIT ALIEN TO YOU, BUT WE CAN HELP. WE'RE YOUR FRIENDS.
TOOT!
THEY SPEAK YOUR LANGUAGE.
WELL, I NEVER...

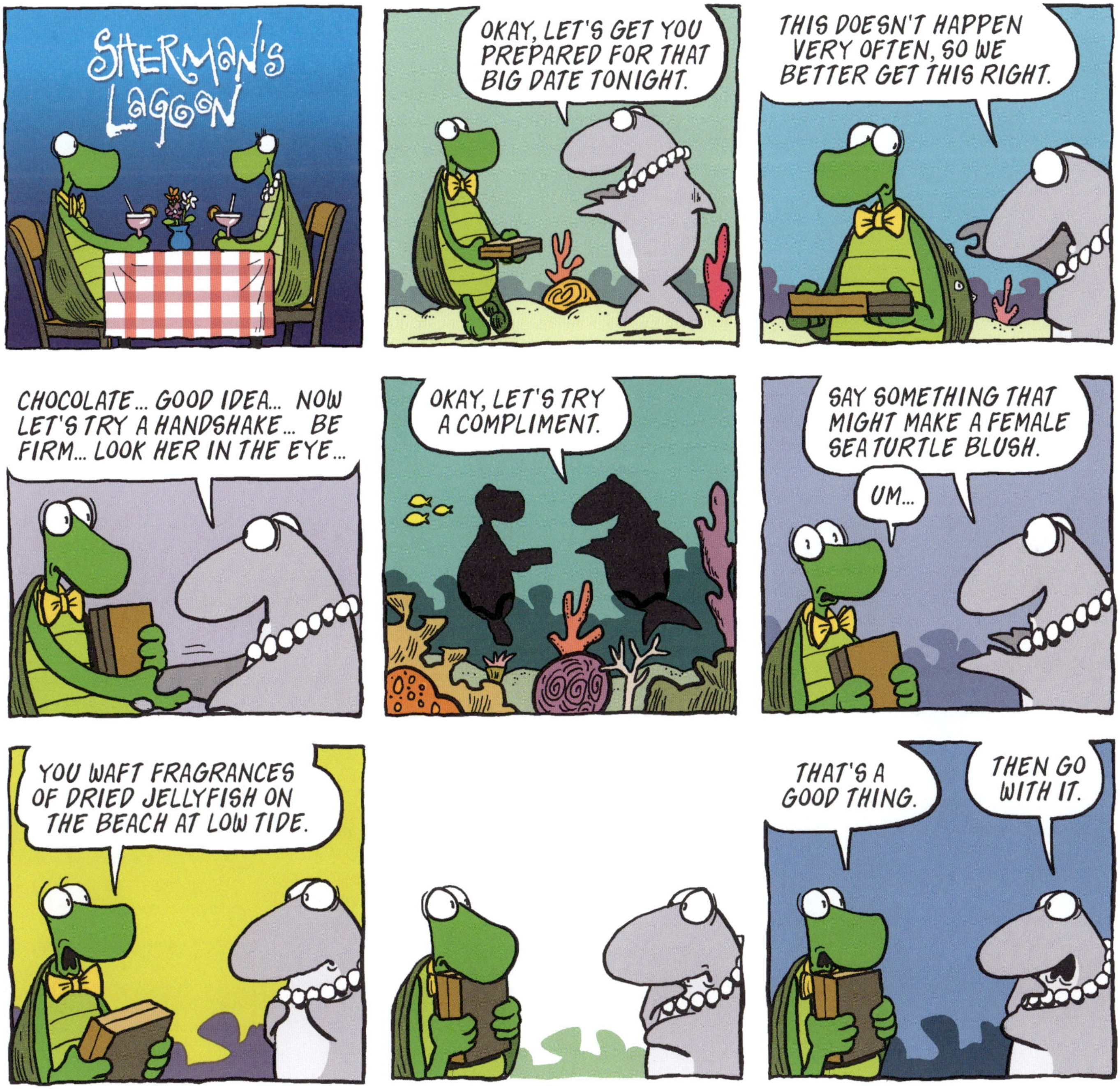
SHERMAN'S LAGOON
OKAY, LET'S GET YOU PREPARED FOR THAT BIG DATE TONIGHT.
THIS DOESN'T HAPPEN VERY OFTEN, SO WE BETTER GET THIS RIGHT.
CHOCOLATE... GOOD IDEA... NOW LET'S TRY A HANDSHAKE... BE FIRM... LOOK HER IN THE EYE...
OKAY, LET'S TRY A COMPLIMENT.
SAY SOMETHING THAT MIGHT MAKE A FEMALE SEA TURTLE BLUSH.
UM...
YOU WAFT FRAGRANCES OF DRIED JELLYFISH ON THE BEACH AT LOW TIDE.
THAT'S A GOOD THING.
THEN GO WITH IT.

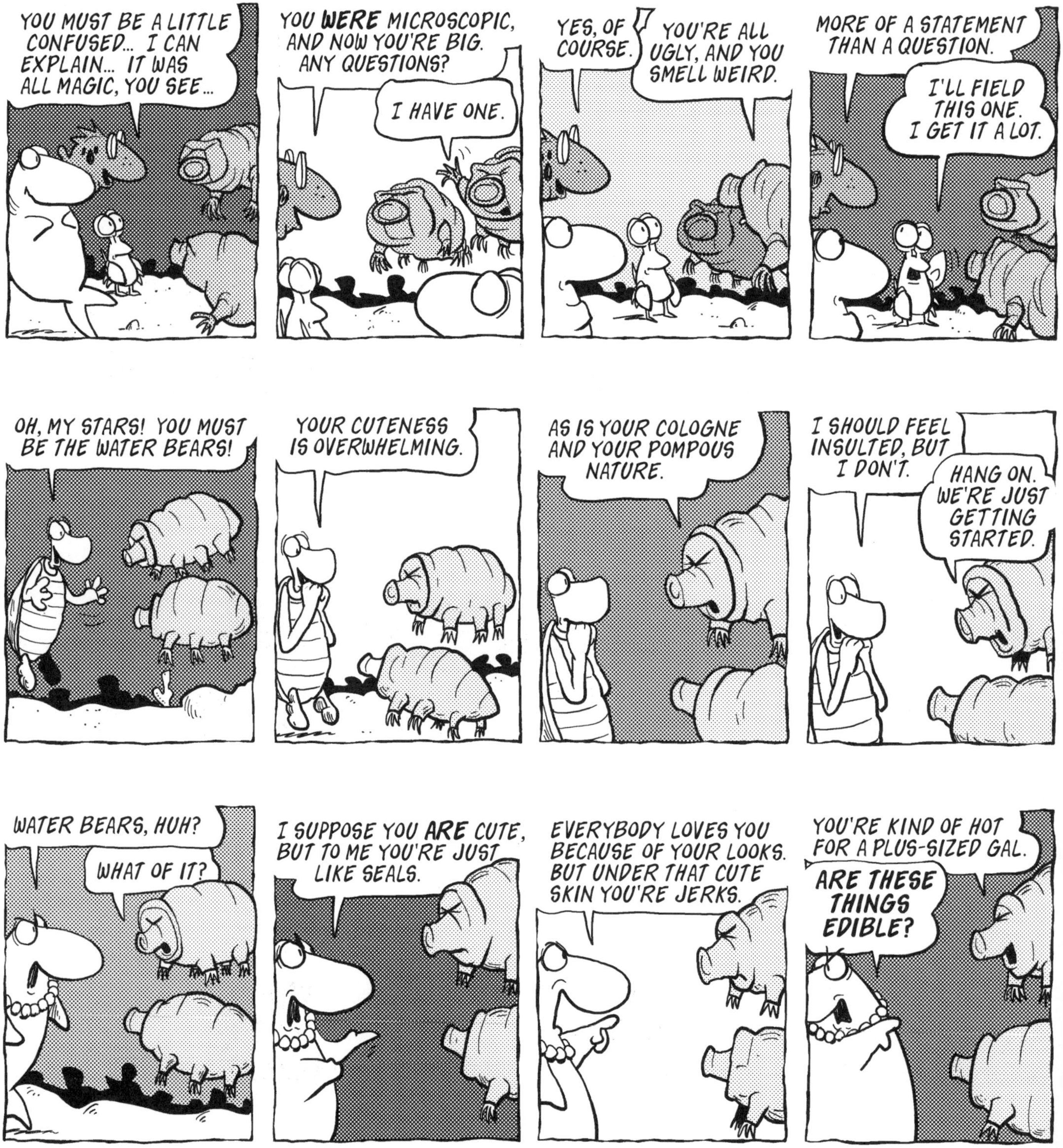
YOU MUST BE A LITTLE CONFUSED... I CAN EXPLAIN... IT WAS ALL MAGIC, YOU SEE...
YOU WERE MICROSCOPIC, AND NOW YOU'RE BIG. ANY QUESTIONS?
I HAVE ONE.
YES, OF COURSE.
YOU'RE ALL UGLY, AND YOU SMELL WEIRD.
MORE OF A STATEMENT THAN A QUESTION.
I'LL FIELD THIS ONE. I GET IT A LOT.
OH, MY STARS! YOU MUST BE THE WATER BEARS!
YOUR CUTENESS IS OVERWHELMING.
AS IS YOUR COLOGNE AND YOUR POMPOUS NATURE.
I SHOULD FEEL INSULTED, BUT I DON'T.
HANG ON. WE'RE JUST GETTING STARTED.
WATER BEARS, HUH?
WHAT OF IT?
I SUPPOSE YOU ARE CUTE, BUT TO ME YOU'RE JUST LIKE SEALS.
EVERYBODY LOVES YOU BECAUSE OF YOUR LOOKS. BUT UNDER THAT CUTE SKIN YOU'RE JERKS.
YOU'RE KIND OF HOT FOR A PLUS-SIZED GAL.
ARE THESE THINGS EDIBLE?

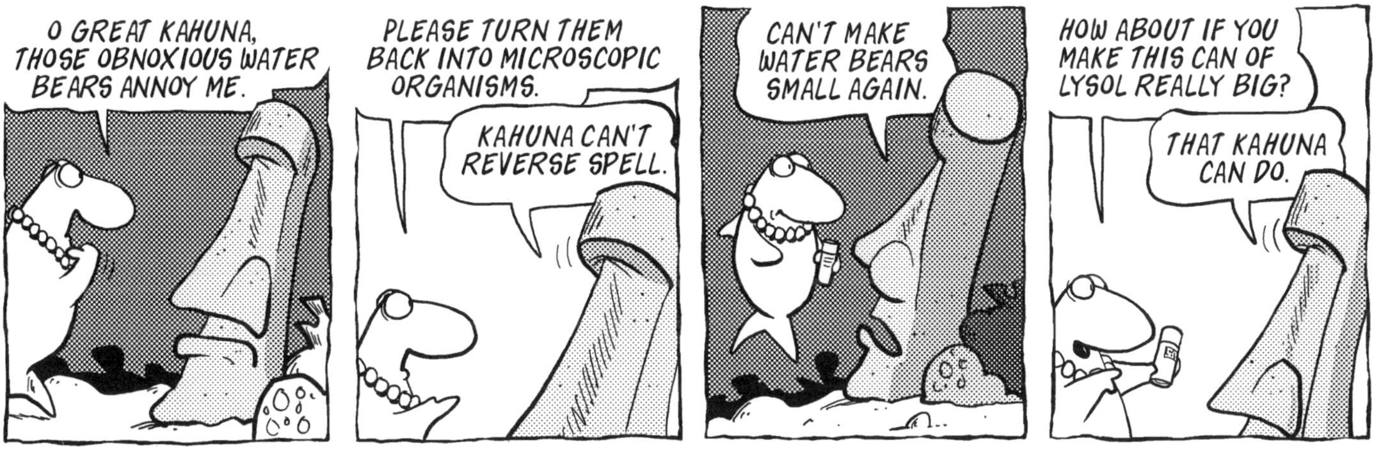
O GREAT KAHUNA, THOSE OBNOXIOUS WATER BEARS ANNOY ME.
PLEASE TURN THEM BACK INTO MICROSCOPIC ORGANISMS.
KAHUNA CAN'T REVERSE SPELL.
CAN'T MAKE WATER BEARS SMALL AGAIN.
HOW ABOUT IF YOU MAKE THIS CAN OF LYSOL REALLY BIG?
THAT KAHUNA CAN DO.

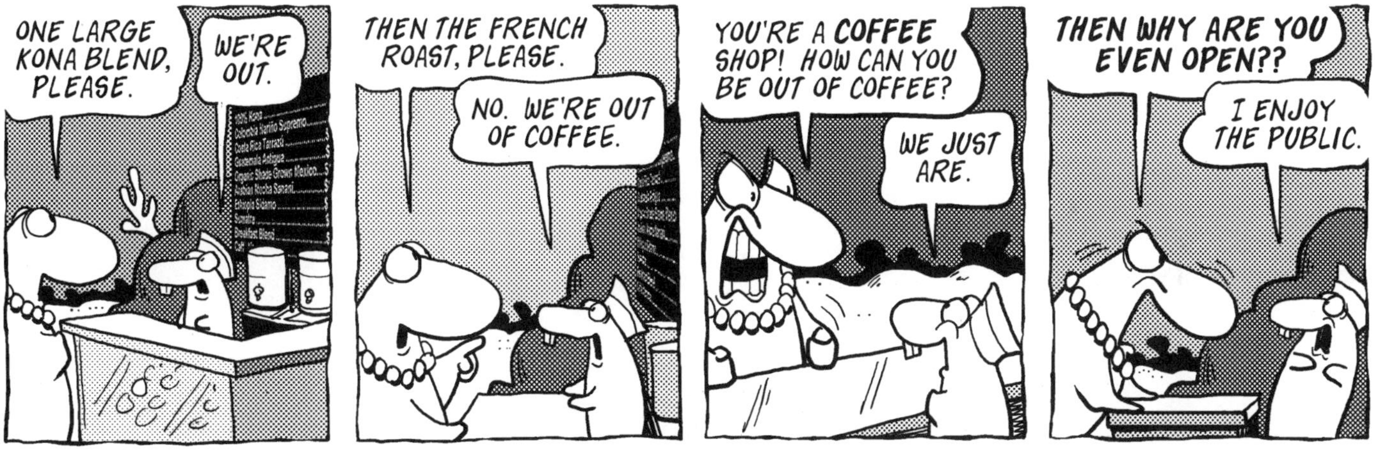
ONE LARGE KONA BLEND, PLEASE.
WE'RE OUT.
THEN THE FRENCH ROAST, PLEASE.
NO. WE'RE OUT OF COFFEE.
YOU'RE A **COFFEE** SHOP! HOW CAN YOU BE OUT OF COFFEE?
WE JUST ARE.
THEN WHY ARE YOU EVEN OPEN??
I ENJOY THE PUBLIC.

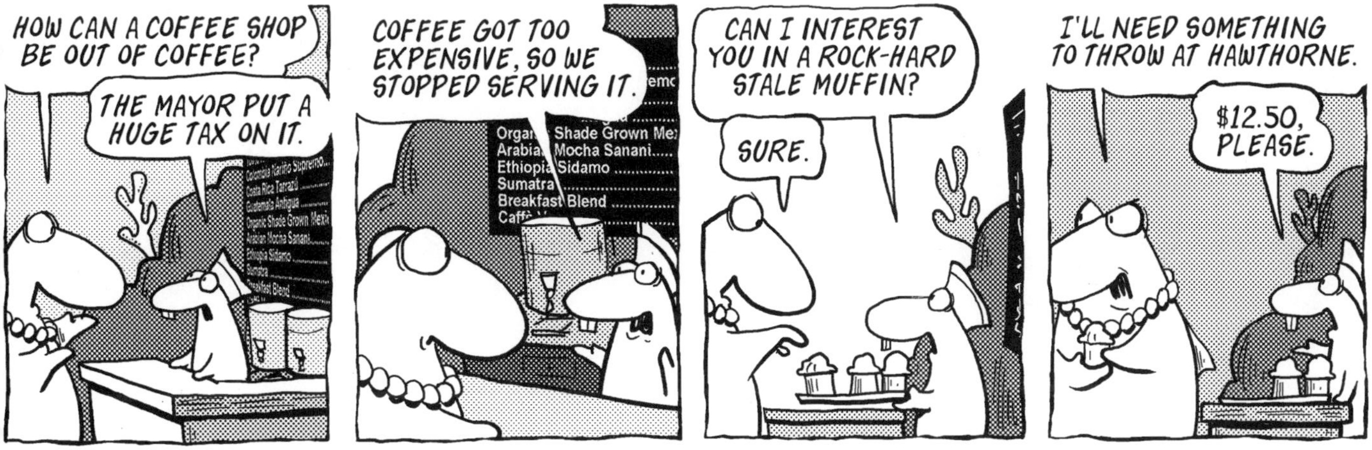
HOW CAN A COFFEE SHOP BE OUT OF COFFEE?
THE MAYOR PUT A HUGE TAX ON IT.
COFFEE GOT TOO EXPENSIVE, SO WE STOPPED SERVING IT.
CAN I INTEREST YOU IN A ROCK-HARD STALE MUFFIN?
SURE.
I'LL NEED SOMETHING TO THROW AT HAWTHORNE.
$12.50, PLEASE.

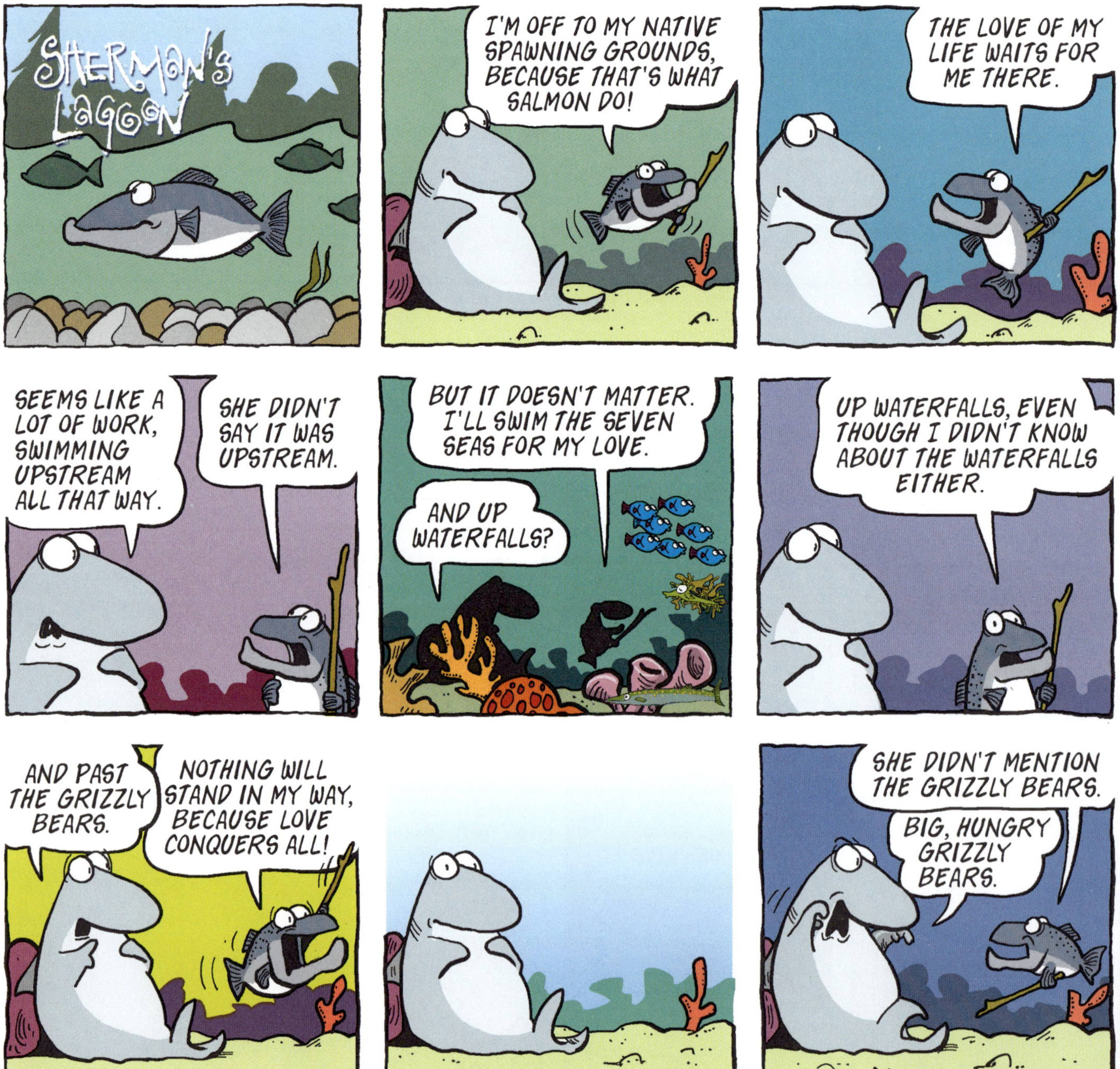
SHERMAN'S LAGOON
I'M OFF TO MY NATIVE SPAWNING GROUNDS, BECAUSE THAT'S WHAT SALMON DO!
THE LOVE OF MY LIFE WAITS FOR ME THERE.
SEEMS LIKE A LOT OF WORK, SWIMMING UPSTREAM ALL THAT WAY.
SHE DIDN'T SAY IT WAS UPSTREAM.
BUT IT DOESN'T MATTER. I'LL SWIM THE SEVEN SEAS FOR MY LOVE.
AND UP WATERFALLS?
UP WATERFALLS, EVEN THOUGH I DIDN'T KNOW ABOUT THE WATERFALLS EITHER.
AND PAST THE GRIZZLY BEARS.
NOTHING WILL STAND IN MY WAY, BECAUSE LOVE CONQUERS ALL!
SHE DIDN'T MENTION THE GRIZZLY BEARS.
BIG, HUNGRY GRIZZLY BEARS.

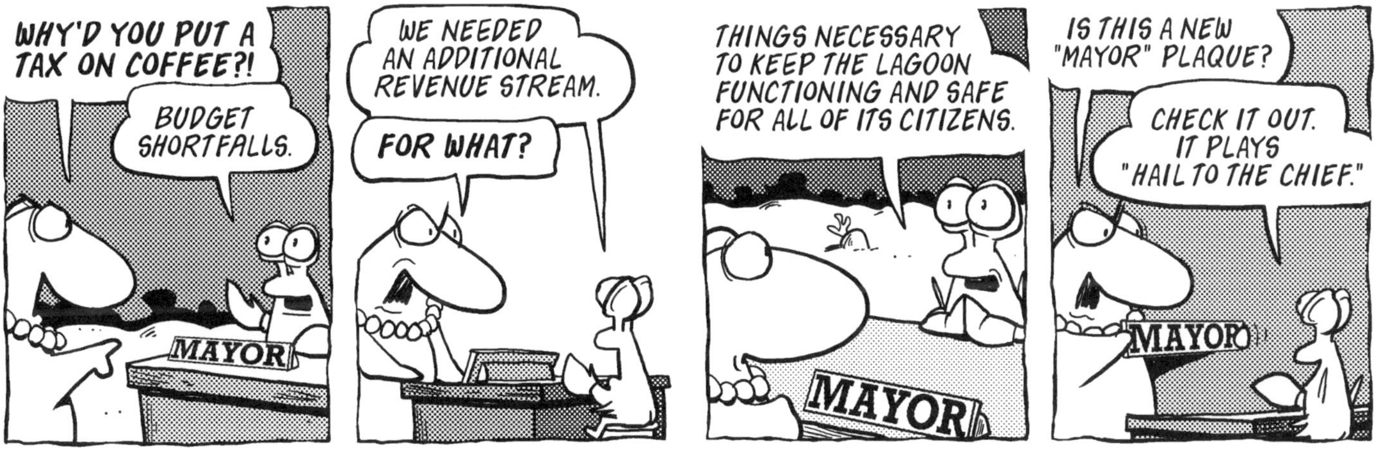
WHY'D YOU PUT A TAX ON COFFEE?!
BUDGET SHORTFALLS.
MAYOR
WE NEEDED AN ADDITIONAL REVENUE STREAM.
FOR WHAT?
THINGS NECESSARY TO KEEP THE LAGOON FUNCTIONING AND SAFE FOR ALL OF ITS CITIZENS.
MAYOR
IS THIS A NEW "MAYOR" PLAQUE?
CHECK IT OUT. IT PLAYS "HAIL TO THE CHIEF."
MAYOR

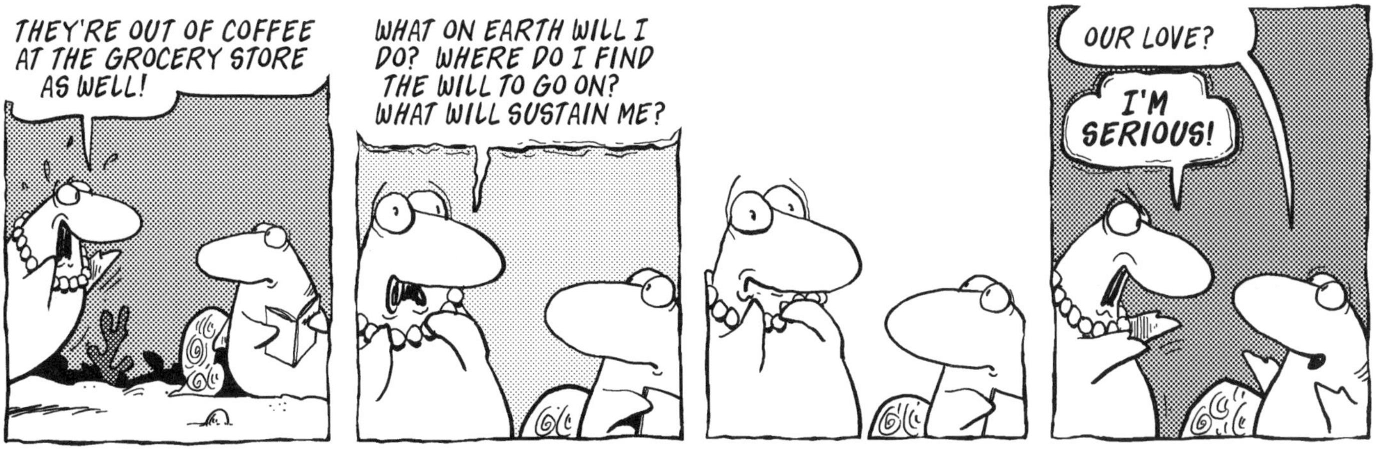
THEY'RE OUT OF COFFEE AT THE GROCERY STORE AS WELL!
WHAT ON EARTH WILL I DO? WHERE DO I FIND THE WILL TO GO ON? WHAT WILL SUSTAIN ME?
OUR LOVE?
I'M SERIOUS!

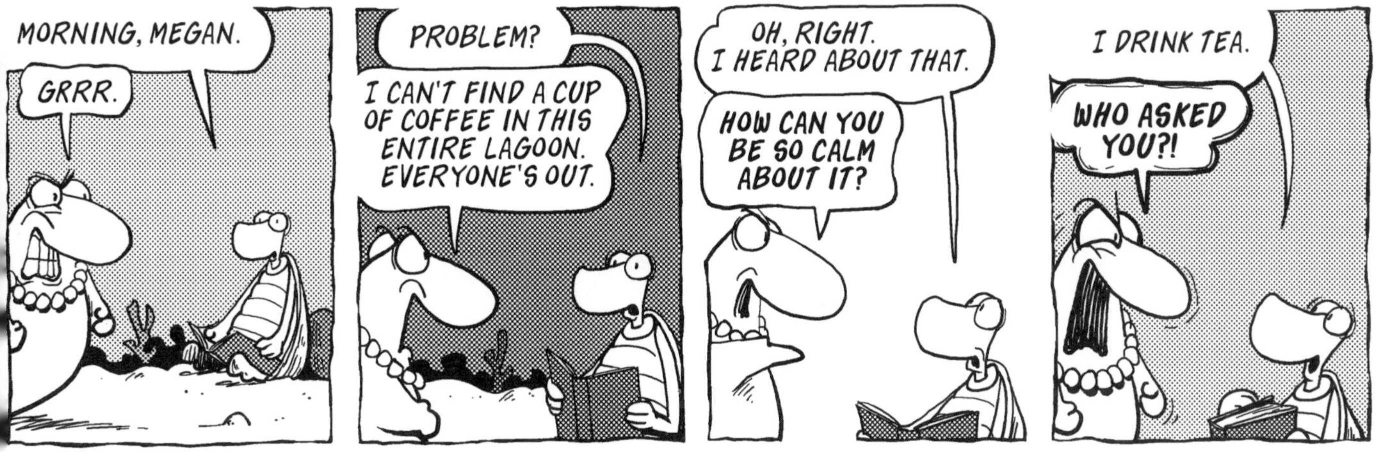
MORNING, MEGAN.
GRRR.
PROBLEM?
I CAN'T FIND A CUP OF COFFEE IN THIS ENTIRE LAGOON. EVERYONE'S OUT.
OH, RIGHT. I HEARD ABOUT THAT.
HOW CAN YOU BE SO CALM ABOUT IT?
I DRINK TEA.
WHO ASKED YOU?!

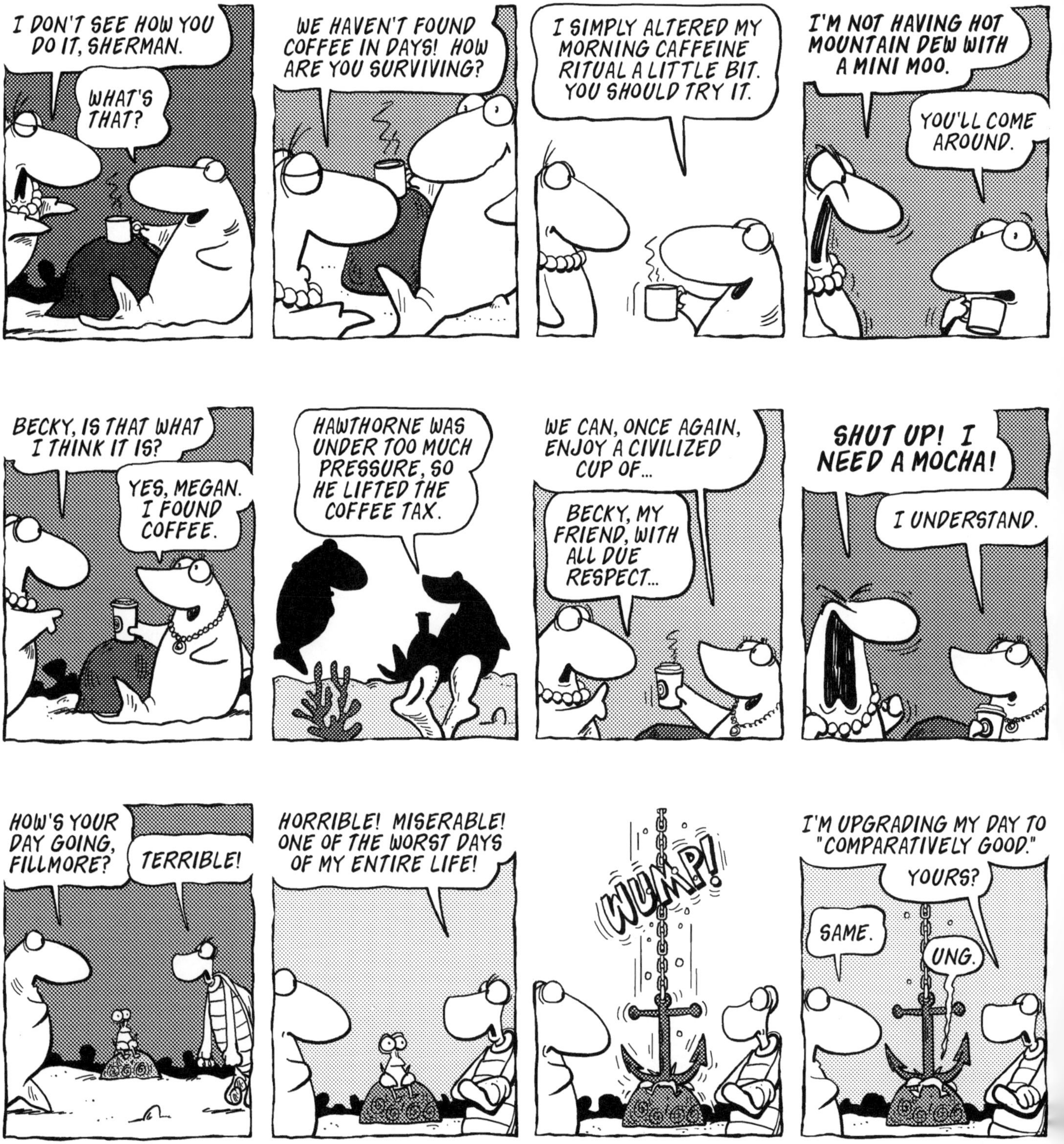
I DON'T SEE HOW YOU DO IT, SHERMAN.
WHAT'S THAT?
WE HAVEN'T FOUND COFFEE IN DAYS! HOW ARE YOU SURVIVING?
I SIMPLY ALTERED MY MORNING CAFFEINE RITUAL A LITTLE BIT. YOU SHOULD TRY IT.
I'M NOT HAVING HOT MOUNTAIN DEW WITH A MINI MOO.
YOU'LL COME AROUND.
BECKY, IS THAT WHAT I THINK IT IS?
YES, MEGAN. I FOUND COFFEE.
HAWTHORNE WAS UNDER TOO MUCH PRESSURE, SO HE LIFTED THE COFFEE TAX.
WE CAN, ONCE AGAIN, ENJOY A CIVILIZED CUP OF...
BECKY, MY FRIEND, WITH ALL DUE RESPECT...
SHUT UP! I NEED A MOCHA!
I UNDERSTAND.
HOW'S YOUR DAY GOING, FILLMORE?
TERRIBLE!
HORRIBLE! MISERABLE! ONE OF THE WORST DAYS OF MY ENTIRE LIFE!
WUMP!
I'M UPGRADING MY DAY TO "COMPARATIVELY GOOD."
YOURS?
SAME.
UNG.

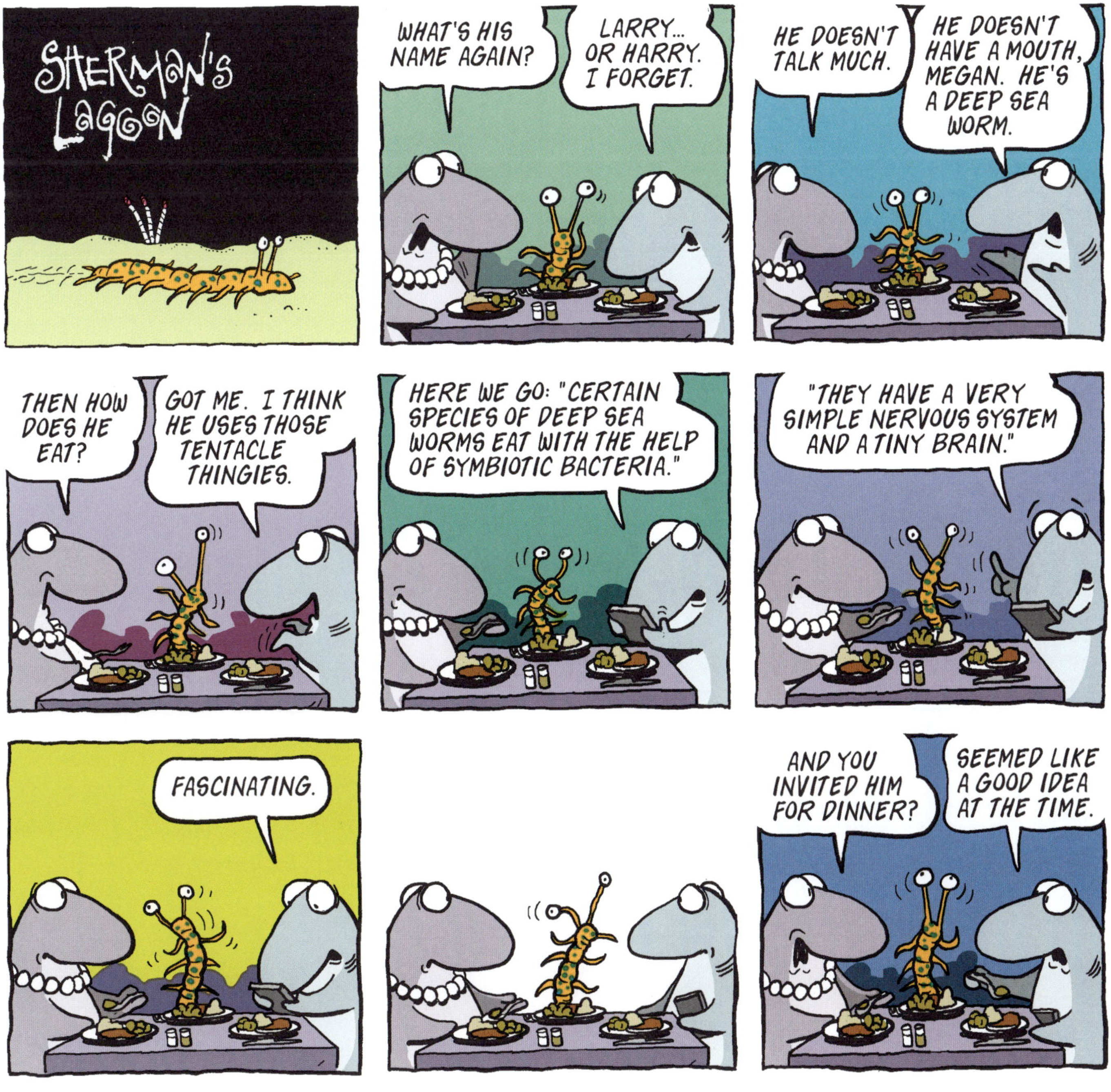
SHERMAN'S LAGOON
WHAT'S HIS NAME AGAIN?
LARRY... OR HARRY. I FORGET.
HE DOESN'T TALK MUCH.
HE DOESN'T HAVE A MOUTH, MEGAN. HE'S A DEEP SEA WORM.
THEN HOW DOES HE EAT?
GOT ME. I THINK HE USES THOSE TENTACLE THINGIES.
HERE WE GO: "CERTAIN SPECIES OF DEEP SEA WORMS EAT WITH THE HELP OF SYMBIOTIC BACTERIA."
"THEY HAVE A VERY SIMPLE NERVOUS SYSTEM AND A TINY BRAIN."
FASCINATING.
AND YOU INVITED HIM FOR DINNER?
SEEMED LIKE A GOOD IDEA AT THE TIME.

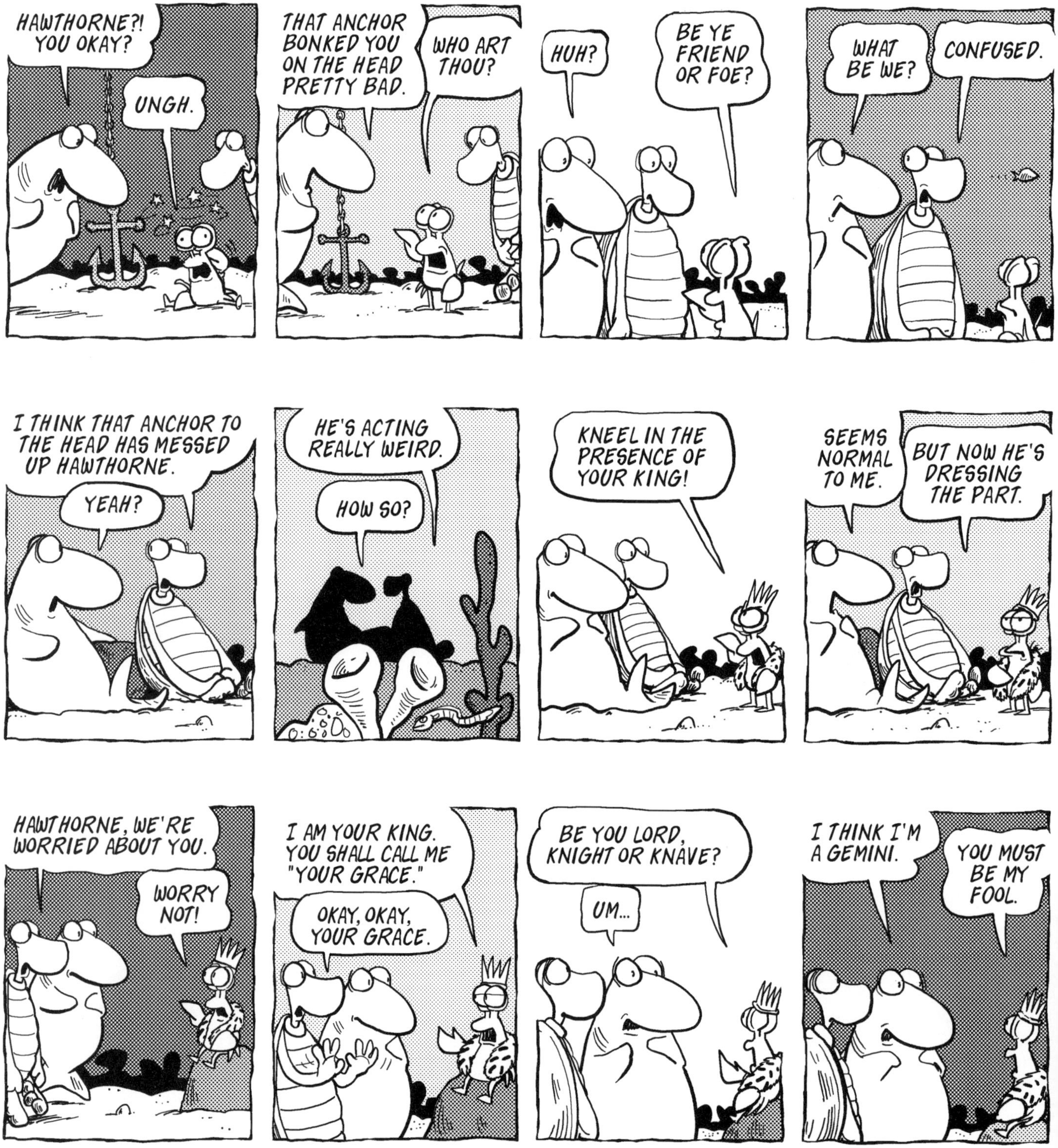
HAWTHORNE?! YOU OKAY?
UNGH.
THAT ANCHOR BONKED YOU ON THE HEAD PRETTY BAD.
WHO ART THOU?
HUH?
BE YE FRIEND OR FOE?
WHAT BE WE?
CONFUSED.
I THINK THAT ANCHOR TO THE HEAD HAS MESSED UP HAWTHORNE.
YEAH?
HE'S ACTING REALLY WEIRD.
HOW SO?
KNEEL IN THE PRESENCE OF YOUR KING!
SEEMS NORMAL TO ME.
BUT NOW HE'S DRESSING THE PART.
HAWTHORNE, WE'RE WORRIED ABOUT YOU.
WORRY NOT!
I AM YOUR KING. YOU SHALL CALL ME "YOUR GRACE."
OKAY, OKAY, YOUR GRACE.
BE YOU LORD, KNIGHT OR KNAVE?
UM...
I THINK I'M A GEMINI.
YOU MUST BE MY FOOL.

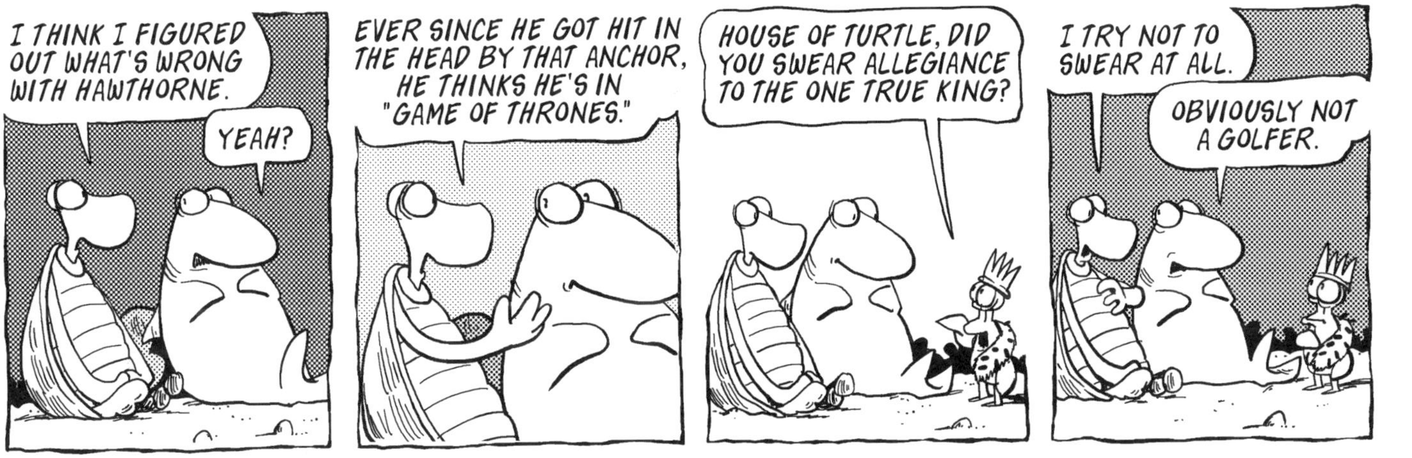
I THINK I FIGURED OUT WHAT'S WRONG WITH HAWTHORNE.
YEAH?
EVER SINCE HE GOT HIT IN THE HEAD BY THAT ANCHOR, HE THINKS HE'S IN "GAME OF THRONES."
HOUSE OF TURTLE, DID YOU SWEAR ALLEGIANCE TO THE ONE TRUE KING?
I TRY NOT TO SWEAR AT ALL.
OBVIOUSLY NOT A GOLFER.

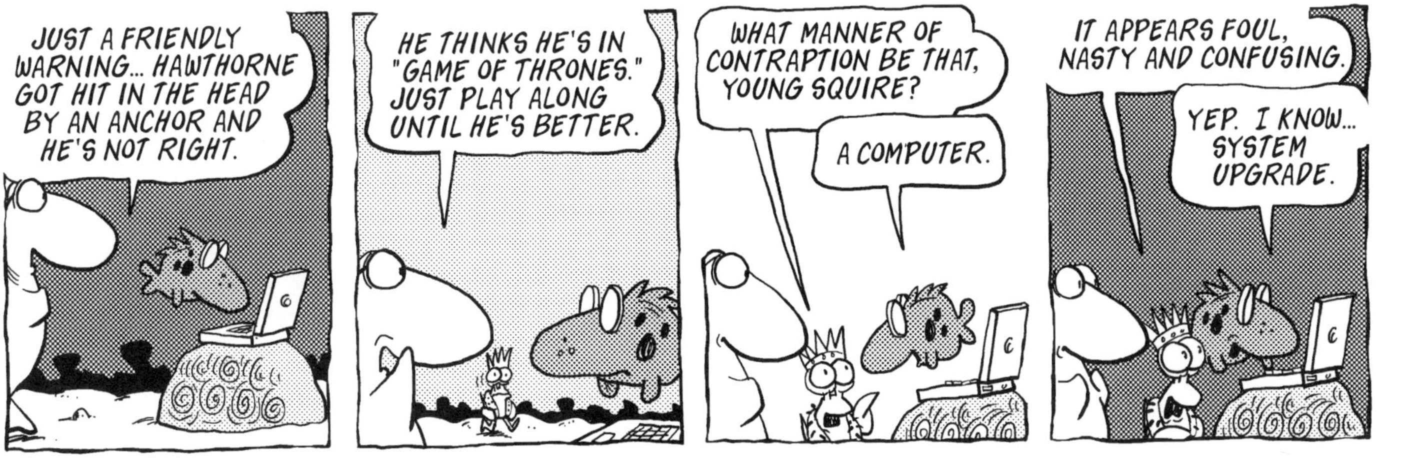
JUST A FRIENDLY WARNING... HAWTHORNE GOT HIT IN THE HEAD BY AN ANCHOR AND HE'S NOT RIGHT.
HE THINKS HE'S IN "GAME OF THRONES." JUST PLAY ALONG UNTIL HE'S BETTER.
WHAT MANNER OF CONTRAPTION BE THAT, YOUNG SQUIRE?
A COMPUTER.
IT APPEARS FOUL, NASTY AND CONFUSING.
YEP. I KNOW... SYSTEM UPGRADE.

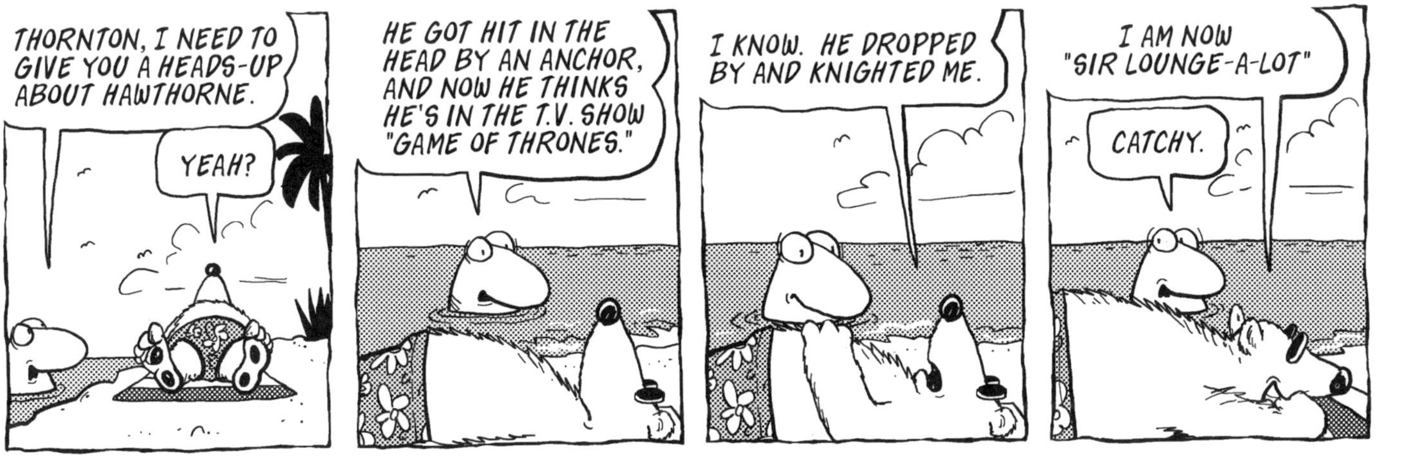
THORNTON, I NEED TO GIVE YOU A HEADS-UP ABOUT HAWTHORNE.
YEAH?
HE GOT HIT IN THE HEAD BY AN ANCHOR, AND NOW HE THINKS HE'S IN THE T.V. SHOW "GAME OF THRONES."
I KNOW. HE DROPPED BY AND KNIGHTED ME.
I AM NOW "SIR LOUNGE-A-LOT"
CATCHY.

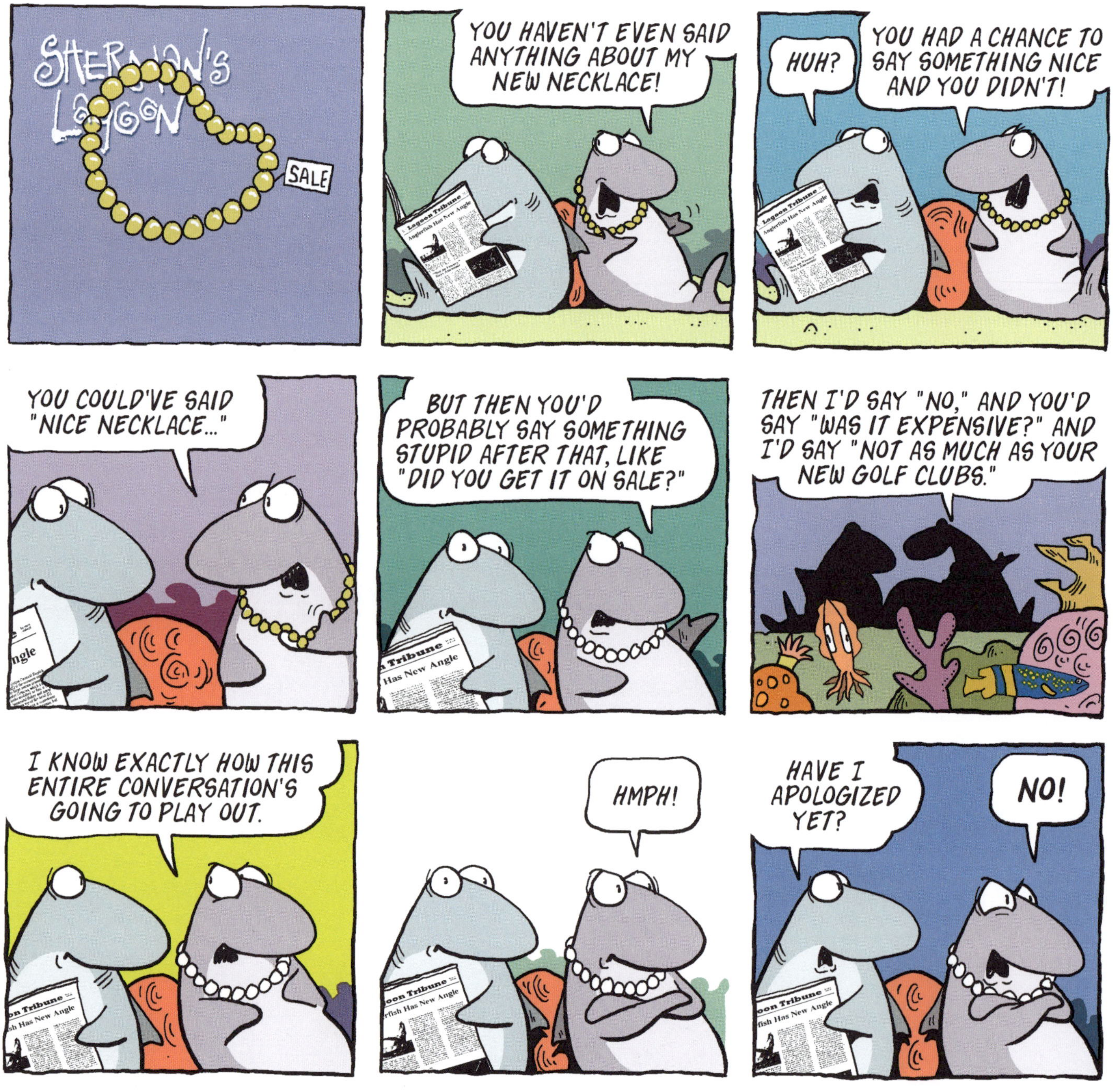
SHERMAN'S LAGOON
SALE
YOU HAVEN'T EVEN SAID ANYTHING ABOUT MY NEW NECKLACE!
HUH?
YOU HAD A CHANCE TO SAY SOMETHING NICE AND YOU DIDN'T!
YOU COULD'VE SAID "NICE NECKLACE..."
BUT THEN YOU'D PROBABLY SAY SOMETHING STUPID AFTER THAT, LIKE "DID YOU GET IT ON SALE?"
THEN I'D SAY "NO," AND YOU'D SAY "WAS IT EXPENSIVE?" AND I'D SAY "NOT AS MUCH AS YOUR NEW GOLF CLUBS."
I KNOW EXACTLY HOW THIS ENTIRE CONVERSATION'S GOING TO PLAY OUT.
HMPH!
HAVE I APOLOGIZED YET?
NO!

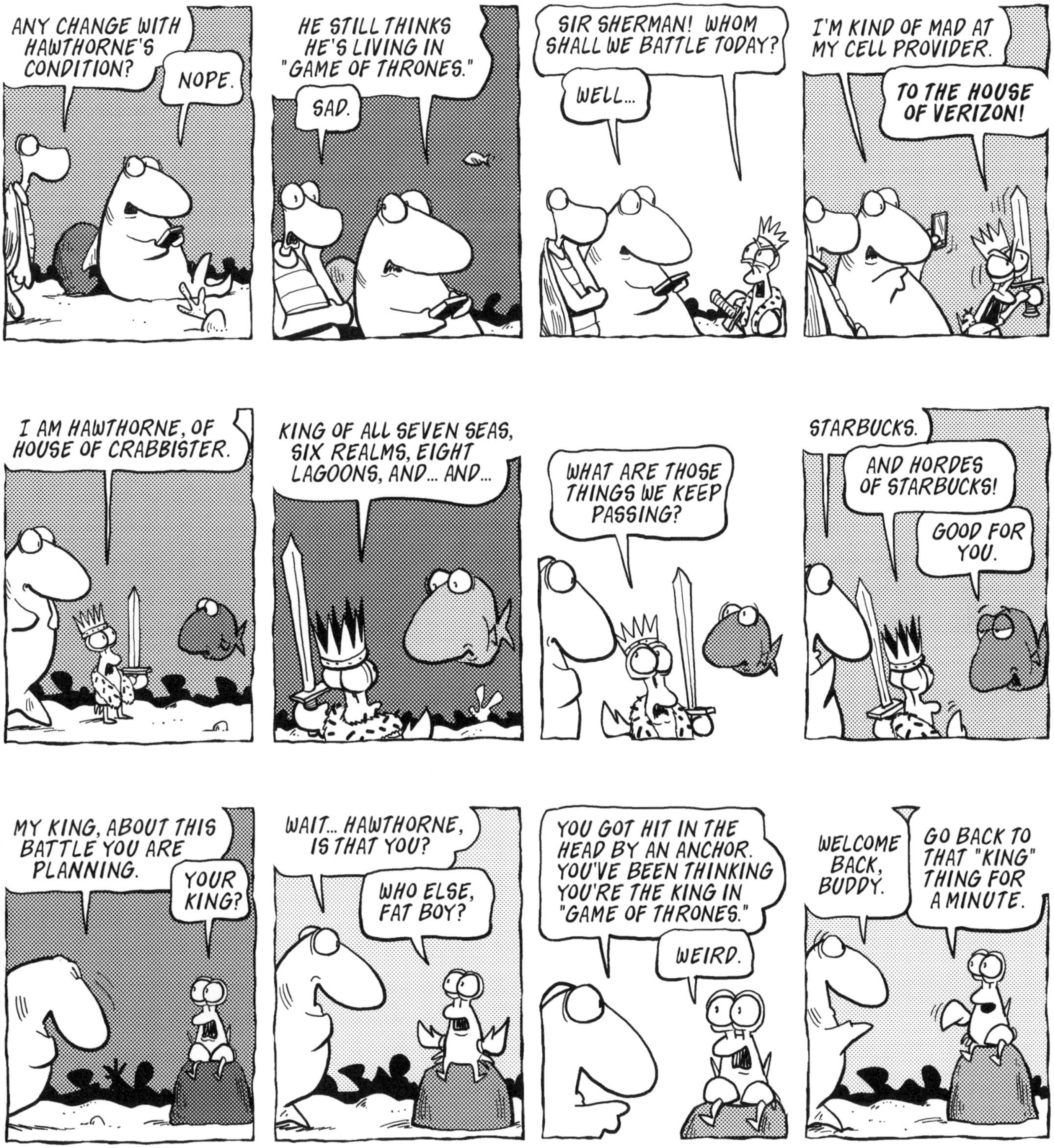
ANY CHANGE WITH HAWTHORNE'S CONDITION?
NOPE.
HE STILL THINKS HE'S LIVING IN "GAME OF THRONES."
SAD.
SIR SHERMAN! WHOM SHALL WE BATTLE TODAY?
WELL...
I'M KIND OF MAD AT MY CELL PROVIDER.
TO THE HOUSE OF VERIZON!
I AM HAWTHORNE, OF HOUSE OF CRABBISTER.
KING OF ALL SEVEN SEAS, SIX REALMS, EIGHT LAGOONS, AND... AND...
WHAT ARE THOSE THINGS WE KEEP PASSING?
STARBUCKS.
AND HORDES OF STARBUCKS!
GOOD FOR YOU.
MY KING, ABOUT THIS BATTLE YOU ARE PLANNING.
YOUR KING?
WAIT... HAWTHORNE, IS THAT YOU?
WHO ELSE, FAT BOY?
YOU GOT HIT IN THE HEAD BY AN ANCHOR. YOU'VE BEEN THINKING YOU'RE THE KING IN "GAME OF THRONES."
WEIRD.
WELCOME BACK, BUDDY.
GO BACK TO THAT "KING" THING FOR A MINUTE.

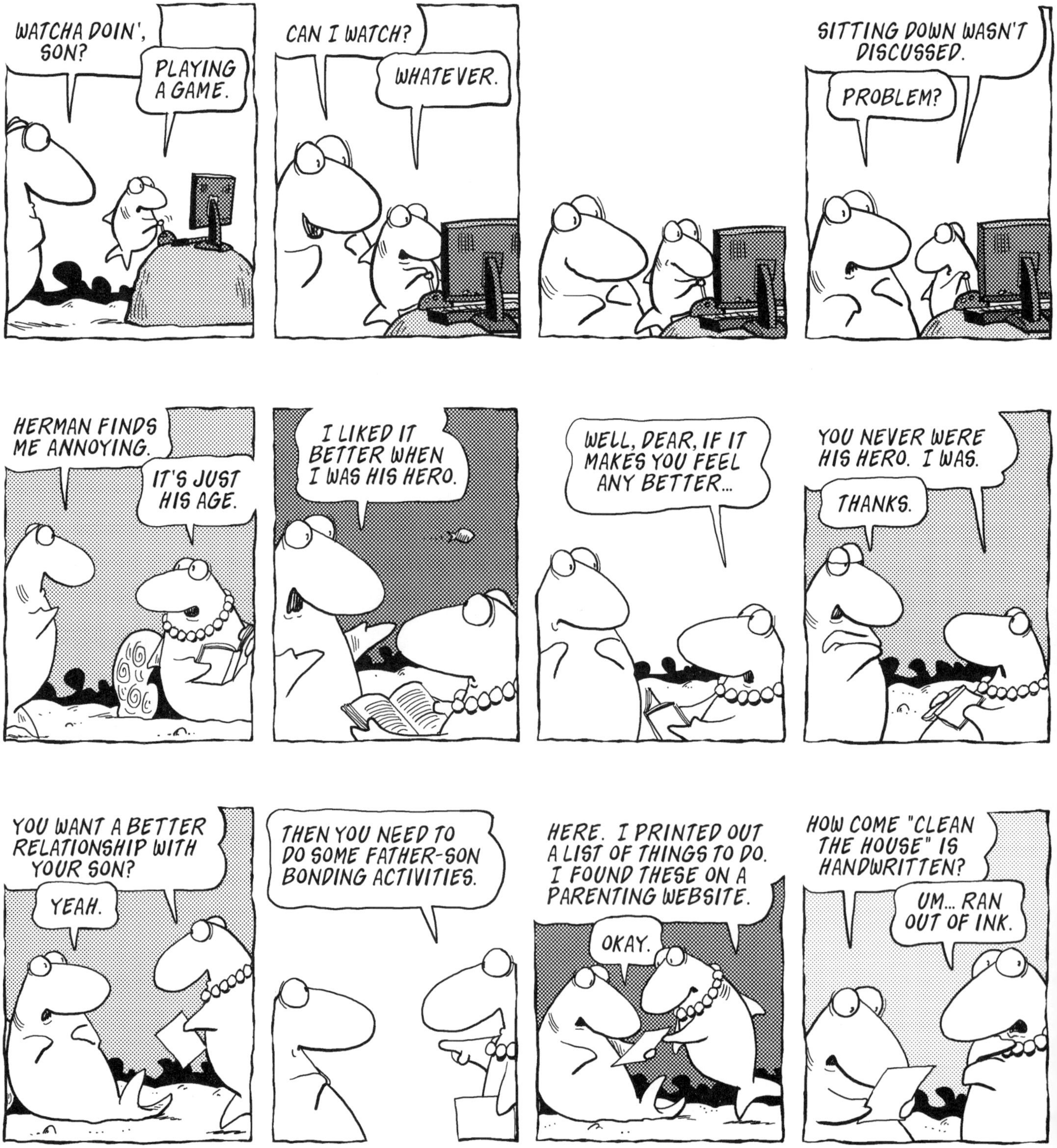
WATCHA DOIN', SON?
PLAYING A GAME.
CAN I WATCH?
WHATEVER.
SITTING DOWN WASN'T DISCUSSED.
PROBLEM?
HERMAN FINDS ME ANNOYING.
IT'S JUST HIS AGE.
I LIKED IT BETTER WHEN I WAS HIS HERO.
WELL, DEAR, IF IT MAKES YOU FEEL ANY BETTER...
YOU NEVER WERE HIS HERO. I WAS.
THANKS.
YOU WANT A BETTER RELATIONSHIP WITH YOUR SON?
YEAH.
THEN YOU NEED TO DO SOME FATHER-SON BONDING ACTIVITIES.
HERE. I PRINTED OUT A LIST OF THINGS TO DO. I FOUND THESE ON A PARENTING WEBSITE.
OKAY.
HOW COME "CLEAN THE HOUSE" IS HANDWRITTEN?
UM... RAN OUT OF INK.

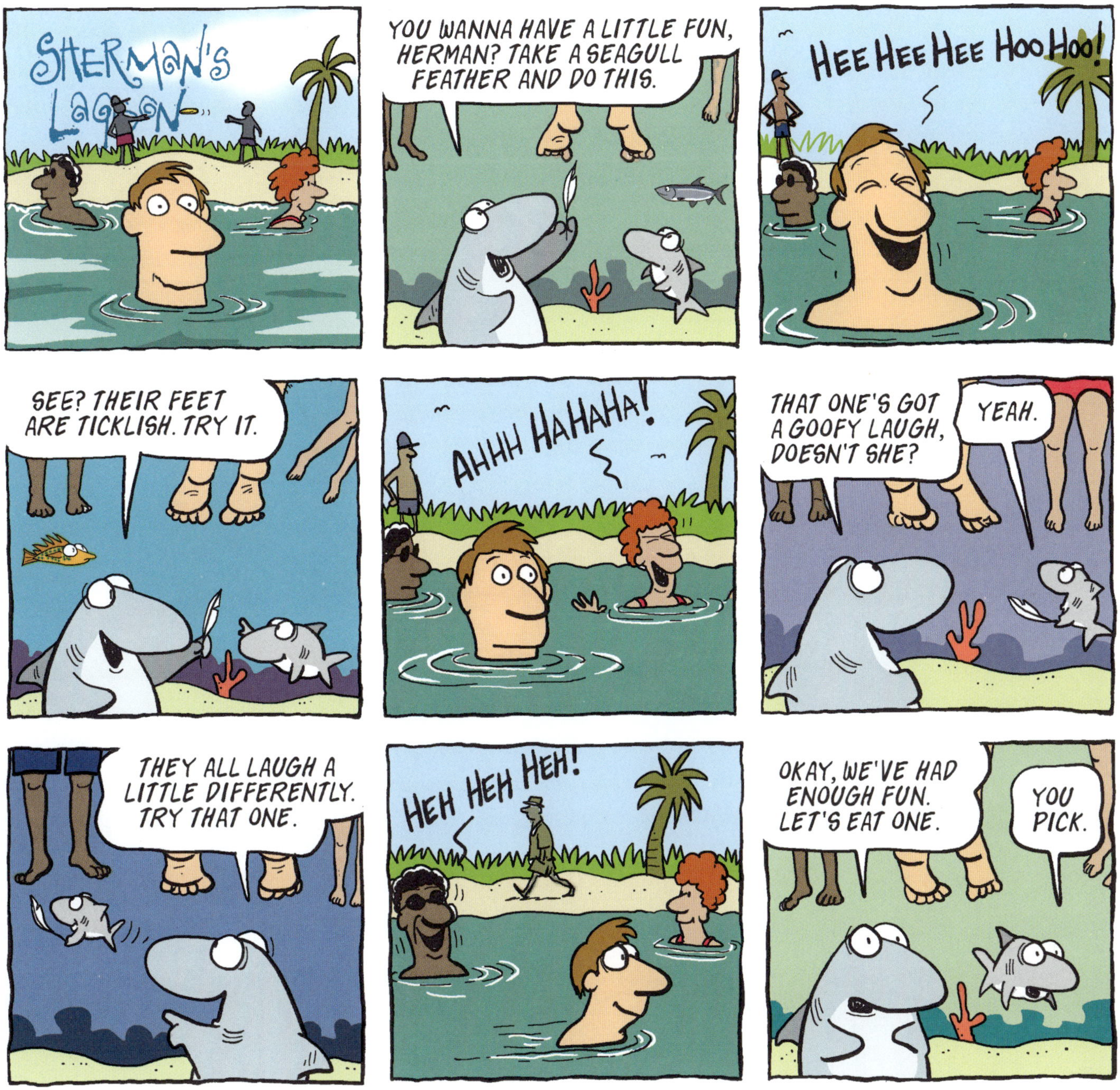
SHERMAN'S LAGOON
YOU WANNA HAVE A LITTLE FUN, HERMAN? TAKE A SEAGULL FEATHER AND DO THIS.
HEE HEE HEE HOO HOO!
SEE? THEIR FEET ARE TICKLISH. TRY IT.
AHHH HAHAHA!
THAT ONE'S GOT A GOOFY LAUGH, DOESN'T SHE?
YEAH.
THEY ALL LAUGH A LITTLE DIFFERENTLY. TRY THAT ONE.
HEH HEH HEH!
OKAY, WE'VE HAD ENOUGH FUN. LET'S EAT ONE.
YOU PICK.

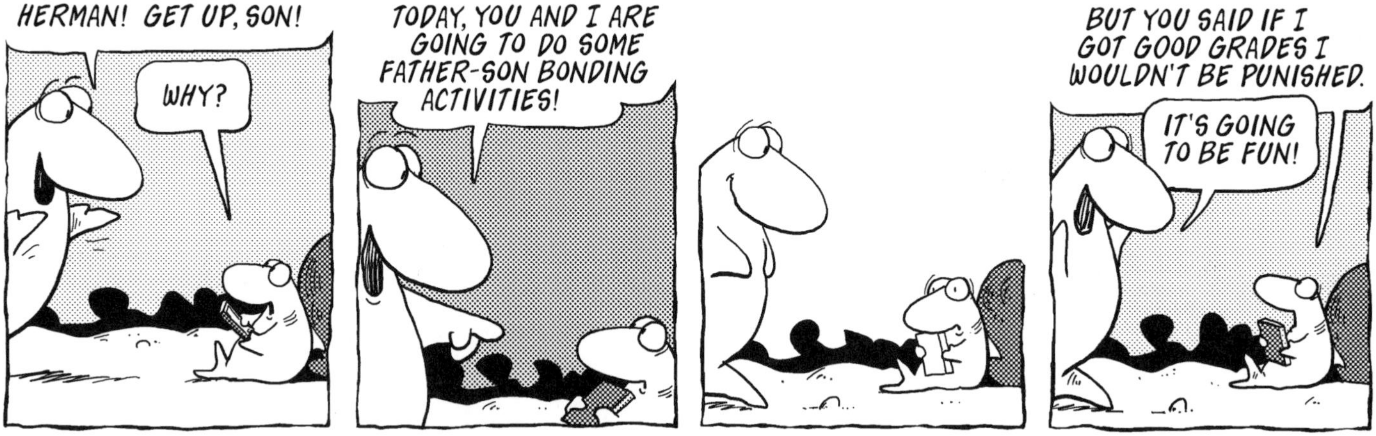
HERMAN! GET UP, SON!
WHY?
TODAY, YOU AND I ARE GOING TO DO SOME FATHER-SON BONDING ACTIVITIES!
BUT YOU SAID IF I GOT GOOD GRADES I WOULDN'T BE PUNISHED.
IT'S GOING TO BE FUN!

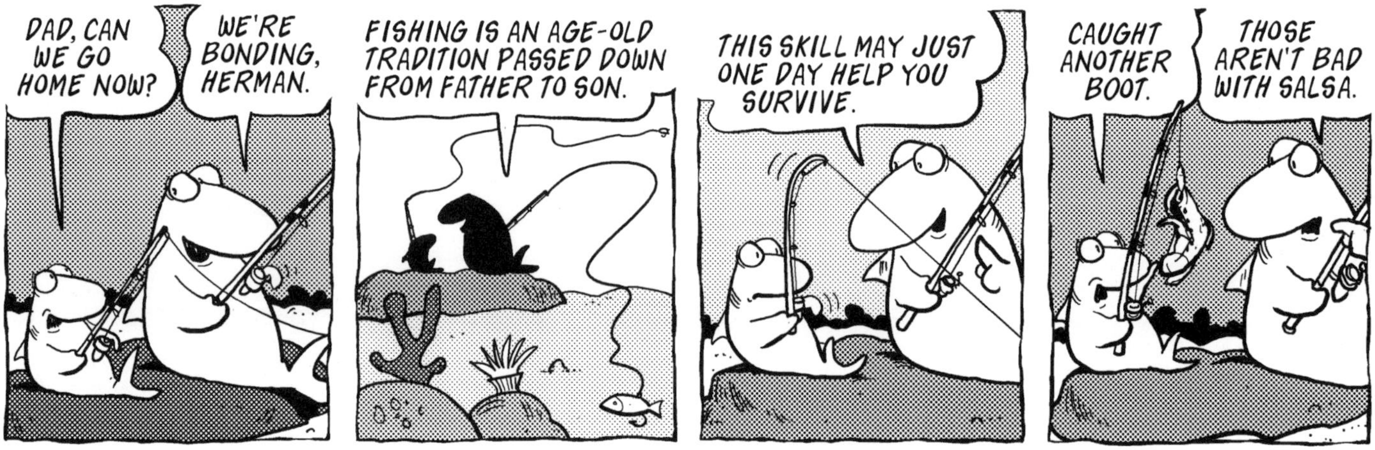
DAD, CAN WE GO HOME NOW?
WE'RE BONDING, HERMAN.
FISHING IS AN AGE-OLD TRADITION PASSED DOWN FROM FATHER TO SON.
THIS SKILL MAY JUST ONE DAY HELP YOU SURVIVE.
CAUGHT ANOTHER BOOT.
THOSE AREN'T BAD WITH SALSA.

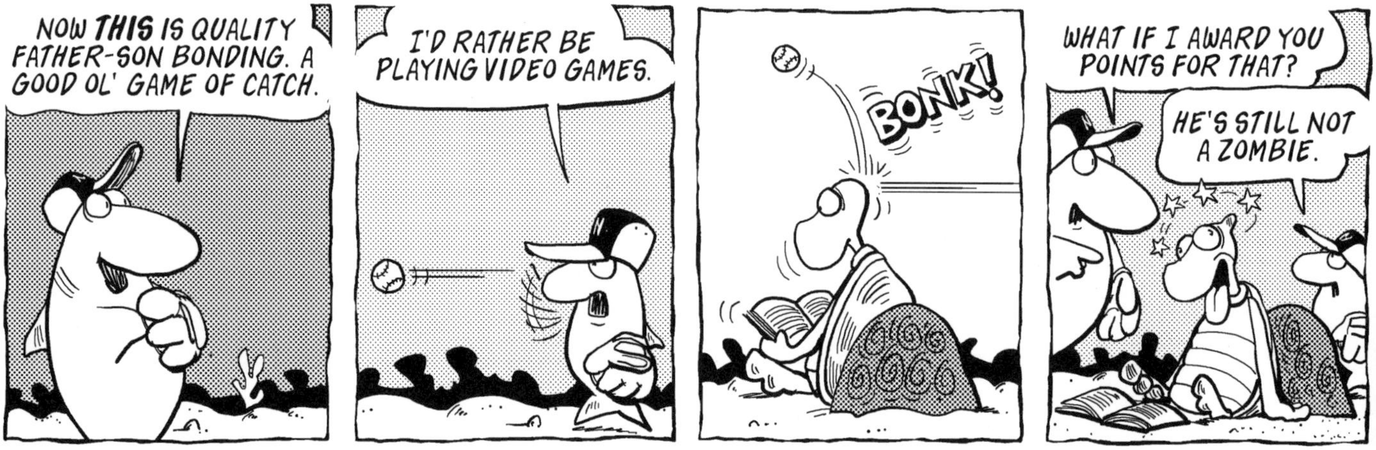
NOW **THIS** IS QUALITY FATHER-SON BONDING. A GOOD OL' GAME OF CATCH.
I'D RATHER BE PLAYING VIDEO GAMES.
BONK!
WHAT IF I AWARD YOU POINTS FOR THAT?
HE'S STILL NOT A ZOMBIE.

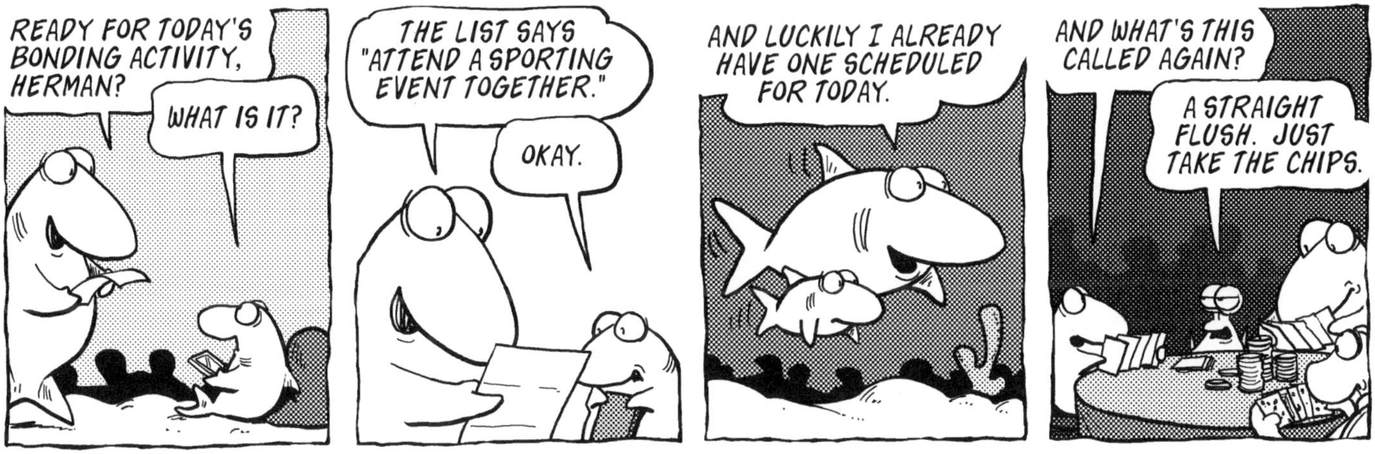
READY FOR TODAY'S BONDING ACTIVITY, HERMAN?
WHAT IS IT?
THE LIST SAYS "ATTEND A SPORTING EVENT TOGETHER."
OKAY.
AND LUCKILY I ALREADY HAVE ONE SCHEDULED FOR TODAY.
AND WHAT'S THIS CALLED AGAIN?
A STRAIGHT FLUSH. JUST TAKE THE CHIPS.

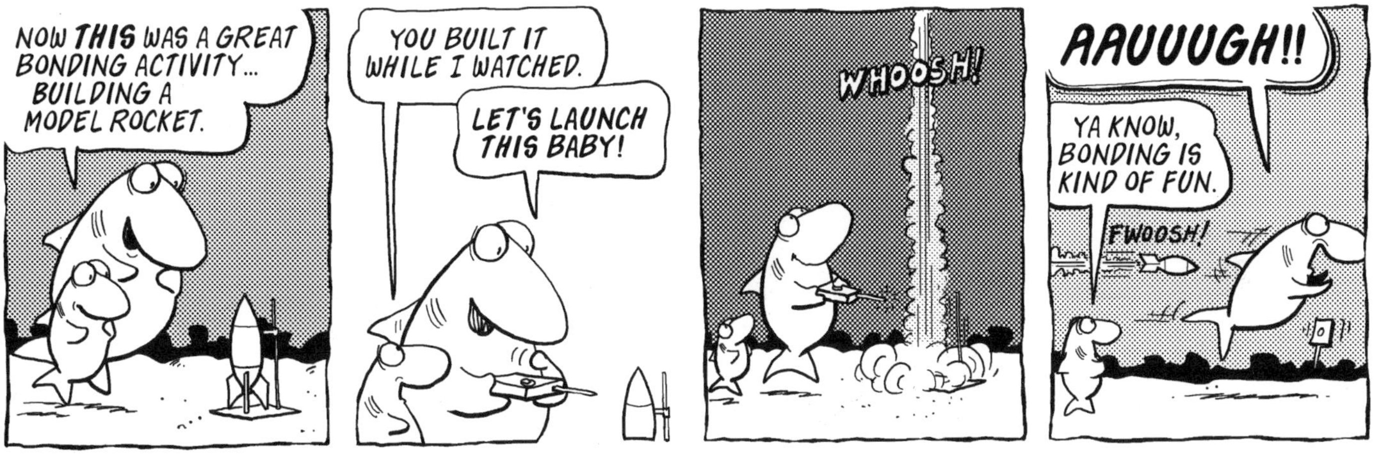
NOW THIS WAS A GREAT BONDING ACTIVITY... BUILDING A MODEL ROCKET.
YOU BUILT IT WHILE I WATCHED.
LET'S LAUNCH THIS BABY!
WHOOSH!
AAUUUGH!!
YA KNOW, BONDING IS KIND OF FUN.
FWOOSH!

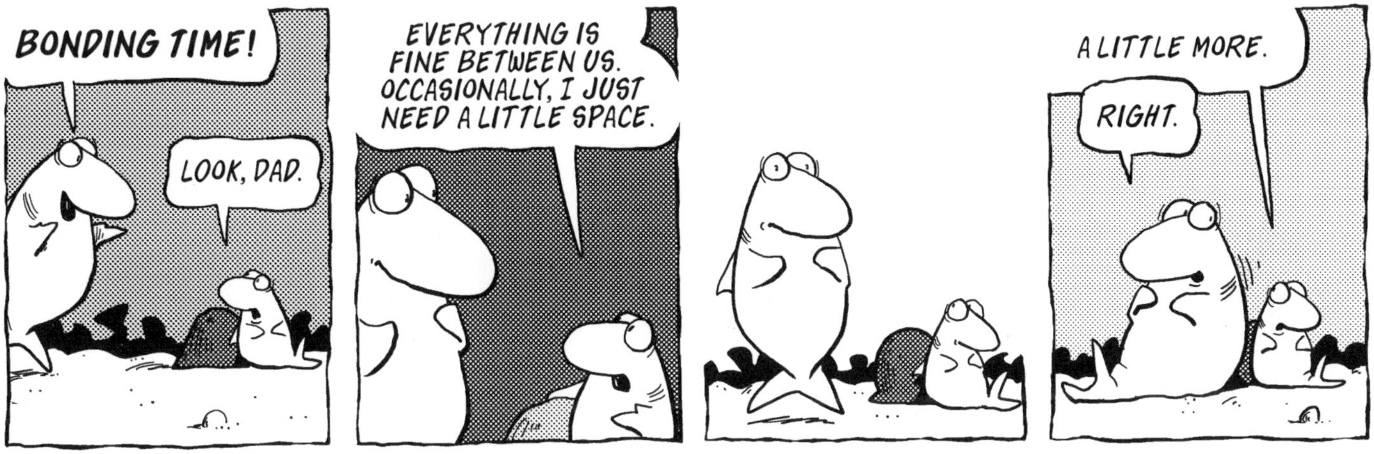
BONDING TIME!
LOOK, DAD.
EVERYTHING IS FINE BETWEEN US. OCCASIONALLY, I JUST NEED A LITTLE SPACE.
A LITTLE MORE.
RIGHT.

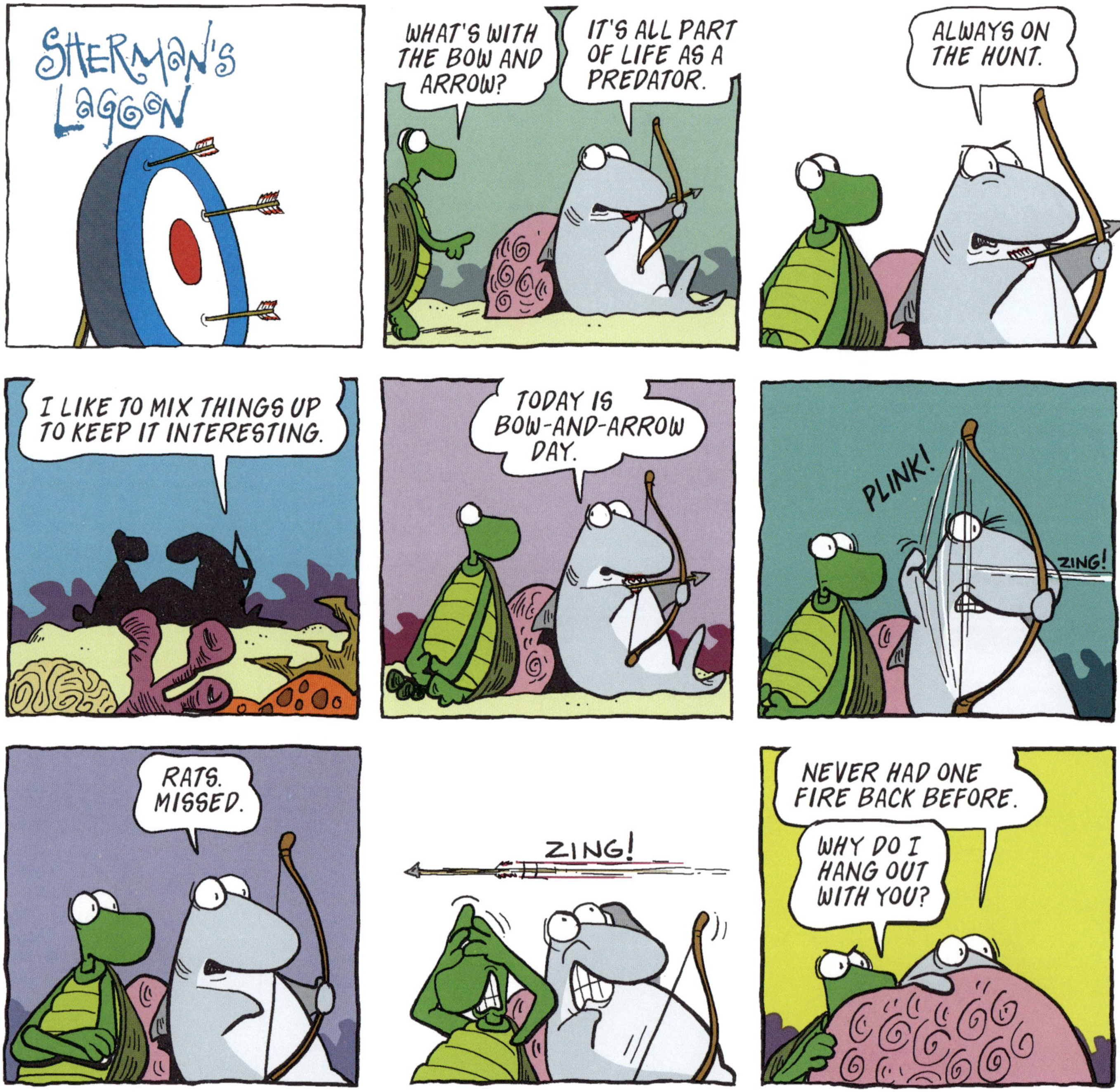
SHERMAN'S LAGOON
WHAT'S WITH THE BOW AND ARROW?
IT'S ALL PART OF LIFE AS A PREDATOR.
ALWAYS ON THE HUNT.
I LIKE TO MIX THINGS UP TO KEEP IT INTERESTING.
TODAY IS BOW-AND-ARROW DAY.
PLINK!
ZING!
RATS. MISSED.
ZING!
NEVER HAD ONE FIRE BACK BEFORE.
WHY DO I HANG OUT WITH YOU?

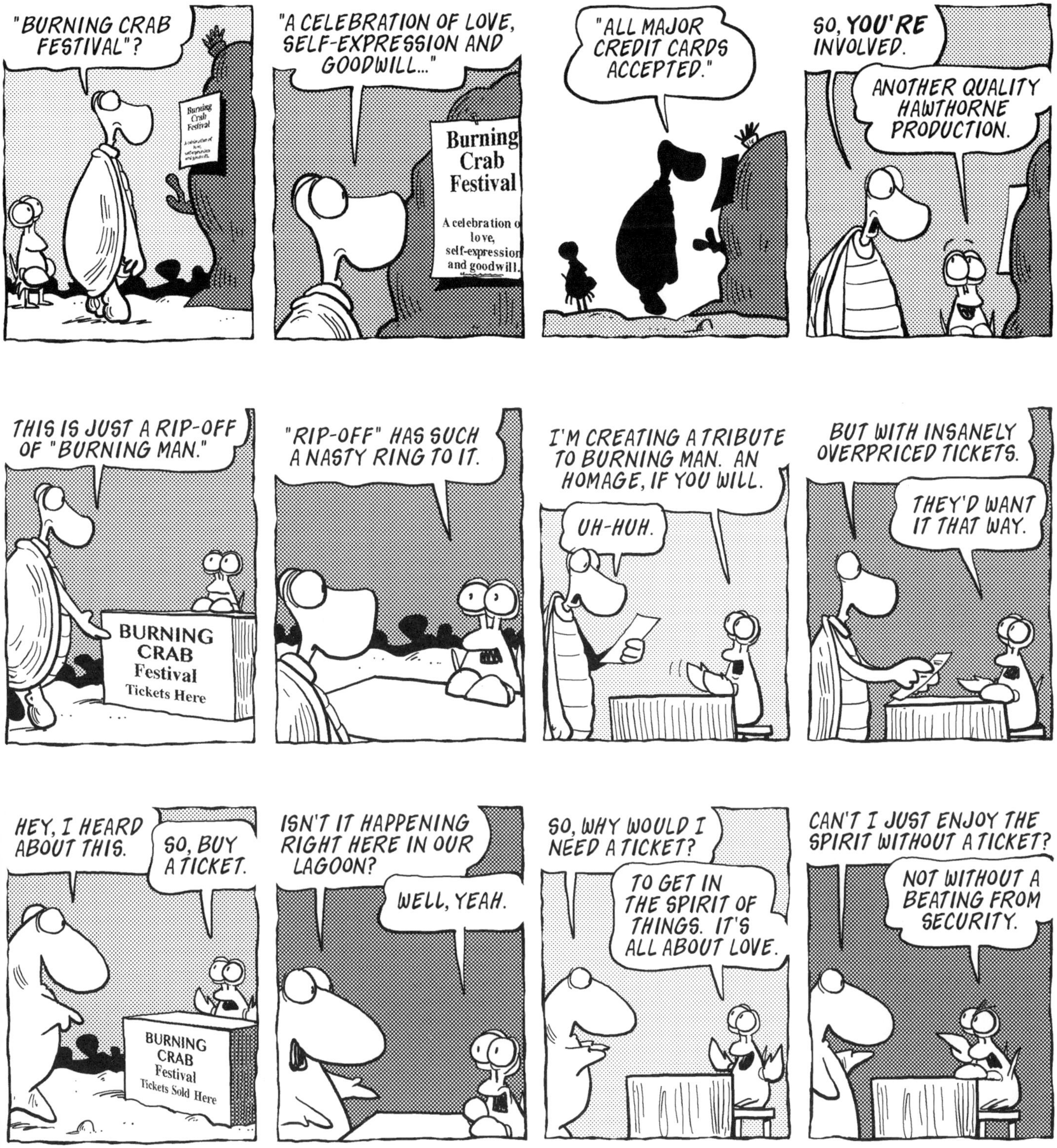
"BURNING CRAB FESTIVAL"?
Burning Crab Festival
"A CELEBRATION OF LOVE, SELF-EXPRESSION AND GOODWILL..."
Burning Crab Festival
A celebration of love, self-expression and goodwill.
"ALL MAJOR CREDIT CARDS ACCEPTED."
SO, YOU'RE INVOLVED.
ANOTHER QUALITY HAWTHORNE PRODUCTION.
THIS IS JUST A RIP-OFF OF "BURNING MAN."
BURNING CRAB Festival Tickets Here
"RIP-OFF" HAS SUCH A NASTY RING TO IT.
I'M CREATING A TRIBUTE TO BURNING MAN. AN HOMAGE, IF YOU WILL.
UH-HUH.
BUT WITH INSANELY OVERPRICED TICKETS.
THEY'D WANT IT THAT WAY.
HEY, I HEARD ABOUT THIS.
SO, BUY A TICKET.
BURNING CRAB Festival Tickets Sold Here
ISN'T IT HAPPENING RIGHT HERE IN OUR LAGOON?
WELL, YEAH.
SO, WHY WOULD I NEED A TICKET?
TO GET IN THE SPIRIT OF THINGS. IT'S ALL ABOUT LOVE.
CAN'T I JUST ENJOY THE SPIRIT WITHOUT A TICKET?
NOT WITHOUT A BEATING FROM SECURITY.

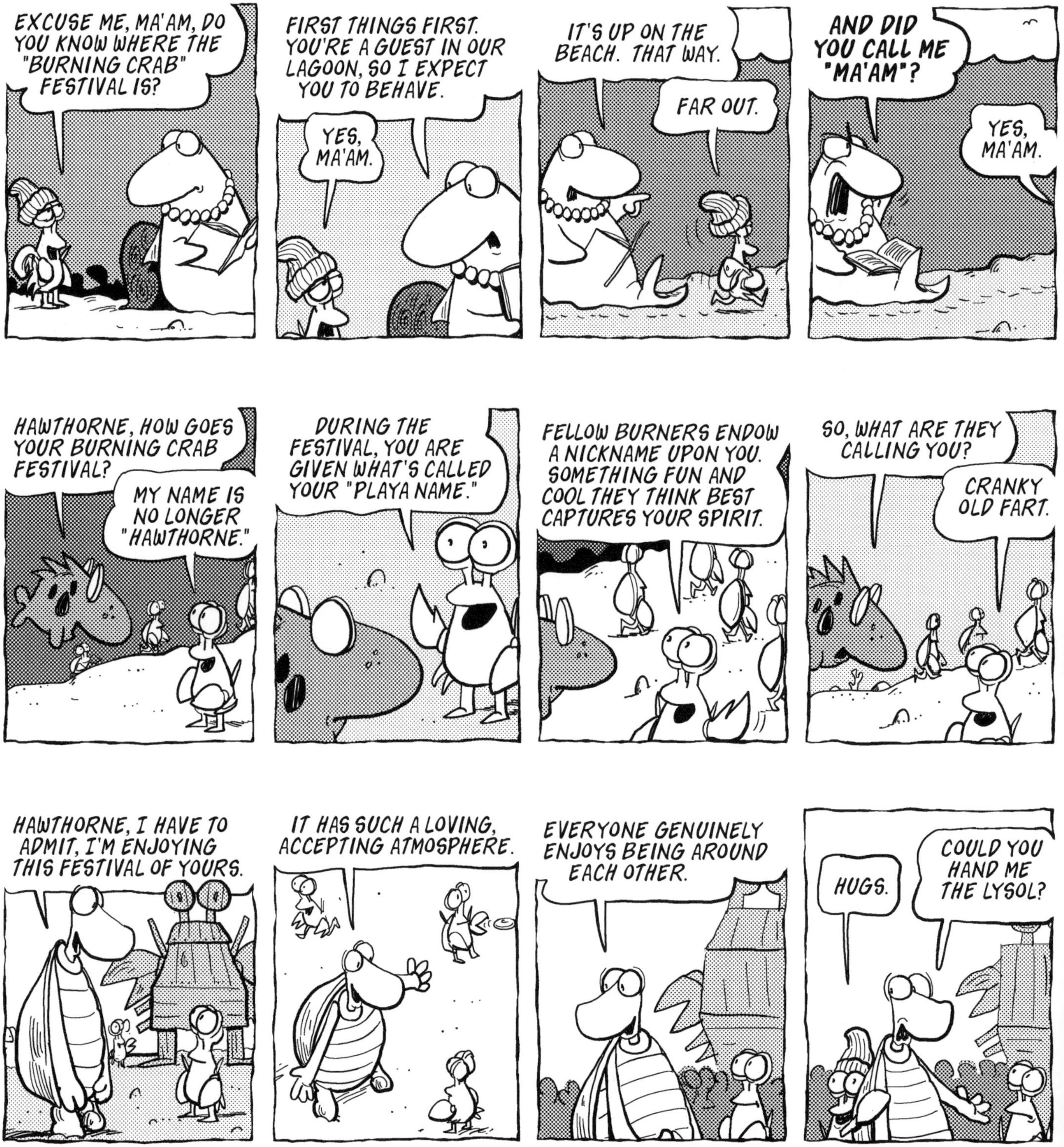
EXCUSE ME, MA'AM, DO YOU KNOW WHERE THE "BURNING CRAB" FESTIVAL IS?
FIRST THINGS FIRST. YOU'RE A GUEST IN OUR LAGOON, SO I EXPECT YOU TO BEHAVE.
YES, MA'AM.
IT'S UP ON THE BEACH. THAT WAY.
FAR OUT.
AND DID YOU CALL ME "MA'AM"?
YES, MA'AM.
HAWTHORNE, HOW GOES YOUR BURNING CRAB FESTIVAL?
MY NAME IS NO LONGER "HAWTHORNE."
DURING THE FESTIVAL, YOU ARE GIVEN WHAT'S CALLED YOUR "PLAYA NAME."
FELLOW BURNERS ENDOW A NICKNAME UPON YOU. SOMETHING FUN AND COOL THEY THINK BEST CAPTURES YOUR SPIRIT.
SO, WHAT ARE THEY CALLING YOU?
CRANKY OLD FART.
HAWTHORNE, I HAVE TO ADMIT, I'M ENJOYING THIS FESTIVAL OF YOURS.
IT HAS SUCH A LOVING, ACCEPTING ATMOSPHERE.
EVERYONE GENUINELY ENJOYS BEING AROUND EACH OTHER.
HUGS.
COULD YOU HAND ME THE LYSOL?

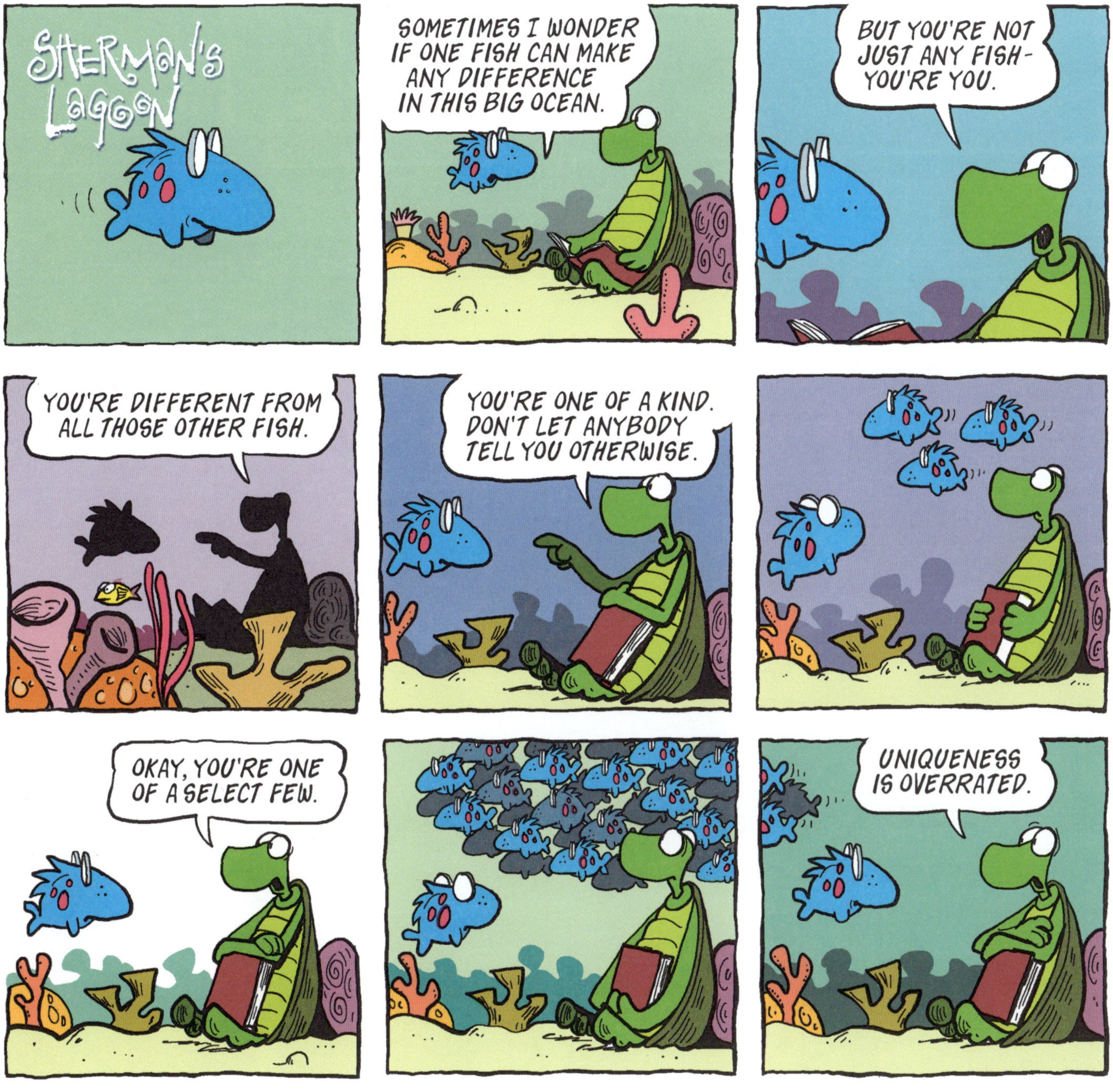
SHERMAN'S LAGOON
SOMETIMES I WONDER IF ONE FISH CAN MAKE ANY DIFFERENCE IN THIS BIG OCEAN.
BUT YOU'RE NOT JUST ANY FISH- YOU'RE YOU.
YOU'RE DIFFERENT FROM ALL THOSE OTHER FISH.
YOU'RE ONE OF A KIND. DON'T LET ANYBODY TELL YOU OTHERWISE.
OKAY, YOU'RE ONE OF A SELECT FEW.
UNIQUENESS IS OVERRATED.

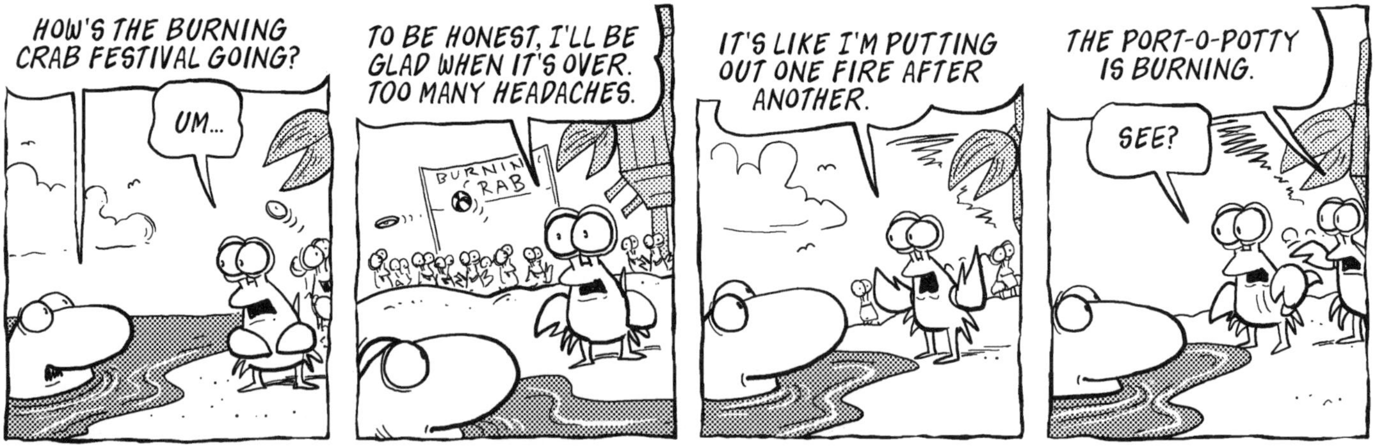
HOW'S THE BURNING CRAB FESTIVAL GOING?
UM...
TO BE HONEST, I'LL BE GLAD WHEN IT'S OVER. TOO MANY HEADACHES.
BURNIN
RAB
IT'S LIKE I'M PUTTING OUT ONE FIRE AFTER ANOTHER.
THE PORT-O-POTTY IS BURNING.
SEE?

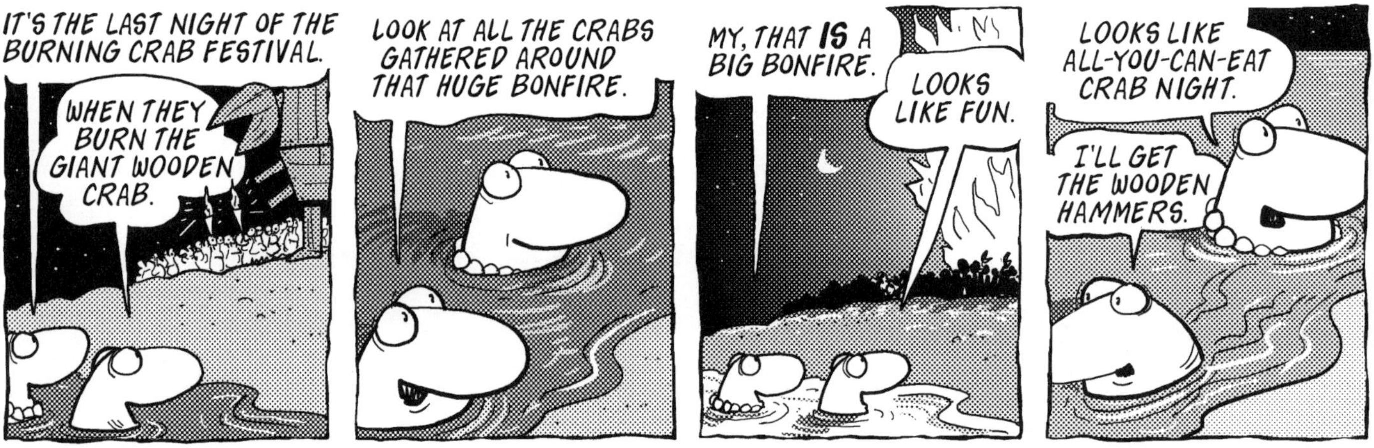
IT'S THE LAST NIGHT OF THE BURNING CRAB FESTIVAL.
WHEN THEY BURN THE GIANT WOODEN CRAB.
LOOK AT ALL THE CRABS GATHERED AROUND THAT HUGE BONFIRE.
MY, THAT **IS** A BIG BONFIRE.
LOOKS LIKE FUN.
LOOKS LIKE ALL-YOU-CAN-EAT CRAB NIGHT.
I'LL GET THE WOODEN HAMMERS.

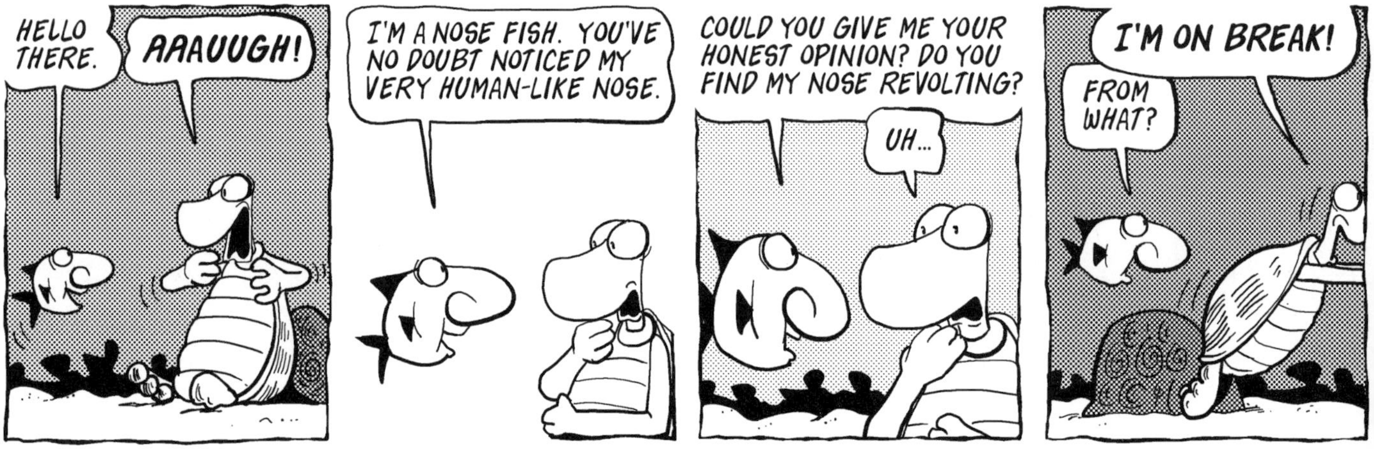
HELLO THERE.
AAAUUGH!
I'M A NOSE FISH. YOU'VE NO DOUBT NOTICED MY VERY HUMAN-LIKE NOSE.
COULD YOU GIVE ME YOUR HONEST OPINION? DO YOU FIND MY NOSE REVOLTING?
UH...
I'M ON BREAK!
FROM WHAT?

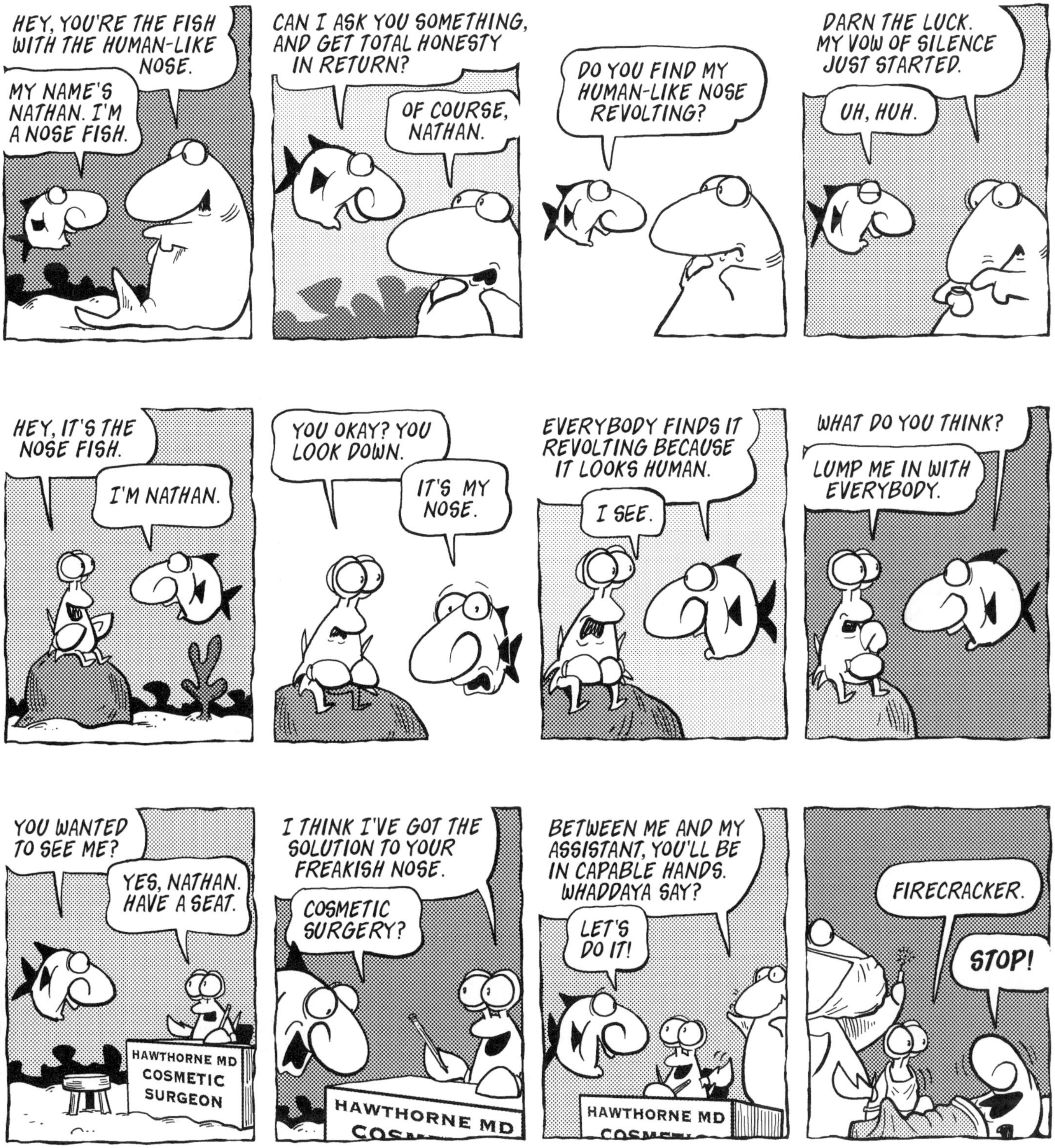
HEY, YOU'RE THE FISH WITH THE HUMAN-LIKE NOSE.
MY NAME'S NATHAN. I'M A NOSE FISH.
CAN I ASK YOU SOMETHING, AND GET TOTAL HONESTY IN RETURN?
OF COURSE, NATHAN.
DO YOU FIND MY HUMAN-LIKE NOSE REVOLTING?
DARN THE LUCK. MY VOW OF SILENCE JUST STARTED.
UH, HUH.
HEY, IT'S THE NOSE FISH.
I'M NATHAN.
YOU OKAY? YOU LOOK DOWN.
IT'S MY NOSE.
EVERYBODY FINDS IT REVOLTING BECAUSE IT LOOKS HUMAN.
I SEE.
WHAT DO YOU THINK?
LUMP ME IN WITH EVERYBODY.
YOU WANTED TO SEE ME?
YES, NATHAN. HAVE A SEAT.
HAWTHORNE MD COSMETIC SURGEON
I THINK I'VE GOT THE SOLUTION TO YOUR FREAKISH NOSE.
COSMETIC SURGERY?
HAWTHORNE MD
BETWEEN ME AND MY ASSISTANT, YOU'LL BE IN CAPABLE HANDS. WHADDAYA SAY?
LET'S DO IT!
HAWTHORNE MD
FIRECRACKER.
STOP!

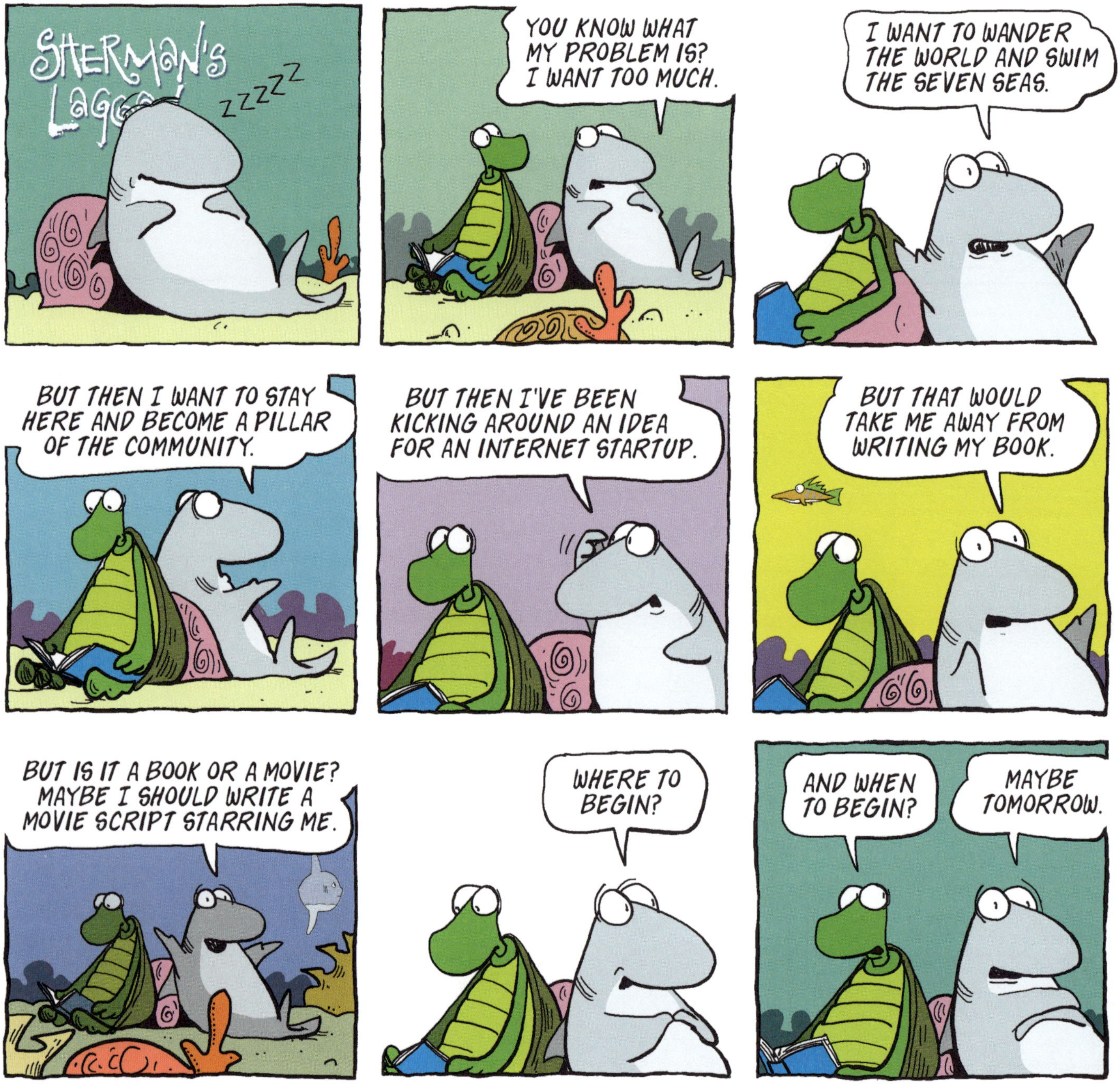
SHERMAN'S LAGOON
ZZZZZ
YOU KNOW WHAT MY PROBLEM IS? I WANT TOO MUCH.
I WANT TO WANDER THE WORLD AND SWIM THE SEVEN SEAS.
BUT THEN I WANT TO STAY HERE AND BECOME A PILLAR OF THE COMMUNITY.
BUT THEN I'VE BEEN KICKING AROUND AN IDEA FOR AN INTERNET STARTUP.
BUT THAT WOULD TAKE ME AWAY FROM WRITING MY BOOK.
BUT IS IT A BOOK OR A MOVIE? MAYBE I SHOULD WRITE A MOVIE SCRIPT STARRING ME.
WHERE TO BEGIN?
AND WHEN TO BEGIN?
MAYBE TOMORROW.

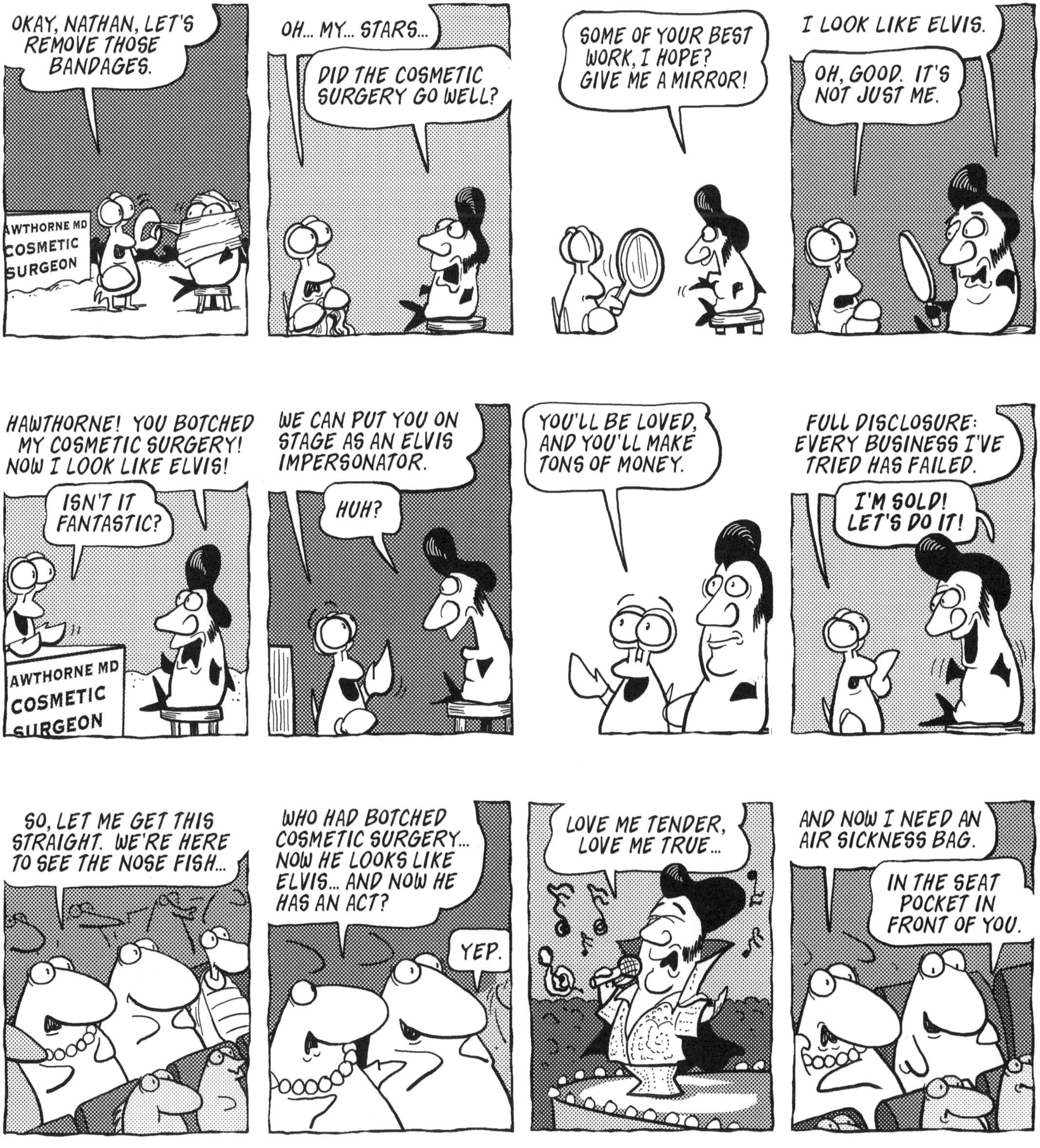
OKAY, NATHAN, LET'S REMOVE THOSE BANDAGES.
AWTHORNE MD COSMETIC SURGEON
OH... MY... STARS...
DID THE COSMETIC SURGERY GO WELL?
SOME OF YOUR BEST WORK, I HOPE? GIVE ME A MIRROR!
I LOOK LIKE ELVIS.
OH, GOOD. IT'S NOT JUST ME.
HAWTHORNE! YOU BOTCHED MY COSMETIC SURGERY! NOW I LOOK LIKE ELVIS!
ISN'T IT FANTASTIC?
AWTHORNE MD COSMETIC SURGEON
WE CAN PUT YOU ON STAGE AS AN ELVIS IMPERSONATOR.
HUH?
YOU'LL BE LOVED, AND YOU'LL MAKE TONS OF MONEY.
FULL DISCLOSURE: EVERY BUSINESS I'VE TRIED HAS FAILED.
I'M SOLD! LET'S DO IT!
SO, LET ME GET THIS STRAIGHT. WE'RE HERE TO SEE THE NOSE FISH...
WHO HAD BOTCHED COSMETIC SURGERY... NOW HE LOOKS LIKE ELVIS... AND NOW HE HAS AN ACT?
YEP.
LOVE ME TENDER, LOVE ME TRUE...
AND NOW I NEED AN AIR SICKNESS BAG.
IN THE SEAT POCKET IN FRONT OF YOU.

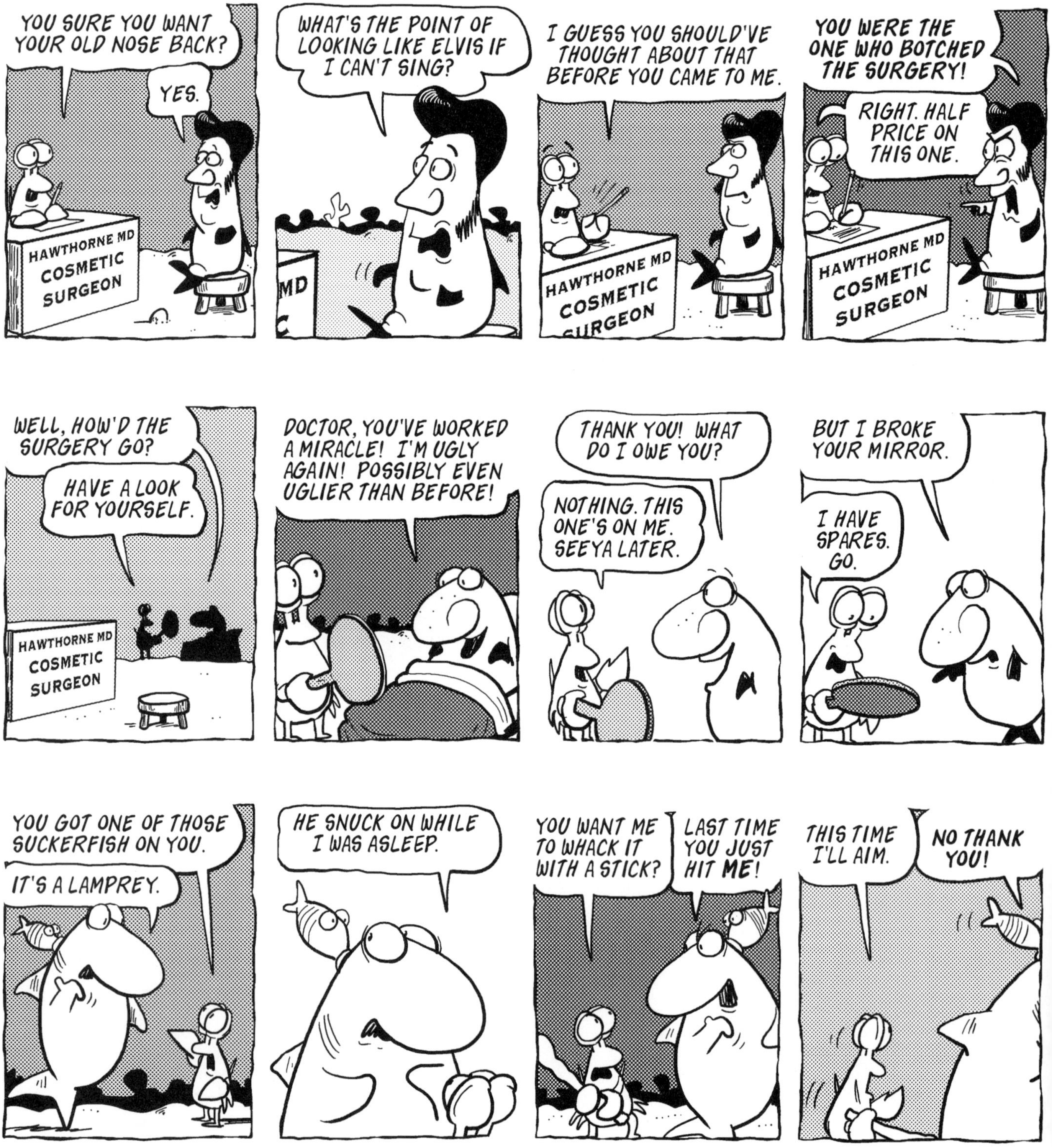
YOU SURE YOU WANT YOUR OLD NOSE BACK?
YES.
HAWTHORNE MD COSMETIC SURGEON
WHAT'S THE POINT OF LOOKING LIKE ELVIS IF I CAN'T SING?
I GUESS YOU SHOULD'VE THOUGHT ABOUT THAT BEFORE YOU CAME TO ME.
HAWTHORNE MD COSMETIC SURGEON
YOU WERE THE ONE WHO BOTCHED THE SURGERY!
RIGHT. HALF PRICE ON THIS ONE.
HAWTHORNE MD COSMETIC SURGEON
WELL, HOW'D THE SURGERY GO?
HAVE A LOOK FOR YOURSELF.
HAWTHORNE MD COSMETIC SURGEON
DOCTOR, YOU'VE WORKED A MIRACLE! I'M UGLY AGAIN! POSSIBLY EVEN UGLIER THAN BEFORE!
THANK YOU! WHAT DO I OWE YOU?
NOTHING. THIS ONE'S ON ME. SEEYA LATER.
BUT I BROKE YOUR MIRROR.
I HAVE SPARES. GO.
YOU GOT ONE OF THOSE SUCKERFISH ON YOU.
IT'S A LAMPREY.
HE SNUCK ON WHILE I WAS ASLEEP.
YOU WANT ME TO WHACK IT WITH A STICK?
LAST TIME YOU JUST HIT ME!
THIS TIME I'LL AIM.
NO THANK YOU!

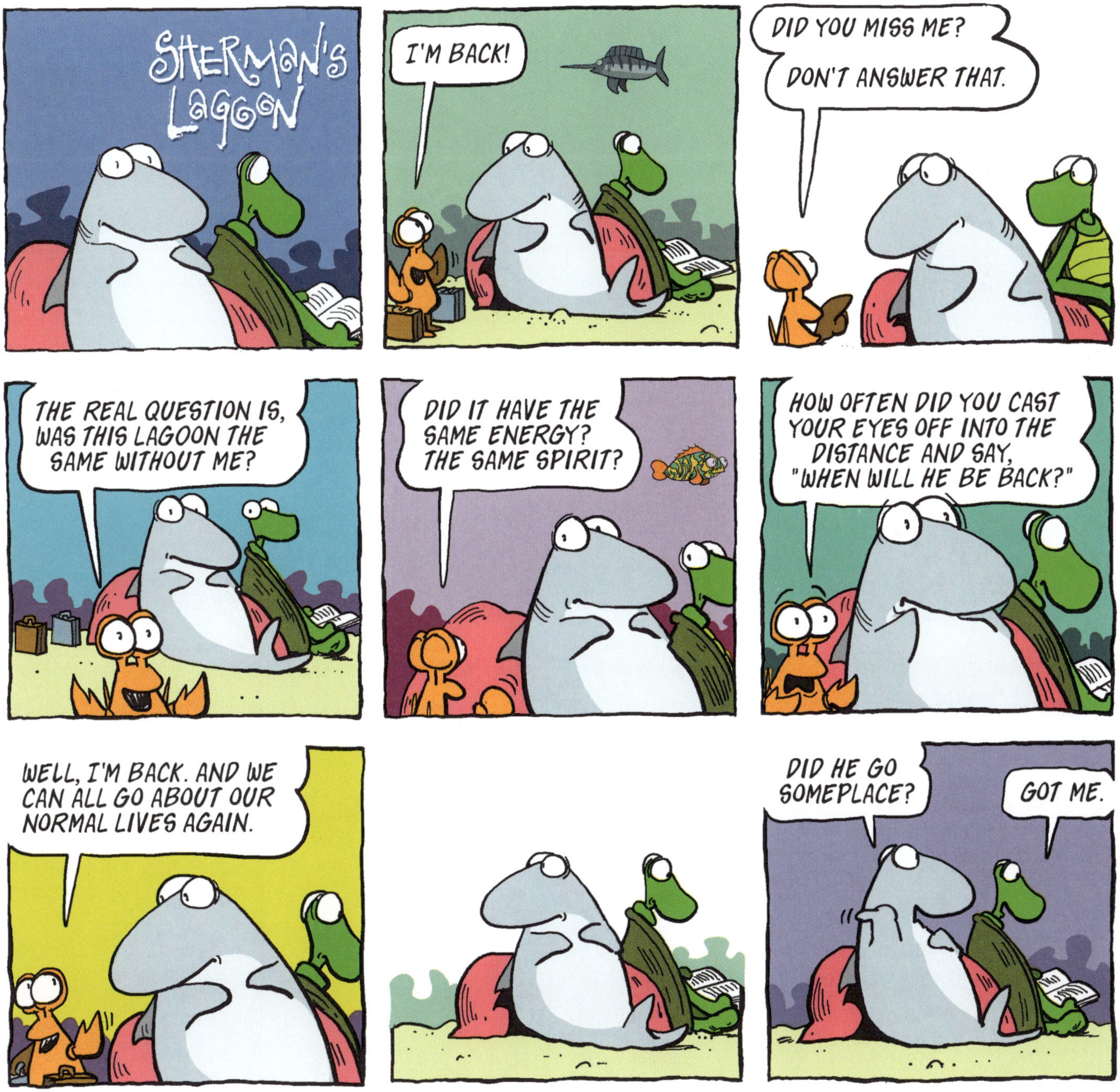
SHERMAN'S LAGOON
I'M BACK!
DID YOU MISS ME?
DON'T ANSWER THAT.
THE REAL QUESTION IS, WAS THIS LAGOON THE SAME WITHOUT ME?
DID IT HAVE THE SAME ENERGY? THE SAME SPIRIT?
HOW OFTEN DID YOU CAST YOUR EYES OFF INTO THE DISTANCE AND SAY, "WHEN WILL HE BE BACK?"
WELL, I'M BACK. AND WE CAN ALL GO ABOUT OUR NORMAL LIVES AGAIN.
DID HE GO SOMEPLACE?
GOT ME.

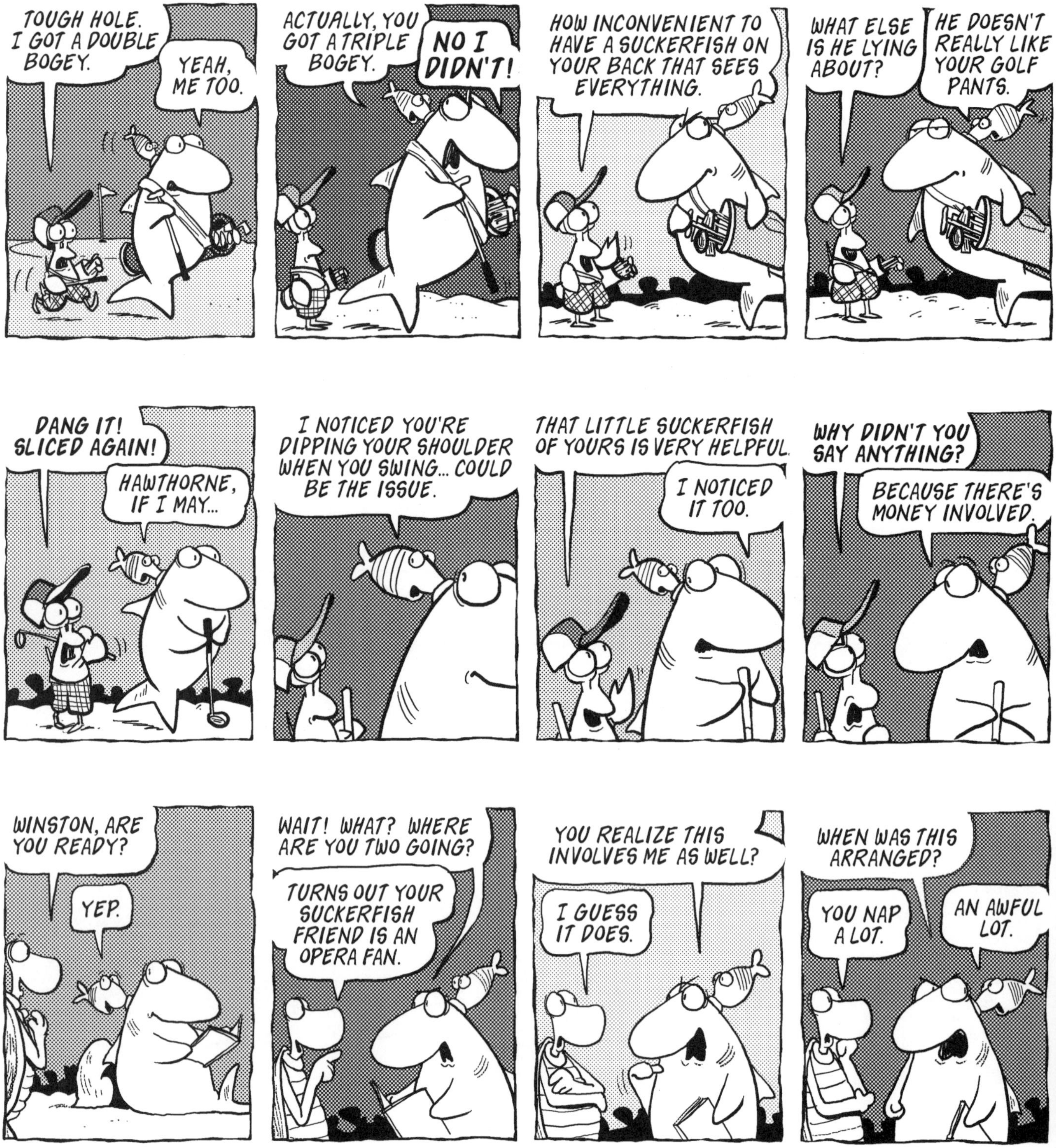
TOUGH HOLE. I GOT A DOUBLE BOGEY.
YEAH, ME TOO.
ACTUALLY, YOU GOT A TRIPLE BOGEY.
NO I DIDN'T!
HOW INCONVENIENT TO HAVE A SUCKERFISH ON YOUR BACK THAT SEES EVERYTHING.
WHAT ELSE IS HE LYING ABOUT?
HE DOESN'T REALLY LIKE YOUR GOLF PANTS.
DANG IT! SLICED AGAIN!
HAWTHORNE, IF I MAY...
I NOTICED YOU'RE DIPPING YOUR SHOULDER WHEN YOU SWING... COULD BE THE ISSUE.
THAT LITTLE SUCKERFISH OF YOURS IS VERY HELPFUL.
I NOTICED IT TOO.
WHY DIDN'T YOU SAY ANYTHING?
BECAUSE THERE'S MONEY INVOLVED.
WINSTON, ARE YOU READY?
YEP.
WAIT! WHAT? WHERE ARE YOU TWO GOING?
TURNS OUT YOUR SUCKERFISH FRIEND IS AN OPERA FAN.
YOU REALIZE THIS INVOLVES ME AS WELL?
I GUESS IT DOES.
WHEN WAS THIS ARRANGED?
YOU NAP A LOT.
AN AWFUL LOT.

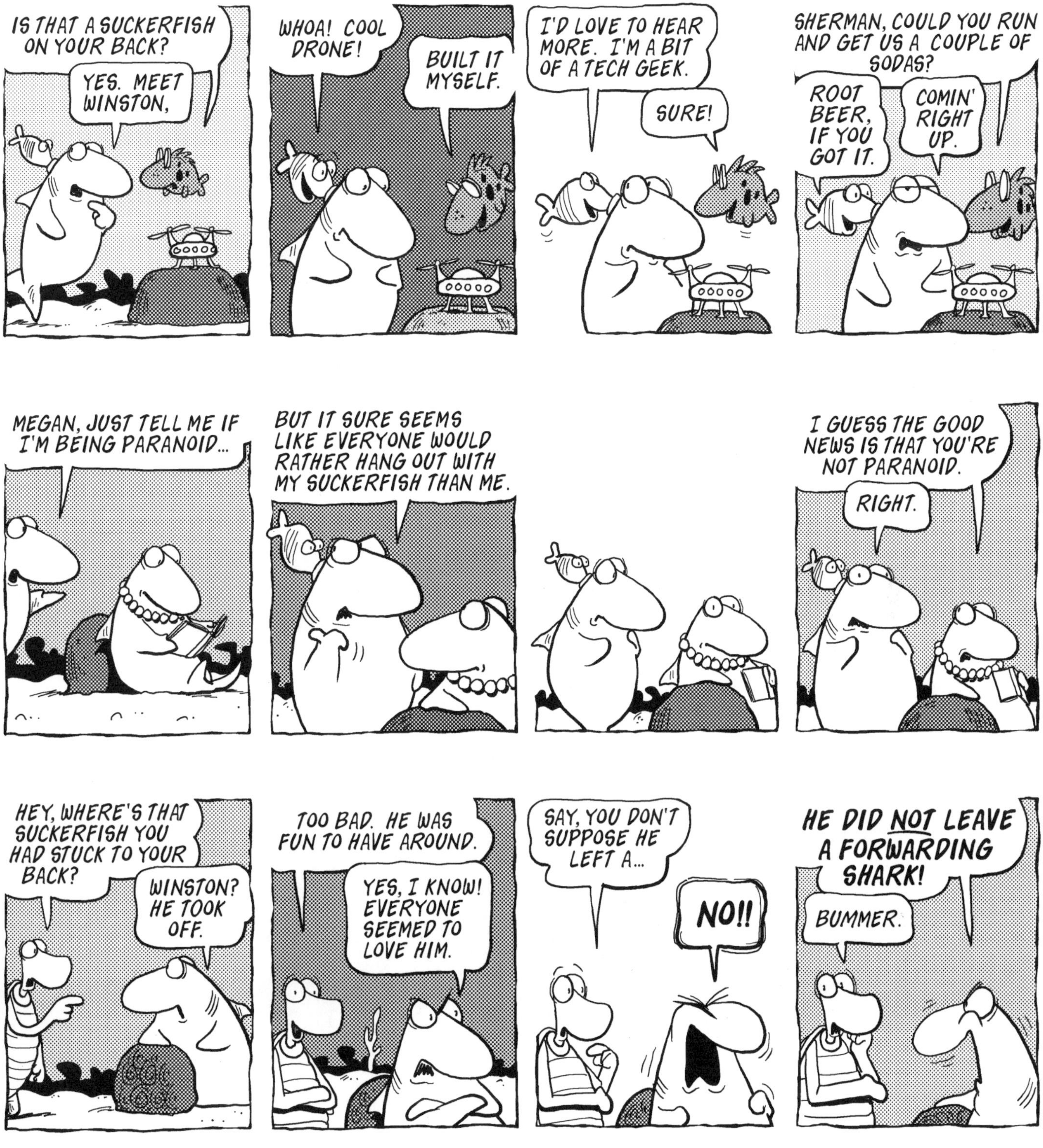
IS THAT A SUCKERFISH ON YOUR BACK?
YES. MEET WINSTON,
WHOA! COOL DRONE!
BUILT IT MYSELF.
I'D LOVE TO HEAR MORE. I'M A BIT OF A TECH GEEK.
SURE!
SHERMAN, COULD YOU RUN AND GET US A COUPLE OF SODAS?
ROOT BEER, IF YOU GOT IT.
COMIN' RIGHT UP.
MEGAN, JUST TELL ME IF I'M BEING PARANOID...
BUT IT SURE SEEMS LIKE EVERYONE WOULD RATHER HANG OUT WITH MY SUCKERFISH THAN ME.
I GUESS THE GOOD NEWS IS THAT YOU'RE NOT PARANOID.
RIGHT.
HEY, WHERE'S THAT SUCKERFISH YOU HAD STUCK TO YOUR BACK?
WINSTON? HE TOOK OFF.
TOO BAD. HE WAS FUN TO HAVE AROUND.
YES, I KNOW! EVERYONE SEEMED TO LOVE HIM.
SAY, YOU DON'T SUPPOSE HE LEFT A...
NO!!
HE DID NOT LEAVE A FORWARDING SHARK!
BUMMER.

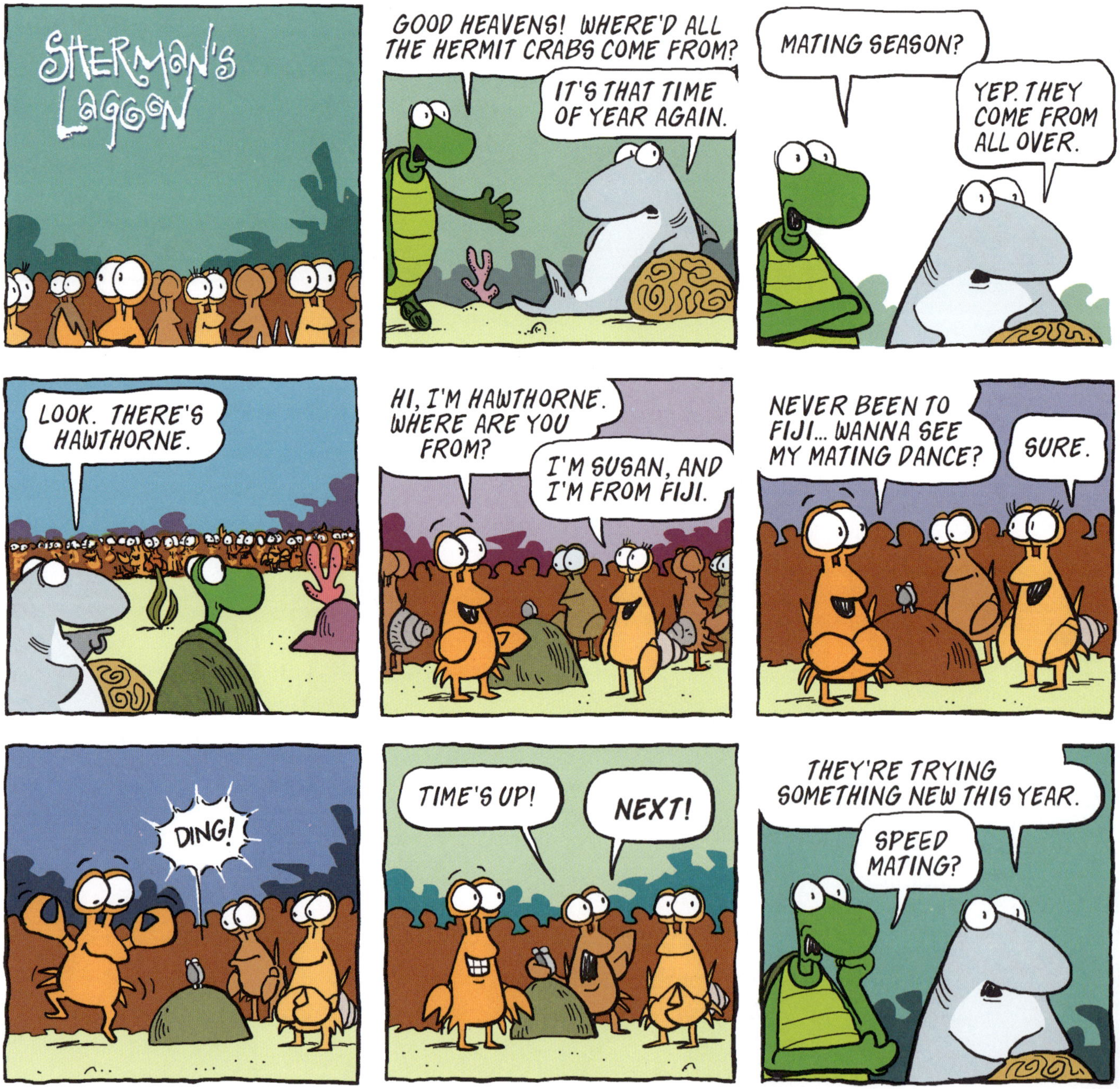
SHERMAN'S LAGOON
GOOD HEAVENS! WHERE'D ALL THE HERMIT CRABS COME FROM?
IT'S THAT TIME OF YEAR AGAIN.
MATING SEASON?
YEP. THEY COME FROM ALL OVER.
LOOK. THERE'S HAWTHORNE.
HI, I'M HAWTHORNE. WHERE ARE YOU FROM?
I'M SUSAN, AND I'M FROM FIJI.
NEVER BEEN TO FIJI... WANNA SEE MY MATING DANCE?
SURE.
DING!
TIME'S UP!
NEXT!
THEY'RE TRYING SOMETHING NEW THIS YEAR.
SPEED MATING?

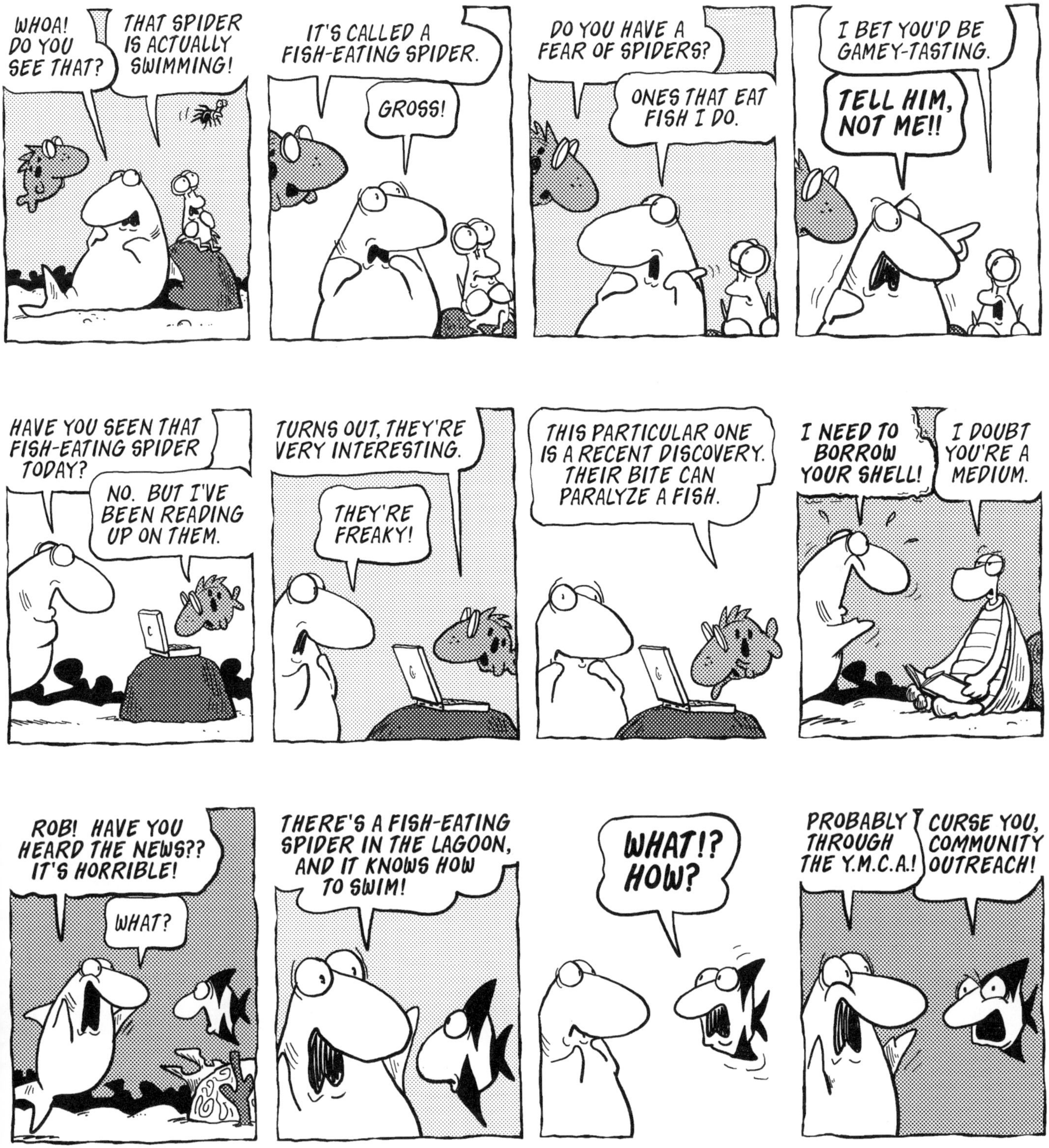

WHOA! DO YOU SEE THAT?
THAT SPIDER IS ACTUALLY SWIMMING!
IT'S CALLED A FISH-EATING SPIDER.
GROSS!
DO YOU HAVE A FEAR OF SPIDERS?
ONES THAT EAT FISH I DO.
I BET YOU'D BE GAMEY-TASTING.
TELL HIM, NOT ME!!
HAVE YOU SEEN THAT FISH-EATING SPIDER TODAY?
NO. BUT I'VE BEEN READING UP ON THEM.
TURNS OUT, THEY'RE VERY INTERESTING.
THEY'RE FREAKY!
THIS PARTICULAR ONE IS A RECENT DISCOVERY. THEIR BITE CAN PARALYZE A FISH.
I NEED TO BORROW YOUR SHELL!
I DOUBT YOU'RE A MEDIUM.
ROB! HAVE YOU HEARD THE NEWS?? IT'S HORRIBLE!
WHAT?
THERE'S A FISH-EATING SPIDER IN THE LAGOON, AND IT KNOWS HOW TO SWIM!
WHAT!? HOW?
PROBABLY THROUGH THE Y.M.C.A.!
CURSE YOU, COMMUNITY OUTREACH!

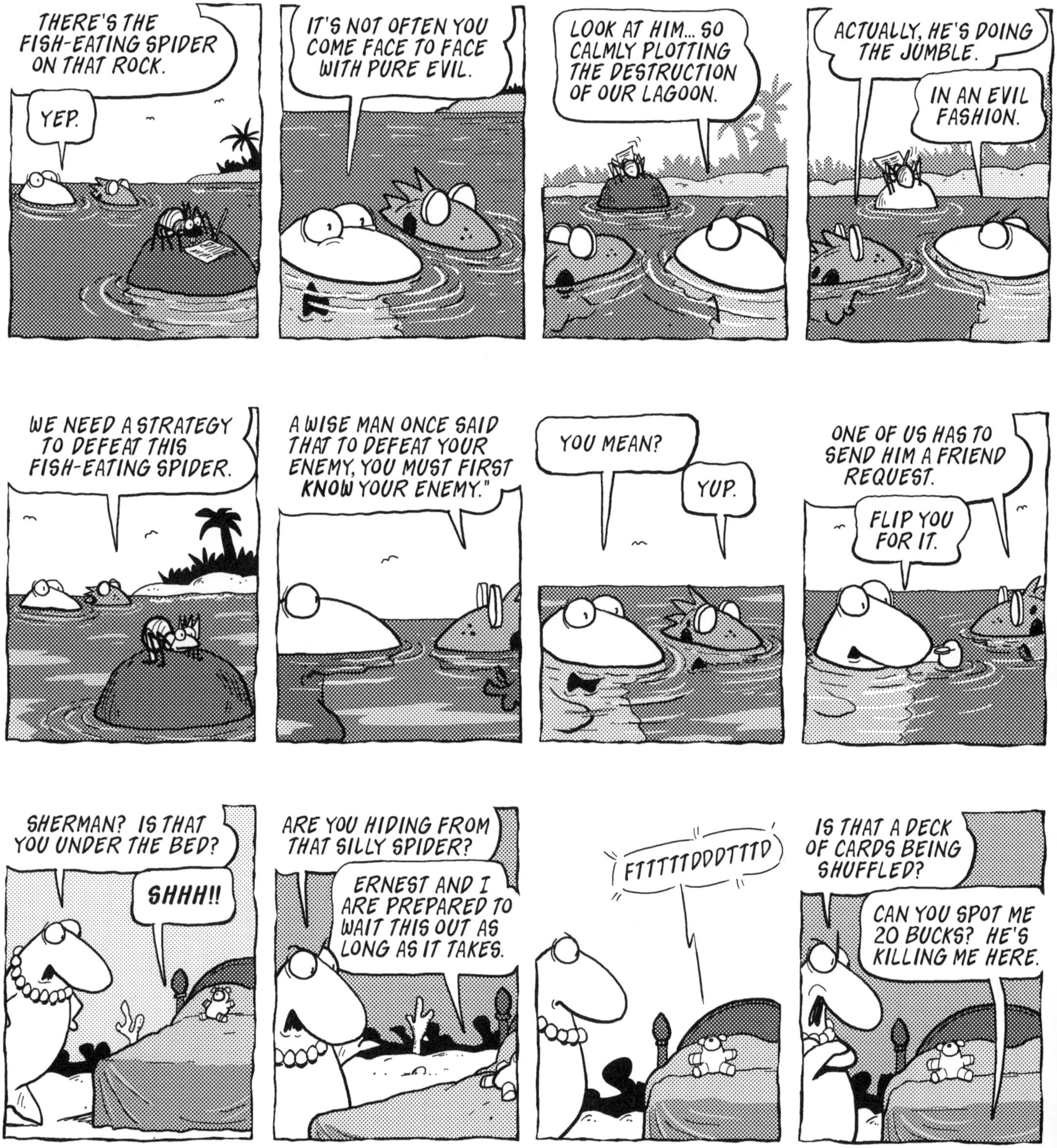
THERE'S THE FISH-EATING SPIDER ON THAT ROCK.
YEP.
IT'S NOT OFTEN YOU COME FACE TO FACE WITH PURE EVIL.
LOOK AT HIM... SO CALMLY PLOTTING THE DESTRUCTION OF OUR LAGOON.
ACTUALLY, HE'S DOING THE JUMBLE.
IN AN EVIL FASHION.
WE NEED A STRATEGY TO DEFEAT THIS FISH-EATING SPIDER.
A WISE MAN ONCE SAID THAT TO DEFEAT YOUR ENEMY, YOU MUST FIRST KNOW YOUR ENEMY."
YOU MEAN?
YUP.
ONE OF US HAS TO SEND HIM A FRIEND REQUEST.
FLIP YOU FOR IT.
SHERMAN? IS THAT YOU UNDER THE BED?
SHHH!!
ARE YOU HIDING FROM THAT SILLY SPIDER?
ERNEST AND I ARE PREPARED TO WAIT THIS OUT AS LONG AS IT TAKES.
FTTTTTDDDTTTD
IS THAT A DECK OF CARDS BEING SHUFFLED?
CAN YOU SPOT ME 20 BUCKS? HE'S KILLING ME HERE.

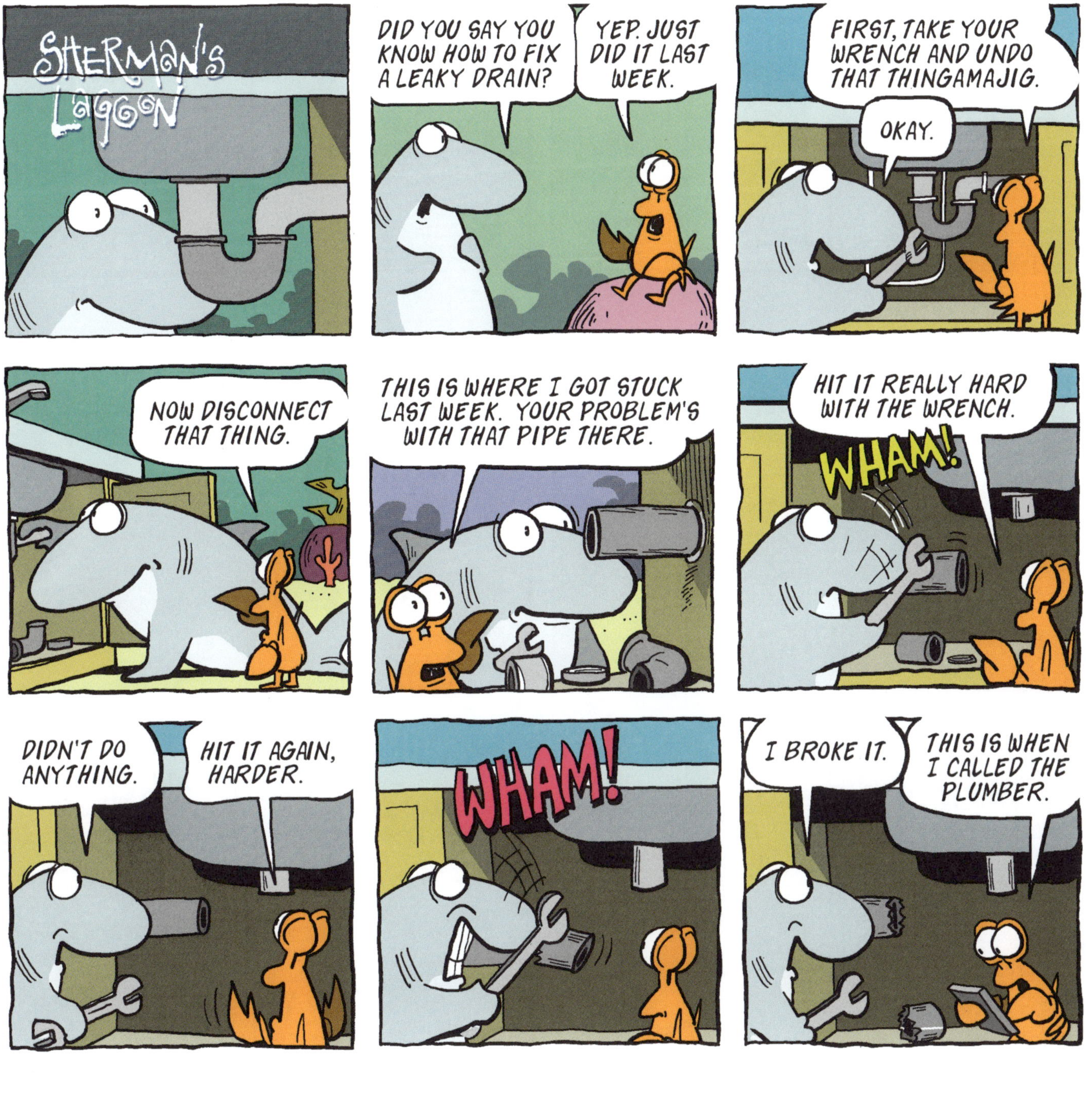
SHERMAN'S LAGOON
DID YOU SAY YOU KNOW HOW TO FIX A LEAKY DRAIN?
YEP. JUST DID IT LAST WEEK.
FIRST, TAKE YOUR WRENCH AND UNDO THAT THINGAMAJIG.
OKAY.
NOW DISCONNECT THAT THING.
THIS IS WHERE I GOT STUCK LAST WEEK. YOUR PROBLEM'S WITH THAT PIPE THERE.
HIT IT REALLY HARD WITH THE WRENCH.
WHAM!
DIDN'T DO ANYTHING.
HIT IT AGAIN, HARDER.
WHAM!
I BROKE IT.
THIS IS WHEN I CALLED THE PLUMBER.

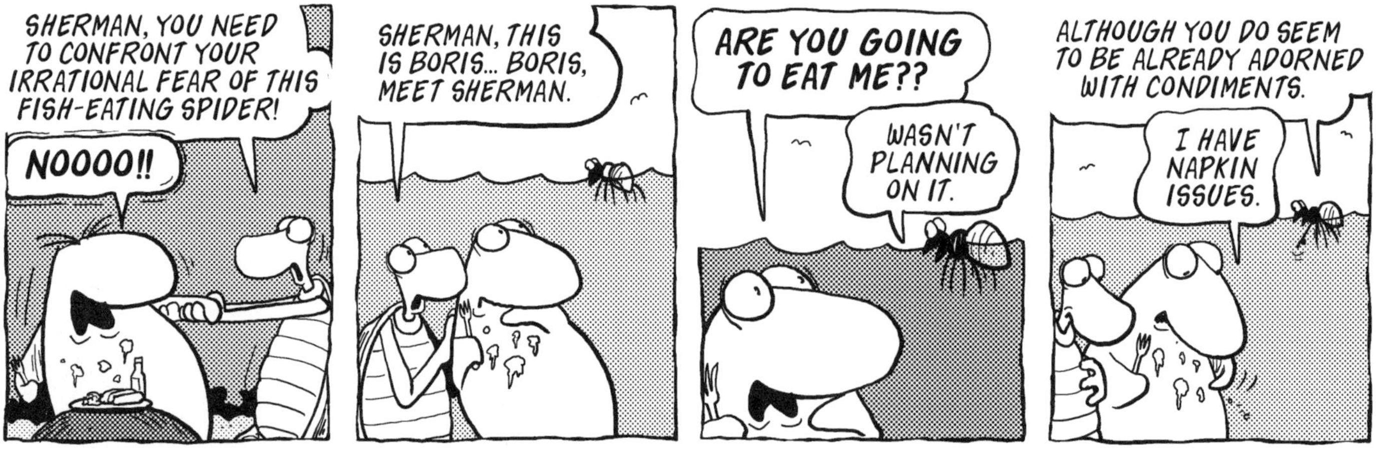
SHERMAN, YOU NEED TO CONFRONT YOUR IRRATIONAL FEAR OF THIS FISH-EATING SPIDER!
NOOOO!!
SHERMAN, THIS IS BORIS... BORIS, MEET SHERMAN.
ARE YOU GOING TO EAT ME??
WASN'T PLANNING ON IT.
ALTHOUGH YOU DO SEEM TO BE ALREADY ADORNED WITH CONDIMENTS.
I HAVE NAPKIN ISSUES.

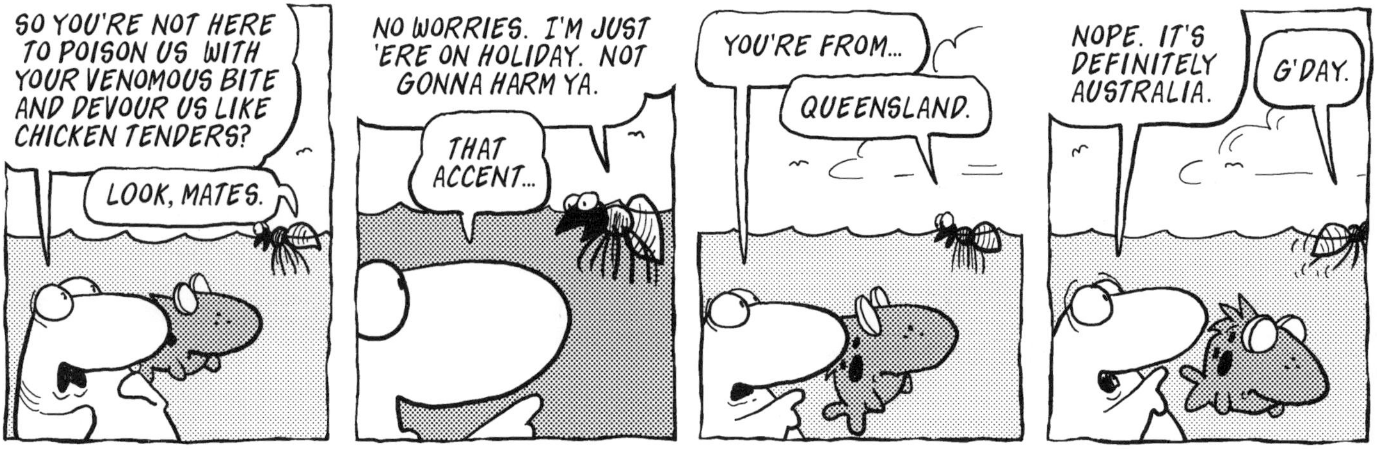
SO YOU'RE NOT HERE TO POISON US WITH YOUR VENOMOUS BITE AND DEVOUR US LIKE CHICKEN TENDERS?
LOOK, MATES.
NO WORRIES. I'M JUST 'ERE ON HOLIDAY. NOT GONNA HARM YA.
THAT ACCENT...
YOU'RE FROM...
QUEENSLAND.
NOPE. IT'S DEFINITELY AUSTRALIA.
G'DAY.

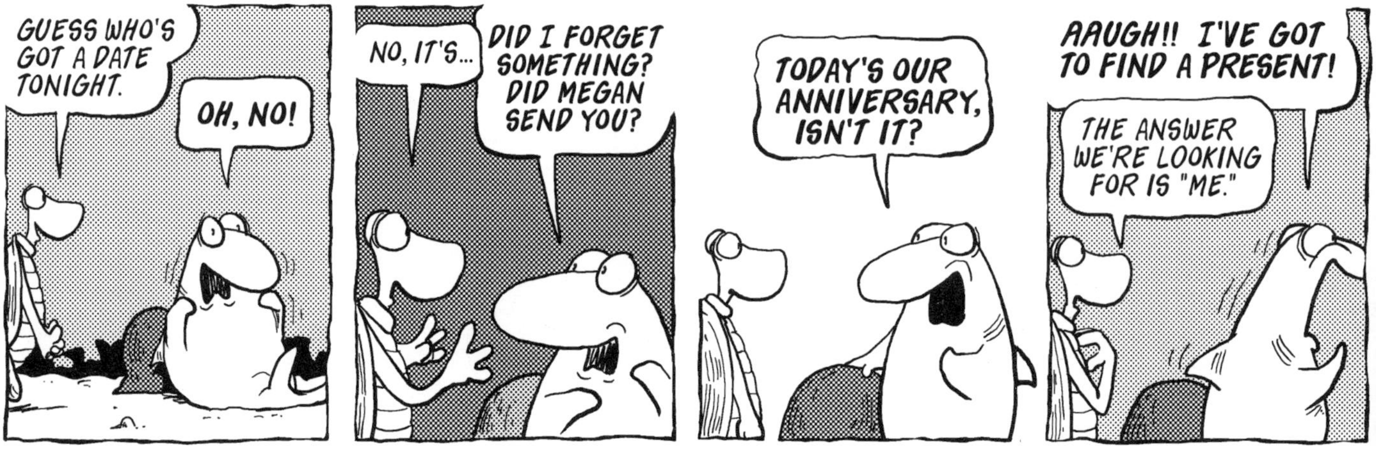
GUESS WHO'S GOT A DATE TONIGHT.
OH, NO!
NO, IT'S...
DID I FORGET SOMETHING? DID MEGAN SEND YOU?
TODAY'S OUR ANNIVERSARY, ISN'T IT?
AAUGH!! I'VE GOT TO FIND A PRESENT!
THE ANSWER WE'RE LOOKING FOR IS "ME."

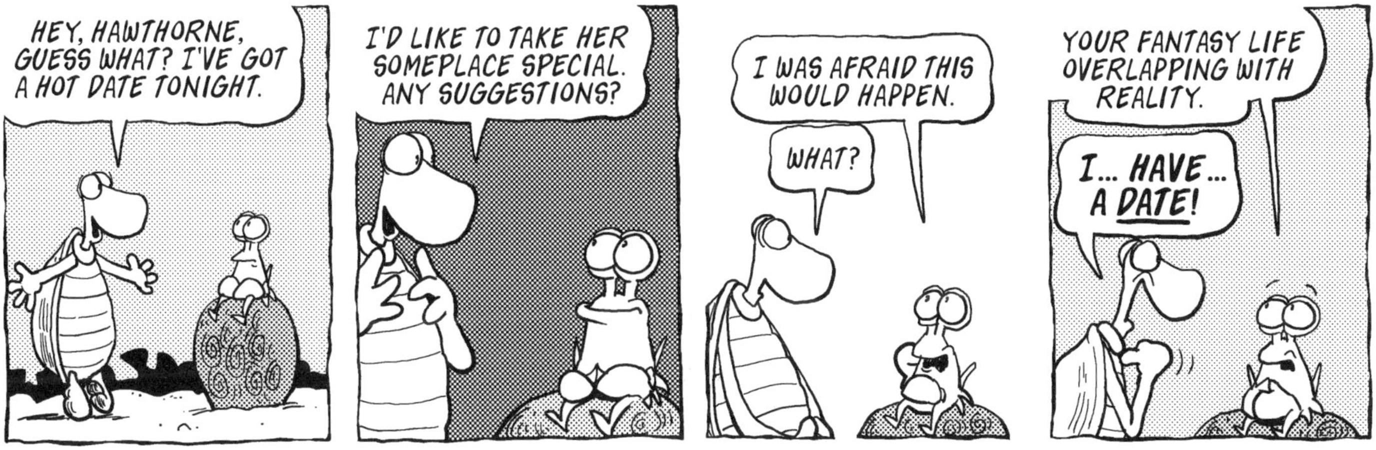
HEY, HAWTHORNE, GUESS WHAT? I'VE GOT A HOT DATE TONIGHT.
I'D LIKE TO TAKE HER SOMEPLACE SPECIAL. ANY SUGGESTIONS?
I WAS AFRAID THIS WOULD HAPPEN.
WHAT?
YOUR FANTASY LIFE OVERLAPPING WITH REALITY.
I... **HAVE**... A **DATE**!

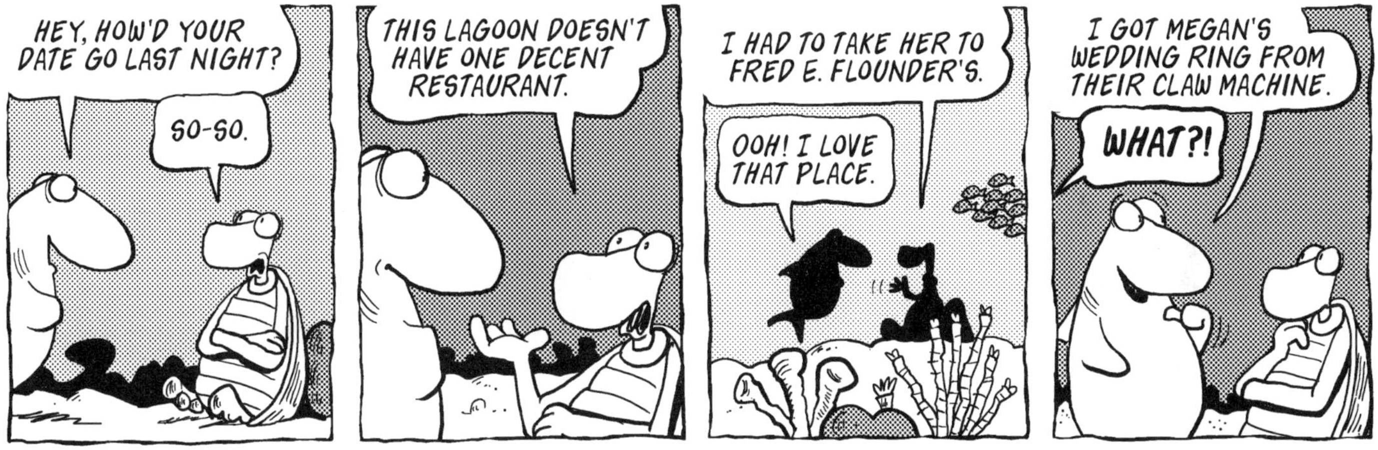
HEY, HOW'D YOUR DATE GO LAST NIGHT?
SO-SO.
THIS LAGOON DOESN'T HAVE ONE DECENT RESTAURANT.
I HAD TO TAKE HER TO FRED E. FLOUNDER'S.
OOH! I LOVE THAT PLACE.
I GOT MEGAN'S WEDDING RING FROM THEIR CLAW MACHINE.
WHAT?!

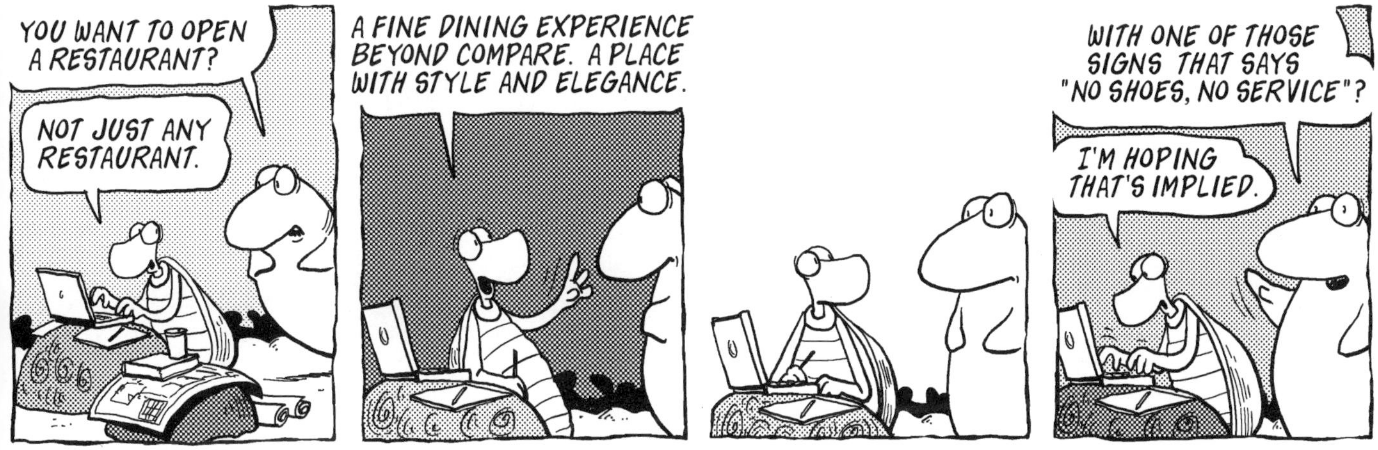
YOU WANT TO OPEN A RESTAURANT?
NOT JUST ANY RESTAURANT.
A FINE DINING EXPERIENCE BEYOND COMPARE. A PLACE WITH STYLE AND ELEGANCE.
WITH ONE OF THOSE SIGNS THAT SAYS "NO SHOES, NO SERVICE"?
I'M HOPING THAT'S IMPLIED.

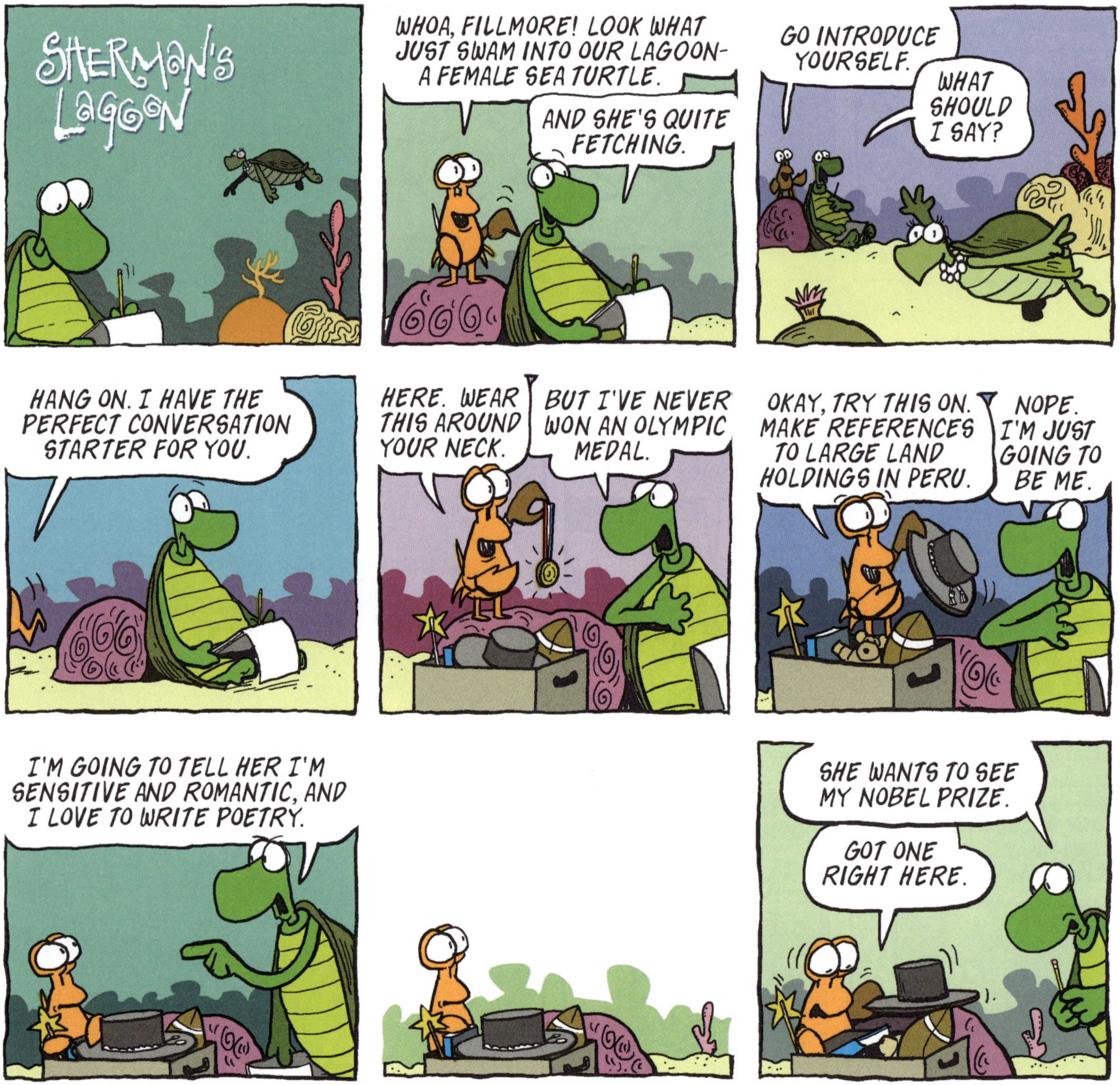
SHERMAN'S LAGOON
WHOA, FILLMORE! LOOK WHAT JUST SWAM INTO OUR LAGOON- A FEMALE SEA TURTLE.
AND SHE'S QUITE FETCHING.
GO INTRODUCE YOURSELF.
WHAT SHOULD I SAY?
HANG ON. I HAVE THE PERFECT CONVERSATION STARTER FOR YOU.
HERE. WEAR THIS AROUND YOUR NECK.
BUT I'VE NEVER WON AN OLYMPIC MEDAL.
OKAY, TRY THIS ON. MAKE REFERENCES TO LARGE LAND HOLDINGS IN PERU.
NOPE. I'M JUST GOING TO BE ME.
I'M GOING TO TELL HER I'M SENSITIVE AND ROMANTIC, AND I LOVE TO WRITE POETRY.
SHE WANTS TO SEE MY NOBEL PRIZE.
GOT ONE RIGHT HERE.

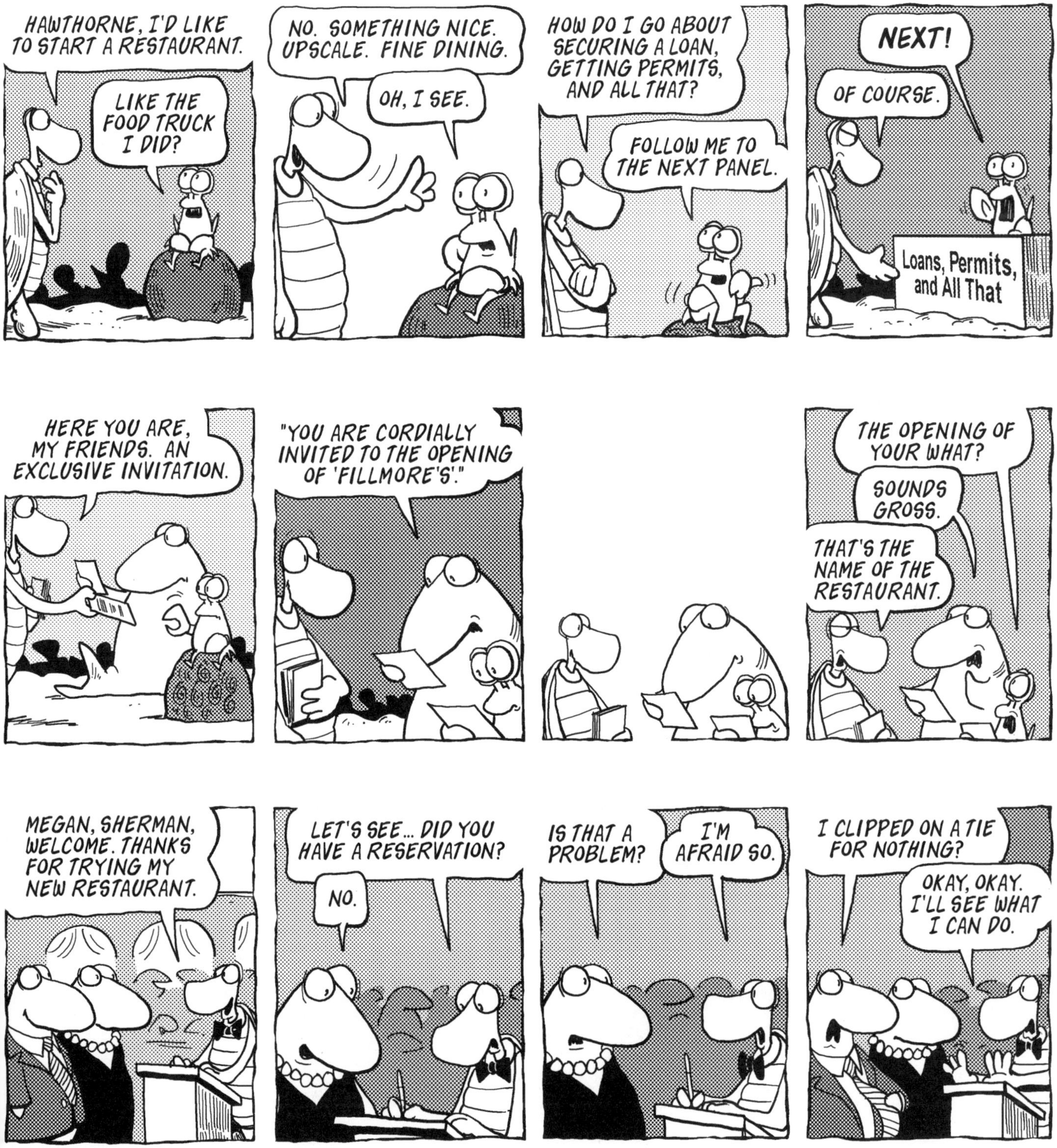
HAWTHORNE, I'D LIKE TO START A RESTAURANT.
LIKE THE FOOD TRUCK I DID?
NO. SOMETHING NICE. UPSCALE. FINE DINING.
OH, I SEE.
HOW DO I GO ABOUT SECURING A LOAN, GETTING PERMITS, AND ALL THAT?
FOLLOW ME TO THE NEXT PANEL.
NEXT!
OF COURSE.
Loans, Permits, and All That
HERE YOU ARE, MY FRIENDS. AN EXCLUSIVE INVITATION.
"YOU ARE CORDIALLY INVITED TO THE OPENING OF 'FILLMORE'S'."
THE OPENING OF YOUR WHAT?
SOUNDS GROSS.
THAT'S THE NAME OF THE RESTAURANT.
MEGAN, SHERMAN, WELCOME. THANKS FOR TRYING MY NEW RESTAURANT.
LET'S SEE... DID YOU HAVE A RESERVATION?
NO.
IS THAT A PROBLEM?
I'M AFRAID SO.
I CLIPPED ON A TIE FOR NOTHING?
OKAY, OKAY. I'LL SEE WHAT I CAN DO.

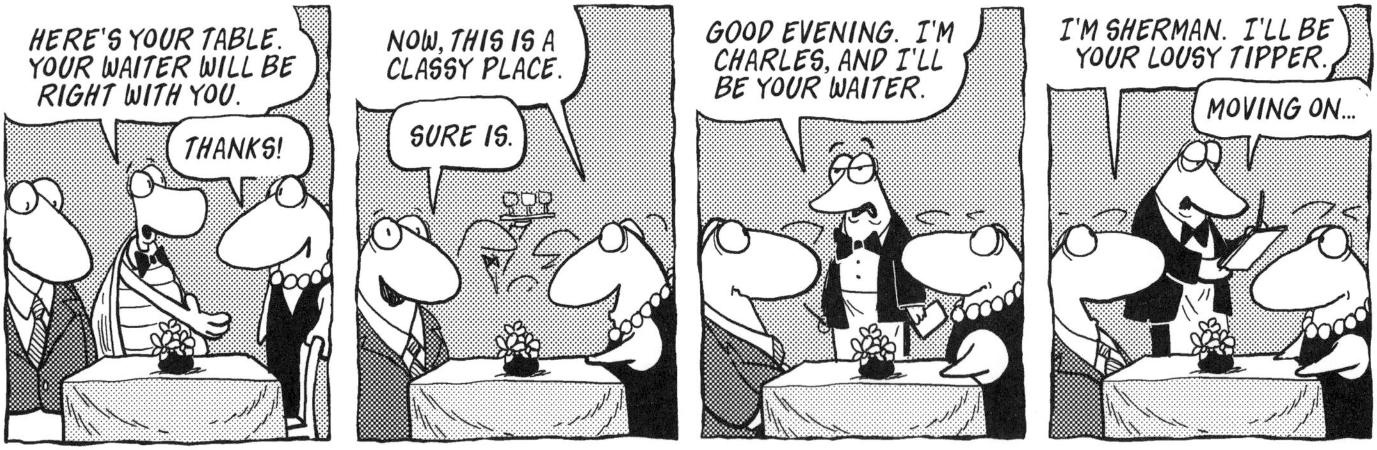
HERE'S YOUR TABLE. YOUR WAITER WILL BE RIGHT WITH YOU.
THANKS!
NOW, THIS IS A CLASSY PLACE.
SURE IS.
GOOD EVENING. I'M CHARLES, AND I'LL BE YOUR WAITER.
I'M SHERMAN. I'LL BE YOUR LOUSY TIPPER.
MOVING ON...

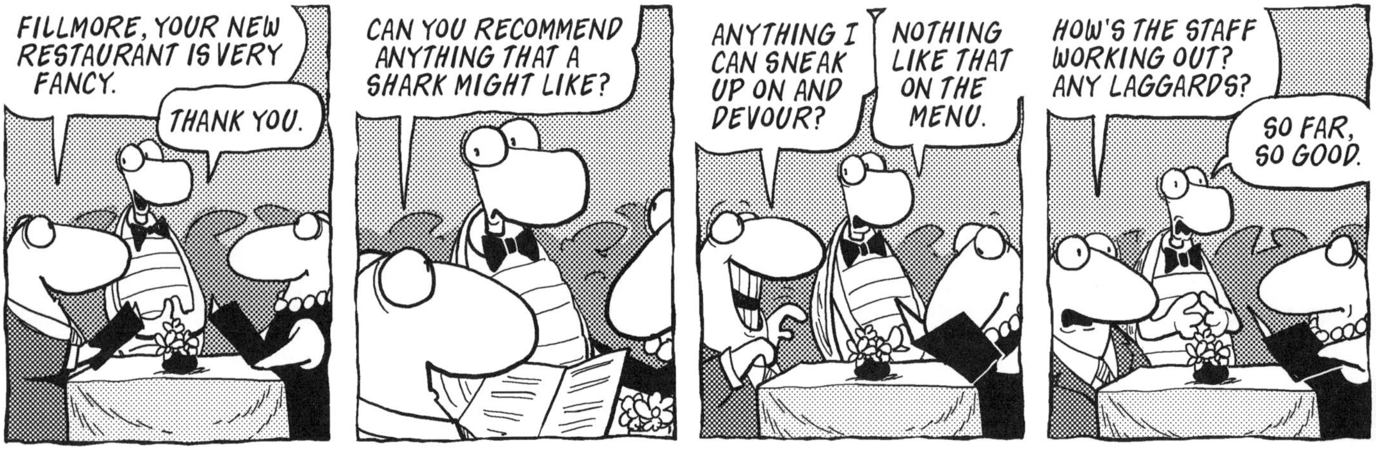
FILLMORE, YOUR NEW RESTAURANT IS VERY FANCY.
THANK YOU.
CAN YOU RECOMMEND ANYTHING THAT A SHARK MIGHT LIKE?
ANYTHING I CAN SNEAK UP ON AND DEVOUR?
NOTHING LIKE THAT ON THE MENU.
HOW'S THE STAFF WORKING OUT? ANY LAGGARDS?
SO FAR, SO GOOD.

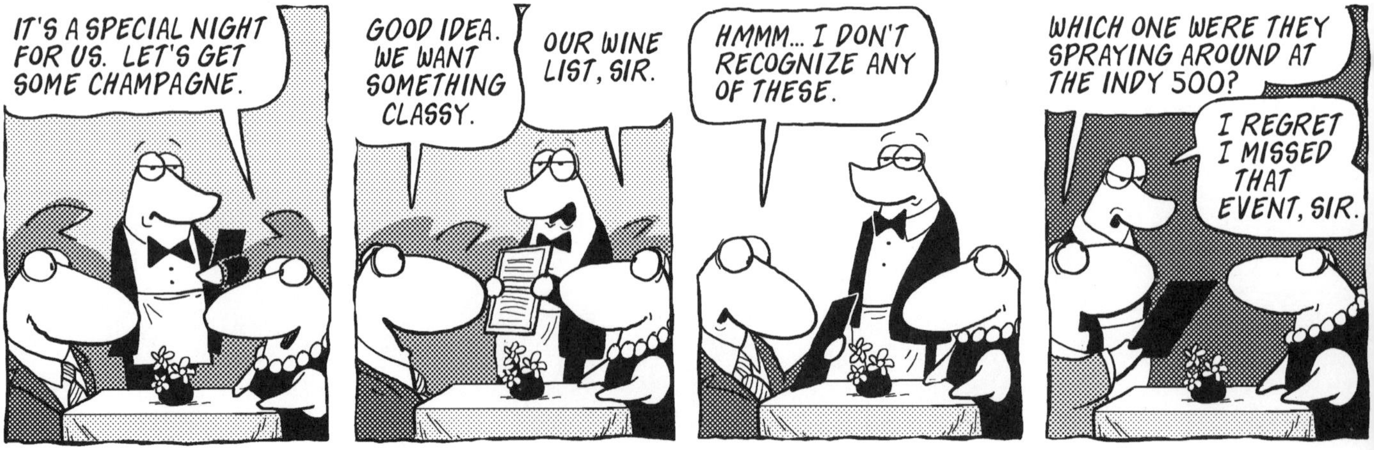
IT'S A SPECIAL NIGHT FOR US. LET'S GET SOME CHAMPAGNE.
GOOD IDEA. WE WANT SOMETHING CLASSY.
OUR WINE LIST, SIR.
HMMM... I DON'T RECOGNIZE ANY OF THESE.
WHICH ONE WERE THEY SPRAYING AROUND AT THE INDY 500?
I REGRET I MISSED THAT EVENT, SIR.

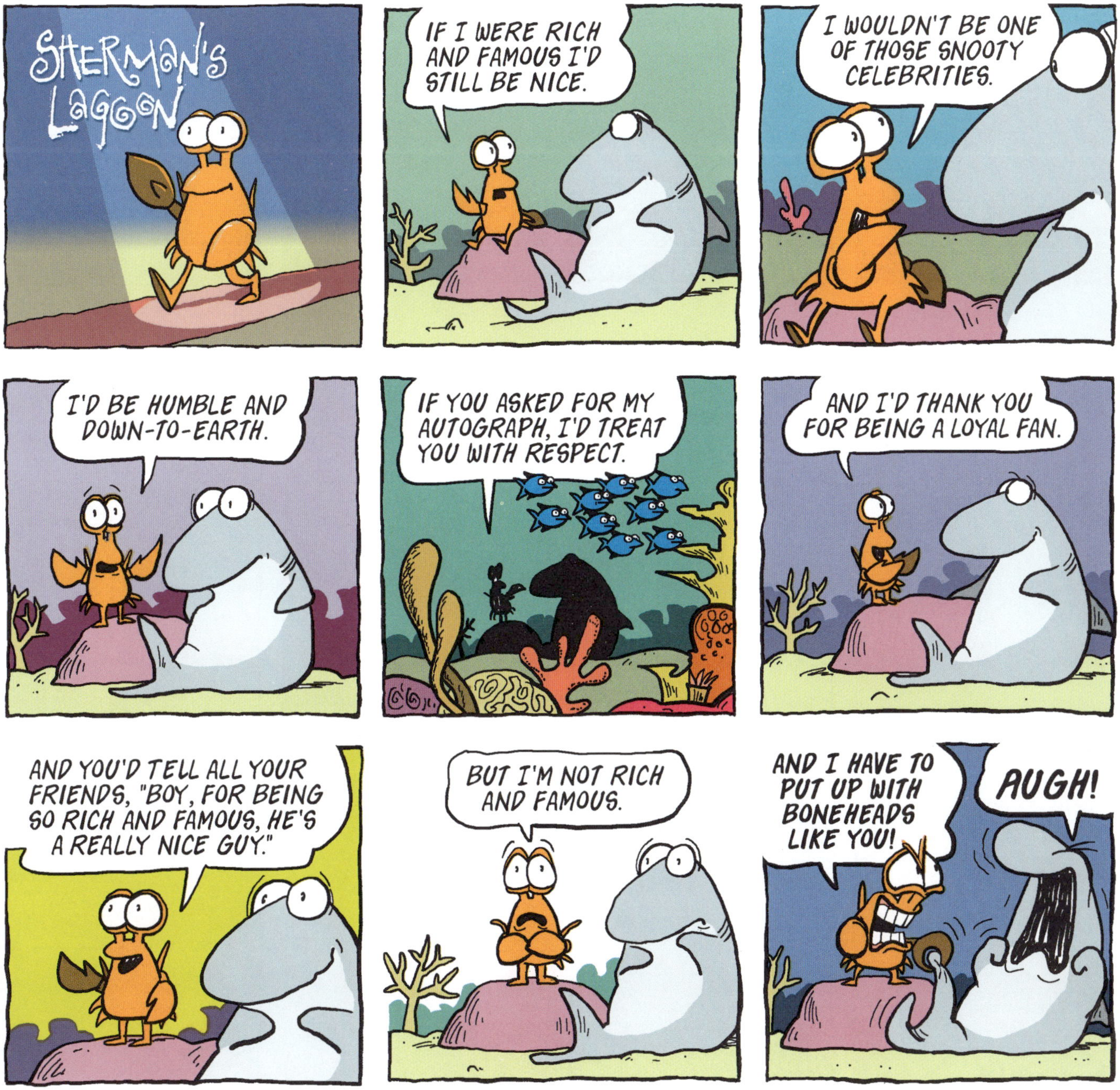
SHERMAN'S LAGOON
IF I WERE RICH AND FAMOUS I'D STILL BE NICE.
I WOULDN'T BE ONE OF THOSE SNOOTY CELEBRITIES.
I'D BE HUMBLE AND DOWN-TO-EARTH.
IF YOU ASKED FOR MY AUTOGRAPH, I'D TREAT YOU WITH RESPECT.
AND I'D THANK YOU FOR BEING A LOYAL FAN.
AND YOU'D TELL ALL YOUR FRIENDS, "BOY, FOR BEING SO RICH AND FAMOUS, HE'S A REALLY NICE GUY."
BUT I'M NOT RICH AND FAMOUS.
AND I HAVE TO PUT UP WITH BONEHEADS LIKE YOU!
AUGH!

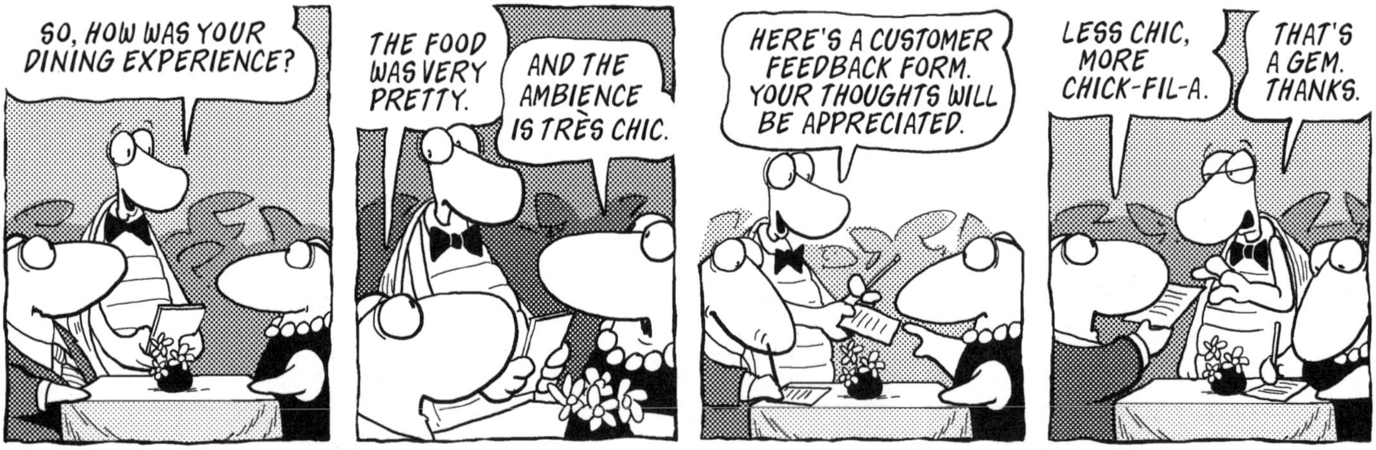
SO, HOW WAS YOUR DINING EXPERIENCE?
THE FOOD WAS VERY PRETTY.
AND THE AMBIENCE IS TRÈS CHIC.
HERE'S A CUSTOMER FEEDBACK FORM. YOUR THOUGHTS WILL BE APPRECIATED.
LESS CHIC, MORE CHICK-FIL-A.
THAT'S A GEM. THANKS.

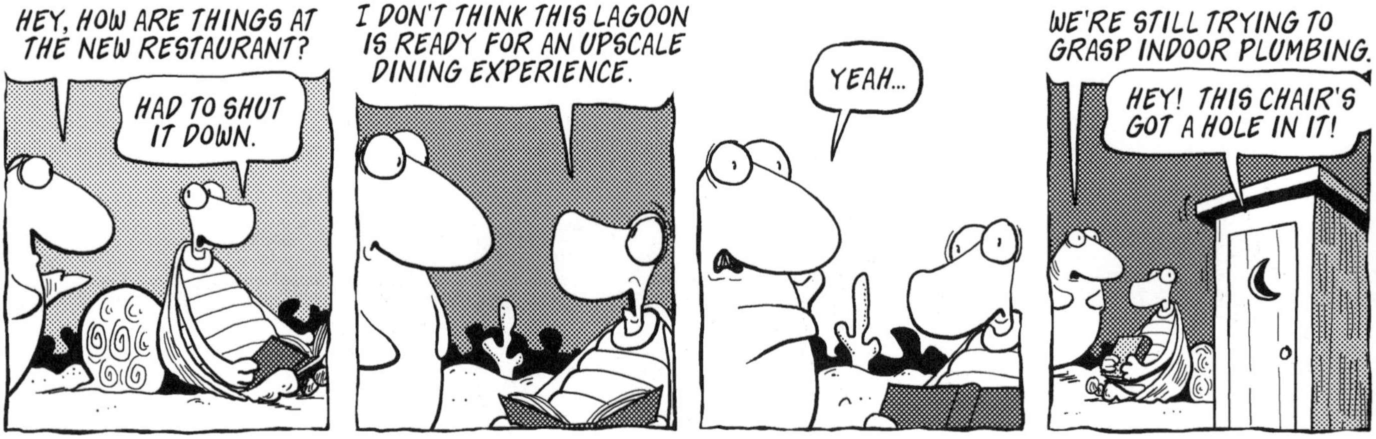
HEY, HOW ARE THINGS AT THE NEW RESTAURANT?
HAD TO SHUT IT DOWN.
I DON'T THINK THIS LAGOON IS READY FOR AN UPSCALE DINING EXPERIENCE.
YEAH...
WE'RE STILL TRYING TO GRASP INDOOR PLUMBING.
HEY! THIS CHAIR'S GOT A HOLE IN IT!

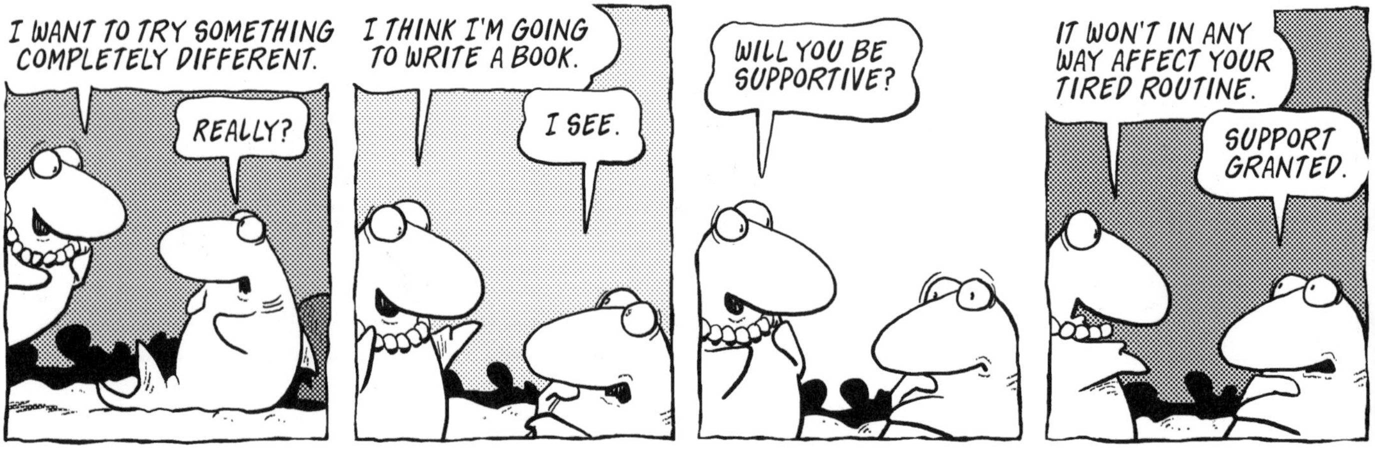
I WANT TO TRY SOMETHING COMPLETELY DIFFERENT.
REALLY?
I THINK I'M GOING TO WRITE A BOOK.
I SEE.
WILL YOU BE SUPPORTIVE?
IT WON'T IN ANY WAY AFFECT YOUR TIRED ROUTINE.
SUPPORT GRANTED.

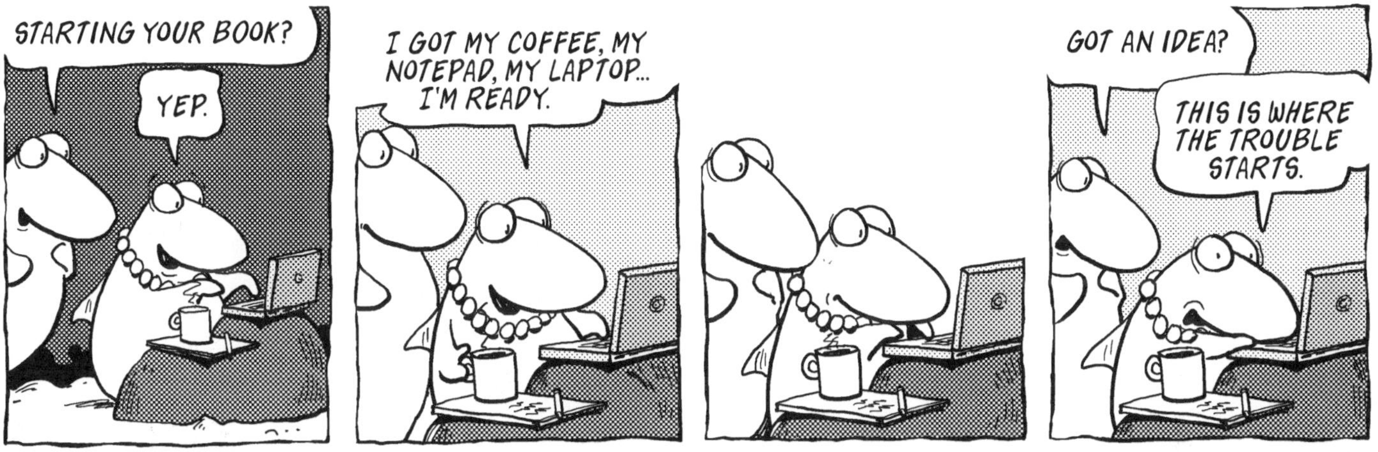
STARTING YOUR BOOK?
YEP.
I GOT MY COFFEE, MY NOTEPAD, MY LAPTOP... I'M READY.
GOT AN IDEA?
THIS IS WHERE THE TROUBLE STARTS.

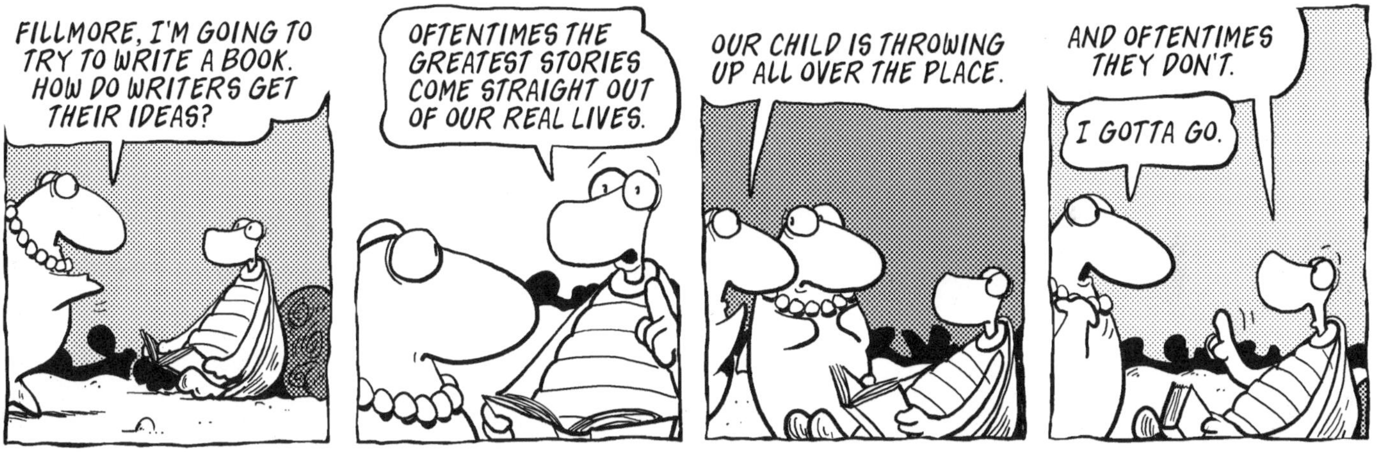
FILLMORE, I'M GOING TO TRY TO WRITE A BOOK. HOW DO WRITERS GET THEIR IDEAS?
OFTENTIMES THE GREATEST STORIES COME STRAIGHT OUT OF OUR REAL LIVES.
OUR CHILD IS THROWING UP ALL OVER THE PLACE.
AND OFTENTIMES THEY DON'T.
I GOTTA GO.

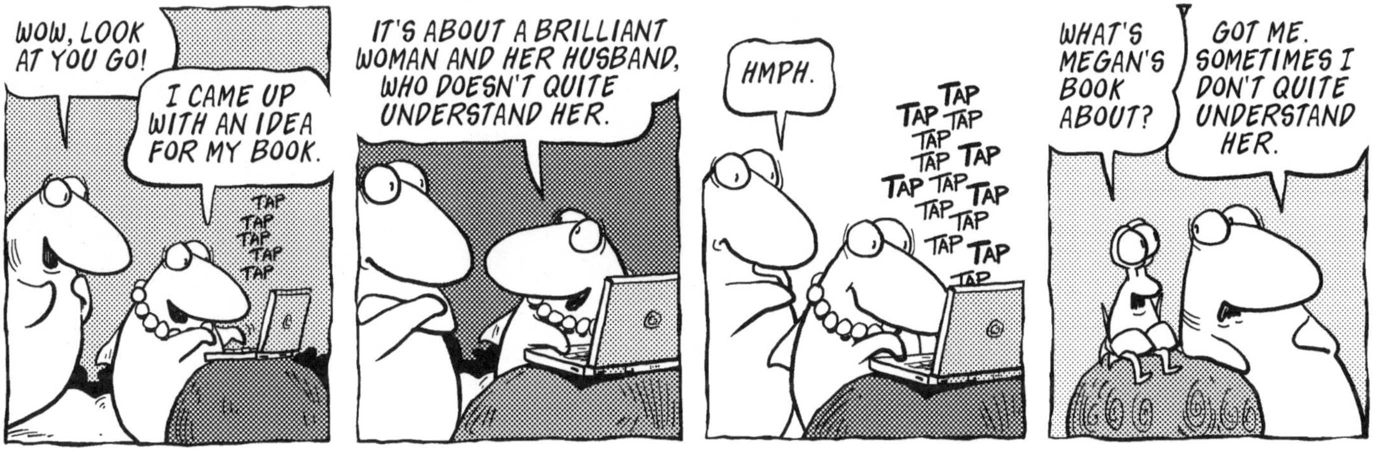
WOW, LOOK AT YOU GO!
I CAME UP WITH AN IDEA FOR MY BOOK.
TAP TAP TAP TAP TAP
IT'S ABOUT A BRILLIANT WOMAN AND HER HUSBAND, WHO DOESN'T QUITE UNDERSTAND HER.
HMPH.
TAP TAP TAP TAP TAP TAP TAP TAP TAP TAP TAP TAP TAP
WHAT'S MEGAN'S BOOK ABOUT?
GOT ME. SOMETIMES I DON'T QUITE UNDERSTAND HER.

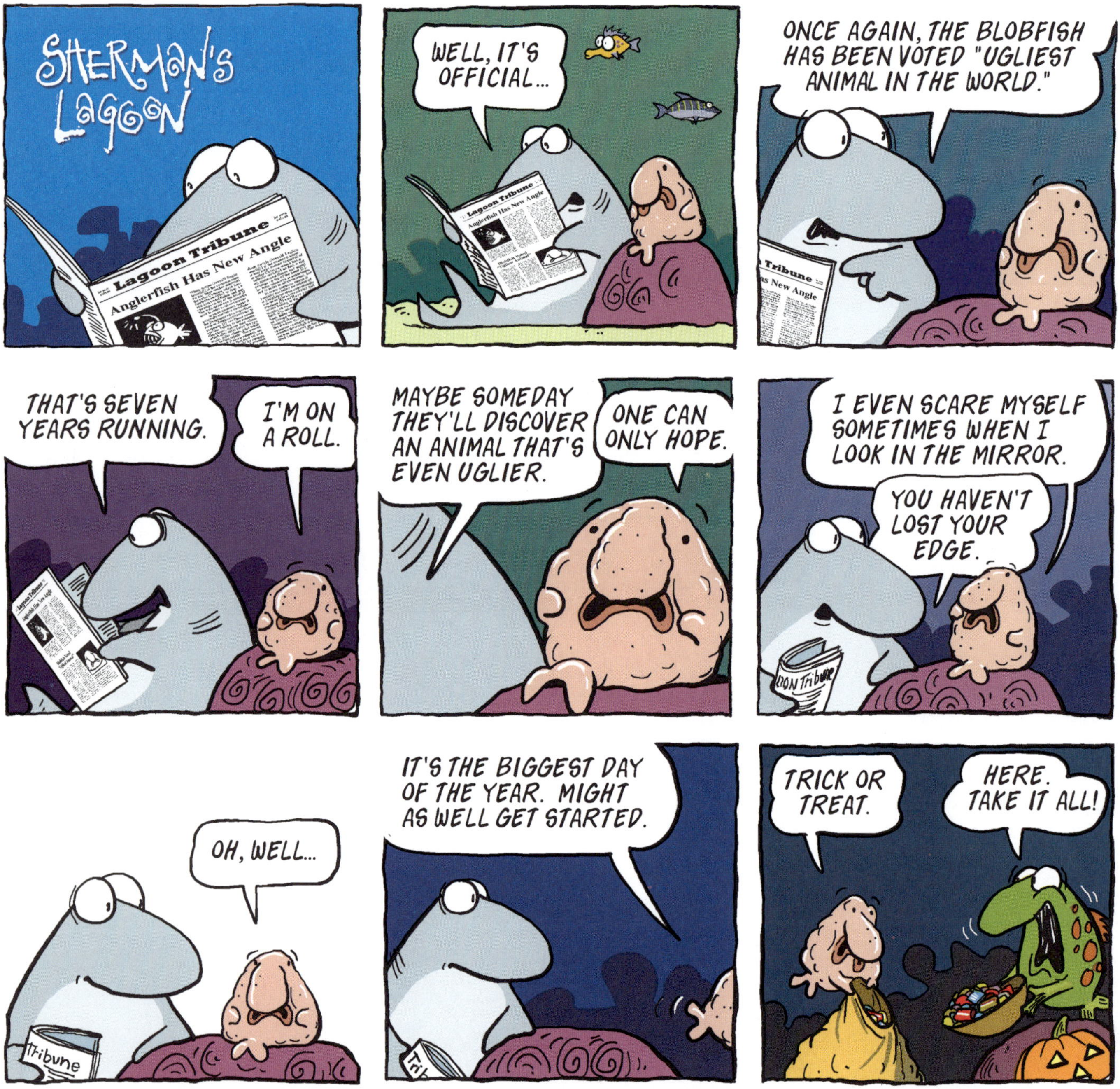
SHERMAN'S LAGOON
Lagoon Tribune
Anglerfish Has New Angle
WELL, IT'S OFFICIAL...
ONCE AGAIN, THE BLOBFISH HAS BEEN VOTED "UGLIEST ANIMAL IN THE WORLD."
THAT'S SEVEN YEARS RUNNING.
I'M ON A ROLL.
MAYBE SOMEDAY THEY'LL DISCOVER AN ANIMAL THAT'S EVEN UGLIER.
ONE CAN ONLY HOPE.
I EVEN SCARE MYSELF SOMETIMES WHEN I LOOK IN THE MIRROR.
YOU HAVEN'T LOST YOUR EDGE.
OH, WELL...
IT'S THE BIGGEST DAY OF THE YEAR. MIGHT AS WELL GET STARTED.
TRICK OR TREAT.
HERE. TAKE IT ALL!

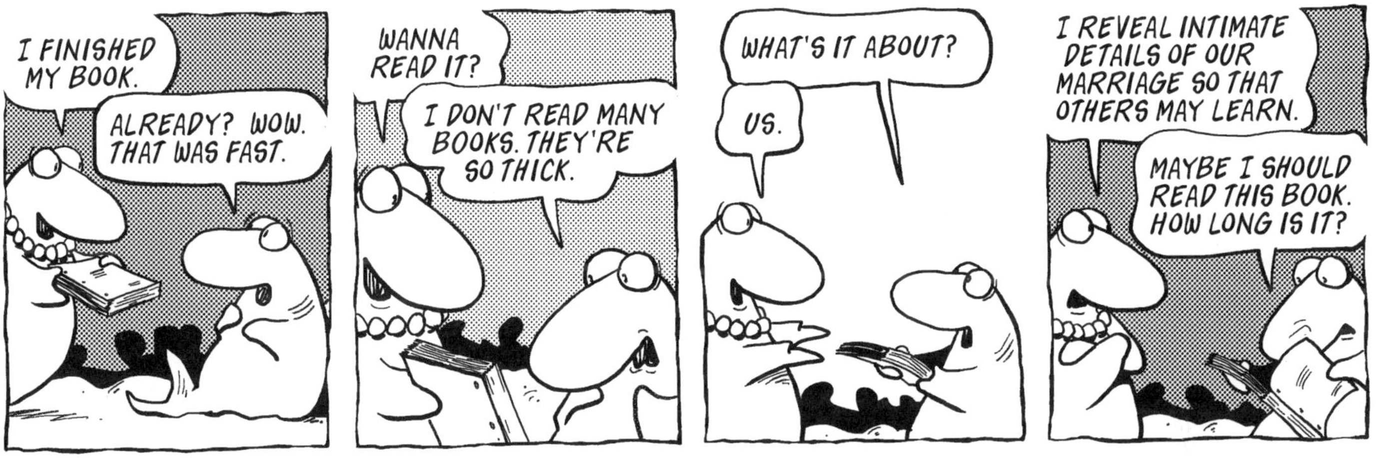
I FINISHED MY BOOK.
ALREADY? WOW. THAT WAS FAST.
WANNA READ IT?
I DON'T READ MANY BOOKS. THEY'RE SO THICK.
WHAT'S IT ABOUT?
US.
I REVEAL INTIMATE DETAILS OF OUR MARRIAGE SO THAT OTHERS MAY LEARN.
MAYBE I SHOULD READ THIS BOOK. HOW LONG IS IT?

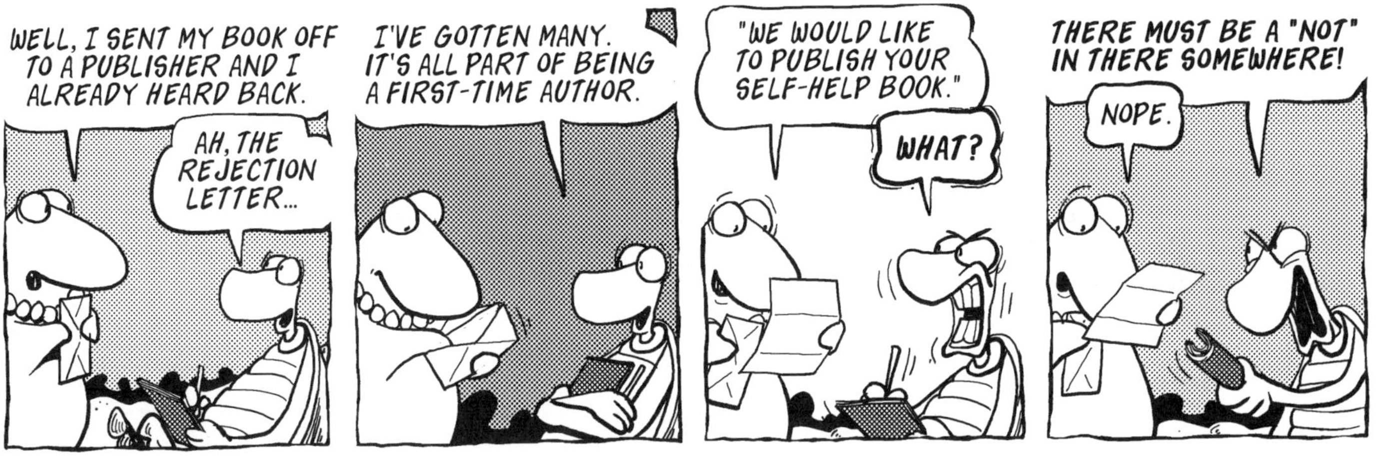
WELL, I SENT MY BOOK OFF TO A PUBLISHER AND I ALREADY HEARD BACK.
AH, THE REJECTION LETTER...
I'VE GOTTEN MANY. IT'S ALL PART OF BEING A FIRST-TIME AUTHOR.
"WE WOULD LIKE TO PUBLISH YOUR SELF-HELP BOOK."
WHAT?
THERE MUST BE A "NOT" IN THERE SOMEWHERE!
NOPE.

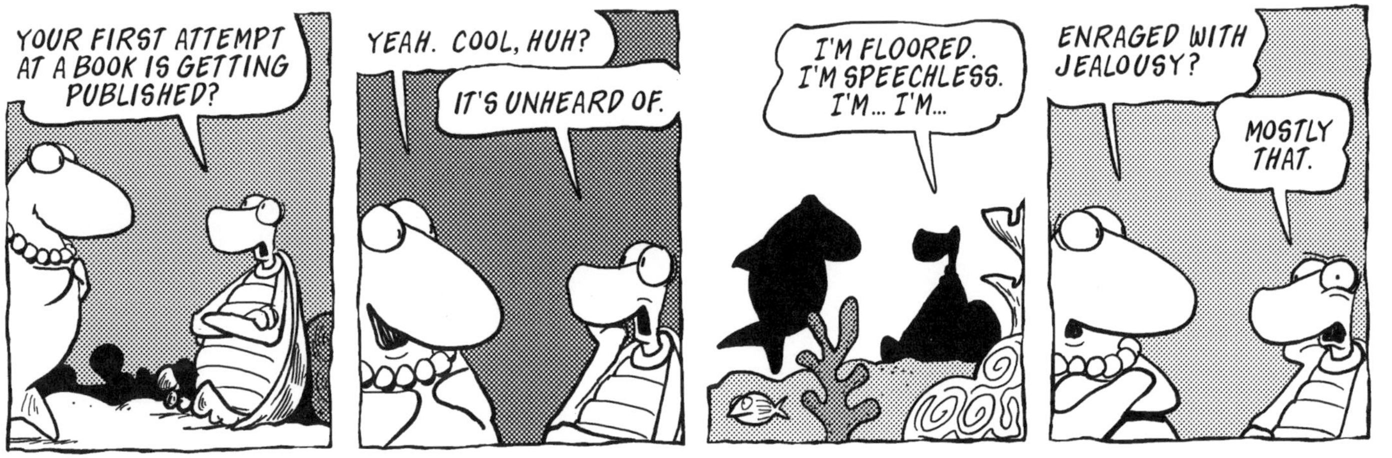
YOUR FIRST ATTEMPT AT A BOOK IS GETTING PUBLISHED?
YEAH. COOL, HUH?
IT'S UNHEARD OF.
I'M FLOORED. I'M SPEECHLESS. I'M... I'M...
ENRAGED WITH JEALOUSY?
MOSTLY THAT.

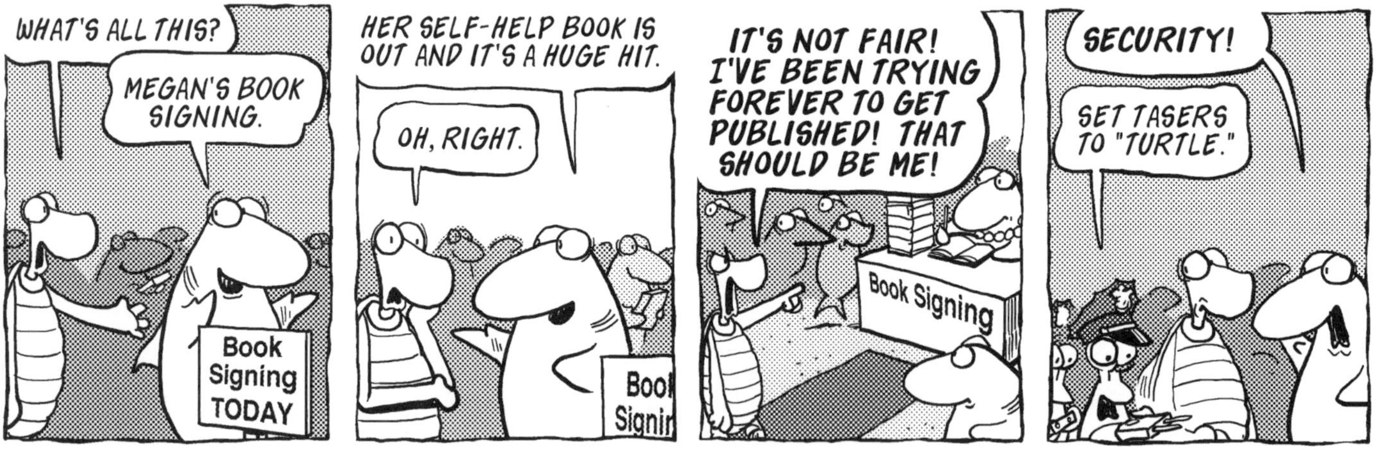
WHAT'S ALL THIS?
MEGAN'S BOOK SIGNING.
Book Signing TODAY
HER SELF-HELP BOOK IS OUT AND IT'S A HUGE HIT.
OH, RIGHT.
IT'S NOT FAIR! I'VE BEEN TRYING FOREVER TO GET PUBLISHED! THAT SHOULD BE ME!
Book Signing
SECURITY!
SET TASERS TO "TURTLE."

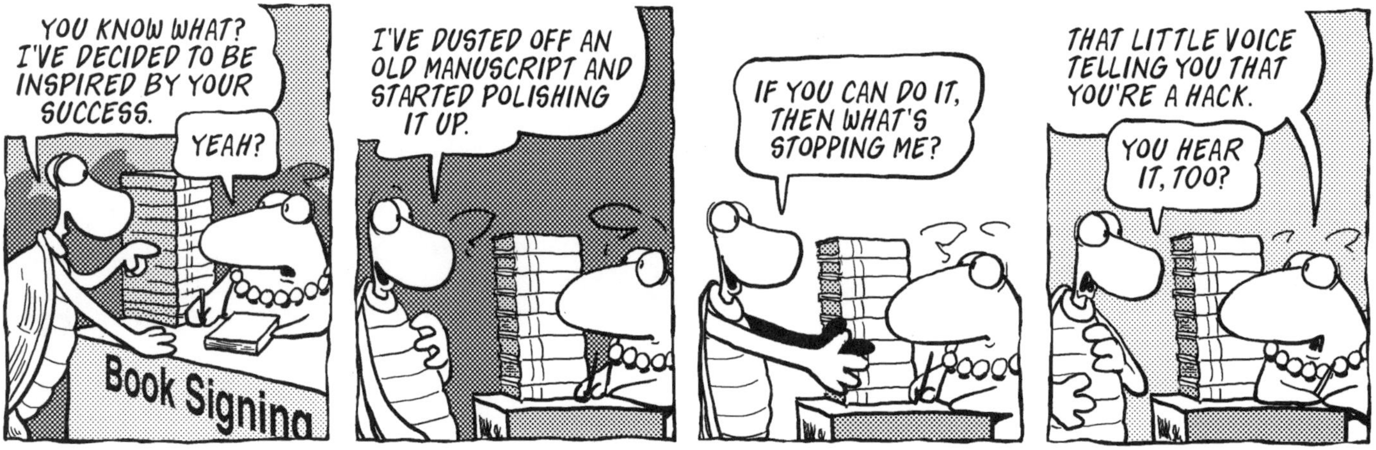
YOU KNOW WHAT? I'VE DECIDED TO BE INSPIRED BY YOUR SUCCESS.
YEAH?
Book Signing
I'VE DUSTED OFF AN OLD MANUSCRIPT AND STARTED POLISHING IT UP.
IF YOU CAN DO IT, THEN WHAT'S STOPPING ME?
THAT LITTLE VOICE TELLING YOU THAT YOU'RE A HACK.
YOU HEAR IT, TOO?

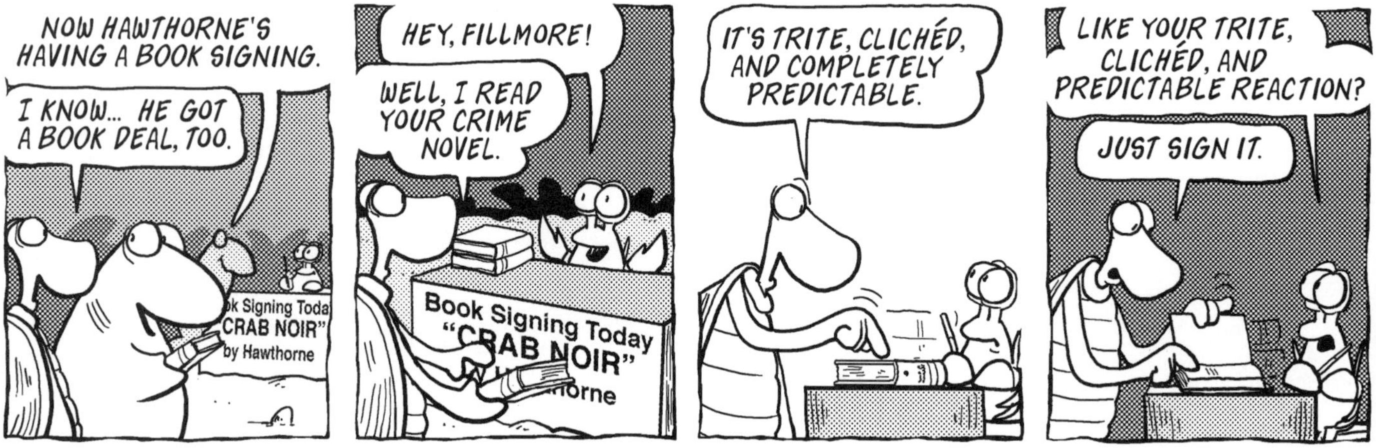
NOW HAWTHORNE'S HAVING A BOOK SIGNING.
I KNOW... HE GOT A BOOK DEAL, TOO.
HEY, FILLMORE!
WELL, I READ YOUR CRIME NOVEL.
Book Signing Today "CRAB NOIR"
IT'S TRITE, CLICHÉD, AND COMPLETELY PREDICTABLE.
LIKE YOUR TRITE, CLICHÉD, AND PREDICTABLE REACTION?
JUST SIGN IT.

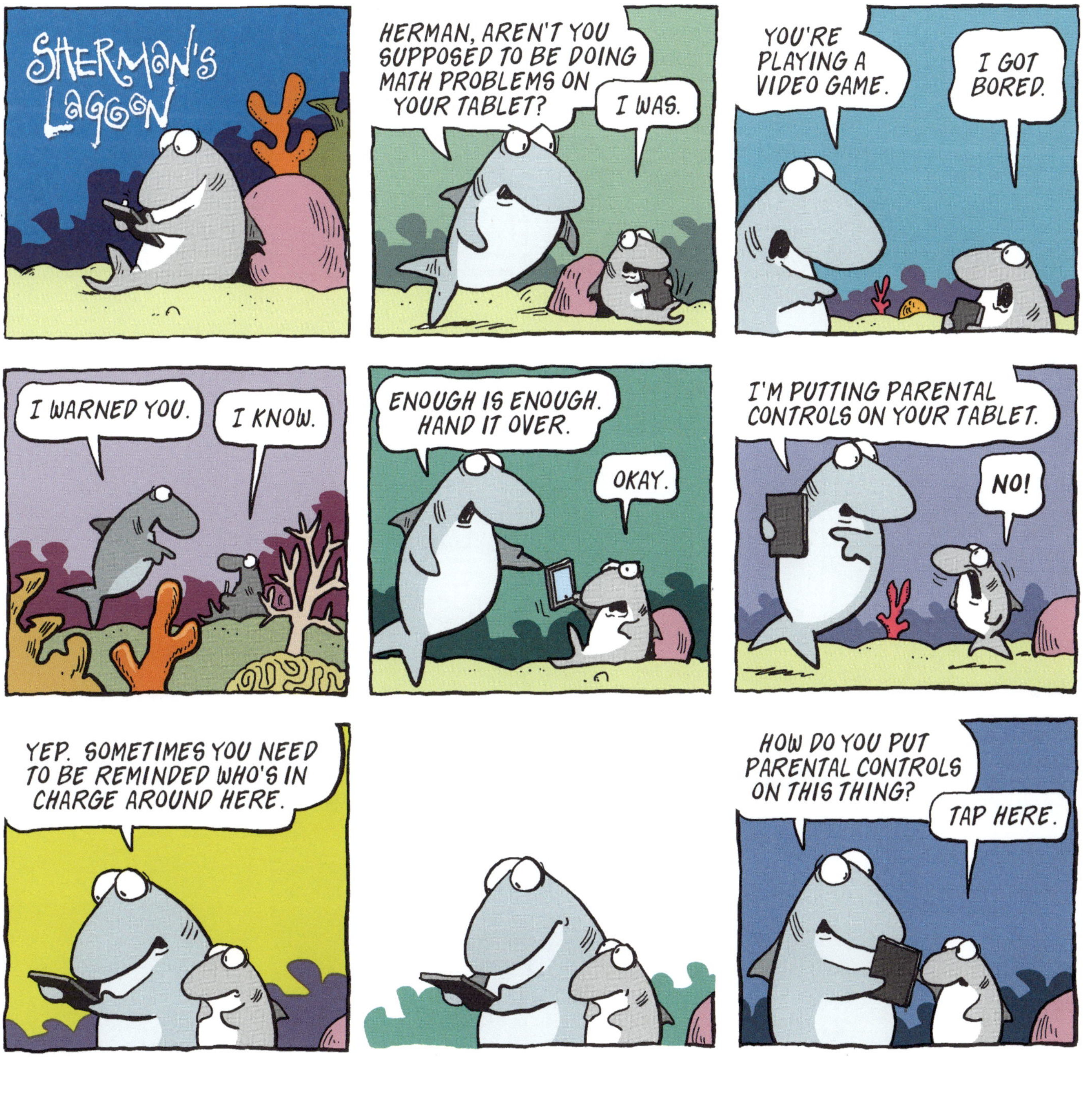
SHERMAN'S LAGOON
HERMAN, AREN'T YOU SUPPOSED TO BE DOING MATH PROBLEMS ON YOUR TABLET?
I WAS.
YOU'RE PLAYING A VIDEO GAME.
I GOT BORED.
I WARNED YOU.
I KNOW.
ENOUGH IS ENOUGH. HAND IT OVER.
OKAY.
I'M PUTTING PARENTAL CONTROLS ON YOUR TABLET.
NO!
YEP. SOMETIMES YOU NEED TO BE REMINDED WHO'S IN CHARGE AROUND HERE.
HOW DO YOU PUT PARENTAL CONTROLS ON THIS THING?
TAP HERE.

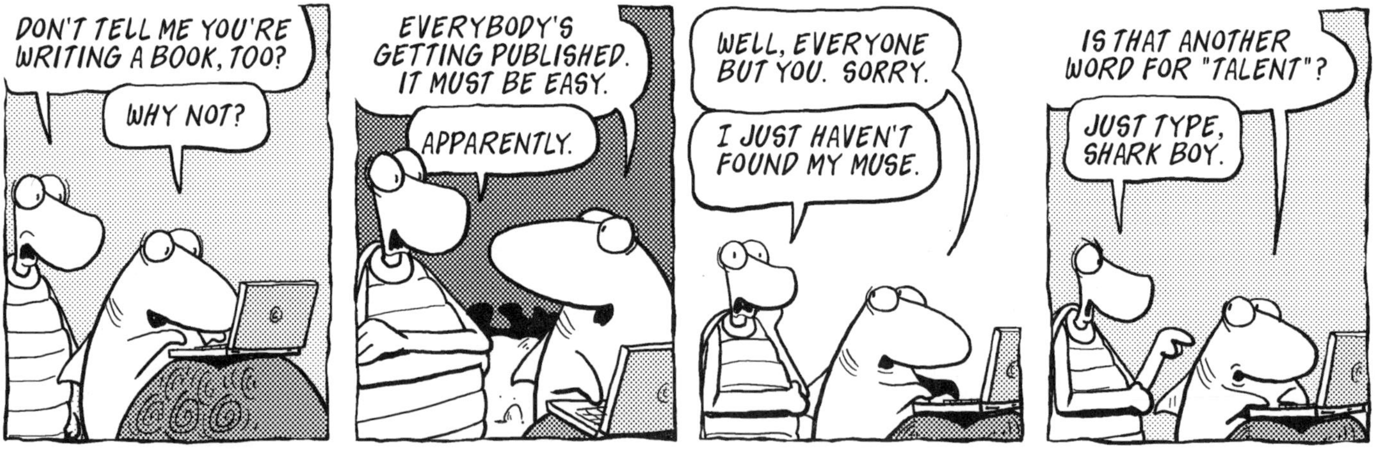
DON'T TELL ME YOU'RE WRITING A BOOK, TOO?
WHY NOT?
EVERYBODY'S GETTING PUBLISHED. IT MUST BE EASY.
APPARENTLY.
WELL, EVERYONE BUT YOU. SORRY.
I JUST HAVEN'T FOUND MY MUSE.
IS THAT ANOTHER WORD FOR "TALENT"?
JUST TYPE, SHARK BOY.

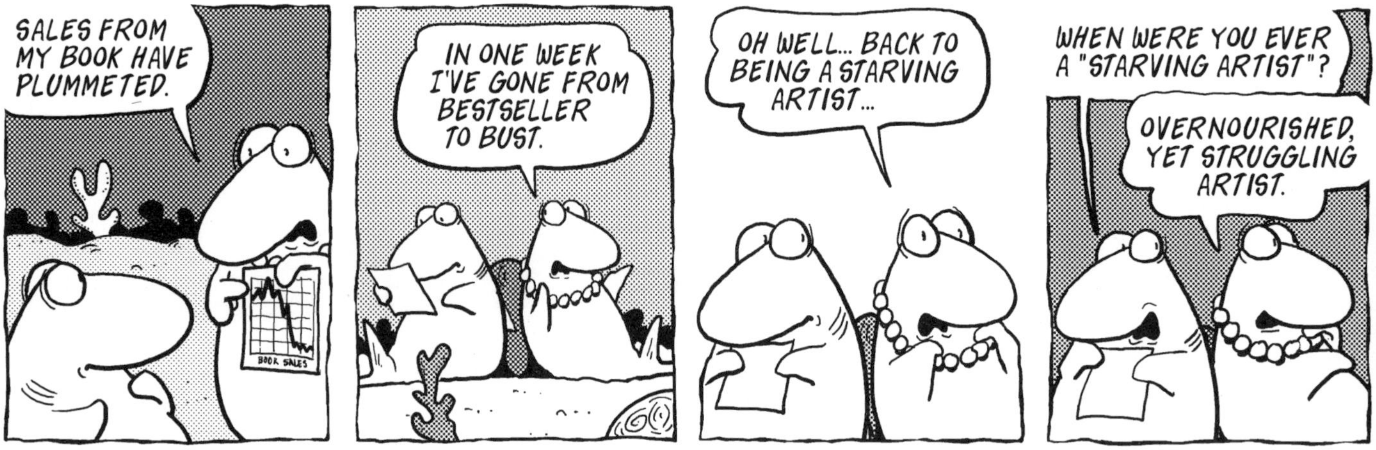
SALES FROM MY BOOK HAVE PLUMMETED.
BOOK SALES
IN ONE WEEK I'VE GONE FROM BESTSELLER TO BUST.
OH WELL... BACK TO BEING A STARVING ARTIST...
WHEN WERE YOU EVER A "STARVING ARTIST"?
OVERNOURISHED, YET STRUGGLING ARTIST.

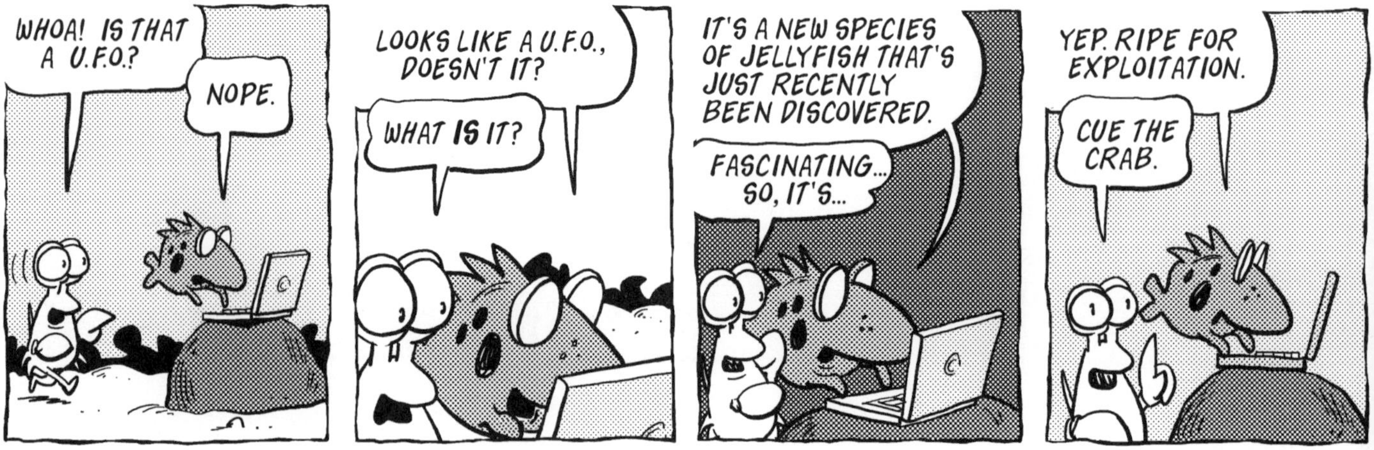
WHOA! IS THAT A U.F.O.?
NOPE.
LOOKS LIKE A U.F.O., DOESN'T IT?
WHAT IS IT?
IT'S A NEW SPECIES OF JELLYFISH THAT'S JUST RECENTLY BEEN DISCOVERED.
FASCINATING... SO, IT'S...
YEP. RIPE FOR EXPLOITATION.
CUE THE CRAB.

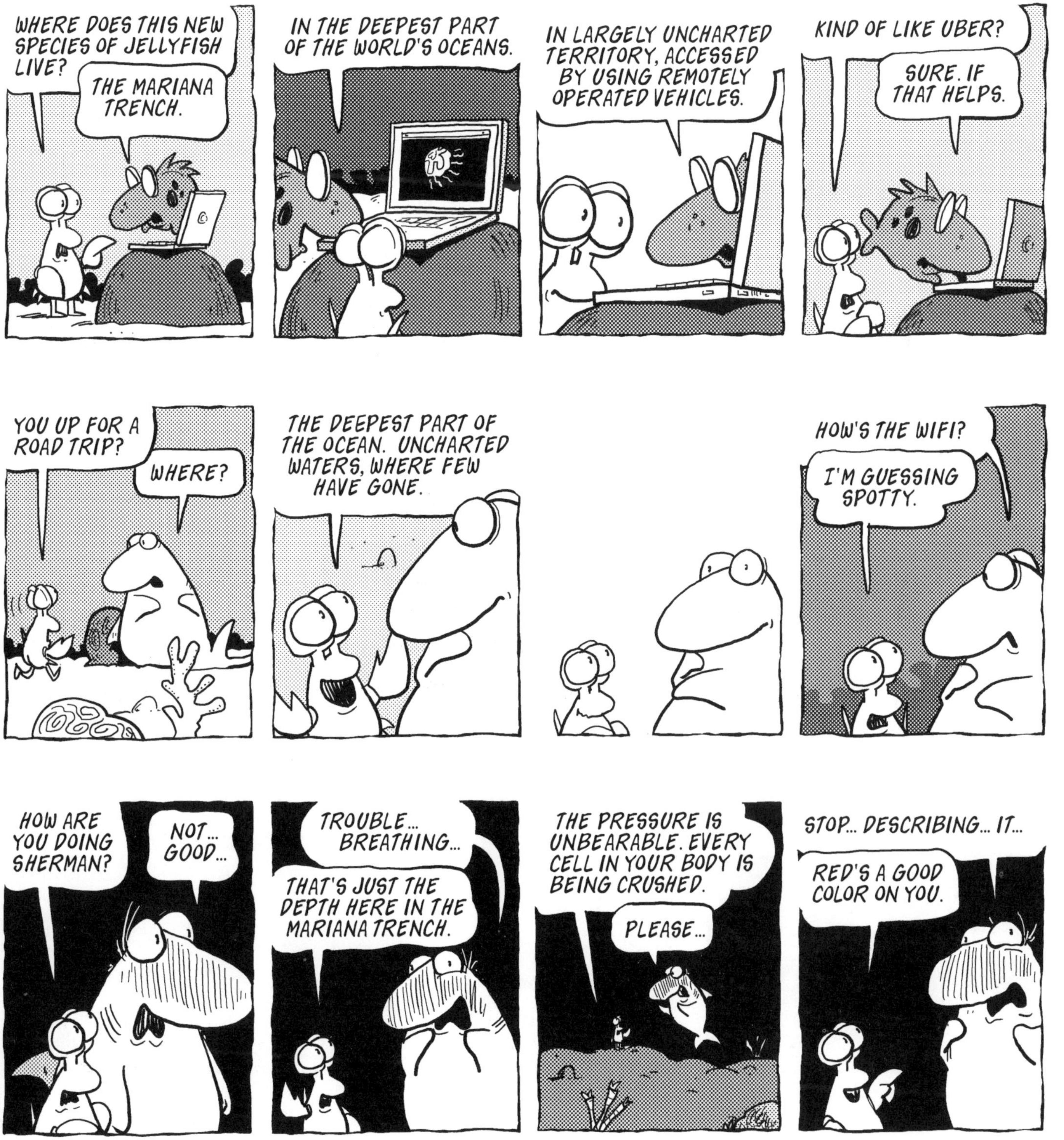
WHERE DOES THIS NEW SPECIES OF JELLYFISH LIVE?
THE MARIANA TRENCH.
IN THE DEEPEST PART OF THE WORLD'S OCEANS.
IN LARGELY UNCHARTED TERRITORY, ACCESSED BY USING REMOTELY OPERATED VEHICLES.
KIND OF LIKE UBER?
SURE. IF THAT HELPS.
YOU UP FOR A ROAD TRIP?
WHERE?
THE DEEPEST PART OF THE OCEAN. UNCHARTED WATERS, WHERE FEW HAVE GONE.
HOW'S THE WIFI?
I'M GUESSING SPOTTY.
HOW ARE YOU DOING SHERMAN?
NOT... GOOD...
TROUBLE... BREATHING...
THAT'S JUST THE DEPTH HERE IN THE MARIANA TRENCH.
THE PRESSURE IS UNBEARABLE. EVERY CELL IN YOUR BODY IS BEING CRUSHED.
PLEASE...
STOP... DESCRIBING... IT...
RED'S A GOOD COLOR ON YOU.

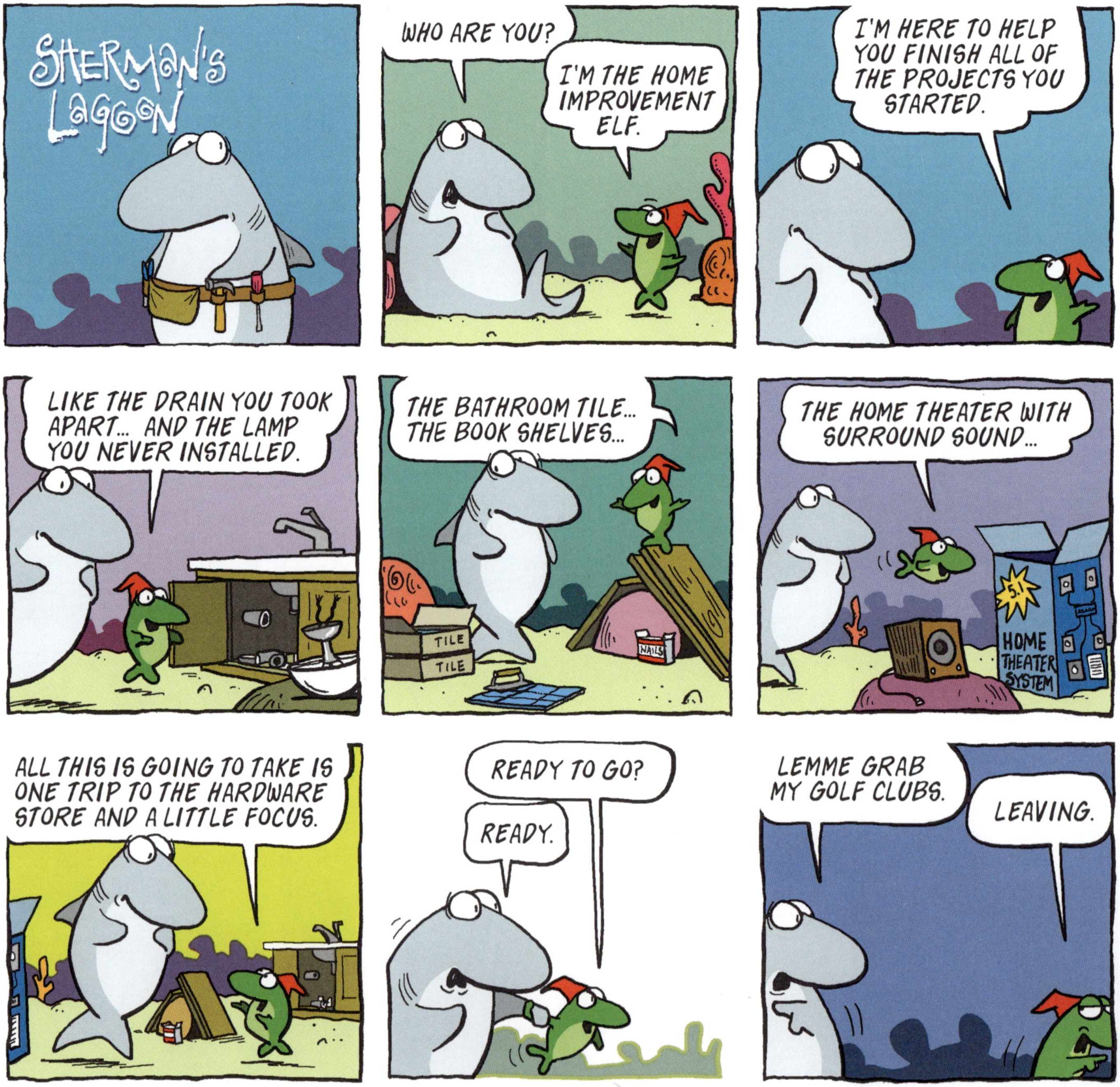
SHERMAN'S LAGOON
WHO ARE YOU?
I'M THE HOME IMPROVEMENT ELF.
I'M HERE TO HELP YOU FINISH ALL OF THE PROJECTS YOU STARTED.
LIKE THE DRAIN YOU TOOK APART... AND THE LAMP YOU NEVER INSTALLED.
THE BATHROOM TILE... THE BOOK SHELVES...
TILE
TILE
NAILS
THE HOME THEATER WITH SURROUND SOUND...
5.1
HOME THEATER SYSTEM
ALL THIS IS GOING TO TAKE IS ONE TRIP TO THE HARDWARE STORE AND A LITTLE FOCUS.
READY TO GO?
READY.
LEMME GRAB MY GOLF CLUBS.
LEAVING.

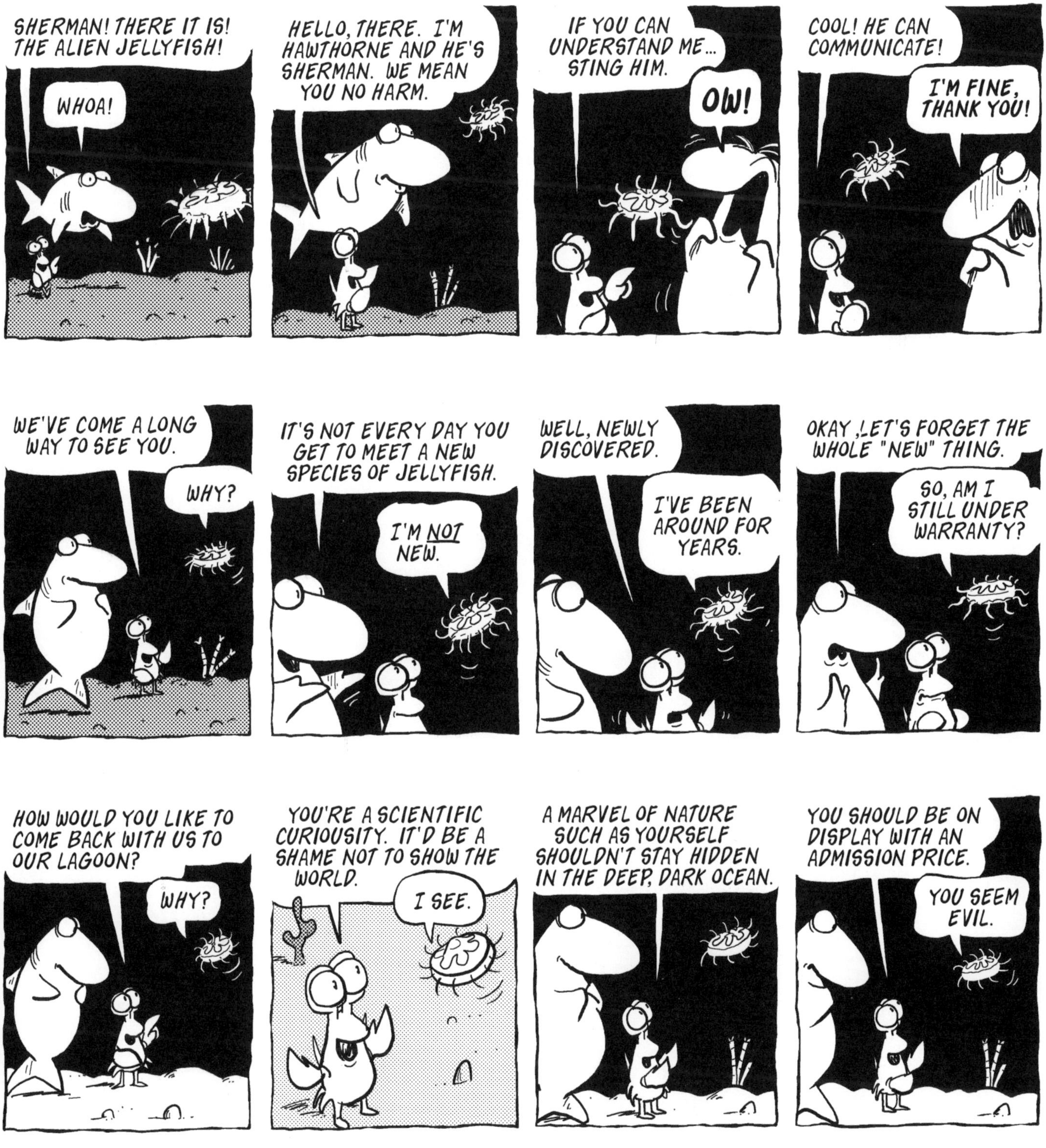
SHERMAN! THERE IT IS! THE ALIEN JELLYFISH!
WHOA!
HELLO, THERE. I'M HAWTHORNE AND HE'S SHERMAN. WE MEAN YOU NO HARM.
IF YOU CAN UNDERSTAND ME... STING HIM.
OW!
COOL! HE CAN COMMUNICATE!
I'M FINE, THANK YOU!
WE'VE COME A LONG WAY TO SEE YOU.
WHY?
IT'S NOT EVERY DAY YOU GET TO MEET A NEW SPECIES OF JELLYFISH.
I'M NOT NEW.
WELL, NEWLY DISCOVERED.
I'VE BEEN AROUND FOR YEARS.
OKAY, LET'S FORGET THE WHOLE "NEW" THING.
SO, AM I STILL UNDER WARRANTY?
HOW WOULD YOU LIKE TO COME BACK WITH US TO OUR LAGOON?
WHY?
YOU'RE A SCIENTIFIC CURIOUSITY. IT'D BE A SHAME NOT TO SHOW THE WORLD.
I SEE.
A MARVEL OF NATURE SUCH AS YOURSELF SHOULDN'T STAY HIDDEN IN THE DEEP, DARK OCEAN.
YOU SHOULD BE ON DISPLAY WITH AN ADMISSION PRICE.
YOU SEEM EVIL.

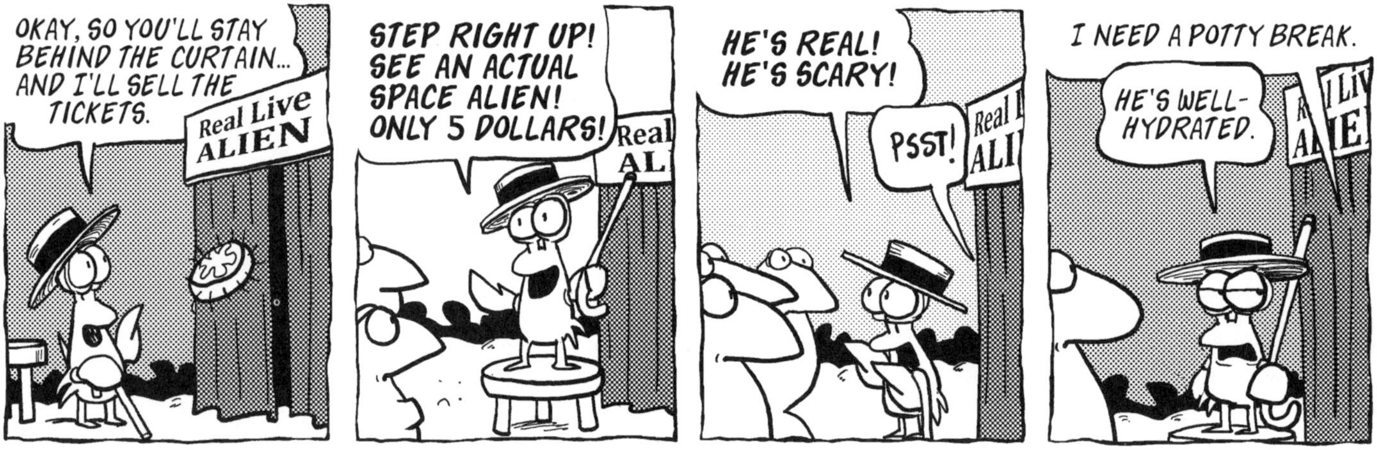
OKAY, SO YOU'LL STAY BEHIND THE CURTAIN... AND I'LL SELL THE TICKETS.
Real Live ALIEN
STEP RIGHT UP! SEE AN ACTUAL SPACE ALIEN! ONLY 5 DOLLARS!
HE'S REAL! HE'S SCARY!
PSST!
I NEED A POTTY BREAK.
HE'S WELL-HYDRATED.

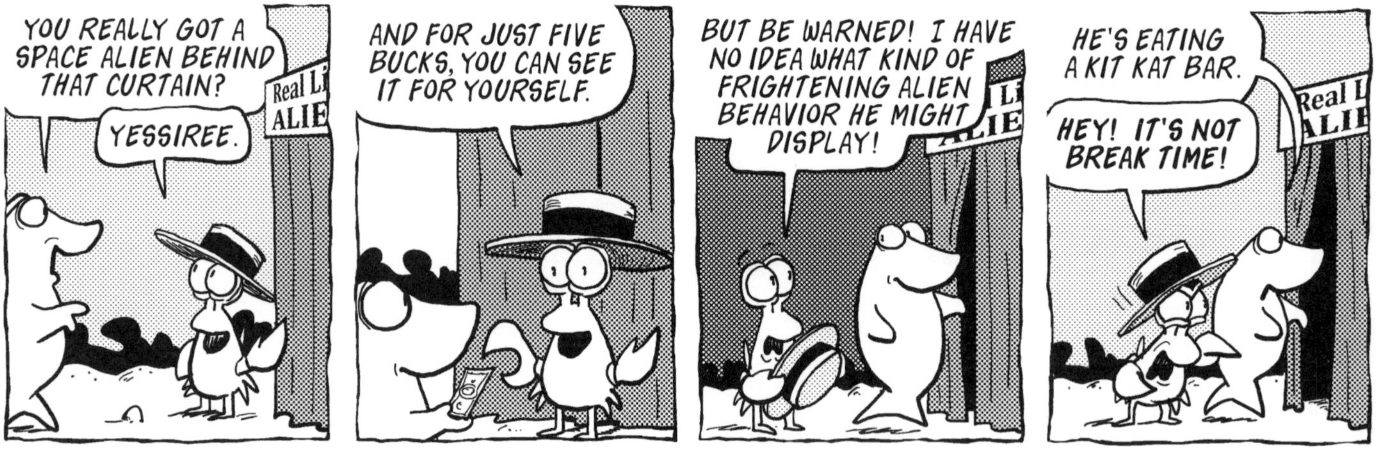
YOU REALLY GOT A SPACE ALIEN BEHIND THAT CURTAIN?
YESSIREE.
AND FOR JUST FIVE BUCKS, YOU CAN SEE IT FOR YOURSELF.
BUT BE WARNED! I HAVE NO IDEA WHAT KIND OF FRIGHTENING ALIEN BEHAVIOR HE MIGHT DISPLAY!
HE'S EATING A KIT KAT BAR.
HEY! IT'S NOT BREAK TIME!

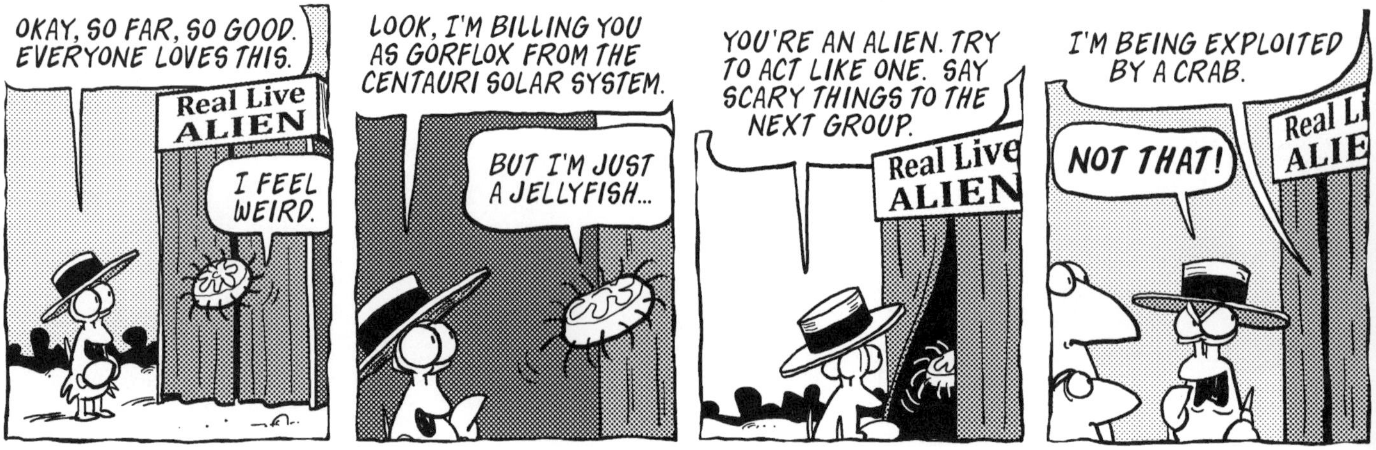
OKAY, SO FAR, SO GOOD. EVERYONE LOVES THIS.
Real Live ALIEN
I FEEL WEIRD.
LOOK, I'M BILLING YOU AS GORFLOX FROM THE CENTAURI SOLAR SYSTEM.
BUT I'M JUST A JELLYFISH...
YOU'RE AN ALIEN. TRY TO ACT LIKE ONE. SAY SCARY THINGS TO THE NEXT GROUP.
Real Live ALIEN
I'M BEING EXPLOITED BY A CRAB.
NOT THAT!

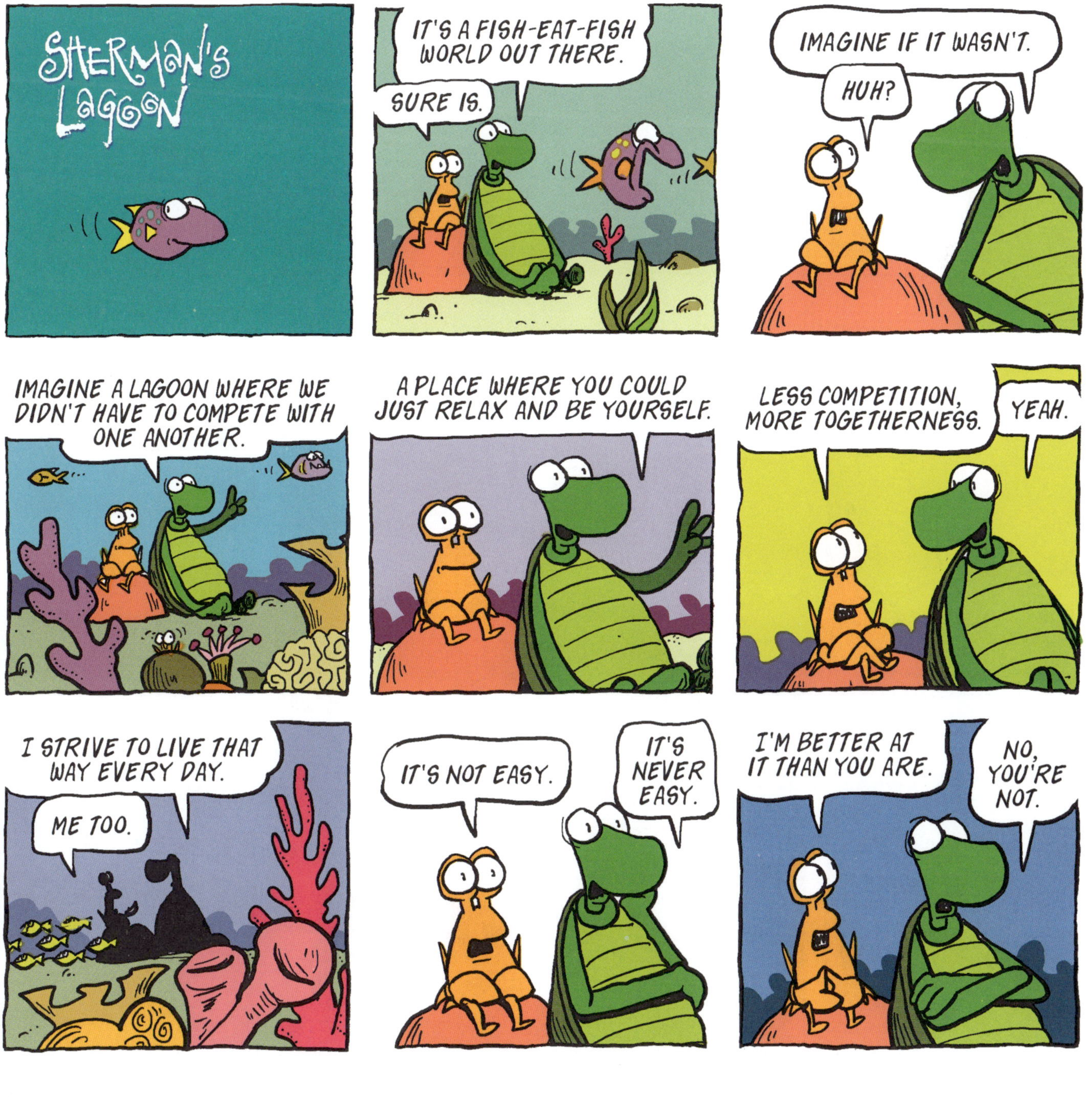
SHERMAN'S LAGOON
IT'S A FISH-EAT-FISH WORLD OUT THERE.
SURE IS.
IMAGINE IF IT WASN'T.
HUH?
IMAGINE A LAGOON WHERE WE DIDN'T HAVE TO COMPETE WITH ONE ANOTHER.
A PLACE WHERE YOU COULD JUST RELAX AND BE YOURSELF.
LESS COMPETITION, MORE TOGETHERNESS.
YEAH.
I STRIVE TO LIVE THAT WAY EVERY DAY.
ME TOO.
IT'S NOT EASY.
IT'S NEVER EASY.
I'M BETTER AT IT THAN YOU ARE.
NO, YOU'RE NOT.

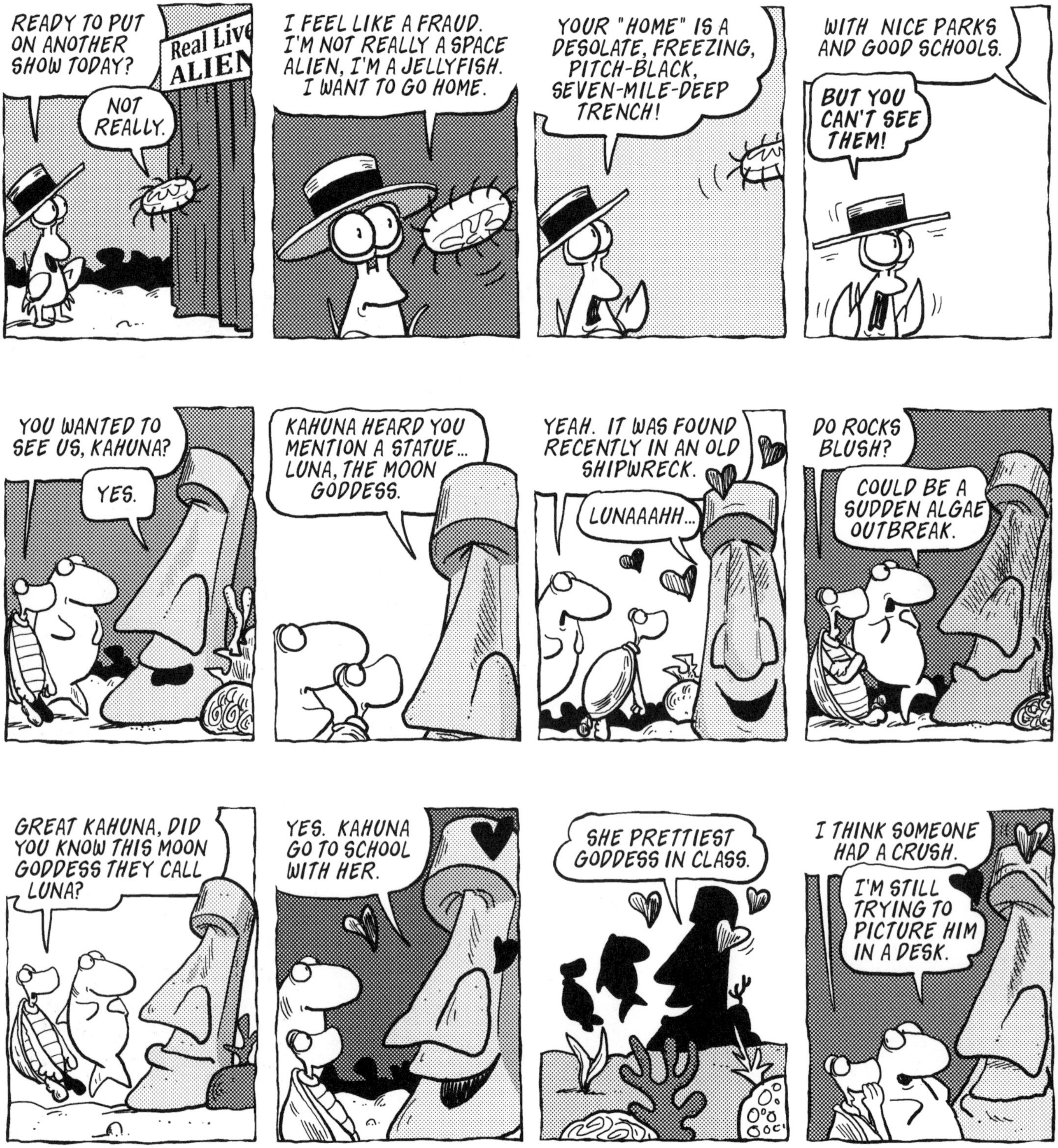
READY TO PUT ON ANOTHER SHOW TODAY?
Real Live ALIEN
NOT REALLY.
I FEEL LIKE A FRAUD. I'M NOT REALLY A SPACE ALIEN, I'M A JELLYFISH. I WANT TO GO HOME.
YOUR "HOME" IS A DESOLATE, FREEZING, PITCH-BLACK, SEVEN-MILE-DEEP TRENCH!
WITH NICE PARKS AND GOOD SCHOOLS.
BUT YOU CAN'T SEE THEM!
YOU WANTED TO SEE US, KAHUNA?
YES.
KAHUNA HEARD YOU MENTION A STATUE... LUNA, THE MOON GODDESS.
YEAH. IT WAS FOUND RECENTLY IN AN OLD SHIPWRECK.
LUNAAAHH...
DO ROCKS BLUSH?
COULD BE A SUDDEN ALGAE OUTBREAK.
GREAT KAHUNA, DID YOU KNOW THIS MOON GODDESS THEY CALL LUNA?
YES. KAHUNA GO TO SCHOOL WITH HER.
SHE PRETTIEST GODDESS IN CLASS.
I THINK SOMEONE HAD A CRUSH.
I'M STILL TRYING TO PICTURE HIM IN A DESK.

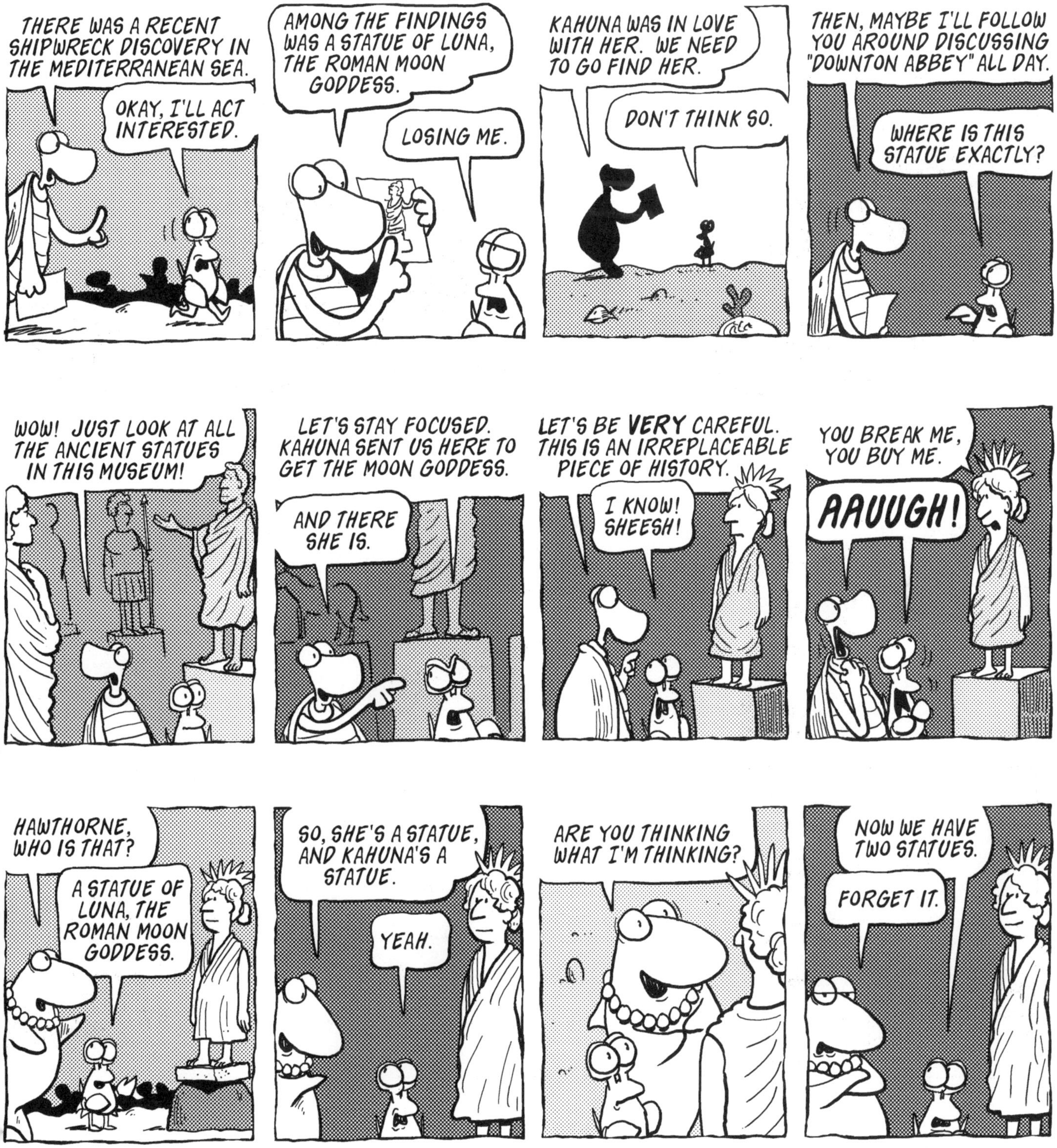
THERE WAS A RECENT SHIPWRECK DISCOVERY IN THE MEDITERRANEAN SEA.
OKAY, I'LL ACT INTERESTED.
AMONG THE FINDINGS WAS A STATUE OF LUNA, THE ROMAN MOON GODDESS.
LOSING ME.
KAHUNA WAS IN LOVE WITH HER. WE NEED TO GO FIND HER.
DON'T THINK SO.
THEN, MAYBE I'LL FOLLOW YOU AROUND DISCUSSING "DOWNTON ABBEY" ALL DAY.
WHERE IS THIS STATUE EXACTLY?
WOW! JUST LOOK AT ALL THE ANCIENT STATUES IN THIS MUSEUM!
LET'S STAY FOCUSED. KAHUNA SENT US HERE TO GET THE MOON GODDESS.
AND THERE SHE IS.
LET'S BE VERY CAREFUL. THIS IS AN IRREPLACEABLE PIECE OF HISTORY.
I KNOW! SHEESH!
YOU BREAK ME, YOU BUY ME.
AAUUGH!
HAWTHORNE, WHO IS THAT?
A STATUE OF LUNA, THE ROMAN MOON GODDESS.
SO, SHE'S A STATUE, AND KAHUNA'S A STATUE.
YEAH.
ARE YOU THINKING WHAT I'M THINKING?
NOW WE HAVE TWO STATUES.
FORGET IT.

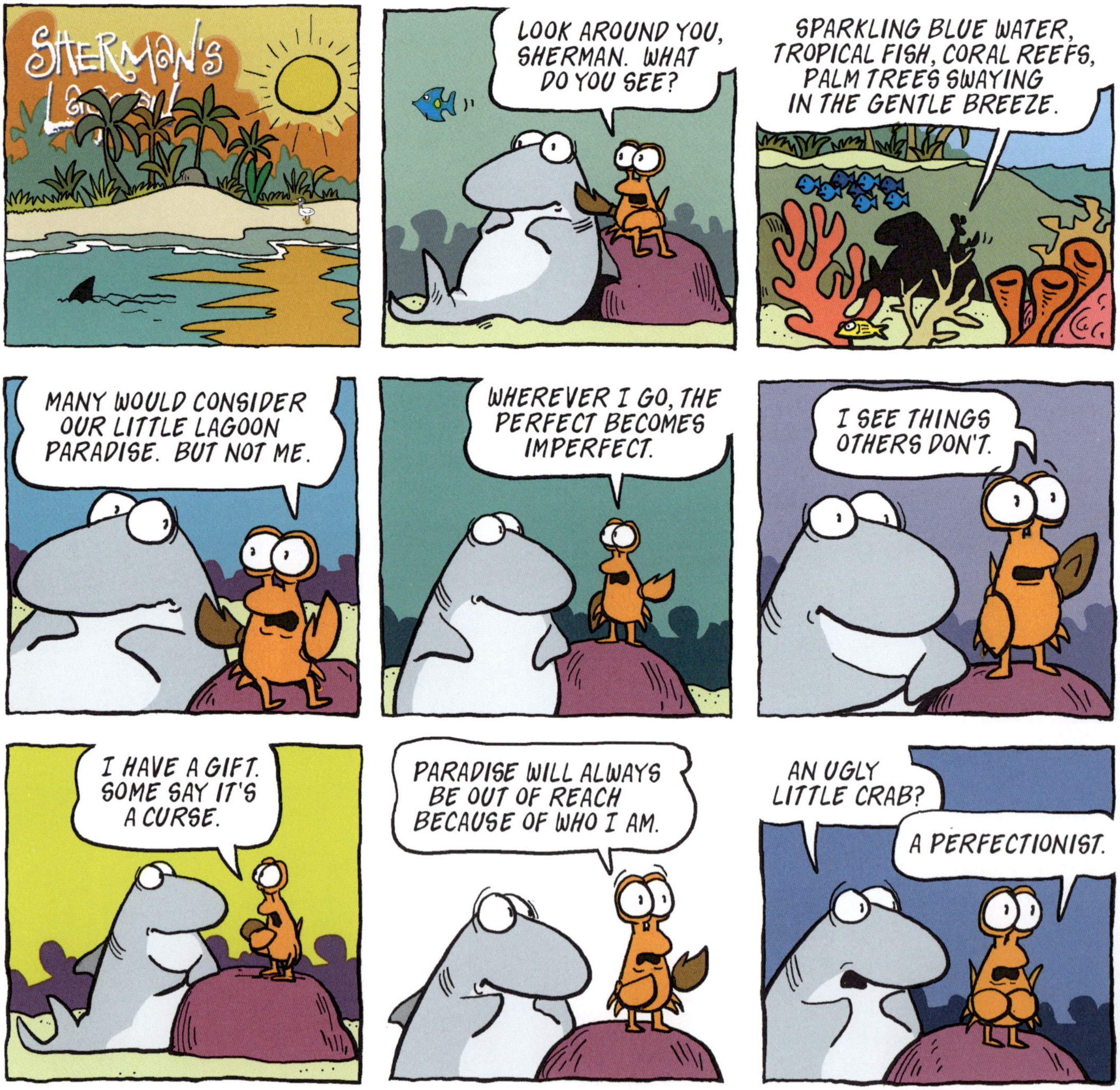
Sherman's Lagoon
LOOK AROUND YOU, SHERMAN. WHAT DO YOU SEE?
SPARKLING BLUE WATER, TROPICAL FISH, CORAL REEFS, PALM TREES SWAYING IN THE GENTLE BREEZE.
MANY WOULD CONSIDER OUR LITTLE LAGOON PARADISE. BUT NOT ME.
WHEREVER I GO, THE PERFECT BECOMES IMPERFECT.
I SEE THINGS OTHERS DON'T.
I HAVE A GIFT. SOME SAY IT'S A CURSE.
PARADISE WILL ALWAYS BE OUT OF REACH BECAUSE OF WHO I AM.
AN UGLY LITTLE CRAB?
A PERFECTIONIST.

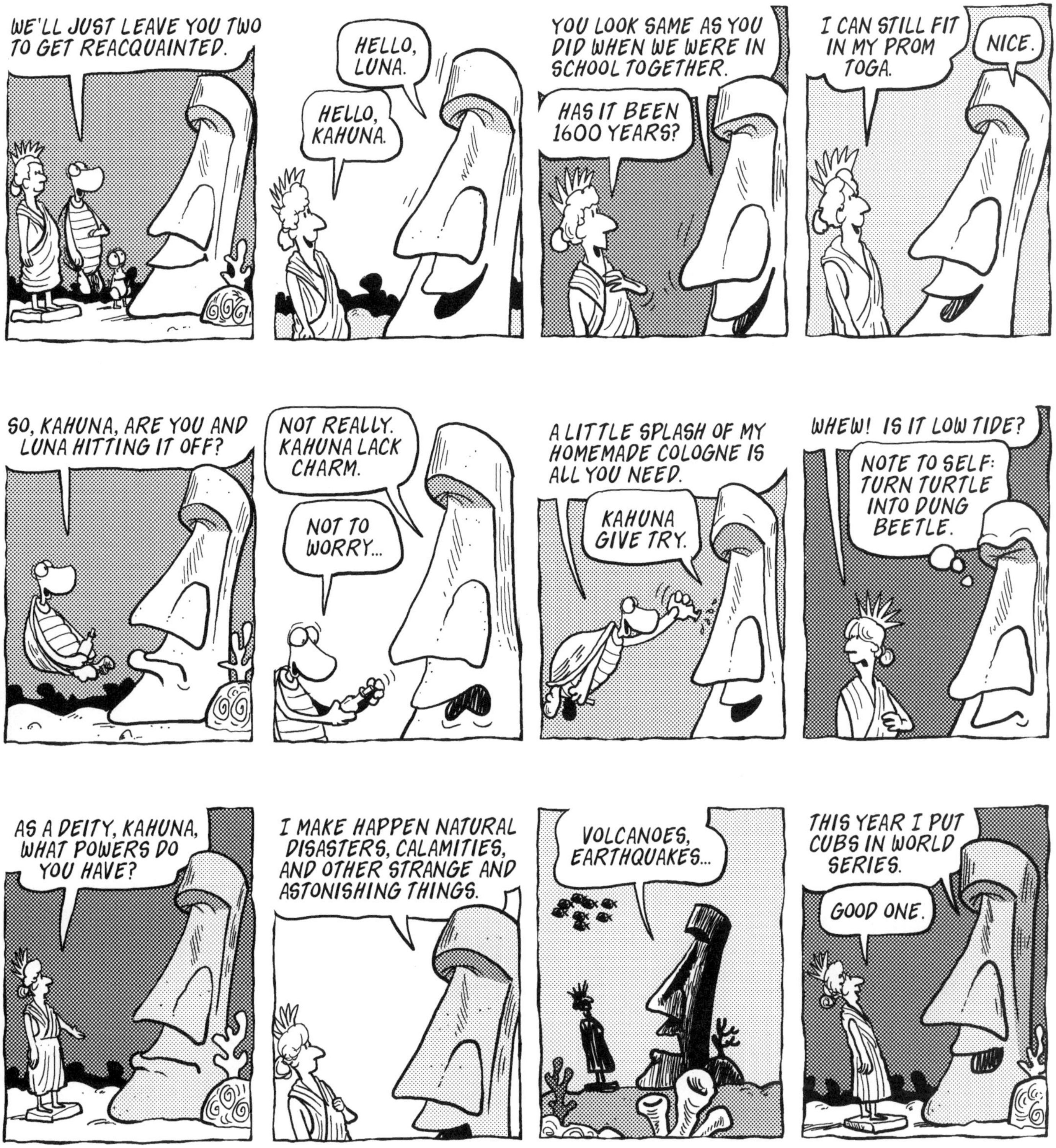
WE'LL JUST LEAVE YOU TWO TO GET REACQUAINTED.
HELLO, LUNA.
HELLO, KAHUNA.
YOU LOOK SAME AS YOU DID WHEN WE WERE IN SCHOOL TOGETHER.
HAS IT BEEN 1600 YEARS?
I CAN STILL FIT IN MY PROM TOGA.
NICE.
SO, KAHUNA, ARE YOU AND LUNA HITTING IT OFF?
NOT REALLY. KAHUNA LACK CHARM.
NOT TO WORRY...
A LITTLE SPLASH OF MY HOMEMADE COLOGNE IS ALL YOU NEED.
KAHUNA GIVE TRY.
WHEW! IS IT LOW TIDE?
NOTE TO SELF: TURN TURTLE INTO DUNG BEETLE.
AS A DEITY, KAHUNA, WHAT POWERS DO YOU HAVE?
I MAKE HAPPEN NATURAL DISASTERS, CALAMITIES, AND OTHER STRANGE AND ASTONISHING THINGS.
VOLCANOES, EARTHQUAKES...
THIS YEAR I PUT CUBS IN WORLD SERIES.
GOOD ONE.

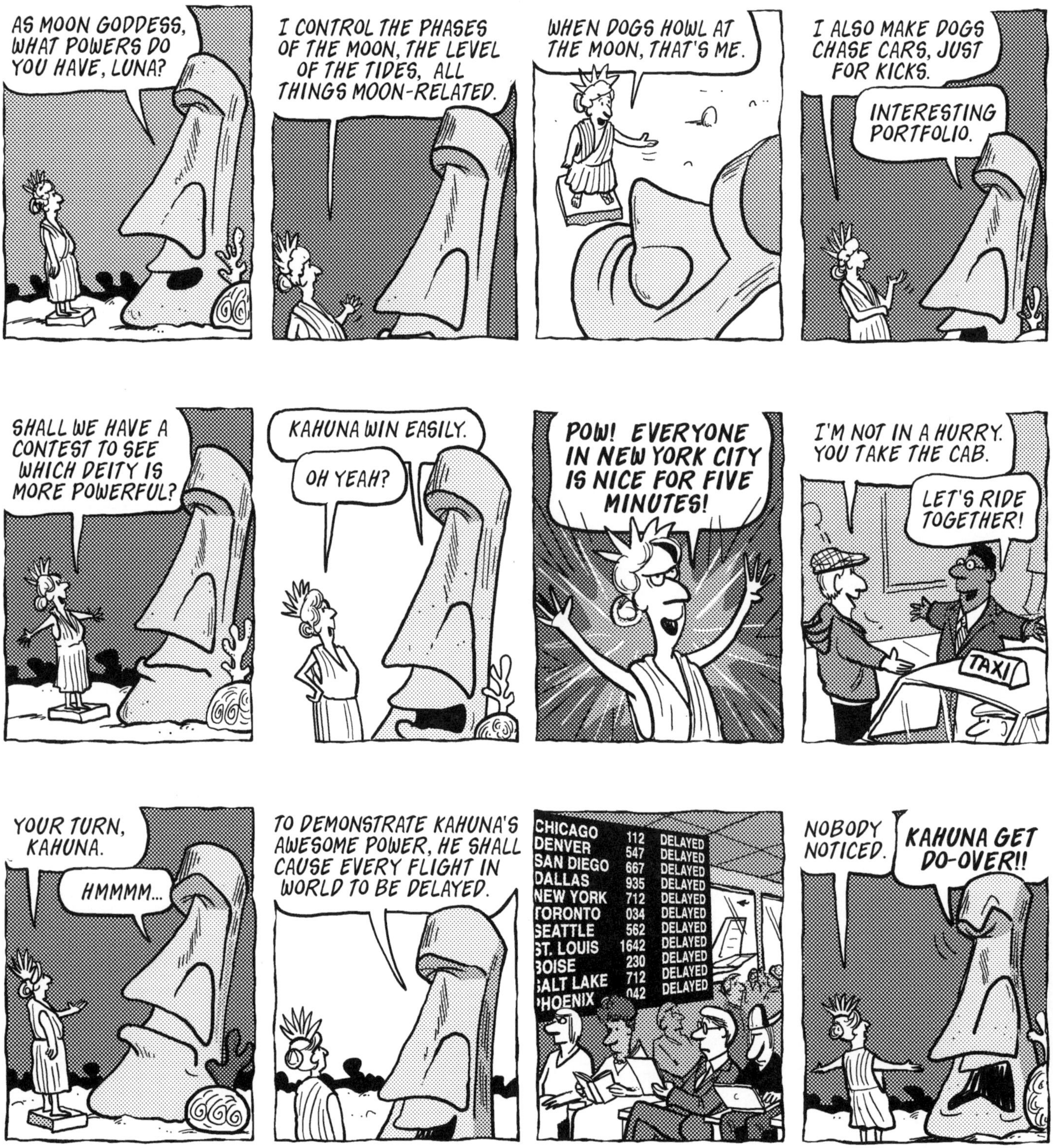
AS MOON GODDESS, WHAT POWERS DO YOU HAVE, LUNA?
I CONTROL THE PHASES OF THE MOON, THE LEVEL OF THE TIDES, ALL THINGS MOON-RELATED.
WHEN DOGS HOWL AT THE MOON, THAT'S ME.
I ALSO MAKE DOGS CHASE CARS, JUST FOR KICKS.
INTERESTING PORTFOLIO.
SHALL WE HAVE A CONTEST TO SEE WHICH DEITY IS MORE POWERFUL?
KAHUNA WIN EASILY.
OH YEAH?
POW! EVERYONE IN NEW YORK CITY IS NICE FOR FIVE MINUTES!
I'M NOT IN A HURRY. YOU TAKE THE CAB.
LET'S RIDE TOGETHER!
TAXI
YOUR TURN, KAHUNA.
HMMMM...
TO DEMONSTRATE KAHUNA'S AWESOME POWER, HE SHALL CAUSE EVERY FLIGHT IN WORLD TO BE DELAYED.
CHICAGO 112 DELAYED
DENVER 547 DELAYED
SAN DIEGO 667 DELAYED
DALLAS 935 DELAYED
NEW YORK 712 DELAYED
TORONTO 034 DELAYED
SEATTLE 562 DELAYED
ST. LOUIS 1642 DELAYED
BOISE 230 DELAYED
SALT LAKE 712 DELAYED
PHOENIX 042
NOBODY NOTICED.
KAHUNA GET DO-OVER!!

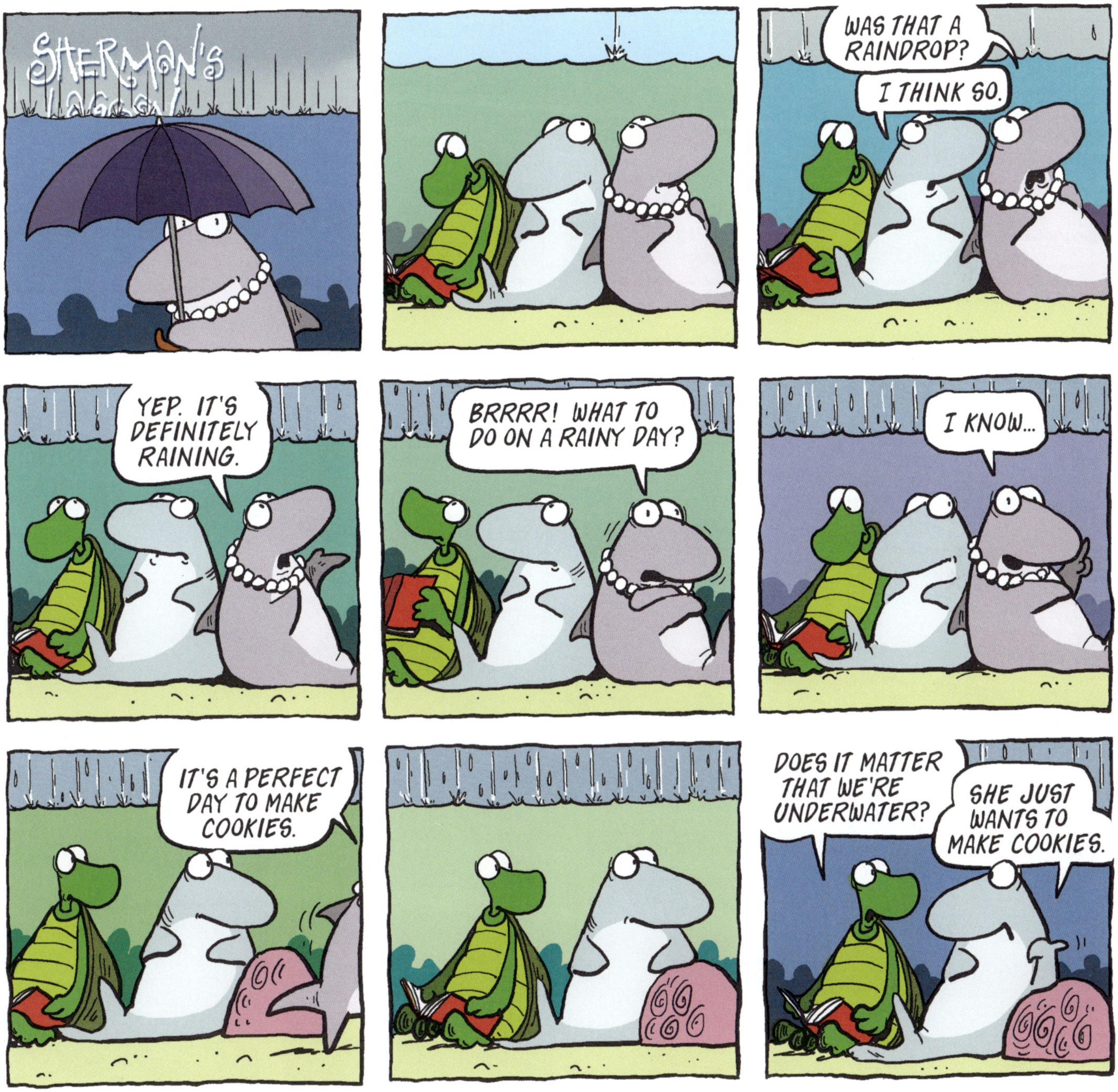
SHERMAN'S LAGOON
WAS THAT A RAINDROP?
I THINK SO.
YEP. IT'S DEFINITELY RAINING.
BRRRR! WHAT TO DO ON A RAINY DAY?
I KNOW...
IT'S A PERFECT DAY TO MAKE COOKIES.
DOES IT MATTER THAT WE'RE UNDERWATER?
SHE JUST WANTS TO MAKE COOKIES.

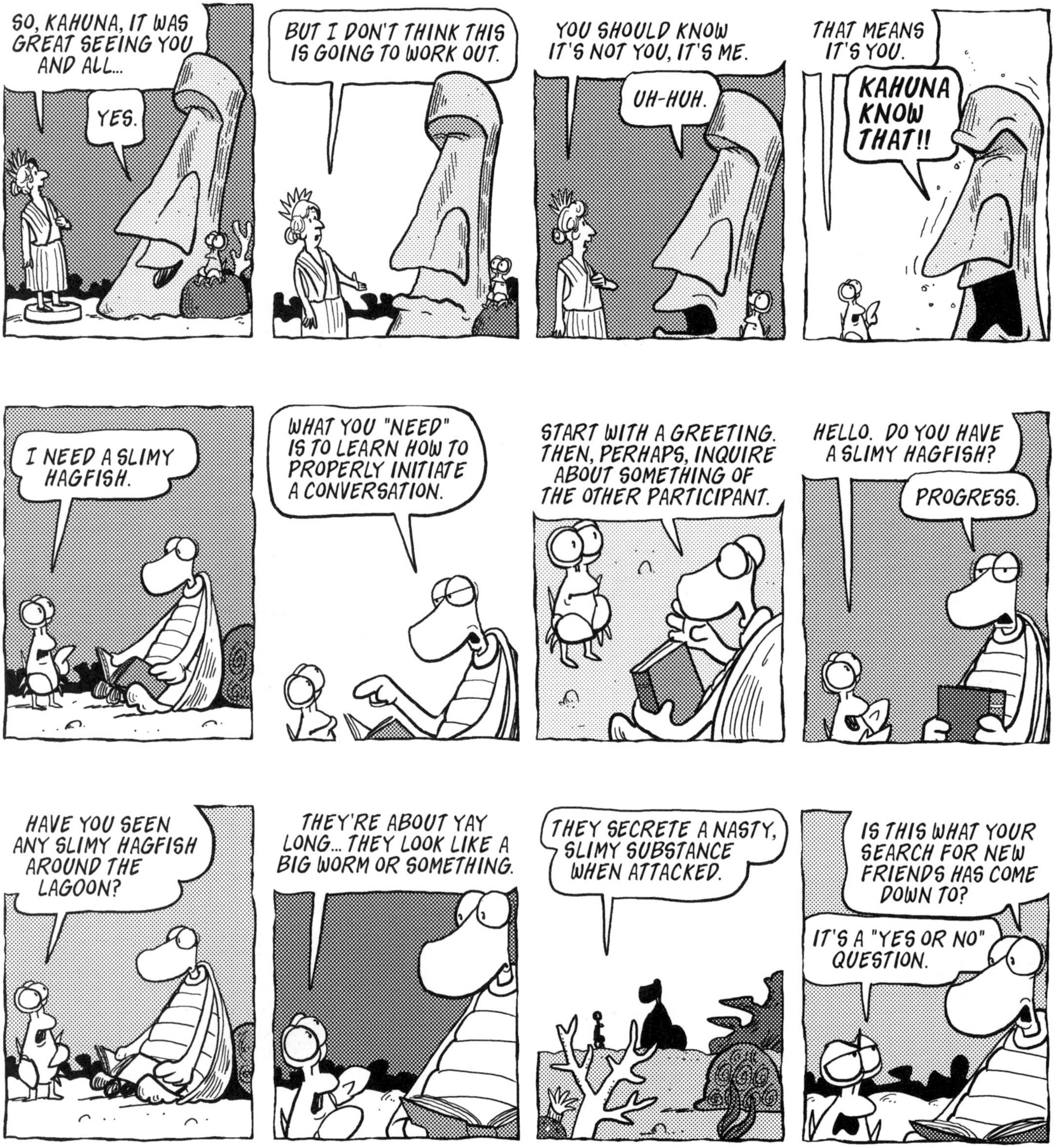
SO, KAHUNA, IT WAS GREAT SEEING YOU AND ALL...
YES.
BUT I DON'T THINK THIS IS GOING TO WORK OUT.
YOU SHOULD KNOW IT'S NOT YOU, IT'S ME.
UH-HUH.
THAT MEANS IT'S YOU.
KAHUNA KNOW THAT!!
I NEED A SLIMY HAGFISH.
WHAT YOU "NEED" IS TO LEARN HOW TO PROPERLY INITIATE A CONVERSATION.
START WITH A GREETING. THEN, PERHAPS, INQUIRE ABOUT SOMETHING OF THE OTHER PARTICIPANT.
HELLO. DO YOU HAVE A SLIMY HAGFISH?
PROGRESS.
HAVE YOU SEEN ANY SLIMY HAGFISH AROUND THE LAGOON?
THEY'RE ABOUT YAY LONG... THEY LOOK LIKE A BIG WORM OR SOMETHING.
THEY SECRETE A NASTY, SLIMY SUBSTANCE WHEN ATTACKED.
IS THIS WHAT YOUR SEARCH FOR NEW FRIENDS HAS COME DOWN TO?
IT'S A "YES OR NO" QUESTION.

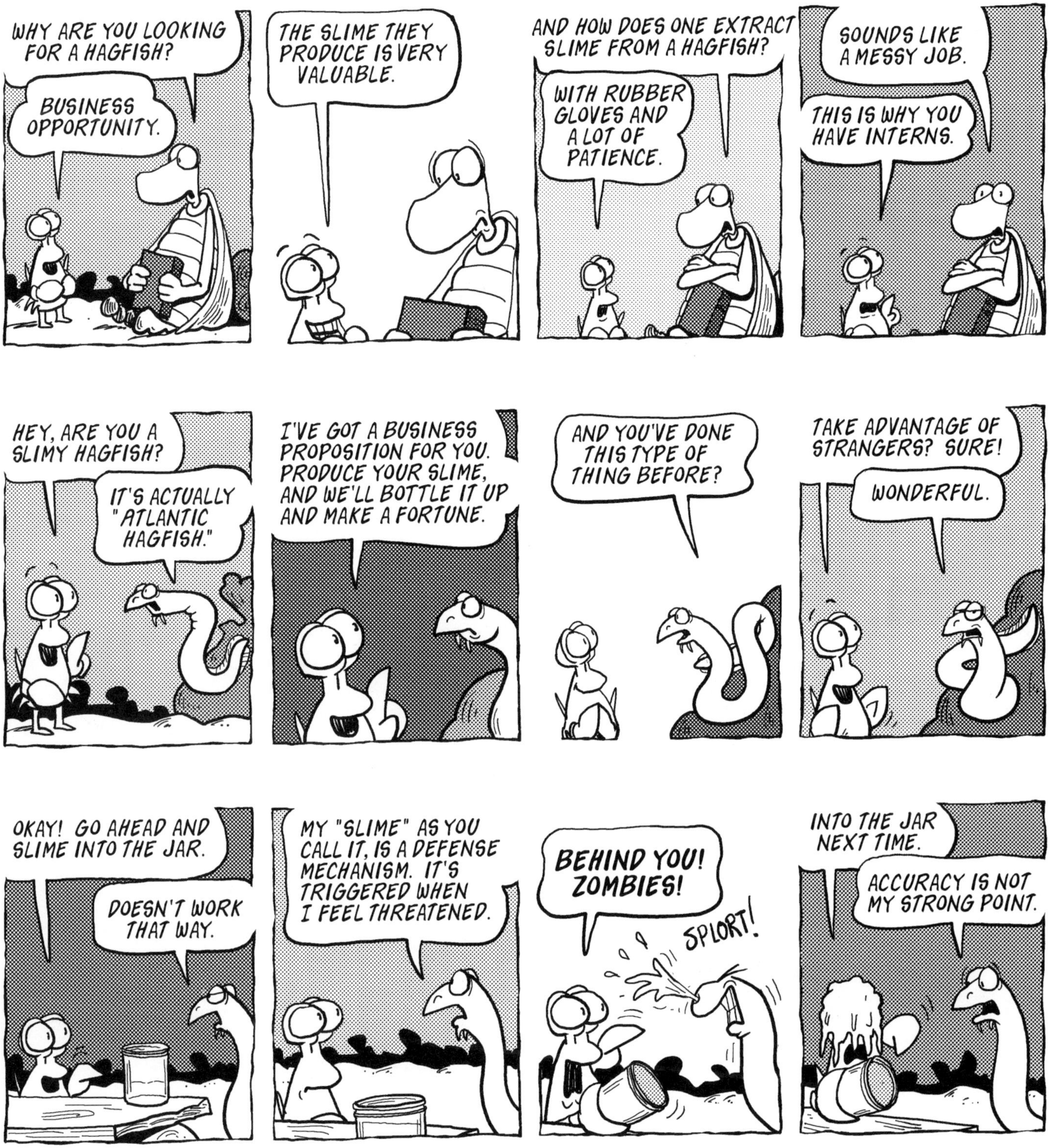
WHY ARE YOU LOOKING FOR A HAGFISH?
BUSINESS OPPORTUNITY.
THE SLIME THEY PRODUCE IS VERY VALUABLE.
AND HOW DOES ONE EXTRACT SLIME FROM A HAGFISH?
WITH RUBBER GLOVES AND A LOT OF PATIENCE.
SOUNDS LIKE A MESSY JOB.
THIS IS WHY YOU HAVE INTERNS.
HEY, ARE YOU A SLIMY HAGFISH?
IT'S ACTUALLY "ATLANTIC HAGFISH."
I'VE GOT A BUSINESS PROPOSITION FOR YOU. PRODUCE YOUR SLIME, AND WE'LL BOTTLE IT UP AND MAKE A FORTUNE.
AND YOU'VE DONE THIS TYPE OF THING BEFORE?
TAKE ADVANTAGE OF STRANGERS? SURE!
WONDERFUL.
OKAY! GO AHEAD AND SLIME INTO THE JAR.
DOESN'T WORK THAT WAY.
MY "SLIME" AS YOU CALL IT, IS A DEFENSE MECHANISM. IT'S TRIGGERED WHEN I FEEL THREATENED.
BEHIND YOU! ZOMBIES!
SPLORT!
INTO THE JAR NEXT TIME.
ACCURACY IS NOT MY STRONG POINT.

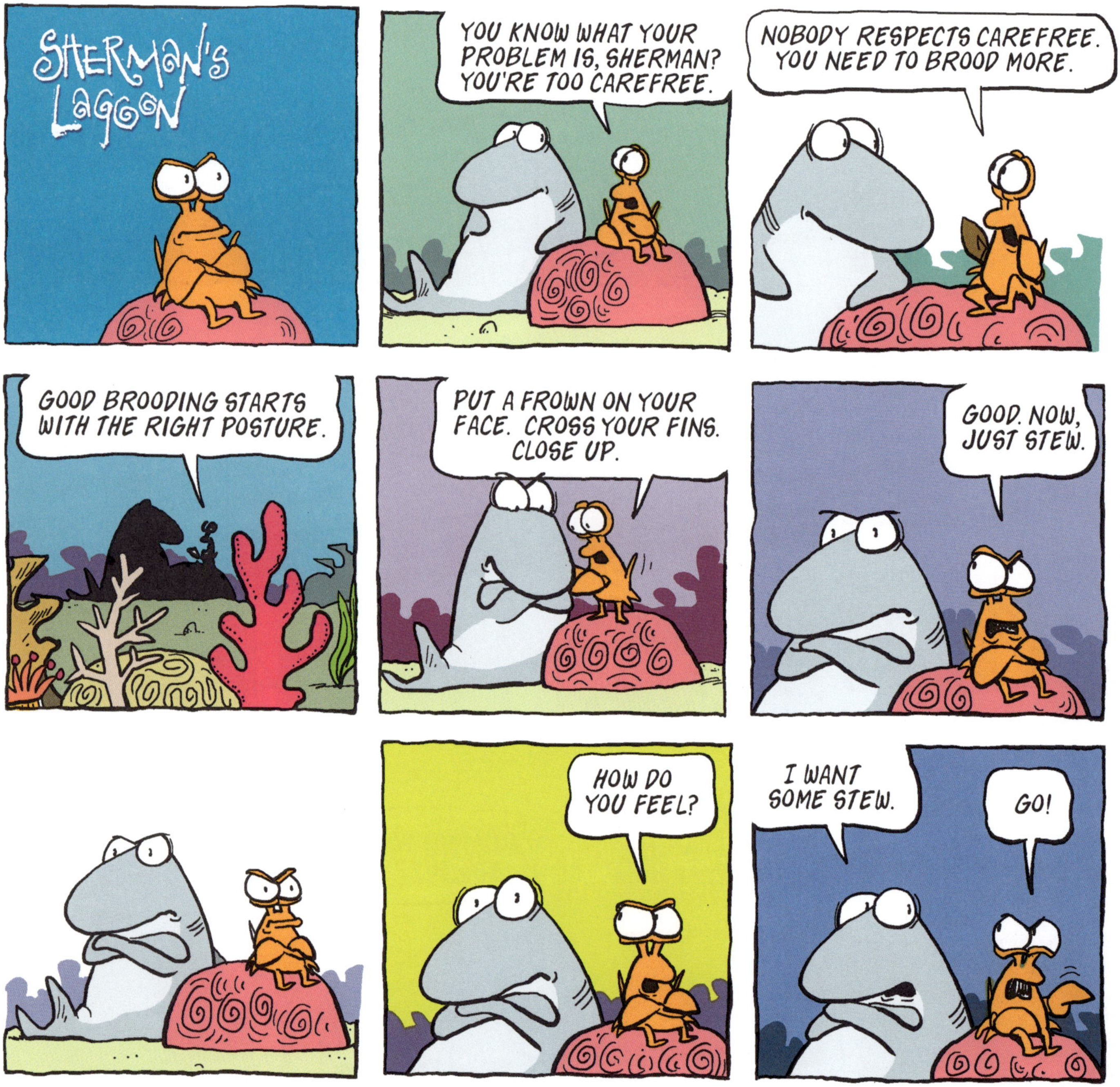
SHERMAN'S LAGOON
YOU KNOW WHAT YOUR PROBLEM IS, SHERMAN? YOU'RE TOO CAREFREE.
NOBODY RESPECTS CAREFREE. YOU NEED TO BROOD MORE.
GOOD BROODING STARTS WITH THE RIGHT POSTURE.
PUT A FROWN ON YOUR FACE. CROSS YOUR FINS. CLOSE UP.
GOOD. NOW, JUST STEW.
HOW DO YOU FEEL?
I WANT SOME STEW.
GO!

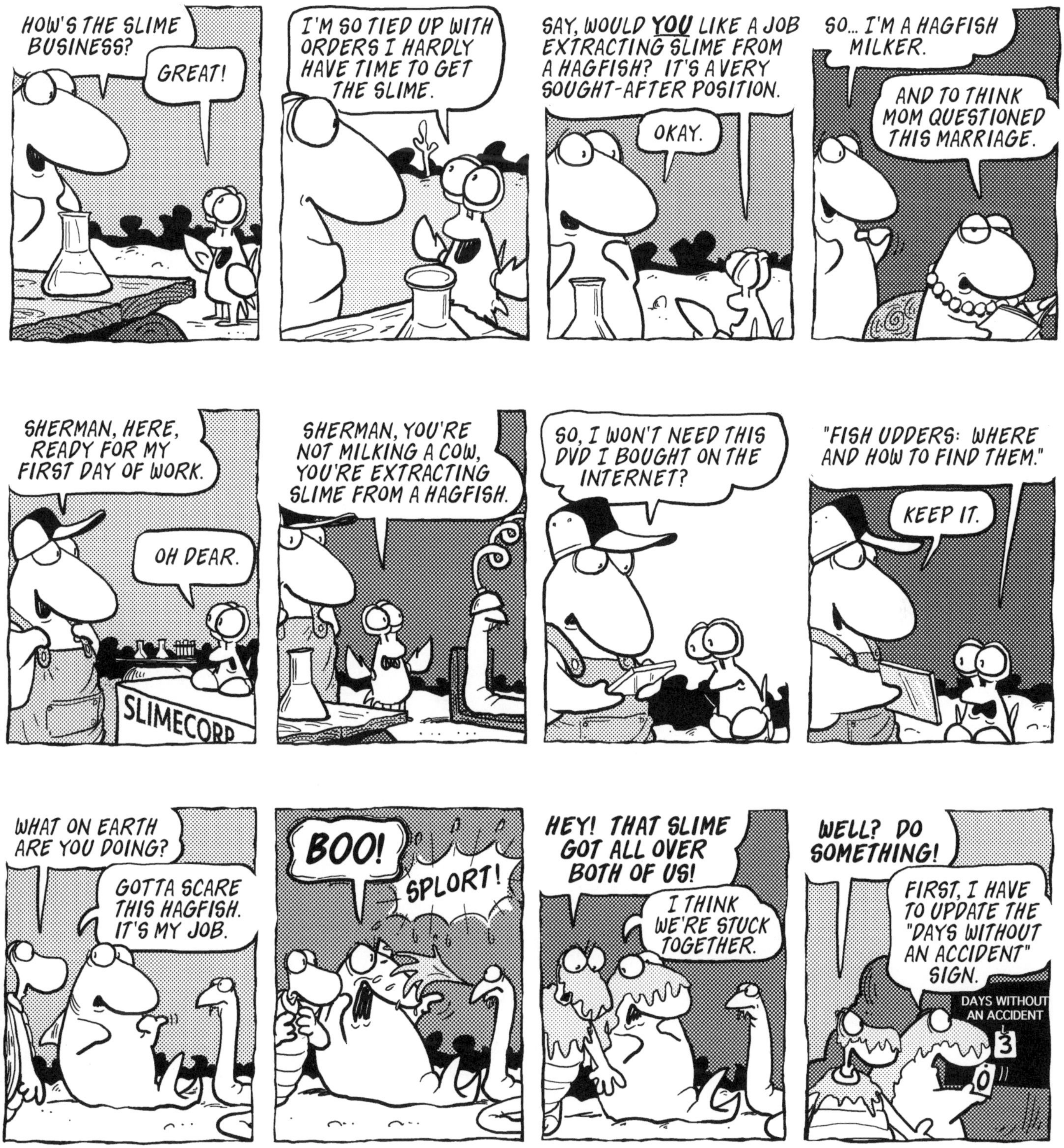
HOW'S THE SLIME BUSINESS?
GREAT!
I'M SO TIED UP WITH ORDERS I HARDLY HAVE TIME TO GET THE SLIME.
SAY, WOULD YOU LIKE A JOB EXTRACTING SLIME FROM A HAGFISH? IT'S A VERY SOUGHT-AFTER POSITION.
OKAY.
SO... I'M A HAGFISH MILKER.
AND TO THINK MOM QUESTIONED THIS MARRIAGE.
SHERMAN, HERE, READY FOR MY FIRST DAY OF WORK.
OH DEAR.
SLIMECORP
SHERMAN, YOU'RE NOT MILKING A COW, YOU'RE EXTRACTING SLIME FROM A HAGFISH.
SO, I WON'T NEED THIS DVD I BOUGHT ON THE INTERNET?
"FISH UDDERS: WHERE AND HOW TO FIND THEM."
KEEP IT.
WHAT ON EARTH ARE YOU DOING?
GOTTA SCARE THIS HAGFISH. IT'S MY JOB.
BOO!
SPLORT!
HEY! THAT SLIME GOT ALL OVER BOTH OF US!
I THINK WE'RE STUCK TOGETHER.
WELL? DO SOMETHING!
FIRST, I HAVE TO UPDATE THE "DAYS WITHOUT AN ACCIDENT" SIGN.
DAYS WITHOUT AN ACCIDENT
3
0

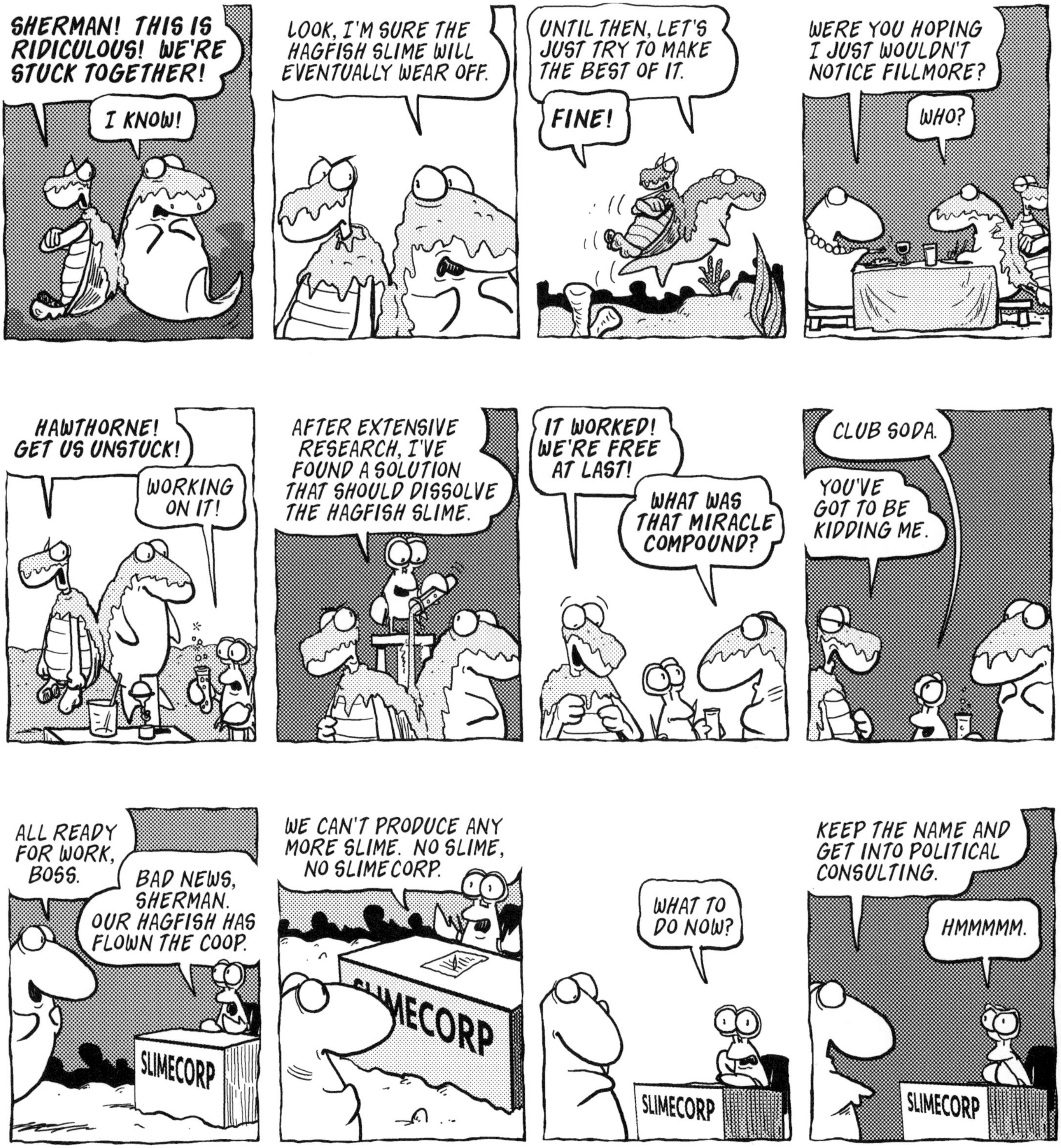
SHERMAN! THIS IS RIDICULOUS! WE'RE STUCK TOGETHER!
I KNOW!
LOOK, I'M SURE THE HAGFISH SLIME WILL EVENTUALLY WEAR OFF.
UNTIL THEN, LET'S JUST TRY TO MAKE THE BEST OF IT.
FINE!
WERE YOU HOPING I JUST WOULDN'T NOTICE FILLMORE?
WHO?
HAWTHORNE! GET US UNSTUCK!
WORKING ON IT!
AFTER EXTENSIVE RESEARCH, I'VE FOUND A SOLUTION THAT SHOULD DISSOLVE THE HAGFISH SLIME.
IT WORKED! WE'RE FREE AT LAST!
WHAT WAS THAT MIRACLE COMPOUND?
CLUB SODA.
YOU'VE GOT TO BE KIDDING ME.
ALL READY FOR WORK, BOSS.
BAD NEWS, SHERMAN. OUR HAGFISH HAS FLOWN THE COOP.
SLIMECORP
WE CAN'T PRODUCE ANY MORE SLIME. NO SLIME, NO SLIMECORP.
MECORP
WHAT TO DO NOW?
SLIMECORP
KEEP THE NAME AND GET INTO POLITICAL CONSULTING.
HMMMMM.
SLIMECORP

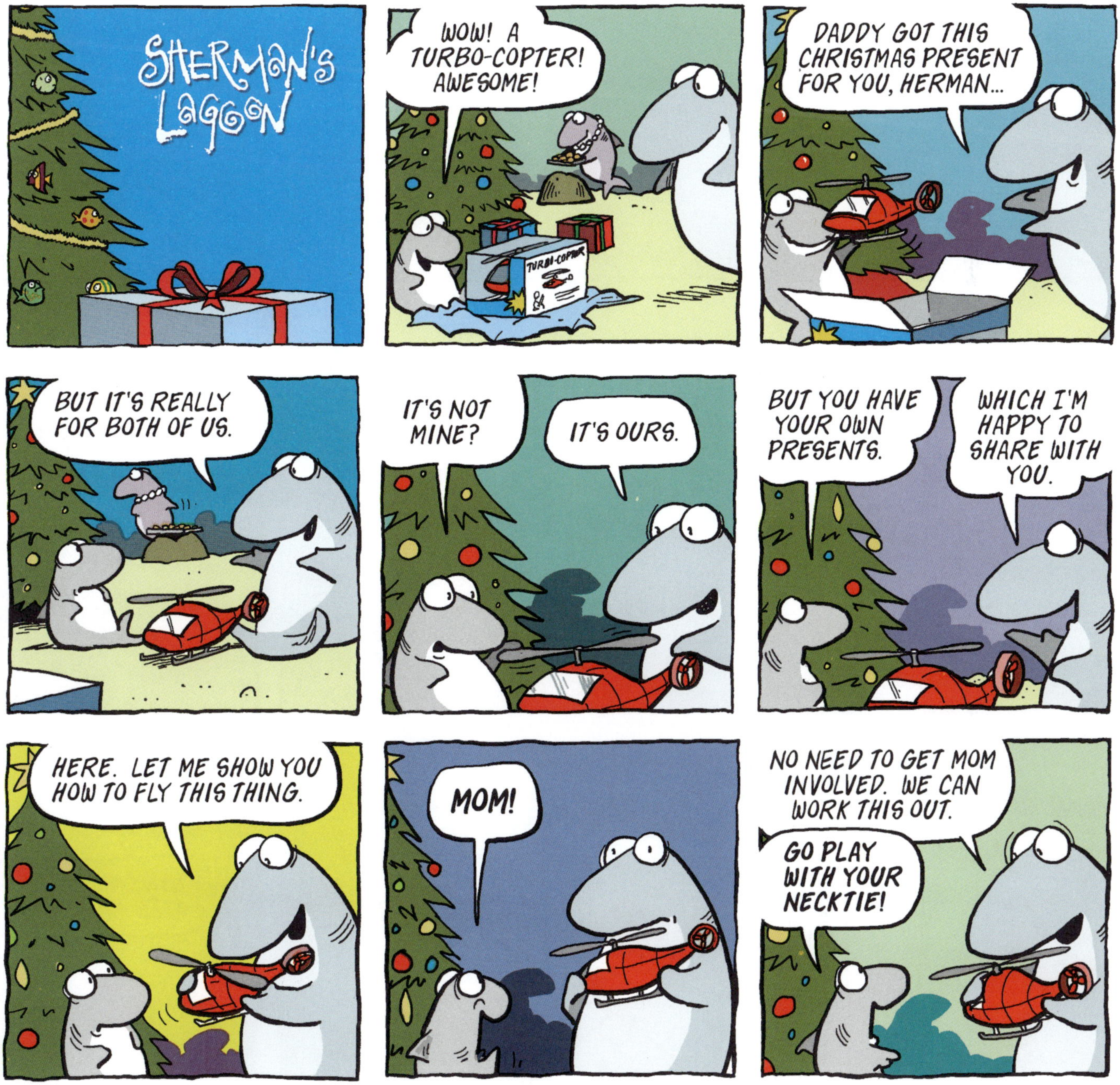

SHERMAN'S LAGOON
WOW! A TURBO-COPTER! AWESOME!
TURBO-COPTER
DADDY GOT THIS CHRISTMAS PRESENT FOR YOU, HERMAN...
BUT IT'S REALLY FOR BOTH OF US.
IT'S NOT MINE?
IT'S OURS.
BUT YOU HAVE YOUR OWN PRESENTS.
WHICH I'M HAPPY TO SHARE WITH YOU.
HERE. LET ME SHOW YOU HOW TO FLY THIS THING.
MOM!
NO NEED TO GET MOM INVOLVED. WE CAN WORK THIS OUT.
GO PLAY WITH YOUR NECKTIE!

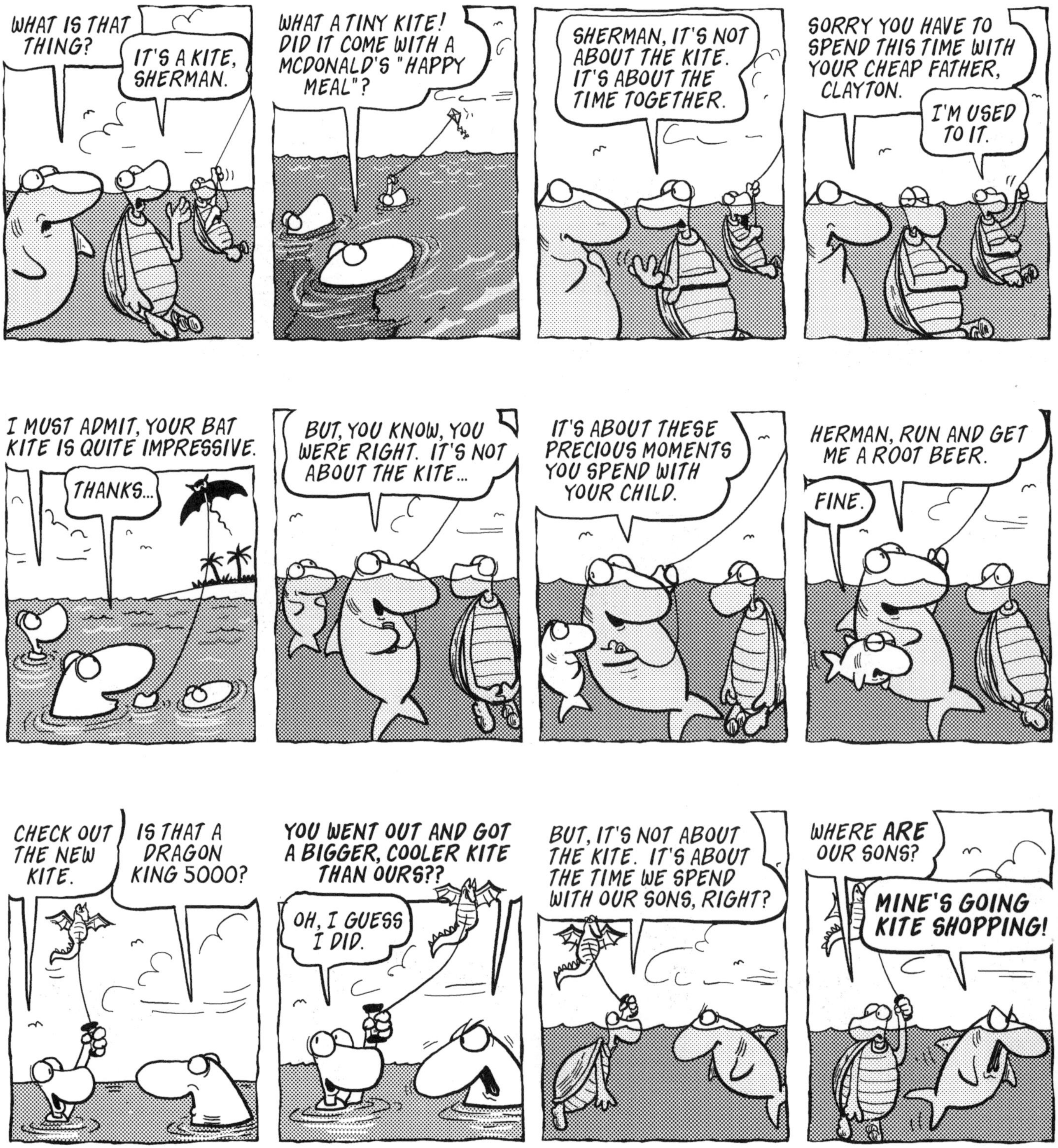
WHAT IS THAT THING?
IT'S A KITE, SHERMAN.
WHAT A TINY KITE! DID IT COME WITH A MCDONALD'S "HAPPY MEAL"?
SHERMAN, IT'S NOT ABOUT THE KITE. IT'S ABOUT THE TIME TOGETHER.
SORRY YOU HAVE TO SPEND THIS TIME WITH YOUR CHEAP FATHER, CLAYTON.
I'M USED TO IT.
I MUST ADMIT, YOUR BAT KITE IS QUITE IMPRESSIVE.
THANKS...
BUT, YOU KNOW, YOU WERE RIGHT. IT'S NOT ABOUT THE KITE...
IT'S ABOUT THESE PRECIOUS MOMENTS YOU SPEND WITH YOUR CHILD.
HERMAN, RUN AND GET ME A ROOT BEER.
FINE.
CHECK OUT THE NEW KITE.
IS THAT A DRAGON KING 5000?
YOU WENT OUT AND GOT A BIGGER, COOLER KITE THAN OURS??
OH, I GUESS I DID.
BUT, IT'S NOT ABOUT THE KITE. IT'S ABOUT THE TIME WE SPEND WITH OUR SONS, RIGHT?
WHERE ARE OUR SONS?
MINE'S GOING KITE SHOPPING!

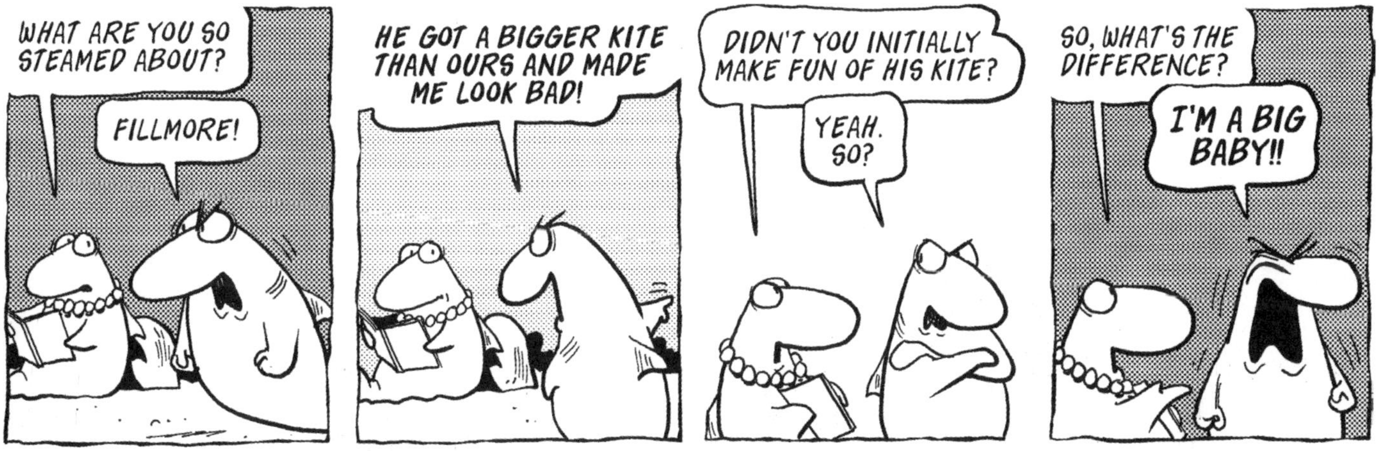
WHAT ARE YOU SO STEAMED ABOUT?
FILLMORE!
HE GOT A BIGGER KITE THAN OURS AND MADE ME LOOK BAD!
DIDN'T YOU INITIALLY MAKE FUN OF HIS KITE?
YEAH. SO?
SO, WHAT'S THE DIFFERENCE?
I'M A BIG BABY!!

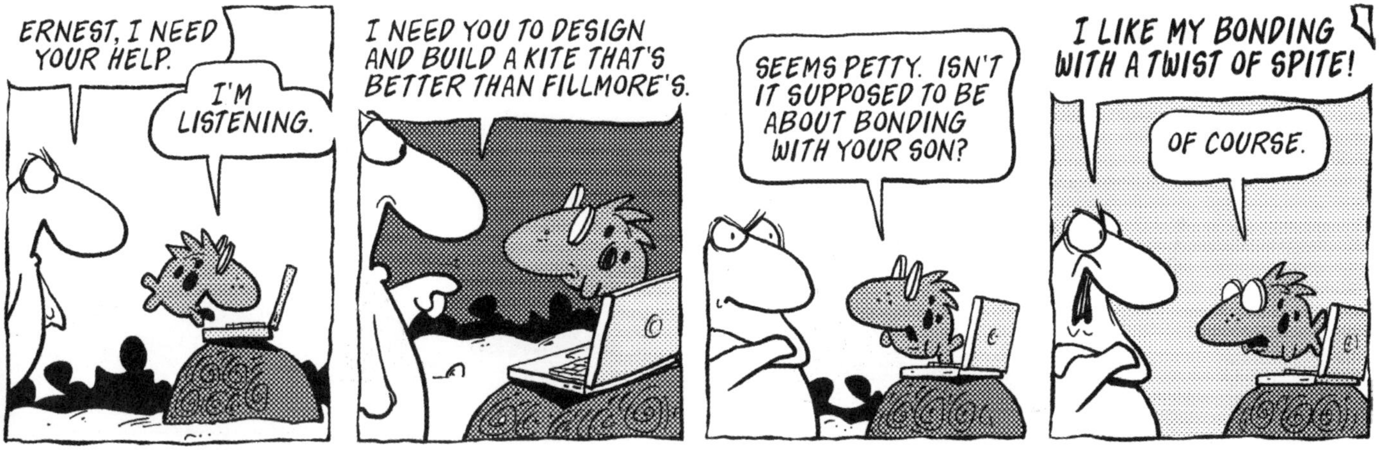
ERNEST, I NEED YOUR HELP.
I'M LISTENING.
I NEED YOU TO DESIGN AND BUILD A KITE THAT'S BETTER THAN FILLMORE'S.
SEEMS PETTY. ISN'T IT SUPPOSED TO BE ABOUT BONDING WITH YOUR SON?
I LIKE MY BONDING WITH A TWIST OF SPITE!
OF COURSE.

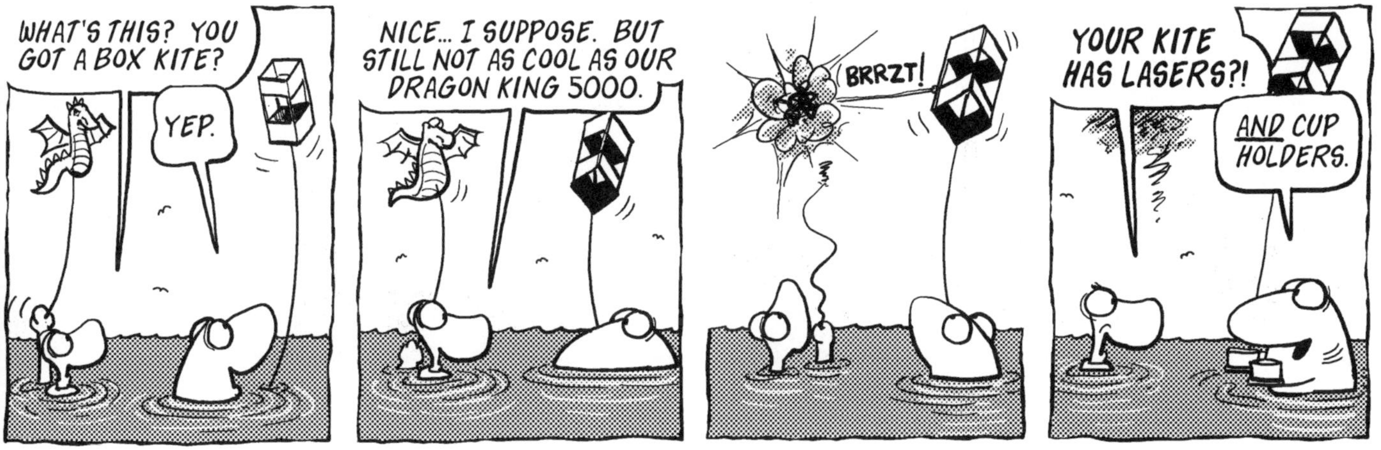
WHAT'S THIS? YOU GOT A BOX KITE?
YEP.
NICE... I SUPPOSE. BUT STILL NOT AS COOL AS OUR DRAGON KING 5000.
BRRZT!
YOUR KITE HAS LASERS?!
AND CUP HOLDERS.

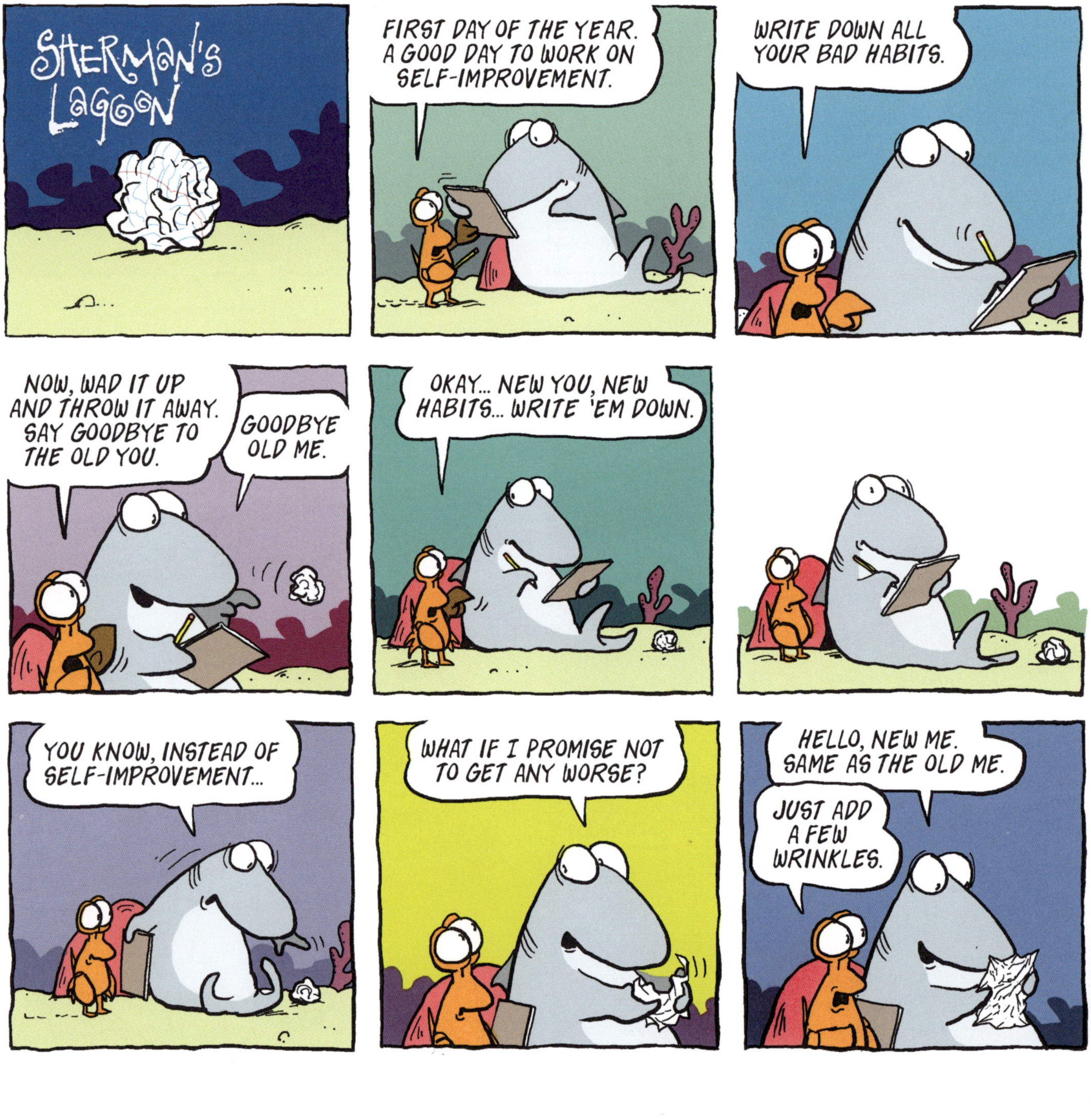
SHERMAN'S LAGOON
FIRST DAY OF THE YEAR. A GOOD DAY TO WORK ON SELF-IMPROVEMENT.
WRITE DOWN ALL YOUR BAD HABITS.
NOW, WAD IT UP AND THROW IT AWAY. SAY GOODBYE TO THE OLD YOU.
GOODBYE OLD ME.
OKAY... NEW YOU, NEW HABITS... WRITE 'EM DOWN.
YOU KNOW, INSTEAD OF SELF-IMPROVEMENT...
WHAT IF I PROMISE NOT TO GET ANY WORSE?
HELLO, NEW ME. SAME AS THE OLD ME.
JUST ADD A FEW WRINKLES.

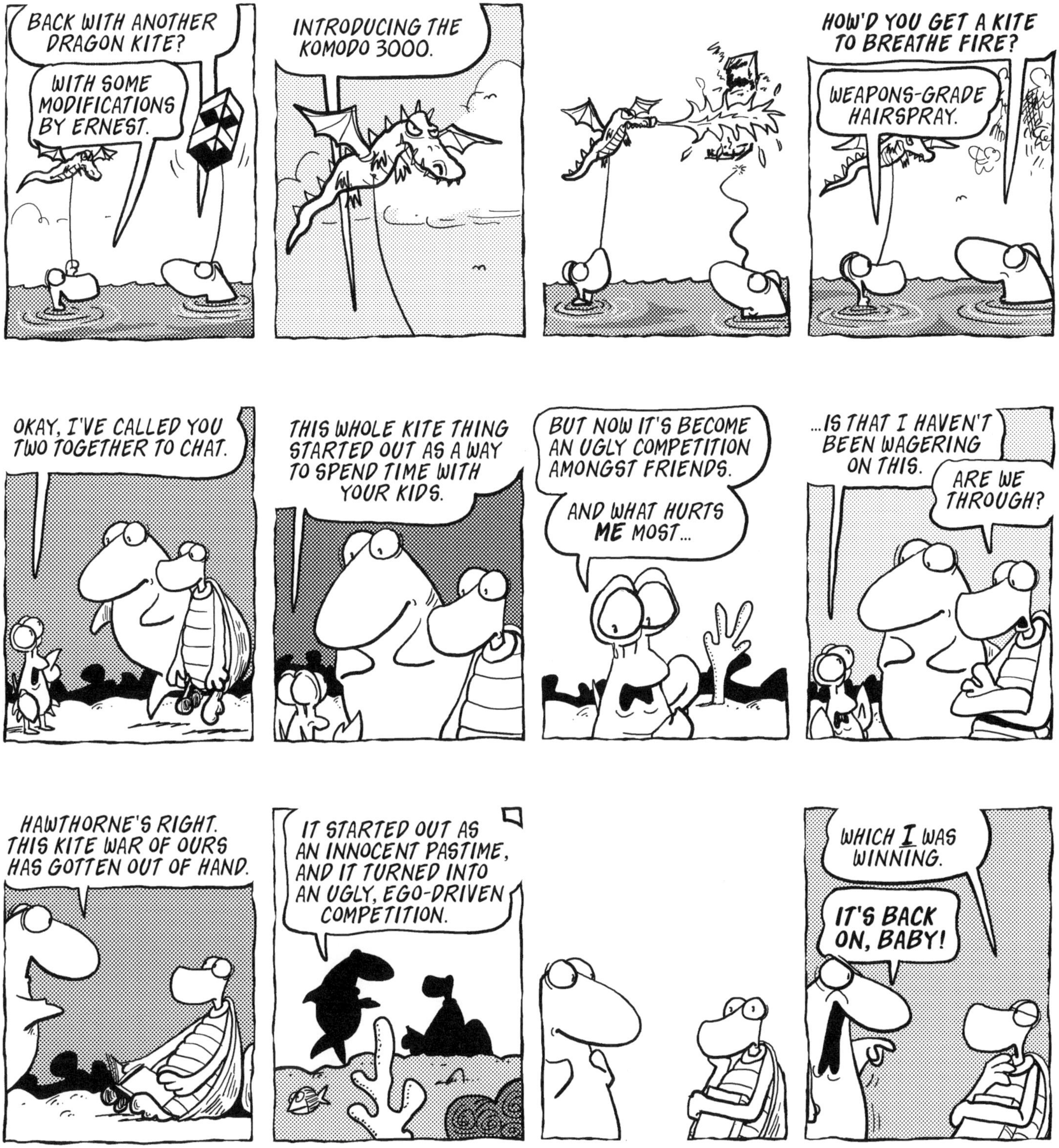
BACK WITH ANOTHER DRAGON KITE?
WITH SOME MODIFICATIONS BY ERNEST.
INTRODUCING THE KOMODO 3000.
HOW'D YOU GET A KITE TO BREATHE FIRE?
WEAPONS-GRADE HAIRSPRAY.
OKAY, I'VE CALLED YOU TWO TOGETHER TO CHAT.
THIS WHOLE KITE THING STARTED OUT AS A WAY TO SPEND TIME WITH YOUR KIDS.
BUT NOW IT'S BECOME AN UGLY COMPETITION AMONGST FRIENDS.
AND WHAT HURTS ME MOST...
...IS THAT I HAVEN'T BEEN WAGERING ON THIS.
ARE WE THROUGH?
HAWTHORNE'S RIGHT. THIS KITE WAR OF OURS HAS GOTTEN OUT OF HAND.
IT STARTED OUT AS AN INNOCENT PASTIME, AND IT TURNED INTO AN UGLY, EGO-DRIVEN COMPETITION.
WHICH I WAS WINNING.
IT'S BACK ON, BABY!

Sherman's Lagoon is syndicated internationally by King Features Syndicate, Inc. For information, write King Features Syndicate, Inc., 300 West Fifty-Seventh Street, New York, NY 10019.

Onward and Downward copyright © 2017 by Jim Toomey. All rights reserved. Printed in China. No part of this book may be used or reproduced in any manner whatsoever without written permission except in the case of reprints in the context of reviews.

Andrews McMeel Publishing, LLC
a division of Andrews McMeel Universal
1130 Walnut Street, Kansas City, Missouri 64106

www.andrewsmcmeel.com

17 18 19 20 21 SDB 10 9 8 7 6 5 4 3 2 1

ISBN: 978-1-4494-8509-2

Library of Congress Control Number: 2017935863

Sherman's Lagoon may be viewed on the Internet at
www.shermanslagoon.com

Learn more about Sylvia Earle's mission to create ocean Hope Spots at: www.mission-blue.org

---
ATTENTION: SCHOOLS AND BUSINESSES

Andrews McMeel books are available at quantity discounts with bulk purchase for educational, business, or sales promotional use. For information, please e-mail the Andrews McMeel Publishing Special Sales Department: specialsales@amuniversal.com